GUSTAV MAHLER: LETTERS TO HIS WIFE

Portrait of Gustav Mahler by Fritz Erler (Lithography based on the portrait of 1905)

GUSTAV MAHLER

Letters to his Wife

Edited by Henry-Louis de La Grange and Günther Weiss
In collaboration with Knud Martner

First complete edition, revised and translated
by Antony Beaumont

Cornell University Press
Ithaca, New York

by the same author

BUSONI THE COMPOSER
ZEMLINSKY
FERRUCCIO BUSONI: SELECTED LETTERS
Edited and translated by Antony Beaumont
ALMA MAHLER-WERFEL: DIARIES 1898–1902
Selected and translated by Antony Beaumont

First published in 1995 by Wolf Jobst Siedler Verlag GmbH, Berlin
First published in the USA in 2004
by Cornell University Press

Typeset by Faber and Faber Limited
Printed in England by Mackays of Chatham, plc

Mahler, Gustav, 1860–1911
    [Glück ohne Ruh'. English]
Gustav Mahler : letters to his wife / edited by Henry-Louis de La Grange and günther
Weiss ; in collaboration with Knud Martner ; revised and translated by Antony Beaumont
from the German edition.
        p. cm.
    "First complete, unabridged edition."
    Includes bibliographical references and index.
    First published in Berlin under title: Glück ohne Ruh' in 1995.
    ISBN 0-8014-4340-7 (cloth)
        1. Mahler, Gustav, 1860–1911 –Correspondence. 2. Mahler, Alma,
1879–1964–Correspondence. 3. Composers–Austria–Correspondence. I. La Grange,
Henry-Louis de, 1924- II. Weiss, Günther, 1933- III. Martner, Knud. IV. Beaumont,
Antony. V. Title.

ML410.M23A413 2004
780'.92–dc22
[B]

                                                            2004052744

                        ISBN 0-8014-4340-7

                    2 4 6 8 10 9 7 5 3 1

Contents

List of Illustrations

ACKNOWLEDGEMENTS

Picture Archive of Austrian National Library, Vienna (Plate 6); International Gustav Mahler Society, Vienna (Plate 55); The Kaplan Foundation, New York (Plate 57); Collection Knud Martner, Copenhagen (facsimiles on pp. 203 and 392; Collection J. Niemann, Wassenaar (Plate 54)

Abbreviations

Abbreviations used for literary references correspond to those used in Henry-Louis de La Grange, *Gustav Mahler*, Vols I–IV

AMD   Alma Mahler-Werfel, Diaries 1898–1902, selected and trans. Antony Beaumont, from the German edition transcribed and ed. by Antony Beaumont and Susanne Rode-Breymann, London, 1998

AML   Alma Mahler-Werfel, Mein Leben, Frankfurt/Main, 1960

AMM1 Alma Mahler, Gustav Mahler, Erinnerungen und Briefe, Amsterdam, 1949

AMM4 Alma Mahler, Gustav Mahler, Erinnerungen, Frankfurt/Main, 1991

MmM   Médiathèque musicale Mahler, Paris

ELM   Alma Mahler-Werfel, Ein Leben mit Gustav Mahler, 2 vols, unpubl.

GMB   Gustav Mahler, Briefe, ed. Herta Blaukopf, Vienna, Hamburg, 1982 (new expanded and revised edition of Gustav Mahler, Briefe 1877–1911, ed. Alma Maria Mahler, Berlin etc., 1924)

Letter headings:
U   hitherto unpublished
[ ]   presumed place and/or date
P   place and/or date according to postmark
E   place and/or date according to ELM

Letters, postcards and telegrams:
< >   text suppressed in ELM and/or AMM
[ ]   text amended or added by the editors
» «   original text in English
« »   text deleted by Mahler

Quotations from the diaries of Alma Mahler-Werfel:
« »   text amended, deleted or added at a later date

Typographical conventions
Original texts by Gustav or Alma Mahler are printed in Roman characters. Editors' commentaries and passages quoted from other sources are printed in italics. As far as possible, Mahler's original underscoring has been retained.

Personal or place names that include the German 'sz' ('ß') are reproduced with 'ss'.

Foreword

After the death of Gustav Mahler in May 1911, it took his widow Alma Maria[*] nearly ten years to bring some semblance of order to her private life. Already in the autumn of 1911 she was briefly but passionately involved with Josef Fraenkel, the doctor who had tended her husband during his final illness. Then she met the painter Oskar Kokoschka and embarked with him on an erotic adventure that threatened to consume them both. In search of calm and stability she turned to the architect Walter Gropius, with whom she had fallen in love in the summer of 1910, and who, perhaps unwittingly, had all but wrecked Mahler's marriage. She married Gropius in the autumn of 1915, but by the following year the relationship had deteriorated to a 'weary sundown',[1] and even the birth of a daughter, Manon, on 5 October 1916, could do nothing to restore it. In 1917 Alma found solace in the arms of the writer Franz Werfel, and in January 1919 she gave birth to a son fathered by him, who died in infancy. In October 1920 she annulled her marriage to Gropius and opted, after much heart-searching, for a stable partnership with Werfel. It was her wish, as she wrote, 'not to place a yoke around his neck . . . no . . . but to live freely at his side for the rest of my life'.[2] In due course the partnership was ratified by marriage, but not until 1929.

Were it not for Werfel, Alma may never have found the courage to 'publish and be damned'. Evidently it was he who urged her to capitalize on Mahler's posthumous papers, of which she was administrator and sole beneficiary, and to write a book of memoirs. The Mahler estate included numerous letters, many of which had been given to Alma by the recipients or their heirs. But the mainstay of the collection was a large bundle of letters, telegrams and postcards which she herself had received from Mahler during their years of courtship and marriage.

Her first idea was for a volume of letters from Mahler to his colleagues and friends. She offered the project to the Viennese publisher E. P. Tal, and its imminent publication was duly announced, as *Gustav Mahlers Briefe I*, in the preface to Paul Stefan's Mahler biography of 1920.[3] Time passed, and the book failed to materialize. In 1923, when Tal published an abridged

---

[*] In 1910 a first volume of Lieder was published under the name of Alma Maria Schindler-Mahler, while as a writer she called herself Alma Mahler-Werfel. Henceforth we shall follow tradition and refer to her simply as Alma.

edition of the 'Mahleriana' of Natalie Bauer-Lechner, entitled *Erinnerungen an Gustav Mahler* (Memories of Gustav Mahler), Alma's project was again announced, this time under the title of *Freundesbriefe* (Letters to Friends).*

Alma had been at loggerheads with Paul Stefan for some years, and her resentment of Mahler's indefatigable chronicler Bauer-Lechner went back even further (cf. pp. 12–13). These old antagonisms now resurfaced, evidently because Stefan had pointed out in his preface to Bauer-Lechner's book that the author, who was a first-class viola player, had been able to discuss musical matters with Mahler at a professional level: 'Had Mahler been conversing with a fellow composer or conductor, he would have spoken differently. But here he was talking to a woman who was herself a practising musician, and to whom music signified not only a means of earning a living but also a vocation.'4 Alma was quick to sense the subtext of this seemingly innocuous remark: that she, the wife, rated by comparison as a mere amateur. In a letter to Schoenberg she complained that Stefan had 'promised to stress that these were <u>not</u> Mahler's words, but those of Frau Bauer-Lechner. Now comes the foreword – enthusiastic (as far as could be said of such a moron) in its praise of the book, and larded with <u>impudent</u> remarks about me. [. . .] In future I shall never let anyone – of that particular fraternity – come anywhere near me.'5

Hence, in 1924, when Alma finally completed her manuscript of *Gustav Mahlers Briefe 1877–1911*, it was published not by E. P. Tal but by the newly founded Paul Zsolnay Verlag. 'It was the time of the [galloping] inflation', she recalled, 'and I complained [to Zsolnay] that by the time my royalties from the previous year for the works of Gustav Mahler had been paid out, they were completely worthless. [. . .] Suddenly Zsolnay had a brainwave: "If you were to bring me Franz Werfel's Verdi novel,6 I could set up a new publishing house on the strength of it." [. . .] Later followed my "Mahler Letters", which had already been promised to another publisher, but we were able to free ourselves of the obligation . . . and after several other books followed the facsimile edition of Gustav Mahler's Tenth Symphony.'7

Already at that time Alma was preparing a second volume of letters, which included reminiscences of her life with Mahler. Before it could be published, several passages had to be modified. As her daughter Anna Mahler later explained (in conversation with Henry-Louis de La Grange), there was too great a risk that Alma's derogatory remarks – about Mahler's friends and relatives, Richard Strauss and his wife Pauline, as well as other well-known figures, both alive and deceased – would lay her and the pub-

---

* E. P. Tal announced several other titles that were never written (or even commissioned), including a monograph on Zemlinsky by Alban Berg.

lishers open to libel charges. By the end of the 1930s the situation had changed. For one thing, Mahler's next of kin were all dead, as were most of his friends of whom Alma had written so disparagingly, including Bauer-Lechner, Emil Freund, Siegfried Lipiner, Friedrich Löhr and Albert Spiegler; for another, Alma was now a fugitive from Nazi Germany, having decided to join Werfel in exile. Thus it was only natural that she should come into contact with Allert De Lange, one of the leading publishers of exiled German authors, who operated from Amsterdam.* In 1940, when De Lange published *Gustav Mahler. Erinnerungen und Briefe* (Gustav Mahler. Memories and Letters), Alma was beyond the jurisdiction of German, Austrian or Swiss courts of law. Even after the war, when Richard Strauss read her book at Baden (Canton Aargau), there was little he could do but pencil his protests into the margin, in the hope that posterity would find them (which it did: see pp. 90–100).

Both typescript drafts of Alma's *Gustav Mahler. Erinnerungen und Briefe* are preserved at the Médiathèque musicale Mahler in Paris. The first, bound in black cardboard and embossed in gold with the title *Ein Leben mit Gustav Mahler 1901–1911*, includes not only letters from Mahler to Alma but also letters to other recipients, dating from 1875 to 1886. The revised version, in two volumes bound in red linen with gold-embossed titles, is entitled *Ein Leben mit Gustav Mahler I* and *II* (henceforth referred to as ELM).

'I wrote this book many years ago,' explains Alma in her preface. 'The sole reason for doing so was that nobody knew Gustav Mahler better than I did. [. . .] I had not originally intended it to be published during my lifetime.'[8] In the first version of her autobiography, published in 1959 under the title *And the Bridge Is Love*, she returned to the question of the *Erinnerungen und Briefe*: 'I was wrong to delay publication of Gustav Mahler's letters for so long and to allow myself to play a secondary role in it. All his friends thought I had something to hide.'[9] Later she adds: 'In Holland [in 1936] I had to give several interviews on the subject of Gustav Mahler; and people urged me to write down everything I had said. I replied that I had already done so long ago. Later, as a result of these newspaper articles, I was visited in Paris by Dr Landauer, a representative of the publisher Allert de Lange, who begged me so long and so hard to assign him the rights to my book on Mahler that I finally gave in, although I had actually promised it to Paul von Zsolnay.'[10]

---

* Amsterdam was the home of two major publishers of exile literature: Querido and De Lange. The German novelist Hermann Kesten and his compatriot Walter Landauer ran De Lange's German department, which published ninety-one books by authors in exile, including Bertolt Brecht, Max Brod, Ödön von Horvath, Joseph Roth and Stefan Zweig.

In June 1940 Holland was invaded and occupied by German troops; Landauer was arrested and deported to Germany, and the correspondence files of De Lange were confiscated and taken to Berlin. Landauer perished shortly before the end of the war, aged forty-three, in the Bergen-Belsen concentration camp. Only in 1991 were the De Lange papers returned to Amsterdam, after an odyssey via Berlin, Dresden, Moscow and Potsdam. Thus Alma's correspondence with Landauer miraculously survived the Holocaust and is now available for research. From her letters it transpires that not only Werfel but also Anna Mahler helped her with the manuscript, and that Werfel himself corrected the proofs. The publishers left the choice of letters entirely to her, and were evidently also content to leave the question of omissions and alterations to her discretion. On 29 December 1938 Alma informed Landauer that the manuscript of *Ein Leben mit Gustav Mahler* was ready, and six months later she acknowledged receipt of the galley proofs. Publication was originally scheduled for the autumn of 1939, but had to be postponed by six months due to the outbreak of war. In the event, Alma agreed to the title suggested by Landauer: *Gustav Mahler. Erinnerungen und Briefe (Gustav Mahler. Memories and Letters)*. In its final form the book included 197 letters, of which 159 were addressed to Alma.

A new impression of the book, identical in content to the 1940 edition, was published in Amsterdam by Bermann-Fischer/Querido in 1949. This version also served as the basis for translations into Czech, Dutch, English, French, Italian, Russian, Spanish and Swedish, published between 1946 and 1993. Altogether three English editions were published, and since these are the forebears of the present volume, they merit particular attention. The first, translated with Alma's seal of approval by Basil Creighton and published by John Murray in 1946, included only eighty-one letters, all addressed to Alma. In 1968 followed an expanded, annotated and commented version, edited by Donald Mitchell. This was also a first attempt to correct Alma's commentaries in the light of independent research. Three further impressions of this edition were published in Britain and the USA (in 1969, 1973 and 1990), the 1973 and 1990 editions being edited by Mitchell in collaboration with Knud Martner. An unauthorized German version of Mitchell's 1969 edition was published in 1979 by Ullstein Verlag, Berlin.

None of these editions included any new source material. It had long been assumed that there were considerably more letters in existence than those which Alma had chosen to publish, but since her collection was not accessible to outsiders, this could not be verified.

*

After Alma's death, on 11 December 1964 in New York, her entire estate, including all her Mahler manuscripts, was inherited by her daughter Anna. A few years later Anna Mahler sold several items from this collection – including all the letters of Gustav Mahler – to a private collector in the USA, Hans Moldenhauer.

The first musicologist to investigate the life and works of Mahler on a systematic basis, Henry-Louis de La Grange, had been on friendly terms with Anna and her mother since the early 1950s. Before parting with these precious manuscripts, Anna therefore permitted him to transcribe or photograph anything he considered of importance to his work. This photographic material, including copies of almost all the letters published in this book, is now housed at the Médiathèque musicale Mahler (formerly Bibliothèque Musicale Gustav Mahler) in Paris, founded by La Grange and Maurice Fleuret in 1985.

The Moldenhauer Archives in Spokane, which Hans Moldenhauer often referred to as his 'Taj Mahal', housed what was probably the largest private collection of Mahleriana in the world. In 1982, as a memorial to his wife Rosaleen, he envisaged the finding of a permanent home for the Archives at The Library of Congress and eight other institutions in Europe and the USA.[11] Günther Weiss inspected the Mahler manuscripts in the Archive in 1983, and in 1989 he completed an inventory of Mahler letters, devoting particular attention to those addressed to Alma. Two years later he published a report on his findings in the German periodical *Musica*.[12]

It took several years before arrangements could be finalized for the transfer of the Mahler letters, as well as other letters[*] and twenty-two musical manuscripts, from the Moldenhauer Archives to a new home. Finally, in 1998, with the support of the Bavarian Landesstiftung and the German federal government, the Archive was acquired by the Bavarian State Library in Munich. At an exhibition in the library from March to May 2003 the collection was presented for the first time to a wider public. At the same time, the library published a lavishly illustrated companion volume,[13] with an essay on Mahler in Munich by Günther Weiss, and detailed accounts of the letters and musical manuscripts by Sigrid von Moisy and Hartmut Schaefer.

The remaining posthumous papers of Alma were bequeathed by Anna Mahler to the University of Pennsylvania in Philadelphia, where the

---

[*] These included fifty-six letters to Mahler's parents-in-law, Carl and Anna Moll, letters to Emil Hertzka (Universal Edition, Vienna), early love letters to Josephine Poisl in Iglau (Jihlava) and five love poems, dating from 1884, to the young soprano in Kassel who inspired the *Lieder eines fahrenden Gesellen*, Johanna Richter.

'Mahler-Werfel Collection' was deposited in the Special Collections of the van Pelt-Dietrich Library Center. For any student of Alma, of Werfel, or indeed of the multitude of artists and writers with whom they both were in contact, this collection contains a mine of information. Central to the collection are the manuscript copies of Alma's early diaries (*Tagebuch-Suiten*). They were published in German in 1997, edited by Antony Beaumont and Susanne Rode-Breymann; an abridged English version followed in 1998. Largely unaffected as they remain by Alma's later impulse to expurgate and distort, they have contributed much to the revision of this book.

One major obstacle to evaluating Alma's posthumous papers is her handwriting (for a facsimile of a relatively legible specimen see p. 45). Researchers may be consoled by the knowledge that even Mahler had difficulty in reading it, at least during the first weeks of their romance (cf. letter 9, second paragraph), and that her composition teacher, Alexander Zemlinsky, once replied to a letter from her in the form of a sackcloth-and-ashes Old Testament parody:

4. [. . .] And the Lord God Zebaoth brought down great misfortunes upon my wicked head;

5. For he sent a written message from his child Alma Maria; and wretch that I am, I strained my sinful eyes a full hour in the hope of divining what she had told me.[14]

When it comes to Alma's typescripts, the problem is less of legibility than of credibility. All her publications draw to a greater or lesser extent on typed copies of her diaries, which she herself prepared, abridging and altering *a piacere* as she went along, before destroying the originals (i.e. with the exception of the early 'suites'). Some passages from these copies went into the making of her Mahler memoirs, while other passages served as source material for her autobiography. A third collection of typescript fragments in the Mahler-Werfel Collection includes material that not even Alma deemed suitable for publication. A few extracts from these later, hitherto unknown diaries have been incorporated into the revised commentaries and annotations of this book. Where appropriate, handwritten addenda, corrigenda and other explanatory notes in the unpublished version of ELM are incorporated in the commentaries and footnotes. The same goes for passages which diverge in any substantial way from the published edition of 1940. ELM has also proved invaluable in cases where the original manuscripts of certain letters are no longer preserved. Here the editors had no choice but to reproduce Alma's transcripts, naturally with a *caveat* about possible abridgement or expurgation.

A further substantial, largely unresearched source of information about Alma and her world is her correspondence with composers, conductors, writers and acquaintances in other walks of life. Here again, in many instances she preserved only typewritten copies of the letters, and sold or destroyed the originals. The same *caveat* therefore applies here as to her copies of Mahler's letters.

Of her own letters Alma rarely kept copies, and since Anna Mahler took no action after her mother's death to organize the return of originals from the recipients or their heirs, the correspondence as preserved leaves an unbalanced impression. However, the posthumous papers of Gropius at the Bauhaus Archive in Berlin include sheaves of letters from Alma, ranging from her first outpourings of love to the final messages of estrangement. These present a very clear picture of her style as it developed over a period of some fifteen years. Well over a hundred letters to Arnold Schoenberg are preserved at the Arnold Schoenberg Center in Vienna, and other archives, both in Europe and the USA, contain further material. Forty years after her death, all these manuscript sources still await the attention of archivists and researchers. A true picture of Alma can emerge only from those documents with which she herself had no chance to tamper. As for her letters to Mahler, we have it on her own authority (as related to La Grange) that she destroyed them, with the sole exception of the letter of 29 November 1901, of which a fair copy is pasted into her diary (cf. facsimile on p. 45).

Of the 159 Mahler letters published in AMM1, only thirty-seven were reproduced in their urtext form; the remaining 125 were abridged or expurgated, the numerical discrepancy (37 + 125 = 162) being explained by the fact that in three instances Alma telescoped two letters into one (87/135, 243/245 and 323/324). The present edition includes a total of 350 items (letters, postcards, telegrams and other messages in diverse forms).

In his letters Mahler sometimes mentions telegrams, postcards or letters that were not preserved in Alma's archive. Alma may have lost them, sold them or even given them away, for at times the spirit moved her to distribute gifts of Mahleriana amongst her friends, and though she will have been unlikely to part with original letters, the possibility cannot be ruled out. Hence even the revisions and additions implemented in this book do not necessarily represent the final word.

The table on p. xx illustrates the statistical difference between the present edition and Alma's original edition of 1940.

Mahler wrote to Alma most frequently when he was on concert tours, hiking in the mountains or resting at his summer house in Maiernigg (later

Year	Letter number	Hitherto unabridged	Hitherto abridged	Hitherto unpublished	Total
1899	1	0	0	1	1
1901	2–16	5	9	1	15
1902	17–21	2	1	2	5
1903	22–57	3	16	17	36
1904	58–127	4	25	41	70
1905	128–158	5	12	14	31
1906	159–192	3	10	21	34
1907	193–246	3	19	32	54
1908	247–265	0	7	12	19
1909	266–300	0	13	22	35
1910	301–350	12	13	25	50
Total		37	125	188	350

Toblach). Whenever Alma accompanied him on his travels, or whenever they were at home together, there can be little doubt that they conversed in much the same tone and on the same range of topics as they corresponded. Conversely, Mahler's studied avoidance of certain topics – notably his work in progress – implies that he steered clear of these issues even when he and Alma were together.

By their very essence, Mahler's letters lack biographical continuity. In this book, for the sake of completing the time-line of his creative life, the letters are therefore interspersed with commentaries. Two further factors motivated this departure from standard editorial practice: the need for background information, which might otherwise have been provided by Alma's half of the correspondence, and the lengthy gaps between some of the groups of letters, which, for the sake of continuity, needed to be filled with at least a backbone of biographical information.

When Mahler was away from home, he normally wrote on stationery provided by the hotel in which he was staying or by the orchestra which he was conducting. Naturally, these letter headings vary in style and layout. For the sake of consistency and clarity, the layout here has been standardized. The same applies to the many telegrams and postcards, with the term 'postcard' covering three different document categories: correspondence cards (usually sent in envelopes), double-sided blank postcards and picture postcards.

In the early twentieth century, cities such as Vienna or Berlin enjoyed the luxury of at least two postal deliveries per day. Since all long-distance post was transported by train, letters dispatched in the late afternoon normally reached their destination by the following morning (at least, over distances that could be covered by a night train). At this time it was standard practice in Germany and Austria for letters to be postmarked not only on reaching the sorting office but also on arrival at their destination. Since the latter was often easier to read, Alma dated many of the letters according to their arrival stamp. 'Because Mahler never dated his letters,' she writes in AML, 'it was not at all easy to sort them into the correct order. I was only able to do so by taking note of their content. Nobody could have done this other than myself.'[15]

Only six of Mahler's letters to Alma include an exact date (letters 24, 145, 328, 271, 337 and 343); some open simply with the day, written out in longhand, but most are entirely devoid of such information. 'The reason [. . .] is quite simple,' Mahler explained (in 1896) to the music critic Max Marschalk. 'I usually have no idea what the date actually is!'[16] Since many of his letters include references to documented events (concerts and opera performances, birthdays etc.), the date on which they were written can usually be deduced. In the case of the letters written on vacation at Maiernigg or Toblach the situation is less clear, for many of these lack concrete points of reference. Unfortunately the accuracy of Alma's own datings leaves much to be desired. The untiring research of La Grange, Mitchell, Martner, Weiss and others, followed by a minute inspection of original postmarks and other fresh 'evidence' at the Bavarian State Library, has meanwhile made it possible to assign reliable datings to many items in the collection.

In several instances Alma obliterated single words, whole lines or even complete passages of Mahler's text. To this end, her distinctive violet ink proved remarkably effective. Even with the aid of forensic chemistry it will probably never be possible to restore those lost words.

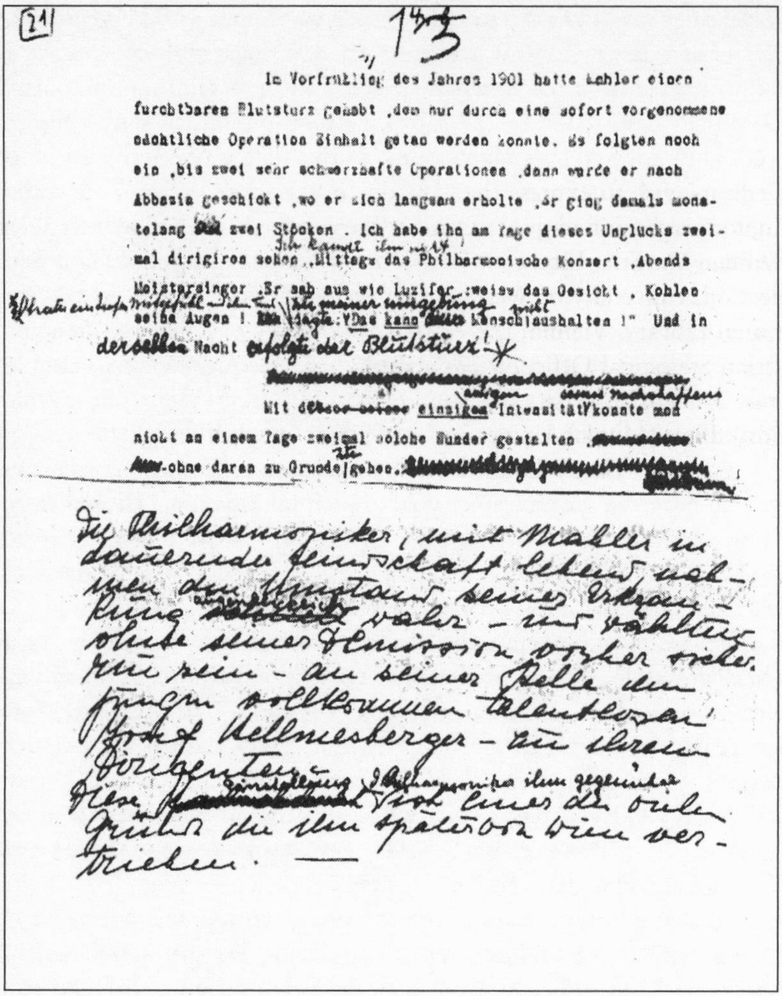

[21]

13

Im Vorfrühling des Jahres 1901 hatte Mahler einen furchtbaren Blutsturz gehabt, dem nur durch eine sofort vorgenommene nächtliche Operation Einhalt getan werden konnte. Es folgten noch ein, bis zwei sehr schmerzhafte Operationen, dann wurde er nach Abbazia geschickt, wo er sich langsam erholte. Er ging damals monatelang mit zwei Stöcken. Ich habe ihn am Tage dieses Unglücks zweimal dirigiren sehen, Mittags das Philharmonische Konzert, Abends Meistersinger. Er sah aus wie Luzifer: weiss das Gesicht, Kohlen seine Augen! [illegible] sagte: "Das kann [illegible] Mensch aushalten!" Und in derselben Nacht erfolgte der Blutsturz! *

Mit [illegible] einzigen Intensität konnte man nicht an einem Tage zweimal solche Wunder gestalten, [illegible] ohne daran zu Grunde gehen.

Die Philharmoniker, mit Mahler in dauernder Feindschaft lebend, nahmen den Umstand seiner Erkrankung [illegible] wahr – und wählten ohne seiner Demission vorher sicher zu sein – an seiner Stelle den jungen vollkommen talentlosen! Josef Hellmesberger – zu ihrem Dirigenten. Diese Einstellung d. Philharmoniker ihm gegenüber ist eines der vielen Gründe die ihn später von Wien vertrieben. —

A page of Alma's typescript for *Ein Leben mit Gustav Mahler*

The editors wish to express their thanks to S. Fischer Verlag, Frankfurt am Main, for permission to quote from the publications of Alma Mahler-Werfel; to William Guthrie, Librarian-in-Charge, Music Library and Mahler-Rosé Collection, University of Western Ontario, London, Ontario; the Austrian National Library, Vienna; the Austrian Academy of Sciences, Vienna; the Austrian Statistical Office, Vienna; Robert E. Becque (Hook of Holland); Gernot Gruber (University of Vienna); Oswald Panagl (Salzburg University); Hendrik Bims (Munich University); and Bernt Hage (Vienna)

Henry-Louis de La Grange, Knud Martner, Günther Weiss

Summer 1995

Preface to the English Edition

Since 1995, when the German edition of this book was first published, two events have served to expand its horizons: the publication in 1997 of the complete text of Alma's early diaries (*Tagebuch-Suiten*), dating from January 1898 to March 1902, and the publication in 2003 by the Bavarian State Library of a catalogue of all Mahler letters acquired from the Moldenhauer Archives.

Until 1997 the Médiathèque musicale Mahler was in possession only of those pages of Alma's early diary that were relevant to Mahler (i.e. part of Suite 23 and the whole of Suite 24), photocopied in the early 1960s. Earlier research on this topic was invariably based on these photocopies, the difficulty of deciphering Alma's hand leading scholars to work from a transcript prepared for the Médiathèque rather than struggle with the original. When transcribing the complete canon of twenty-one *Tagebuch-Suiten* for publication, it became clear to the editors, Susanne Rode-Breymann and myself, that this first transcript was far from accurate, and that some of the pages had been wrongly ordered, leading to substantial errors of chronology.

In cataloguing the letters at the Bavarian State Library, Monika Köstlin and Sigrid von Moisy discovered to their consternation that no less than twenty-one items had gone astray, and that others were in urgent need of conservation. For the first time, however, it was now possible to scrutinize the envelopes and verso sides of postcards, which were not included in La Grange's collection of photographed copies. With the aid of this new material, it has been possible to revise many of the datings in the German edition, and to assign reliable datings to several items hitherto dated only putatively.

For Rode-Breymann and myself, the German version of this book (*Ein Glück ohne Ruh'*) provided invaluable information for the annotation of the *Tagebuch-Suiten*. Its publication also demonstrated, however, that Mahler's letters to Alma intersected on many levels with the *Tagebuch-Suiten*, and that a definitive edition of the one would have to be fully correlated with the other. It is above all in this sense that the English edition has been revised ('updated' might be the more appropriate word). In the light of information from the *Tagebuch-Suiten*, the opening section ('Overtures') has been extended to cover considerably more ground than the original 'Präludium'. Likewise, commentaries and annotations throughout the book have been corrected and expanded in the light of recent research, and extra annotations included where appropriate, necessary or possible. A number of errors, of the kind that inevitably creep into a project of this size and scope, have been corrected.

Although this is by no means the first time that Mahler's letters to Alma have been put into English, over half of the items in this book appear in print for the first time. Apart from the admirable work of Creighton, a team of translators, led by Alice Frank and Roy MacDonald, has been occupied for years with the translating of texts for the authoritative four-volume Mahler monograph of La Grange. Other English-language writers on Mahler, when quoting from Alma's letters, have helped themselves as best they could.

Once the stiffness of unfamiliarity has been softened by a few months of marriage, Mahler's style of correspondence with Alma is generally simple, direct and astonishingly down-to-earth. In a manner akin to that of his musical style, he spikes his language with witticisms and *double entendres*, colloquialisms and quotations from librettos and classical works of literature. A translator must be prepared to take all this in his stride, but where passages of particular linguistic curiosity occur, I have included the corresponding German words or phrases (Saxon, Berlin, Viennese . . .) in the footnotes. For the Bavarian dialect with which Mahler mimics the speech of Richard Strauss and his wife Pauline there exists no adequate English equivalent.*
Mahler's poems constitute a further obstacle to translation, particularly those dating from the summer of 1910. Creighton and Mitchell considered them 'well-nigh impossible to translate effectively' and included only a few of them in their editions. Naturally, a complete edition cannot follow that example, even if some of the poems – whether left on a table or at the head of the stairs in the Toblach summer house – do not strictly count as letters. It seemed essential to retain the original scansion and structure of this poetry, even if semantic accuracy sometimes had to be sacrificed to the demands of rhyme and rhythm. By way of compensation, the original German text of each poem is reproduced in the appendix.

In early twentieth century Austro-Germany the use of florid opening and closing formulae – 'Highly esteemed Sir', 'I remain, Sir, your obedient servant' etc. – was still the general rule, even between husband and wife. These opening and closing formulae can sound ludicrous in translation, and in some contexts they are better omitted. With Mahler this is not the case: his greetings are brief, plain and sincere, hence eminently translatable.

* Alma's impression of the dialect spoken by Strauss and his wife, as 'notated' in AML, is equally graphic.

No hard and fast rules have been applied to the question of place names. 'Helsinki' is substituted for 'Helsingfors', since the Swedish name has been out of currency for almost a century; however, the names of cities and towns in formerly German-speaking regions – Göding (now Czech), Lemberg (now Ukrainian), Breslau (now Polish) etc. – have been left unaltered, with present-day equivalents in parentheses. Strictly speaking, 'Toblach' should have been replaced by 'Dobbiacco', for the town has been under Italian jurisdiction since the mid-1920s. Yet the Austrian name is synonymous with Mahler: in Italian, the flavour would have been quite wrong.

For help in revising and translating this book I would like to express my warmest thanks to Henry-Louis de La Grange (who has, in fact, masterminded the whole project), Alena Parthonnaud and the entire staff of the Médiathèque musicale Mahler, Paris; also Nancy Shawcross, curator of Special Collections, van Pelt-Dietrich Library Center, University of Pennsylvania in Philadelphia; Monika Köstlin (author) and Sigrid von Moisy (editor), who were responsible for the Mahler Acquisitions Catalogue, Bavarian State Library, Munich, Manuscripts Department; Oliver Hilmes, who shared with me much invaluable information that he had gathered for his biography of Alma, (*Witwe im Wahn*, Munich, 2004); Knud Martner, who checked the proofs and made numerous suggestions for corrections and improvements; Ingrid Schneider, who helped check the translations; Lee Watson, the postman at 3 Queen Square, who gave us expert advice on motorcycles; and Otto Hagedorn, who co-ordinated the bibliographical information and helped check the inventory of letters.

Antony Beaumont
Summer 2004

Introduction: A crossing of paths

> . . . and all things are true so far as they are,
> nor is there any falsehood, unless when
> that is thought to be, which is not.
> *Confessions of St Augustine*

Gustav Mahler and Alma Maria Schindler were married in the Karlskirche in Vienna on 9 March 1902. The bride was twenty-one-and-a-half years old, her groom a few months short of forty-two. Apart from their substantial age difference, it seems to have been the very disparity of their intellectual and social backgrounds that drew them together. Mahler was attracted to Alma by her beauty, her alert mind and emotional intensity. Though aware that he possessed by far the broader outlook, he trusted in Alma's ability and willingness to learn from him.

In their respective circles, both were highly regarded. For the young Stefan Zweig, to catch sight of Mahler on the street was 'something of a personal triumph which one could proudly relate to one's school-friends the following day'.[1] As for Alma, daughter of a celebrated painter whose death was still lamented in court circles ten years after the event, she was known to be intelligent, musical and exceptionally good-looking.

Mahler had been appointed Director of the Vienna Court Opera (*Hofoperndirektor*) by decree of the Kaiser in 1897. Zweig recalls that the decision was controversial: 'When Mahler was appointed Hofoperndirektor at the age of thirty-eight, fingers wagged and heads shook in disbelief that such a "young man" should be given charge of Vienna's leading cultural institution. People forgot that Mozart had completed his life's work by the age of thirty-six, Schubert indeed by the age of thirty-one.'[2] For Mahler himself, the appointment, which came as the just reward for years of indefatigable toil, marked the zenith of his career.

His father, Bernard Mahler, was born in 1827 in the small town of Lipnitz (Lipnice), approximately seventy miles south of Prague. Having set out in life as a simple carter, Bernard Mahler left no stone unturned to improve his social standing and widen his intellectual horizon. He was an avid reader (amongst fellow carters he was known as the 'coach-box scholar') and tried his hand at various professions, until at the age of thirty he acquired the lease of a small inn not far from his father's distillery in Kalischt (Kaliště), a small village in southern Bohemia. There, in 1857, he married Marie Herrmann and founded a family. Marie was ten years his junior, the second of seven daughters of a soap-boiler named Abraham Herrmann from the nearby town of Ledec.

During the first half of the nineteenth century, the right of abode for Jews in Austro-Hungary was strictly regulated. In 1860 this legislation was relaxed slightly, and Bernard Mahler lost no time in taking advantage of the new freedom of movement. In October of the same year he moved his small business across the Moravian border to the industrial town of Iglau (Jihlava), an isolated outpost of German culture in a predominantly Czech-speaking area of the Hapsburg Empire. There were two large churches in the town, as well as a small theatre which was used for occasional performances of opera and operetta. In the course of time Iglau had also become the home for a thriving, German-speaking Jewish community.

Here the Mahler family prospered and grew, until in 1879 Marie gave birth to her fourteenth child (of eleven sons and three daughters, several died in infancy, and one son, Ernst, died in his teens). Over a period of fifteen years Bernard Mahler established himself as a successful businessman, noted for his acumen, diligence and ambition. Thus he rose from humble beginnings to become a respected member of Jewish middle-class society.

The Mahlers' first son had died in infancy, and when the family moved to Iglau their second son, Gustav, was just four months old. Even if the circumstances of his birth (on 7 July 1860) were scarcely propitious, in one respect he was particularly fortunate: he had inherited in full measure his father's ambition, determination and self-confidence. At the age of three he was given a small accordion, and soon he had taught himself to play simple tunes and folk songs. As a result he was allowed to take piano lessons, and since there were several first-rate music teachers in Iglau, he made rapid headway, giving his first public concert at the age of ten.

As a child, and later also during his adolescence, Gustav was considered something of a daydreamer. He loved to spend his free time reading and making music, but made little outward show of the feelings and impressions aroused in him by his literary and musical discoveries. By the age of fifteen he had made such striking progress, both with piano playing and composition, that a family friend urged his reluctant father to take him to Vienna. Armed with a letter of introduction to the celebrated pianist Julius Epstein, Gustav went to audition at the Conservatory. He had played for hardly ten minutes when Epstein interrupted him. 'Herr Mahler,' he said, turning to

Bernard, 'your son is a born musician. [. . .] In this case I know that I am not wrong. This young man has spirit, but he should not be made to purvey wines and spirits like his father.'³

Two months later, in September 1875, Gustav Mahler enrolled for a three-year course at the Vienna Conservatory. There, by and by, he was able to develop his natural gifts. He also stayed on as an external pupil at Iglau grammar school (*Gymnasium*), where in 1877 he passed his final examinations (*Matura*) albeit with some difficulty. Parallel to his studies at the Conservatory, he also enrolled at the University.

During his years of study Mahler composed mainly chamber works; of his first attempts at orchestral writing many remained incomplete. The only score to have survived at all from this early period is the first movement of a piano quartet, composed at the age of about sixteen and a half. Though skilfully crafted, it reveals little individuality. At this stage, Mahler was clearly more concerned to satisfy his teachers' fondness for pastiche than to cultivate an original style. His strategy seems to have paid off, for having won first prize for piano in 1876, at his graduation in 1878 he also won first prize for composition.

All signs indicate that Mahler was by now aware of his exceptional gifts and dreamt of a career as a composer. However, his first two years after leaving the Conservatory were the most unhappy period of his entire youth. To eke out at least a modest living, he was obliged to give piano lessons, but this meagre income and an equally meagre grant from his father scarcely sufficed to make ends meet. Apart from these financial constraints, which caused him frequently to change his living quarters, a personal crisis was precipitated by his unrequited love for the daughter of the chief telegrapher in Iglau, Josephine Poisl. Three Lieder, composed for her, helped him to concentrate his creative energies, for soon afterwards he completed his first major work – his 'child of sorrow' as he later often described it – the cantata *Das kla-gende Lied* for soloists, chorus and large orchestra. Just before he completed the score, in the spring of 1880, he found himself at a turning point: weary of the lack of direction and the self-torment of his existence in Vienna, he decided to look for a conducting post in a provincial theatre. In the event he found employment for a summer season at Bad Hall, not far from Linz in Upper Austria. His principal task was to conduct performances of operetta, mainly for the benefit of patients who had come there to take the waters. Even if this activity was not exactly the fulfilment of a musical dream, it strengthened his resolve to make a career in theatre. Thereby he could earn an honest living, and later perhaps also make his mark as a composer.

Once the contract at Bad Hall had expired, it was by no means easy for the inexperienced young Kapellmeister to find further employment. A whole year elapsed before Mahler found another post, this time at the Landestheater in Laibach (Ljubljana), the capital city of Slovenia. Meanwhile, in September 1881 he had entered *Das klagende Lied* for the Beethoven Prize, but the jury, chaired jointly by Johannes Brahms, J. N. Fuchs and Hans Richter, rejected it out of hand.

Mahler's contract in Laibach expired after only six months, and once again he had to muddle through for a lengthy period (nine months in all) without a permanent engagement. Then in January 1883 he secured himself a three-month contract at Olmütz (Olomouc). This was his first breakthrough. His interpretations of Méhul's *Joseph* and Bizet's *Carmen* caused such a stir that, on the strength of a one-week trial period, he was offered a full-time contract at the Royal Theatre in Kassel. Here, in the course of two seasons, he developed those characteristics for which he later became both famous and notorious: a highly individual approach to the great classics, a fastidious ear for detail, an interest in stage production that far transcended purely musical considerations and a no-tolerance attitude towards lax discipline. Together with these qualities went the will power and uncompromising honesty he had inherited from his father.

In Kassel, where Mahler's authority was still limited, such qualities endeared him neither to his superiors nor his subordinates. Several times he was reprimanded by the Intendant and even disciplined for infringing the strict theatre regulations. Nevertheless, he became known for his indefatigable style of rehearsing, and he scored a particular success with a performance of Mendelssohn's oratorio *St Paul* at the Kassel Music Festival in June 1885.

Once again it was an unhappy love affair, this time with Johanna Richter, a soprano in the ensemble of the Kassel Hoftheater, that led to the composition of a masterpiece: the *Lieder eines fahrenden Gesellen*.

Already in January 1885 Mahler had signed a three-year contract with the Stadttheater in Leipzig for the post of 2nd Kapellmeister, to take effect from July 1886. But then, in the spring of 1885, his Kassel contract came to a sudden end, and he found himself without employment for the following season. In desperation, Mahler approached the director of the Neues Deutsches Theater in Prague, Angelo Neumann, who immediately offered him a contract as 1st Kapellmeister.

In Prague, Mahler had his first opportunity to conduct Mozart and Wagner, as well as a work with which he was to remain closely associated for the rest of his life: Beethoven's *Fidelio*. Here, too, he was attacked 'in the

4

name of hallowed tradition' and reprimanded for his interpretative idiosyn-
crasies. But he had already grown immune to criticism, and adhered unerr-
ingly to his principles. Towards the end of the season, serious disagreements
arose between him and Neumann over the tempi for the ballet music in
Gounod's *Faust*. But evidently the dispute left no lasting antagonism on
Neumann's part, and anyway Mahler left Prague soon afterwards, in July
1886, to take up his post at Leipzig.

Here too, the critics took him to task for his tempi. For Mahler himself
this was less of an irritation than his subordinate position at the Stadttheater
vis-à-vis Arthur Nikisch, himself a rising star in the firmament of world-class
conductors. In the spring of 1887 Nikisch was ill for several weeks, and
Mahler was required to take over several of the operas that would normally
have been conducted by his colleague. When Nikisch returned, Mahler
expected to continue conducting at least some of these works, but Nikisch
refused, and the fracas ended with Mahler resigning at the end of the season.

One of many friendships forged during this Leipzig period was with Carl von
Weber, grandson of the famous composer and a Captain in the Saxon army.
Weber showed Mahler the sketches for his grandfather's unfinished opera *Die
drei Pintos*, of which he had prepared a revised libretto, and succeeded in persuading him to prepare a stageworthy version and add extra musical numbers
where necessary. Despite the triviality of its libretto, at the world première in
Leipzig on 20 January 1888 the work scored a remarkable success. Soon it was
being performed all over Germany, and Mahler became something of a household name, albeit as arranger rather than as composer or conductor.

This unexpected success served to bolster his confidence in his own
compositions. It was at this time that he completed his *First Symphony* and
the symphonic movement *Todtenfeier*, which later became the first movement of his *Second Symphony*. Once again he fell passionately in love – this
time with Marion, wife of his friend Carl von Weber and a mother of three
children. The two planned to elope, but at the last moment their plans were
thwarted. The finale of the *First Symphony* gives voice to the despair and
hopelessness of Mahler's situation at this time.

Mahler left Leipzig in May 1888. Shortly afterwards, Angelo Neumann
invited him back to Prague to conduct a new production of *Die drei Pintos*
due to open in early August. Mahler remained in Prague to conduct further
performances, but in early September there followed a further disagreement with Neumann, which led to Mahler leaving Prague and returning to
Iglau. Soon afterwards he was invited to Budapest to audition for the post
of musical director at the Royal Opera. His appointment was announced

on 1 October. Thus, at the age of twenty-eight, Mahler took charge of a major opera house.

He made his Budapest début with *Das Rheingold* and *Die Walküre* in January 1889. The success was overwhelming, and the Hungarian press acknowledged that he had achieved remarkable results in a very short time. Since the *Ausgleich* of 1867 between Hungary and Austria, nationalism had been gaining ground throughout the Hapsburg empire. Mahler was accordingly instructed that his ensemble should be recruited as far as possible from within Hungary, and the gaps filled with Italians rather than Germans or Austrians. Nobody objected to the fact that he himself was a German-speaking Jew from Bohemia, or that Wagner provided the mainstay of his repertory, for at this stage he was *persona grata* in Budapest. But in January 1891 the post of Intendant was filled by the Magyar nationalist Count Géza Zichy, who made it clear that the chief conductor in his theatre would have to be a Hungarian. Therefore, at the end of March Mahler resigned. In return he received compensation to the tune of 25,000 fl. to cover his immediate material needs.

A regular visitor to Budapest was Johannes Brahms, who was very impressed by Mahler's interpretation of *Don Giovanni*. For Mahler it was a stroke of luck to have won the admiration of this most influential of musicians. On the negative side, the world première of his *First Symphony* in November 1899 (performed under the title of *Symphonic Poem*) was a complete fiasco. During his remaining time in Budapest he succeeded in completing only two albums of songs from *Des Knaben Wunderhorn*, which he had begun in Leipzig.

As from March 1891 Mahler was under contract as 1st Kapellmeister at the Stadttheater in Hamburg. At first sight this was a relatively modest position compared to his directorship in Budapest, for he now bore no responsibility for artistic decisions. Admittedly he was working with finer singers than ever before, but other aspects of his work in Hamburg left much to be desired. The size of the repertoire in particular strained him severely (he had to conduct anything up to 150 performances per season). Rehearsal time was inadequate, the orchestra was mediocre, productions were poor, and sets and costumes often shabby; above all, the director, Bernhard Pollini, was less interested in artistic quality than in balancing his books. Inevitably, he and Mahler were constantly at loggerheads.

When Mahler took office in Hamburg he made the acquaintance of Hans von Bülow, at that time the high priest of German conductors, who had settled there in 1885. Bülow immediately recognized Mahler's exceptional talent as an interpreter (he called him the 'Pygmalion' of the Hamburg Opera), but could make nothing of his music. After the death of von Bülow in 1894, Mahler was appointed his successor as conductor of the Subscription Concerts.

In Hamburg, as elsewhere, the critics took issue with Mahler's unaccustomed tempi and his orchestral retouchings of the classics. These negative reactions, as well as frequent quarrels with Pollini, strengthened Mahler's resolve to seek his fortunes in Vienna. 'At the sound of the doorbell', recalled Bruno Walter, 'he would often exclaim, "And now comes the call to be lord and master of the southerly regions."'[4] Indeed, Mahler used every resource at his disposal to obtain a conducting post at the Vienna Hofoper.

During his period in Budapest both of Mahler's parents had died, as well as his married sister Poldi. From then on he considered himself responsible for his two surviving sisters and his two brothers. Otto, the youngest, had studied music and was about to embark on a career as an opera conductor when, in 1895, he committed suicide.

Mahler spent the summer months of the years 1893 to 1896 with his sisters Justine and Emma in the Salzkammergut, at Steinbach on the Attersee. Here he completed his *Second* and *Third Symphonies*. To avoid being disturbed by holiday-makers, he had grown accustomed to working in a purpose-built lakeside 'composing shack' (*Komponierhäuschen*). Every year he would call on Brahms, who was in the habit of spending his vacations at nearby Bad Ischl.

A frequent guest at Steinbach was Natalie Bauer-Lechner, violist of the Soldat-Roeger Quartet and a friend of Mahler's from Conservatory days. He valued Bauer-Lechner for her intelligence and first-rate musicianship; furthermore, she shared his tastes in literature and music. Bauer-Lechner stood in awe of Mahler, but also tended to impose on him. Mahler was aware that she kept a diary, in which she wrote down everything that he said in her presence, including comments on his work in progress. He enjoyed talking to her and was of the impression that she, as an ardent admirer, probably understood him better than his own family and most of his closer friends. Natalie's *Mahleriana* were not published until long after his death, and even then only in abridged form.* Her book presents a detailed and riveting chronicle of Mahler's life from 1893 to 1901, i.e. of the summers in Steinbach and later in Maiernigg during which he was working – virtually under her nose – on the *Second*, *Third* and *Fourth Symphonies*, as well as some sections of the *Fifth*.

* An English translation of the original version by Dika Newlin (ed. Peter Franklin, London, 1980) was followed by an expanded German edition, *Gustav Mahler in den Erinnerungen von Natalie Bauer-Lechner* (ed. H. Killian and K. Martner, Hamburg 1984).

In 1895, two years before Mahler was appointed Director of the Vienna Hofoper, Pollini had engaged the Viennese dramatic soprano Anna von Mildenburg for his Hamburg ensemble. Mahler spent countless hours coaching her in her new roles. In the process he fell in love with her. In Hamburg their relationship became an open secret, and idle gossip threatened to jeopardize their careers. The relationship ended only when Mahler left for Vienna in April 1897, and though Mildenburg joined his ensemble in 1898, history did not repeat itself. From now on, the two kept their distance, and eventually Mildenburg found a sympathetic partner in the writer Hermann Bahr, whom she married in 1909. Mahler assured Alma that his affair with Mildenburg had been entirely platonic, but the tone and content of his correspondence with her leaves no doubt as to its true nature. She was a passionate woman, but also temperamental, domineering and intolerant.

At that time, Mahler's ideal of a wife and partner, as outlined in a letter to the Czech composer Josef B. Foerster, was quite the opposite: 'Remember, above all, that I simply cannot abide the sight of a woman who looks unkempt, uncombed or sloppily dressed; and then, above all, I need my solitude. As a creative artist I am utterly reliant on it. In other words, my wife would have to agree to live separately from me: maybe she would take the front rooms, while I occupied the rear of the house, with my own entrance. She would have to be prepared to see me only at certain times of the day, and at such times she would have to appear looking her best and tastefully dressed. Finally, she would have to agree not to reproach me, not to feel rejected, discouraged or disparaged if sometimes I did not feel inclined to see her at all. In other words, she would have to be imbued with qualities that one cannot find even in the finest, most obsequious of women.'[5] If Mahler ever fell in love, Foerster prophesied, he would immediately throw such rigid principles to the wind.

During his Hamburg years, Mahler kept himself informed about every significant event at the Vienna Hofoper. The director, Wilhelm Jahn, had been in office for seventeen years and was beginning to show signs of old age; in particular, he was losing his sight, and it was generally known that he would soon have to stand down. In the spring of 1896, Mahler, aided by Bauer-Lechner and von Mildenburg, contacted Rosa Papier, a mezzo-soprano who knew Mahler from his Kassel performance of *St Paul*, in which she had participated. Since then Papier had abandoned her performing career and returned to Vienna, where she was in great demand as voice teacher at the Conservatory (Mildenburg herself had been one of her students). Papier's relationship with Eduard Wlassack, administrative director to the Intendant, enabled her to exert considerable influence on backstage affairs at the Hofoper.

Mahler's achievements at Budapest and Hamburg, both as conductor and administrator, had won him wide acclaim. Nevertheless, there were still several obstacles to his appointment as Hofoperndirektor in Vienna. In a city where anti-Semitism was rampant, his Jewish background was a particular problem. His alleged irritability, dictatorial manner and uncompromising perfectionism also weighed against him, and thanks to Mildenburg, he enjoyed a reputation as an unbridled womanizer, for in Hamburg she had done all she could to make their relationship public.

Fortunately the court of Franz Josef I was largely free of anti-Semitic prejudice. The Kaiser himself let it be known that he would never allow decisions to be dictated to him by anti-Semites. That this was no empty talk is witnessed by his refusal to ratify the election in 1895 of Karl Lueger, leader of the anti-Semitic Christian Socialist Party, as burgomaster of Vienna. Nevertheless, it was considered advisable to handle the question of Mahler's engagement in Vienna with the greatest discretion. On the advice of Rosa Papier and Eduard Wlassack, in February 1897 Mahler took the essential step of converting to Catholicism. The music critic Ludwig Karpath not only published a detailed description of the events leading up to Mahler's engagement in Vienna, but also published an interview with Mahler on the topic of his conversion. 'The fact is that my longing to escape the hell of Pollini's theatre in Hamburg made me think about withdrawing from the Jewish covenant. That is what is so ignominious about the whole affair. I do not deny that this step – motivated, as one might say, by the instinct for self-preservation – cost me a considerable effort, even though at heart I was not at all averse to the idea.'[6]

In the hope of fulfilling his dearest ambition, Mahler turned to anyone and everyone in Vienna who might be willing or able to help. By this time Brahms was already severely ill, but Mahler knew he could count on the support of Brahms's friend and ally, Eduard Hanslick – the 'Bismarck of music critics', as Verdi once described him.

On 8 April 1897, five days after the death of Brahms (which happened also to be the date of the founding of the Vienna Secession), it was officially announced that Mahler had been appointed Hofopernkapellmeister. His début, with *Lohengrin* on 11 May, was unanimously praised by the critics. The rest was only a matter of time. In July Mahler was promoted to the rank of deputy director, and on 15 October to director.

At once he launched into a programme of internal and external reform. Late-comers would in future be permitted to take their seats only at suitable breaks in the performance, efforts would be made to curb the influence of the claque, and a number of well-loved singers were to be dismissed because, in Mahler's opinion, they paid too little attention to the question of fidelity to the score, which for him was of cardinal importance. Productions of standard works were to be improved, a larger portion of the repertory was to be dedicated to Mozart and Wagner, and, where possible, the operas of Wagner would in future be given without cuts. At first the public viewed Mahler's reforms with considerable suspicion, for concerts and opera performances – indeed all artistic presentations – in Vienna were considered first and foremost to be social events. The vast majority failed to understand the reasoning behind these drastic new measures. Mahler's opponents described him as a tyrant, a devil, a dangerous and inhuman revolutionary. But fortunately there were also serious music-lovers who appreciated his religious devotion to his art and acknowledged him to be an interpreter of genius.

In court circles Mahler's efforts found unreserved support, particularly from the Lord Chamberlain (*Obersthofmeister*) Count Liechtenstein and his deputy Count Montenuovo, the man who bore ultimate administrative responsibility for the Hofoper. As Bauer-Lechner recalls, 'Count Liechtenstein summoned Mahler to discuss an argument about a ballet conductor, and tactfully suggested – for he was very impressed with Mahler – that he should avoid fuelling the fires of those who complained of his irascibility and impatience. Mahler countered by pointing out that discipline at the Hofoper was appalling, that the level of performance had suffered for many years due to slipshod attitudes and woefully low standards, and that such shake-ups were absolutely necessary. He could only call the house to order if he went to work with the utmost severity. Many people actually agreed with him, he added, and indeed *wished* for such "disputes". In future he would therefore be grateful if the Count were to summon him only at times when there had not been at least two such disputes every week.'7

A potentially disruptive situation arose in the autumn of 1898, when the new Intendant, August von Plappart, tendered the draft of a revised contract for Mahler, which would have drastically curbed his powers. It stipulated, namely, that for each and every artistic decision, whether concerned with casting, repertoire or stage design, the Hofoperndirektor would in future be required to submit a written application, to be approved or rejected by the Intendant. The conflict raged for twelve months, with Mahler insisting that he, and only he, was qualified to take such decisions. Eventually he got his way, though not without the support of Montenuovo.

In the autumn of 1898 the Vienna Philharmonic voted for Mahler to assume the directorship of their Sunday midday concert series. Although this was a considerable extra burden, Mahler was glad for the chance to conduct symphonic music as an adjunct to his operatic repertory. For two and a half years, despite occasional disagreements with the orchestra and the customary cavils about his tempi and orchestral retouchings, he dominated the musical scene in Vienna. His programmes included his own works (the *First* and *Second Symphonies* and a selection of his orchestral songs), but neither the public nor the press managed to come to terms with his music. In Berlin, Hamburg and Weimar his first two symphonies fared little better; only in Munich did he find a positive echo with a jubilantly received performance of the *Second Symphony* in October 1900.

Mahler was now forty years old. Compared with the great masters of the past he had composed relatively little. In order to make time for creative work between his professional duties he decided to purchase a permanent summer residence. With the aid of a loan from his sister Justine, in September 1899 he bought a plot of land overlooking the lake at Maiernigg on the Wörthersee. Building work began soon afterwards, and in 1900 his *Komponierhäuschen* was put up in the woods nearby, while the house itself was completed the following year.

As a result of his negative experiences with Mildenburg, Mahler took great care to shield his private life from the public gaze. However, it soon became known that he had fallen in love with the young coloratura soprano Selma Kurz, who had him to thank for her engagement at the Hofoper. The relationship did not last long, for both parties were too concerned about the detrimental effect it might have on their careers. If there was any truth to the gossip circulating in Vienna at the time, Mahler was also entangled, if briefly, with two other sopranos at the Hofoper: Rita Michalek, who sang in the world première of the *Fourth Symphony*, and Marie Gutheil-Schoder, who was widely considered to be the finest artiste in Mahler's ensemble. Documentary evidence indicates that both these relationships were purely platonic. Nevertheless, the rumours were sufficiently widespread for Mahler's future father-in-law, Carl Moll, to warn his stepdaughter Alma that Mahler was a notorious playboy.[8]

On Sunday, 24 February 1901 Mahler conducted the sixth midday concert of the Philharmonic season; the same evening he conducted a performance of *The Magic Flute* at the Hofoper. In AML, Alma claims to have attended both performances ('I saw him conduct twice that day'[9]). In fact, she did nothing of the sort. Her diary reveals that she went to the midday concert (a programme of Weber, Dvořák and Bruckner), but spent the evening at home with friends, playing *Die Meistersinger* to amuse herself.[10] This did not deter her from providing an eye-witness account of the evening performance:* 'He [Mahler] looked like Lucifer: white in the face, his eyes like black coals. I felt profoundly sorry for him, and said to the people sitting near me: "This is more than the man can endure." [. . .] It was the unique intensity of his interpretative art that enabled him to create two such miracles in one day without destroying himself.'[11]

Whatever she later thought up (or repeated from hearsay), during the night of 24–25 February Mahler nearly died of an intestinal haemorrhage. His life was saved by the speedy reaction and presence of mind of two doctors. For fear of a relapse he underwent an operation ten days later at the Sanatorium Loew, after which he was ordered to spend three weeks convalescing. Easter week was spent at the resort of Abbazia (Opatija) on the coast of Istria. From there he wrote to the management of the Vienna Philharmonic that his doctors had advised him to resign his post as conductor of the Sunday concerts. Shortly afterwards it came to his notice that the orchestra had anyway been intending to replace him, and that negotiations were under way with Josef Hellmesberger Jr. Mahler was particularly angered and offended by this decision: Hellmesberger, who was at best a mediocre conductor, scarcely rated as an adequate successor; Mahler also felt that he had done more for the orchestra's material benefit than any of his predecessors.

The following summer saw the completion of three songs for the cycle of *Kindertotenlieder*, a Rückert song ('Um Mitternacht'), a further *Wunderhorn* song ('Der Tambourg'sell') and the funeral march of the *Fifth Symphony*. The American psychoanalyst Stuart Feder has drawn attention to the connection between Mahler's haemorrhage in February 1901 and the obsession with death in these compositions. He has also formulated the remarkable theory that there was a connection between Mahler's experiences of February 1901 and his subconsciously strengthened wish to found a family, which he evidently considered the only way to free himself of his death fixation.[12]

In *Mahleriana*, Bauer-Lechner gives an idyllic description of the spring of 1901 in Abbazia.[13] No less idyllic is her account of the following summer, the first that Mahler spent in his newly completed villa at Maiernigg.[14] It was her fondest hope that Mahler would one day marry her – but it was not to be. The break with Natalie is documented on a page of Alma's typescript of EML that she later pasted over. No doubt this version of the story corresponded largely with what Mahler himself had told her:

'He fended her off, she persisted, and matters finally came to a head with the following dialogue, which remained a catch-phrase in our house.

* As if to corroborate her *faux pas*, Alma writes that Mahler was conducting *Die Meistersinger* that evening. It was in fact the 110th anniversary of the world première of *Die Zauberflöte*.

'Bauer: "Marry me for heaven's sake!"

'Mahler: "No!"

'Bauer: "Why not?"

'Mahler: "Because I don't love you and never shall. I could only ever love a beautiful woman."

'Bauer: "But I am beautiful! Just ask Henriette" (Henriette Mankiewicz, a kitsch painter and an old friend of Mahler's).'

Natalie's confession of her true feelings led to an immediate and irrevocable break between the two. Later Mahler complained to Alma that Natalie had been too hasty in seeking comfort in the arms of a lover: she could have waited a little longer . . .

At this time, according to Alma, Mahler also became aware that his sister Justine was in love with the concertmaster of the Vienna Philharmonic, Arnold Rosé. On several occasions Alma asserts that Mahler felt betrayed by his sister and was disappointed that she had behaved so badly towards him. Here, too, her account is more than questionable, for Arnold Rosé was one of Mahler's closest friends; indeed, the two often spent their summer vacations together. It is also hard to believe that Mahler, who was by no means the 'moralist' Alma often tried to make him out to be, should by this time have been unaware of his sister's true feelings for Rosé. At any rate, none of the many letters to his sister, whether written before or after her marriage, reveal any trace of this alleged annoyance. Apart from this, Mahler had every reason to be grateful to his sister. Already in Budapest she had taken charge of the household; in Hamburg she rendered the same service for him; likewise, in Vienna they shared an apartment (at Auenbruggergasse 2) until shortly before their respective wedding days.

As the year 1901 drew to a close, Mahler was delighted by the prospect of starting a new life with Alma, a young woman whom he truly and profoundly loved. It was no doubt a great relief to him that his resolve to marry had left the way free for his sister Justine to found her own family.

Alma's autobiography, *Mein Leben*, opens with a reverence to her father: 'I am the daughter of a great monument, as it were. My father [. . .], the model for my childhood, was the son of an old patrician family. He was the leading landscape painter of the Austrian monarchy.'[15] When Emil Jakob Schindler died of peritonitis in August 1892, aged fifty, Alma was thirteen years old. To the end of her days, her father remained a powerful and decisive influence on her.

Schindler was known as the leading exponent of 'atmospheric impressionism', an Austrian equivalent to the school of Camille Corot. He first become aware of the *plein air* painters of Fontainebleau, Théodore Rousseau, Charles-François Daubigny and Jean-François Millet (the so-called 'Ecole de Barbizon'), at the First International Art Exhibition (Munich, 1869). This experience persuaded him to concentrate on outdoor painting. Where French artists limited their use of colour to a canon of tone-on-tone painting, Schindler's keen eye led him to portray sunlight in pure, bright and strongly contrasting colours, turning the motifs themselves into abstract objects. His particular interest centred on emanations of light and weather. Sometimes he would dedicate complete series to one motif, recording the way it changed according to weather conditions, the time of day or the changing seasons.

Alma's father was by no means the 'son of an old patrician family', as she would have it. His great-grandfather was in fact a scythe-smith from the Steyr Valley (Upper Austria), and though his grandfather enjoyed a certain affluence, as owner of a cotton-mill in Fischamend, under the proprietorship of Emil's father, Julius, the mill was destroyed by fire, leaving the family destitute. In the early years of his career Schindler was as poor as the proverbial church mouse, and evidently also lived beyond his means. The story is told that he once lacked the money for a pair of new shoes; indeed, that he had not even paid for the previous pair. In order to keep going until he had completed his next picture, he rented a so-called monthly fiacre, complete with driver. Once the painting was sold, he paid the driver, then went off and bought new shoes.

To arrive at the affluence from which Alma benefited so greatly in her childhood, he worked hard and with an unshakable sense of his own worth. As a young unknown in Paris, he had made the acquaintance of Hans Makart, the 'grand master of the Hapsburg industrial revolution',[16] who soon came to appreciate his exceptional talent. For an entire winter Makart put his Vienna studio at his young colleague's disposal. This studio, in the Gusshausstrasse, was also the scene of Makart's legendary costume festivals. On such occasions the room would be festooned with roses, society ladies came dressed in renaissance costumes from Makart's personal collection, and the guests sat at tables laden with exotic dishes and fine wines. Here Schindler witnessed a world half-way between dream and reality, awakening images that provided the incentive for his own rise to a position of respect in high society.

The breakthrough came in 1878, when he was awarded the Karl-Ludwig Medal in Munich for his painting *Moonrise in the Prater*. As a result, two wealthy Viennese patrons offered a guarantee to purchase all his future work. Thus the prize instantly brought him into contact with the very clientele he had been hoping to reach; even the Kaiser and Prince-Regent Luitpold of Bavaria soon numbered amongst his clients and friends. A further mark of distinction was his winning the Reichel Prize in Vienna. From 1885 onwards Schindler led a life of material comfort. He sold his house at Bad Goisern (near Ischl) and rented a romantic manor house at Plankenberg, not far from Vienna.

Alma was thus born with a silver spoon in her mouth. For all the comfort of her surroundings, her father nevertheless took great pains to further her intellectual and artistic talents. Alma recalls having been fascinated from earliest childhood by her father's work in the studio, but also by his passion for music. For, apart from being a painter of distinction, Schindler possessed a fine tenor voice and was a particular connoisseur of the Lieder of Schubert.

Even if it was Schindler who exerted the prime influence on Alma, her talent for music seems largely to have been inherited from her mother. Anna Sofie Schindler (née Bergen) was born in Hamburg on 20 November 1857 as the second of nine children. The 'official' version of her life-story, as recounted in AML, was that her father, who owned a small brewery in Hamburg, sent her to Vienna in 1876 or 1877 to take voice lessons at the private academy of a highly regarded teacher by the name of Adele Passy-Cornet. The reality, as revealed in AMD, was not quite as grand: 'Mama told us about her youth: how one night she (the whole Bergen family) had to flee from the island of Veddel, because after the war the payments weren't coming in, but Grandpa didn't want to declare himself bankrupt, and they didn't even have enough money for the rent – how their mother, who was suffering from puerperal fever after having her twelfth child, was carried out of bed and out of the house by the children – how, at eleven years of age, Mama became a ballet dancer, how she played walk-on parts for a whole year and became the breadwinner for the whole family – how later she became a nanny, had to wash nappies and sleep in the cooks' room – how she became an au-pair girl, «then a cashier at the baths» and finally a singer.'[17]

First mention of Anna Bergen as a singer is found in the *Fremden-Blatt* for 17 December 1877. The article describes an attraction typical of Viennese *Fasching*, a *divertissement* written specially for the occasion and performed by an *ad hoc* troupe of amateurs and semi-professionals. Schindler sang the lead tenor, and Anna had the honour of playing his counterpart: 'The Künstlergenossenchaft [Artists' Union] opened its salon for the season two days ago with a revival of *Lenardo und Blandine.** As Lenardo, Herr Schindler commands a comic talent that would do credit to any professional actor. New to the production was Frl. Bergen, who has been engaged as prima assoluta for the current season at the delightful Theater an der Wien.

---

* *Lenardo und Blandine*, parodistic operetta by Franz Mögele, based on the poem by G. A. Bürger.

The young lady worked hard with her voice, but in the humour-saturated atmosphere of a "Gschnas" [masked ball] as thrown in these surroundings, she has not yet found her footing.'[18]

For the 1878/79 season Anna Bergen secured herself an engagement at the Ring-Theater, where she made her first appearance on 19 October 1878 in Josef Forster's comic opera *Die Wallfahrt der Königin*, partnering the tenor Fritz Schrödter and under the baton (at least in later performances) of the young Felix Mottl. Soon afterwards she auditioned successfully for the Stadttheater in Leipzig and accepted a full-time contract there.

However, at the turn of the year she was still in Vienna, having dissolved her Leipzig contract. A notice in the *Fremden-Blatt* for 28 December 1878 explains why she did so:

'An engagement has recently been announced which should be of considerable interest in Viennese artistic circles. One of our finest landscape painters, Herr Emil J. Schindler, is to marry the young singer Julie [*sic*] Bergen (actually Bergk von Bergen-op-Zoom), who made her name at her début in the Ring-Theater. The bride and groom first met through the amusing operetta performances at the Künstlerhaus, where, as is generally known, Herr Schindler with his pleasing tenor voice has always played a central role, while his female counterparts have changed almost every year. In such operettas, the soprano and tenor are called upon to poke fun at the all-embracing power of Amor. But sometimes that god grows malicious and revenges himself in appropriate form by transforming comedy into bitter earnest.'[19]

The wedding took place on 2 February 1879 in Vienna. Alma was born almost exactly eight months later. 'On 31 August,' wrote Schindler in his diary, 'I became a father: a natural outcome of getting married. Why I married, I cannot say. I could say that I did so because I loved my Anna, but that is not and cannot be the reason. Only those should marry who can lie down and die the very next day, without leaving their nearest and dearest to die of starvation – but not those who love. It was a reprehensible act. Whether I am happy, whether Anna is happy: it makes absolutely no difference. All that counts is whether there is money in the house. And there isn't even enough to pay for my funeral.'[20]

In AML Alma confirms that her mother's first years as the wife of a little-known artist were a 'struggle for daily bread'.[21] Here, at least, the published account is corroborated by her diary: 'And then the first years of her marriage – the debts – and Papa who, when things were at their worst, would simply roll over on his stomach and sleep round the clock. And Carl [Moll], who would run from one usurer to the next and pawn everything he could lay his hands on.'[22]

Alma's attitude towards her mother was one of constant vacillation. She recalls that her parents sometimes argued, and asserts that it was always her mother who was to blame. Two years after Schindler's death, Anna married Carl Moll, who had studied with Schindler and later also managed his business affairs. Alma was shattered to observe her mother's rapid change of allegiance. She herself never came to terms with this marriage or accepted Moll as her new father, and this was certainly the reason for many of the resentful remarks she made about him. In AML she describes him as 'an eternal student of my father', who 'completed one course after another until the time of his death, much to the detriment of his meagre talent'.[23] In fact, Moll was a talented and successful painter in his own right, who joined with Gustav Klimt and other progressive artists in 1897 to found the Vienna Secession.

As for Anna, she was evidently as much a libertine as her daughter. In August 1881 she gave birth to a second daughter, Grete, by the painter Julius Berger.* And later, when Alma herself sought solace in an erotic adventure with the young architect Walter Gropius, Anna Moll thought nothing of acting as their go-between.

While Alma never came fully to terms with her stepfather or forgave her mother for remarrying, Mahler, who was himself almost as old as his in-laws, was fond of them both. His letters to Alma frequently close with greetings to 'Mama and Carl'. In her own edition of these letters, Alma often omitted these passages, as well as many other positive remarks about Anna and Carl Moll.

Emil Jakob Schindler's home had been a meeting place for musicians, painters, writers, architects and politicians: very much the same company that Alma herself later liked to keep. Unforgettable for her was the moment (she was just eight years old) when her father summoned her and Grete, and told them the story of Goethe's *Faust*. When he had finished, he gave them a copy of the book, with the words, 'This is the finest work of literature in the world.'[24]

The highlight of Alma's childhood years was a lengthy journey to Dalmatia, undertaken by Emil Jakob Schindler in 1887–8 in search of material for an ambitious publication that was to be entitled *The Austro-Hungarian Monarchy in Words and Pictures*, as well as to fulfil a lucrative commission by the banker Hermann Horwitz.[25] The expedition ended with a lengthy sojourn on the isle of Korfu. 'We rented an upright piano from the town,' Alma recalls, 'and it was here that I, at nine years of age, began to compose.'[26]

* Some sources ascribe Grete's fatherhood to the art historian Alfred Lichtwark.

The death of Alma's beloved father caused a painful hiatus in the life of the adolescent girl and left deep psychological scars. In 1896 she participated in the unveiling in the Vienna Stadtpark of a memorial statue, sculpted by Edmund Hellmer. From then on, her father was the 'monumental' yardstick against which she measured every man she encountered, from Klimt and Zemlinsky to Werfel and beyond. Even at her funeral in December 1964 her father was still present, in the form of a portrait displayed behind the catafalque.[27]

In her memoirs Alma discusses only her father's side of the family in any detail. Thereby she attaches particular importance to her great-uncle, Alexander Schindler, a member of parliament for the Austrian Liberal Party, who is best remembered for having taken the initiative in the abolishment of corporal punishment in the Austrian army. Alma was fascinated by the theatrical aspect of her great-uncle's life and particularly impressed by the fact that he had published novels under the pseudonym Julius von der Traun. She also recounts that he was a notorious wastrel and once indeed so heavily in debt that he was obliged to sell his stately home at Schloss Leopoldskron near Salzburg.* When the moment came for him to take his leave, he made his way to the waiting coach through a double rank of candle-bearing servants in livery, specially 'staged' by him for the occasion. Alma stresses that her father was himself a 'born aristocrat' and had spent some years of his youth at his uncle's stately home.

To compensate for the loss of her father's artistic and intellectual guidance, Alma plunged into a life of restless activity. She took counterpoint lessons with the blind organist Josef Labor, and sight-read her way through every piece of music she could lay her hands on, from Bach to Offenbach. The greatest discovery for her was the music of Wagner. Day after day she would sit at the piano, singing and playing through Wagner operas; in the process she overstrained her vocal chords (until then, allegedly, she had possessed a pleasing lyric soprano voice). An attack of the measles left her slightly deaf, but she was adept at concealing the fact, and those unaware of her impediment are said to have taken pleasure in the way she would lean forward to listen to them, fondly imagining that this was her way of showing interest in the conversation.

The death of Alma's father left her in dire need of someone to protect and guide her. In the salon of Anna and Carl Moll, male visitors were particularly taken by the talented young lady with her apparently unquenchable thirst for knowledge and exceptionally good looks. It did not take her long to grow

---

* Max Reinhardt later lived at the same address.

accustomed to being admired, and soon she discovered just how much sway it gave her over people. The first to share her 'largely positive outlook on life' was Max Burckhard, who until 1898 had been director of the Vienna Burgtheater, where he was the first to stage Austrian productions of Ibsen, Gerhart Hauptmann and other leading modern playwrights.

On one occasion Burckhard made a sizeable contribution to Alma's library by presenting her with a Christmas present of two laundry baskets full of classical works of literature. In AML Alma writes that she was seventeen years old at the time and 'utterly uninformed' on literary matters.[28] Once again she stands corrected by her own diary. At Christmas 1898, according to AMD, she received 'ten volumes of the writings of Wagner' from an unnamed donor,[29] and the following year she again received 'books etc.', but they paled into insignificance beside such presents as a 'skunk fur, chinchilla fur, blouses, writing paper, a green handbag' and no less than 'six pairs of gloves'.[30] Burckhard's basket-loads – thirty books in all* – actually arrived at Christmas 1900, by which time Alma was twenty-one years old.

Of her friendship with Burckhard she wrote, 'Everyone in my immediate vicinity was shallow, so I had to find everything out for myself. Max Burckhard was the first to take control of my vacillating spirits. We were both wild about Nietzsche, for he was a revolutionary modernist. But I didn't care for Burckhard as a man, and I found his erotic advances repulsive. Apart from that, we always agreed on everything, and in the long run that grew tiresome.'[31]

When Alma entered into a clandestine (and entirely chaste) relationship with Gustav Klimt, the tedium was over. As *spiritus rector* of the Vienna Secession, Klimt was a frequent guest at the Molls'. But when they invited him to join them in the spring of 1899 on the last stage of an extended Italian tour, they had no idea of the fires that were kindling between him and Alma. 'We were all in Genoa,' Alma recalls, 'my "family" and Klimt, who was in pursuit of me. Our love was cruelly destroyed by my mother. In violation of every code of honour, she read the hesitant remarks in my diary, and thus kept herself informed about every stage of the love affair. The worst of it was that she read that Klimt had kissed me.'[32] From then on Alma's parents did their utmost to keep Klimt at bay.

Alma never forgave her mother for having encroached upon her intimate thoughts and feelings at this extremely delicate stage of her development. Even in old age she spoke fondly of Klimt, 'the most gifted of them all, a man

---

* The authors were Grillparzer, Shakespeare, Uhland, Schopenhauer, Gottfried Keller and Knud Hamsun; there was also a domestic encyclopaedia.

who at the age of thirty-five was already at the height of his powers, hand-some in every sense of the word and already very famous. His good looks and my fresh youthfulness, his genius, my talent, the profound musicality of our existence, had tuned us both to the same key. I was criminally inexperienced in the art of loving – and he fulfilled me and found me wherever I was.'[33]

Having been forcibly prevented from loving Klimt, Alma reacted by with-drawing into her shell. 'I started composing again, in search of a way to express my grief,'[34] she writes. But then, on 26 February 1900, she met the man who was to guide her 'unruly attempts at composing' (*wilde Komponiererei*) onto 'earnest'[35] paths: the composer and conductor Alexander Zemlinsky. As from 18 October he was her teacher; the following spring (on 10 April to be exact), after months of self-imposed restraint on both sides, he became her lover. In AMD the reader is fobbed off with a story about Zemlinsky playing the prelude to *Tristan* while Alma gazed into his eyes, then sunk into his arms.[36] In fact, the wooing and winning of her 'beloved Alex' was no instan-taneous event but a lengthy process, fraught on both sides with difficulties. AMD tells the story frankly, unsparingly and in great detail; this is not the place to retell it. The cardinal lesson she learnt from her love for Zemlinsky was that she was perfectly capable of loving a man even if he was not good-looking. Here, as later with Franz Werfel, it was the 'mental acuity and strength' of her partner to which she felt irresistibly drawn.[37]

When the paths of Alma Schindler and Gustav Mahler first crossed, she was caught on the horns of a dilemma: her family circle had lost all appeal for her and, though reluctant to forego her life of leisure and luxury, she was determined to break out on her own. Even if she still had much to learn, she saw her future primarily as a composer.

As for Mahler's music, when Alma later admitted that she had been held in Mahler's 'mysterious and powerful sway',[38] she was speaking of the con-ductor and Hofoperndirektor, not the creative artist. Before her marriage she had already taken a strong dislike to his music, or at least as much as she knew of it, and during ten years of marriage she found little reason to revise that opinion. After his death she enjoyed the role of 'Mahler's widow', but was less happy about having to attend performances of his works and give a verdict on them. On the ninth anniversary of Mahler's death, 18 May 1920, she summed up the situation with brutal frankness: 'I am by no means per-fectly in agreement with his music. To me it often sounds outlandish, some-times even disagreeable. The Sixth and Seventh Symphonies do affect me deeply though.' Then, in pencil, an afterthought: 'u.d.L.v.d.E' ('and *Das Lied von der Erde*').[39]

Ten years later she still thrilled to the sound of the *Seventh Symphony:*[*] 'It was like being in a fairy-tale – blissful – lost in a dream [. . .] – once again I experienced all the torments of privation and fulfilment. Today my belief in Gustav was so strong. Sometimes I had tried to wash it away, to avoid living too much in the past.' When Webern conducted the *Sixth*, later the same day,[†] she wrote that she could 'scarcely bear to sit through the last movement, for it drew me so very close to him again. [. . .] I still feel the same pain as twenty years ago.'[40] But the dream gradually faded, the pain dulled into oblivion. In 1960 and 1961, when the world celebrated two anniversary years in succession, Alma seems to have enjoyed the limelight more than the music. A century after his birth and fifty years after his death, being Mahler's widow still gave her every opportunity to win friends and influence people. But the music played at her funeral, which she had herself chosen, included not one note of Mahler.

[*] Seventh Philharmonic Concert at 12.00 midday on Sunday, 14 December 1930 (Alma writes '1932'); Vienna Philharmonic Orchestra conducted by Clemens Krauss.
[†] Third Workers' Symphony Concert in the Grosser Musikvereinsaal at 8.00 p.m. on 14 December 1930; Vienna Symphony Orchestra conducted by Anton Webern (the programme opened with three pieces for mixed chorus by Hanns Eisler). In AML Alma writes of the Krauss and Webern performances in consecutive paragraphs, but does not mention that they were given on the same day.

Overtures (1898–1900)

Alma perpetuated the myth that she first met Mahler in November 1901 at a dinner party hosted by her friend Bertha Zuckerkandl. In fact, she had already made contact with him, if fleetingly, in the summer of 1899. Her decision to suppress all mention of this early encounter (or indeed of several subsequent 'sightings' in Vienna) was doubtless motivated by her desire to create a legend rather than merely leave a straightforward account of events as they occurred. The same standpoint determined her decision to suppress or abridge passages from Mahler's letters. The aim was not so much to deify Mahler as to create an unsullied monument to an ideal marriage, whereby she, the ideal helpmate and long-suffering partner, would stand just as high and proudly on the pedestal as her celebrated husband. Hence, in her eyes it would hardly have been appropriate to reveal that she had once swooned – like any other impressionable teenage girl – at the mere sight of him.

In the absence of the first three suites of Alma's diaries, which have not survived, our story begins with Suite 4, of which the first entry is dated 25 January 1898.* By that time Mahler had already conducted no less than twenty-one different works at the Hofoper, including new productions of Dalibor *(Smetana),* Djamileh *(Bizet),* Eugene Onegin, The Flying Dutchman, Zar und Zimmermann *(Lortzing) and* Die Zauberflöte, *and had impressed his indelible stamp on a number of repertoire productions, notably* Der Freischütz, Don Giovanni, Lohengrin, Tristan *and the entire* Ring. *There can be no doubt that Alma attended at least some of these performances prior to January 1898, for she was an avid opera-goer and, already at the age of eighteen, a committed Wagnerite. Her first recorded impression of Mahler as a conductor dates from 11 February 1898:*

Siegfried [. . .]
Oh, it was wonderful! It didn't finish until 11:30. Mahler had opened all the cuts. As far as I'm concerned it could have lasted till dawn.[1]

Later that year she thrilled for the first time to the aspect of Mahler on the

---

* As preserved, the manuscripts of Alma's early diaries (*Tagebuch-Suiten*) begin in January 1898 and end in March 1902. She appears to have kept no diary again until the summer of the same year.

rostrum of the Grosser Saal of the Vienna Musikverein (the famous 'Golden Hall'), conducting a symphony concert with the Vienna Philharmonic.

Sunday, 4 December 1898
We didn't get up until 10:45 – got dressed and went straight to the Philharmonic Concert.* It was wonderful. As for Mahler – I'm virtually in love with him.²

Hence, it was only natural that one of Alma's oldest friends, Theobald Pollak,† should present her soon afterwards with a precious souvenir:

Saturday 31 December 1898 (New Year's Eve)
After dinner we played tombola . . . Dr Pollak gave me [a picture of] Mahler, my beloved Mahler, with his autograph.³

Mahler was not the only artist at the Hofoper to whom Alma felt particularly attracted. Another was the Danish heldentenor Erik Schmedes. The man was the quintessence of a Wagnerian hero: tall and strapping, blond and blue-eyed. However, in his private life he was a heavy drinker and, by all accounts, a wife-beater. Though at least vaguely aware of these flaws in his character, Alma delighted in flirting with him. Schmedes responded in kind and also rewarded her with snippets of backstage gossip, including the latest on Mahler and his most recent flame, the soprano Margarethe Michalek.

Friday 3 March 1899
He [Schmedes] told me the most awful things about Mahler: The poor man is so deeply in love (he laid much stress on this phrase, repeating it four or five times in true Burgtheater style, as if addressing a large crowd). He keeps pinching her cheek, and during rehearsal he kisses her repeatedly. All that smooching – it makes you sick. Such words are scarcely designed to brighten a man's halo. But what do I care about his personal affairs? It's the artist that I love.⁴

During the summer months, the better-off Viennese families would flee the torpid heat of the city and rent a house in the mountains or at a lakeside resort. Alma's family was no exception. By preference they spent their summers

---

* Programme: Brahms, *Second Symphony*; Dvořák, *A Hero's Song*, op. 111 (first performance in Vienna); Haydn, *String Quartet*, op. 76, no. 3 *('Emperor')* in Mahler's version for string orchestra; Mendelssohn, overture to Shakespeare's *A Midsummer-Night's Dream*.
† Recalling that Pollak 'was not baptized, and committed to the Jewish faith', Alma recounts that in 1892 her father used his influence to obtain a post for him at the Ministry of Railways, which he held for the rest of his active life (AML, 18).

in the idyllic surroundings of the Salzkammergut. Here Alma and her half-sister Grete could swim or go boating, wander in the forests or explore the countryside on their bicycles. In 1899 the family rented a villa at Stambach near Goisern, a few miles to the north of the Hallstädter See.

Friday 7 July 1899
On 23 June the whole clan was in Hallstatt. I stayed home, because I had an ear-ache and stomach pains. When they returned, they told me that Mahler was there too, indeed that they had spoken to him. They recounted even the tiniest details.
And then, the day before yesterday, this postcard arrived . . .[5]

1[U]   Aussee, 5 July 1899[P]

Sole authenticated and copyrighted signature:
<u>Gustav Mahler</u>.
Imitators are liable to prosecution.

[Alma's Diary, 7 July 1899, contd]
One further thing: they said they had sent me a postcard, and that Mahler had signed it. Gustav [Geiringer]* allegedly gave it to the waiter, but the card

---

* The pianist, composer and voice teacher, Gustav Geiringer. He was married to the actress Christine von Bukovics.

never arrived. So the day before yesterday Gustav told me the whole story: not a living soul had ever set eyes on Mahler, the whole thing was pure fiction, a pack of lies. At my cost the story had kept them heartily amused for two whole weeks. Then a few days ago Anton Geiringer* arrived here. On the way, in Ischl, he met Dr Boer,† who was about to drive to Aussee to call on Mahler. They let him into their little secret, and he passed it on to Mahler, who, just for fun, really did write to me. The whole thing was arranged very cleverly, and I'm delighted about the postcard.[6]

If Alma had missed her chance to meet Mahler that day, she made amends for it – in her own, distinctive way – a few days later.

Tuesday 11 July 1899
P.M. to Gosaumühle with Hanna, Christine, Gustav and Ernst.‡ [. . .]
We were just leaving Gosaumühle when Mahler rode towards us on his bicycle, behind him an old woman,§ followed by his sister and [Arnold] Rosé. I cycled past as quick as a flash. The Geiringers dismounted, the others too. Mahler asked if this was the road to Hallstatt. Christine said it wasn't, and offered to show him the way. By this time I was riding more slowly. They caught up with me and said: 'Mahler is following us.'
He soon caught up with us, and rode alongside about four or five times. Every time, he struck up a conversation. Shortly before Hallstatt he dismounted. We were pushing our bikes, and he started up another conversation, staring hard at me. I jumped onto my bike and rode off into the distance. The Geiringers were angry: they'd wanted to introduce me, and he was expecting it too. Judging by the way he looked at me, he appears to have perceived the connection between myself and the postcard – which I found most embarrassing. Anyway I felt absolutely no urge to meet him. I love and honour him as an artist, but as a man he doesn't interest me at all. I wouldn't want to lose my illusions either.[7]

Other friends of Alma's family, the Maggs, had bought a piano arrangement of one of Mahler's symphonies (presumably the Second*), and about a fort-*

---

* Anton Geiringer, Kommerzialrat and theatre director.
† Orig.: 'Boyer'. Dr Ludwig Boer, physician at the Vienna Hofoper.
‡ i.e. Hanna Moll (Carl Moll's sister-in-law), Gustav Geiringer, his wife Christine and their son, Ernst. The latter was about the same age as Alma.
§ Presumably Natalie Bauer-Lechner. An unpublished passage in her *Recollections of Mahler*, dated 'July 1899', records that Mahler was often driven to a rage during his summer vacation by 'named and unnamed female admirers who pursued him and bombarded him with requests for his autographs, photos etc.'

night after Alma's strange meeting with Mahler on the road to Hallstatt they came over to the Molls' to try it through. These were probably the first notes of Mahler's music that Alma ever heard.

Tuesday 29 August 1899
Dr Egger,* Mrs Magg, Mrs Sternlich and Paul Magg [. . .] came over to rehearse the Mahler symphony, which they played in a version for two pianos, eight hands. It sounded hideous – a potpourri of Wagner operas.[8]

From then on, Alma's diaries record numerous fleeting glimpses of her idol. According to her friend Gretl Hellmann, who was introduced to Mahler in December 1899, the Herr Operndirektor was known to 'trim his sails to the wind'.[9] Though aware of other alleged flaws in Mahler's personality – and Viennese society never ran short of such tittle-tattle – Alma was keen to find out more about him. Another old friend of the Molls, the soprano Lilli Lehmann, offered to make an appointment for Alma to meet him in his office at the Hofoper. 'I'd go,' she wrote, 'no question of it. You have to grab such chances whenever they arise.'[10] In the event, she decided not to go, but after that, whenever she caught sight of Mahler in Vienna, she would record the event with evident delight in her diary. Once, while out walking with Christine Geiringer, she bumped into him on the Ringstrasse. 'He greeted her,' writes Alma, 'but all the while he was staring at me.'[11] On another occasion she sighted him in the Prater three times in succession,[12] and a few days later she saw him there again, this time in the company of Schmedes.[13] A further opportunity for a meeting arose when Max Burckhard took her to dinner at Restaurant Hartmann, which also happened to be one of Mahler's favourite eating places.[14] There he sat, only a few tables away, but Alma made no effort to approach him. She had her reasons . . .

Thursday 10 May 1900
At the Tonkünstlerverein I asked Dr Horn[†] why he hadn't greeted me, and he got someone to tell me that his attitude was like mine towards Mahler: since he knows that I know that he's fond of me, he avoids all contact. – And actually he's right. If you are too well aware of someone's feelings for you, the quality of the friendship deteriorates.[15]

On 26 February 1900 Alma was invited to a dinner party at the home of Friedrich Spitzer, a prosperous amateur musician and patron of the arts. Here she made the acquaintance of several people close to Mahler, including

---

* Dr Friedrich von Egger-Möllwald, a government official.
† The solicitor Dr Richard Horn, a close friend of the Conrat family (cf. footnote on p. 29).

the twenty-eight-year-old composer Alexander Zemlinsky, whose opera Es war einmal . . . *had recently received its highly successful world première under Mahler at the Hofoper.*

Monday 26 February 1900
We took our seats at table. To my one side sat Dr Hans Fuchs, son of the deceased Kapellmeister,* [. . .] to the other – Zemlinsky. Naturally I spoke only with him. First we talked about Schmedes – and became so abusive that Zemlinsky said: 'If we can think of someone with whom neither of us has a bone to pick – we'll down a glass of punch in their honour.' – After a while we did indeed think of somebody: Gustav Mahler. We drained our glasses. I told him how greatly I venerated him and how I longed to meet him. 'Why don't you make an appointment with him at his office? He'd be terribly pleased.' 'I wouldn't mind if I did.'
We were more or less rapturizing over him, when suddenly Dr Fuchs turned to us and said: 'Mahler is a scoundrel.' We were both flabbergasted. And in a quiet, sad voice he poured out his tale of woe: 'My father hated him as long as he lived. He took years off his life.' – Yet I know perfectly well that Fuchs died of blood poisoning. Some people even claim that his son was to blame. It all struck me as unspeakably infantile. All the same I fell silent. And Z. said softly: 'You've gone all quiet. Has Fuchs dampened your enthusiasm for Mahler?' 'No,' I replied, 'on the contrary.'[16]

In his official position as secretary of the Vereinigung bildender Künstler Österreichs, Carl Moll travelled to Paris in May 1900 to supervise the hanging of paintings by prominent Secessionists in the Austrian Village of the World Exhibition. Since Mahler was there to conduct three concerts with the Vienna Philharmonic, Moll seized the opportunity and asked him to sign a postcard for Alma.

Monday 25 June 1900
This card arrived this morning. An autograph – from my Mahler.[†]

---

* The 'deceased Kapellmeister' was Johann Nepomuk Fuchs, who had conducted at the Hofoper from 1880 until his death in 1899. Zemlinsky had studied composition with him at the Vienna Conservatory from 1890–92.
† The other signatory is Dionys Magg, presumably a member of the Magg family mentioned on p. 27.

AVENUE DES CHAMPS ELYSEES LA NUIT. PARIS

Later that year Mahler conducted the Viennese première of his First
Symphony *at a Sunday midday concert of the Philharmonic Society. For
Alma it was a further opportunity to come to grips with his music.*

Sunday 18 November 1900
In the morning: Gretl [Hellmann]. We played through the Mahler symphony.
At noon the Philharmonic concert:
  Beethoven: 'Prometheus' overture
  Schumann: 'Manfred' overture
  G. Mahler: Symphony no 1 in D major
The 'Prometheus' overture, 'Manfred' – say no more. They exist, plain and
simply, and they're beautiful too. Which you can't say of the Mahler symphony. Certainly it's done with talent, but with the greatest naivety and
refinement, and not in the best sense of the word. An unbelievable jumble of
styles – and an ear-splitting, nerve-shattering din. I had never heard anything
like it. It was exhilarating, but no less irritating. I arrived at the Conrats',[*]
my pulses raging, scarcely able to speak.[17]

---

[*] Hugo Conrat, a prosperous businessman and honorary treasurer of the Wiener
Tonkünstlerverein. He and his wife Ida had been close friends of Brahms, and were still a
mainstay of Viennese cultural life. At their apartment in the Walfischgasse they regularly held
soirées and dinner parties for artists, writers, musicians, journalists and politicians.

And so the name of Mahler vanishes from Alma's early diaries for almost a year, from the day, on which she saw every illusion of her hero as a great composer thrown to the winds, until 7 November 1901, when she finally plucked up the courage to speak to him. During the intervening twelve months she completed the transformation from teenage girl to young lady, a process that was sped on its way by her intense, tormented love affair with Zemlinsky. Inevitably, she still took notice of Mahler, if only because she still attended his concerts and opera performances. But if she occasionally caught sight of him in the street or at a restaurant, she made no further mention of it. She was totally engrossed in her 'beloved Alex'.

THE LETTERS

1901

On Saturday 2 November 1901 Alma summed up her feelings for Zemlinsky in a few words:

All my thoughts are centred on this one man, this ugly, sweet little man. [. . .] <u>Nothing</u> about him is disagreeable, unappetizing, I love everything about him.[1]

That same afternoon, while out walking on the Ringstrasse, she met her friends Emil and Bertha Zuckerkandl.

Zuckerkandl was an eminent anatomist, but also a man of high intellect and full of humour. Immediately he asked me: 'We're expecting Mahler to drop in some time this week. Wouldn't you like to come along? – I know that you take an interest in him.' I declined, for the truth was that I had no wish to meet Mahler. The previous summer, when it had seemed almost inevitable, I had myself managed to avoid a meeting.[2]

So Alma stayed away, and Mahler also made his excuses. A week later Bertha Zuckerkandl repeated her invitation, and this time Mahler accepted, chiefly because he wanted to see Bertha's sister, Sophie Szeps, whom he had met the previous summer in Paris. Alma accepted the invitation too, but brought Carl Moll with her as chaperon.*

At table, she was ushered to a place between two of her former lovers, Gustav Klimt and Max Burckhard. As soon as dinner was over she headed straight for Mahler, with the intention of drawing him into a conversation about Zemlinsky. In view of the success of Es war einmal . . . *the previous year, Mahler had agreed to introduce Zemlinsky's new three-act ballet* Der Triumph der Zeit *into the repertoire of the Hofoper. The work was all but completed when Mahler at last found time, during his summer vacation at Maiernigg, to read Hugo von Hofmannsthal's scenario. Completely baffled by it, Mahler had summoned the poet to his office at the Hofoper and declared the work to be unstageable.*

Once the guests had left table and formed into little groups, our conversation turned to the subjectivity of beauty. 'Beauty'. According to Mahler the bust

---

* Sophie Szeps was married to the engineer Paul Clemenceau, a brother of the well-known French politician Georges Clemenceau.

of Socrates was beautiful. I agreed with him wholeheartedly and ventured the opinion that Alexander von Zemlinsky, the musician, was beautiful too. Mahler shrugged his shoulders and said that was going too far. My hackles were raised, so I intentionally turned the conversation to Zemlinsky.

'While we're on the subject: tell me why you won't perform his Hofmannsthal ballet "Das gläserne Herz"?* After all, you gave him your promise.' 'Because I don't understand it,' Mahler retorted.

Thanks to Zemlinsky I had a precise knowledge of the scenario, which was indeed rather confusing. 'Let me outline the plot and explain what it means.' Mahler smiled: 'I'm all ears.'

To which I replied, 'But not until you have explained "Die Braut von Korea"' (a ballet which had a regular place in the repertoire and was a model of confusion and stupidity).† Mahler laughed out loud, revealing a mouth of glistening white teeth. He asked me about my studies, and I told him I was taking composition lessons with Zemlinsky. He asked me to bring some of my work to him at the Opera.[3]

Alma's diary gives a slightly differing account of this meeting, notable above all for the inclusion of her stepfather in the list of guests, and for her striking impression of Mahler pacing up and down the room like a caged beast.

Thursday 7 November
In the evening: at the Zuckerkandls'.
Made the acquaintance of Mahler.
Present were: Mrs Clemenceau, Burckhard, Spitzer, Mahler and his sister & – Klimt. With the latter I barely spoke two words – was perfectly calm. Nor with Mahler at first – but then: A highly interesting controversy arose concerning Alex's ballet – about artistic cross-fertilization in a time of cultural decay. He denied the justification of ballet as an art-form in its own right etc. Klimt, Carl, he and I led the discussion. Then it turned to Alex personally. He described him as limited – in a certain sense he's right too. He described the ballet «Hofmannsthal» as unperformable.
«By the way, I don't understand it.»
I'm <u>dreadfully</u> sorry to hear it.
«My reply:
I can explain the scenario to you but first you should expound Die Braut von

---

* Orig.: 'Das goldene Herz'. *Das gläserne Herz* is the title of Act I of *Der Triumph der Zeit*.
† The ballet *Die Braut von Korea*, with music by Joseph Bayer and scenario by Josef Hassreiter, opened at the Hofoper in May 1897 and was given for the last time on 2 May 1901.

Korea to me – one of the most stupid ballets ever to have been staged.»
He said he found it very good of me that I spoke of Alex with such respect, and it was also a good sign for Alex that, when you knew him better, you got to like him.
He asked me to bring him one of my pieces – even wanted to know exactly <u>when</u> I would call. I promised to come as soon as I had something worthwhile. That wasn't enough for him – he asked me at least to make an appointment. –
I must say, I liked him <u>immensely</u> – though he's dreadfully restless. He stormed about the room like a savage. The fellow is made <u>entirely</u> of oxygen. When you come close to him, you get burnt.
Tomorrow I shall tell Alex <u>some</u> of this . . . [4]

Evidently Mahler had half recognized Alma from their previous encounters. 'Strangely enough,' she recalls in AMM4, 'he noticed me at once; not only because of my face, which was still beautiful in those days, but also because of my harsh, nervous manner. Through his glasses he scrutinized me hard and long.'[5] Clearly he had already fallen for this beautiful, bright-eyed, sharp-tongued young creature. In the highest of spirits he invited her, together with Sophie Clemenceau and Bertha Zuckerkandl, to attend a rehearsal of The Tales of Hoffmann *the following morning at the Hofoper. As arranged, they met up with him at 11.00 a.m. at the stage door.*

Friday 8 November
In the morning to Zuckerkandls' – she, Mrs Clemenceau & I to the Opera. Mahler gave us a warm welcome and led us through the many corridors into the auditorium, carrying my coat. As he took his leave, he said:
Fräulein, don't forget: 'An honest man's word is as good as his bond.'
It was the dress rehearsal of 'The Tales of Hoffmann'. The second act fantastically atmospheric, the effect of the third unbelievably dramatic. Gutheil masterly. Mahler came twice to the railing & spoke to us – really kind. Astonishing what he can hear and see all at once – when a doubling is out of tune, when the lighting is wrong, when a singer makes an ungainly movement – unbelievable.
Afterwards he led us out again.[6]

Max Burckhard was the first to tell Alma of the impression she had made upon Mahler. That same evening she wrote:

Yesterday B. accompanied Mahler on his way home. B. ventured the opinion: 'Miss Schindler is a sensible, <u>interesting</u> young lady, don't you think?'

35

M. replied: 'I didn't care for her at first. I thought she was just a doll. But then I realized that she's also very intelligent. Maybe my first impression was because one doesn't normally expect such a good-looking girl to take anything seriously.'
Today he «Zemlinsky» brought me my songs.[7]

During a break in the rehearsal of Hoffmann, *Mahler took the three ladies into his office. Alma paid little heed to Mahler's conversation with Bertha and Sophie, but thumbed instead through the orchestral scores scattered about the room. Mahler asked whether she had slept well. 'Excellently,' she replied. 'I didn't sleep a wink,' he replied.* [8]

At first he seems to have made little more impression on Alma than in the summer of 1899, for at this time she was still head over heels in love with Zemlinsky. The day after the Hoffmann *rehearsal she mused about him in her diary:*

Saturday 9 November
Something new has occurred to me: art is the outcome of love. While for a man love is a tool for creativity, for a woman it is the prime mover. I was never less productive than when I was in love. I sit at the piano, waiting and waiting – & nothing comes. I can concentrate on nothing else.
I took a careful look at the songs that Alex brought round. They're very morbid but also very beautiful. My songs give me untold pleasure.
I just sit & dream. Thinking of him – you, my beloved. If only I knew:
a) if he does not give himself entirely, whether my nerves would suffer, and
b) if he were to give himself entirely, whether there would be any unpleasant consequences. Both alternatives are equally dangerous, yet I madly desire his embrace. I shall never forget the touch of his hand on my most intimate parts. Such fire, such a sense of joy flowed through me. Yes, one can be entirely happy, there is such a thing as perfect joy. In the arms of my beloved I have known it. One little nuance more, & I would have become a god. –
Once again: everything about him is holy to me. I would like to kneel before him & kiss his loins – kiss everything, everything.
Amen![9]

Alma had difficulty in keeping her surging feelings under control. The following day she noted:

My thoughts were less of Alex, thank God, and I was calmer. Otherwise I shall drive myself to distraction.[10]

On 11 November she attended the opening night of The Tales of Hoffmann. *Apart from recording the event in her diary, she mentions a young architect, Dr Felix Muhr, who had been a rival for her affections since the previous winter. His name also features in her correspondence with Mahler and Zemlinsky.*

Afterwards Muhr, whom we couldn't shake off. He joined us for dinner. Felt dreadful all day. Stomach pains. –
Acts two and three – fabulous.[11]

And on Wednesday 12 November she adds:

P.M. at home. Worked, but with no inclination or desire – entirely without inclination «& desire!». I can't even think of writing to Alex. I feel absolutely nothing for him. –[12]

A few days later she received a blank envelope containing an anonymous poem.

2   [Vienna, November 1901][E]

It happened overnight.
Who would have thought it right
That harmony and counterpoint
Should put a heart so out of joint.

And in that single night
It struck me with such might!
In one long homophonic line
All voices and all parts combine!

It happened in the night,
A vigil 'twas till light,
And now, when someone comes to call,
I rush to see who's in the hall.

'An honest man . . . his word'!
Since first those words I heard,
Their counterpoint has swelled and grown.
I watch the door and wait alone!

The pages of Alma's diary for the week beginning 13 November, the proba-
ble time when the poem was delivered, are no longer preserved. Evidence
suggests that she destroyed them. In AMM4 she recalls:

My mother looked sternly at the anonymous letter, which the postman had
just delivered. She took it out of my hands and asked who could possibly
have sent it. I said it could only be from Mahler. But she laughed, saying I
shouldn't be so rash as to believe that a man like Mahler would send poems
to a young girl, and a stranger at that; no, someone was having a joke at my
expense. But deep down inside me I knew the poem could <u>only</u> be from
him.[13]

The diary resumes on 19 November. The previous evening Alma's mother
had taken her to the Opera, where Bruno Walter had conducted Gluck's
Orpheus and Eurydice *(the performance was followed by the ballet* Coppélia
by Léo Delibes). During the interval Alma met Mahler yet again. This
encounter radically changed her attitude towards him:

Yesterday evening:
Orpheus – Gluck
I was thoroughly bored, but there was the Director's box & I stared up into
it and Mahler stared down . . . At first he didn't recognize me, but then he
did. I just kept on staring. After 'Orpheus' we went into the foyer . . .
Suddenly M. was there. He asked:
Is that your mother?
I introduce her – the Hennebergs* withdraw. He invites us up to his office –
we follow. He offers us tea . . . We talk about everything under the sun – he
is fascinating, kind. Mama invites him to call – he accepts. Let's hope he
really does come. We shook hands with vigour. From the gist of what he said,
it appears that it was he who wrote the poem. – I shan't do anything of the
kind. We stared at each other, stared and stared . . .
<u>Alexander von Zemlinsky</u> – <u>who is he?</u>
Dinner at Hartmann. With B. Was he jealous![14]

In AMM4 Alma fills in further details of the occasion:

After the performance we met up with Moll and Max Burckhard in a restaurant. My mother gave a perfectly innocuous account of our adventure, but it
made its effect. Moll was furious: 'You mean to say you let that lecher invite
a young girl into his office?!'

* Hugo and Marie Henneberg, old friends of Alma and her family.

Rumour had it that Mahler, the ascetic, was a roué who took advantage of his position to make advances to every female singer in his ensemble. But in fact he was a child and was terrified of women! With me, a foolishly inexperienced young girl, he was off his guard.

As a man of the world, Max Burckhard immediately grasped the consequences of the situation, consequences which neither Mahler nor I could yet envisage.

'The other night,' observed Burckhard, 'he was madly in love.'

'I didn't notice anything,' I replied.

'Then what would you do if he were to offer you his hand in marriage?'

'I would accept it,' I replied calmly. I had no idea that Mahler had left the Zuckerkandls at the same time as Burckhard, and that on their way home he had asked all manner of questions about me. Only years later did Mahler tell me about that conversation. Burckhard told him nothing at all. All he said was, 'Those who know Fräulein Schindler know who she is, and those who don't know her never will.' That really roused his interest.

After 'Orpheus', Burckhard exerted all his influence and intellect to rid me of my feelings for Mahler which, as he could clearly see, were beginning to burgeon. 'It would be a sin for a person as good-looking and well-bred as you', he said in his frivolous way, 'to darken your character by marrying a degenerate older man like him.* Just think of the offspring – it would be a sin! And besides: fire and water go together, but not fire and fire! He would stifle you, not vice versa, and that would be a terrible waste of your talent.'

In short, he did his best to prevent the marriage. But whatever his aim was, I simply longed for the following Saturday, when Mahler was due to call. Later on, admittedly, when I awoke from years of silence, during which I never had a moment to myself, during which I had watched in horror as my life was being whittled away, sometimes I recalled those words of his.

On the Thursday afternoon, having moved my lesson with Robert Gound forward from the Saturday, I was struggling to concentrate on figured basses, when suddenly the chambermaid rushed into the room. 'Gustav Mahler is here!' He was known to everyone, even in the servants' quarters. And with that my study of counterpoint was at an end.[15]

This account contradicts what Alma herself wrote in her diary for 8 November (pp. 35–6): she was, in fact, well aware that Burckhard and Mahler had left the house at the same time, and that she had been the subject of conversation

---

* In ELM: '[. . .] to make a piggery of your racial pedigree by marrying a rickety, degenerate Jew.'

on their way home. As it transpires, there was not even any in truth in the allegation that this was her last counterpoint lesson with the composer Robert Gound.

In AMD, Alma gives the impression of having been in command of the situation. Her diary tells a different story:

Wednesday 20 November
It's just too dreadful, I should be ashamed of myself . . . but <u>Mahler's</u> picture is graven in my heart. I will pluck out this poisonous weed – make room for the other again – my poor Alex. – If only the poem had come from him. If only!
I could hate myself!

Friday 22 November
I'm expecting Alex to call. He probably won't – I haven't written to him again . . . My longing is for ⊖. – How dreadful is my punishment.
Alex was here. He spoke no loving word, «didn't kiss me». As explanation he gave me the letter – «we kissed each other once, just once. My longing for him again knows no bounds.»
In the evening: Burckhard – pretty tedious. And Alex is in dissolute company this evening. Alas, poor Alex. –[16]

Zemlinsky's letters to Alma from the spring and early summer of 1901 reveal intimate details of a relationship that was now foundering.
'I have gone through days of fearful expectation; unceasing hope and anxiety in the face of reality. Please understand, dear, dear Fräulein Alma! Reality has brought me nothing but disappointment. In my thoughts, my feelings, I was happy, perfectly happy. I am in the throes of a great, hopeless passion, my adoration has with time become so strong, but also so firm and categorical that I can say: it can never end!!'[17]
'Your Mama, for whom I otherwise have the greatest respect, does not ask: does he love you, but: has he got money. [. . .] Love in exchange for love, that is all I know. I can and will not be denigrated. All my pride rises in rebellion. After all, I do have some standing – perhaps just as much as that entire band of artists, those poseurs and prigs, whose company you respectfully cultivate. [. . .] With a cruelty quite your own, you omit not even the most trivial arguments. Dr Muhr with his money-bags! I retort: Mr Zemlinsky with his talent! There. [18]
'I love you much more passionately than I can ever show – but as master, not as slave!! I can only be the master! [. . .] You say I am frightfully ugly? Very well! I thank God for it. And I thank God that so many young ladies

have ignored that ugliness and found the path to my soul, have never so much as mentioned it; I know I need not be ashamed on that account, that I am still a person of some value.'[19]

On 25 November Mahler was in Munich to conduct the Kaim Orchestra in the world première of his Fourth Symphony (soloist: Margarethe Michalek). Public response was tepid, and the following day Mahler returned to Vienna in a state of depression. That same evening he conducted a further performance of The Tales of Hoffmann, and two days later followed his unannounced visit to the Molls.*

Alma's room was strewn with books. Mahler gave them a cursory glance, but when he discovered a complete edition of the works of Nietzsche, he advised her to throw it on the fire. Alma felt obliged to put in a good word for her favourite philosopher. Then Anna Moll came upstairs to invite Mahler to dine with them: 'There's paprika chicken and Burckhard. Do join us.' 'I'm not particularly fond of either,' he replied, 'but I'll stay all the same.'[20]

Before dinner, Mahler and Alma walked to the post office in Döbling, where he called his sister Justine to tell her he would not be home for dinner. According to Alma, it was the first time in the nine years that he and his sister had lived together that he had ever done this. Carl Moll, who was following a few paces behind, recalls the occasion in his unpublished memoirs: 'Side by side, unhesitatingly close, and yet strangers!'[21] The comments in Alma's diary strike a more forthright note than the flowery account in AMD:

Thursday 28 November
Mahler was here – I can think only of him, only of him. He had to make a telephone call. We walked to Döbling together. He told me how much he liked me. I didn't tell him how much I liked him. We talked of many things – not everything . . .
A barrier stands between us – Alex . . . He doesn't know it, but senses it nonetheless! – I'm not <u>certain</u>, but I <u>believe</u> I love him «Mahler»! I want to be honest. Recently I have no longer felt anything for Alex.[22]

On their way back from Döbling, Alma recalls in AMM4 that Mahler came straight to the point: 'Marrying someone like me isn't at all easy. I am completely independent and must remain so. Materially I can commit myself to nothing and nobody, and my appointment at the Hofoper could terminate at any time.'[23]

---

* Carl Moll and his family had moved into their new villa on the Hohe Warte (Steinfeldgasse 8) only a few weeks previously, on 1 October.

Alma was less taken aback by Mahler's words about his precarious exis-
tence as an artist – she was only too well aware of such things in her own
family – than by the fact that he showed virtually no interest in her point of
view. Instead, he delivered a monologue on the subject of 'his wishes, his mis-
*sion in life'.*24

Having arrived back home, they went up to Alma's room where, 'without
really wanting it to happen', 25 *she let him embrace her for the first time. As*
she recalls, Mahler now spoke 'as if it were a foregone conclusion that we
would get married as soon as possible. As far as he was concerned, our brief
conversation on the way home had already decided the matter. Why then
*should we wait?'*26

Later she recalled every detail of dinner that evening. Other than Max
Burckhard, another guest was present, evidently Wilhelm Legler, who had
studied with Alma's stepfather and married her sister Grete the previous
year. This, at any rate, is the most likely interpretation of the abbreviation 'L.'
in Mahler's next letter.

At table, Mahler bubbled with charm and esprit, defending Schiller against
Alma and Burckhard, who disliked him, and reciting the great poet's verses
by heart.

Alma wrote: 'I felt that only he could shape my life, I sensed his true worth
and his significance, which placed him streets ahead of every other man I had
*met.'*27

The following day Mahler sent her copies of all his published songs,
together with a message (facsimile on p. 43).

3 Postcard   [Vienna, 29 November 1901]

In all haste, dear Fräulein Alma, I have sought out copies of all my vocal
works published to date, and have pleasure in sending them to you (how sad
for me that I cannot deliver them in person).* Meanwhile I console myself
with the agreeable thought that you will be obliged to spend some of your
time with me, and that you will therefore be thinking of me. – When I come
next Monday (until which time I shall be counting the hours like a schoolboy), I shall be happy to play whichever pieces you wish or need to hear.
It was very 'cosy and snug' yesterday, despite all the 'anxiety'. I could sense
it on my way home, once I had taken my leave of L. and was on my own.

---

* These will have been the three volumes of *Lieder und Gesänge* (Mainz, 1892), *Lieder eines*
fahrenden Gesellen (Vienna, 1897) and the twelve *Gesänge aus Des Knaben Wunderhorn*
(Vienna, 1899/1900).

Everything lovable and beautiful was still resounding within me – and went on vibrating through my dreams.
These cordial greetings in all haste, dear Fräulein Alma, from your   Gustav Mahler

Alma recorded these events in her diary entry for 29 November. Once again, this account differs considerably from the version in AML:

Friday 29 November

8.00 a.m. The walk was lovely yesterday – through <u>snow and wind</u>. Initially we didn't know what to say. Then he told me how much he had been thinking about me & how worried he was, because his life was preordained. Only his art – and now his thoughts are of other things.

Later this too: to maintain <u>complete</u> freedom of action. His sister has always helped him. He wouldn't object in the least to tendering his resignation right away. But if he was committed to somebody else, the situation would be quite different.

Well, I said, what if that person also possessed a modicum of artistic sensibility?

We want to get to know each other, that's our mutual wish. My thoughts are only of him – memories of the other are already fading.

. . . The day before yesterday Muhr said:

Well then, when are we going to marry?

In the evening I went up to my room. I don't know why, but I was ashamed. Now I regret every kiss, every caress, every amorous glance. – The hour of <u>remorse</u> has come!

I would have wished to meet him pure, <u>completely</u> pure! But that can no longer be. Now I feel – the stains will <u>never</u> fade.

B[urckhard] doesn't bother me as much . . . He didn't get his money's worth this evening – brought me flowers & a book by Ibsen. But Alex, whom I would be depriving of years of his life, and to whom in my last letter I still swore:

You are the <u>only</u> man to whom I would give myself!

And now: I am glad I never yielded to his entreaties – and anyway, I never should have done so. – My lips are «profaned!»

At midday Mahler sent me all his songs, which disappointed me because they struck me as insincere. I shall tell him as much too. –[28]

The first page of Alma's letter of thanks is reproduced in facsimile on p. 45. At this stage she was careful to avoid voicing any direct criticisms of Mahler's music.

Saturday, 29 November 1901

Dear Herr Director,

Many, many thanks! I will not write about the songs, but would like to tell you about them, and I also have some questions. How I look forward to next Monday! – I would much like you to read what Maeterlinck has to say about

44

'silence'. I was forcibly reminded of it during our first, beautiful walk. – It was a uniquely beautiful & wonderful experience. You will need to grow accustomed to my handwriting – therefore I shall close for now. I send you a warm clasp of the hand and warmest greetings. Until Monday. Alma M. Schindler

The same day she wrote in her diary:

Alex called, a little peeved about M[ie],* but otherwise as sweet as ever. I had the feeling: <u>that's</u> where I belong. —29

Until their next meeting, on Monday 2 December, Alma again confided all her personal and artistic conflicts to her diary:

Saturday 30 November
A battle is raging within me. Alex versus Mahler. My trust for Mahler is boundless.
Yesterday, Alex and I discussed his songs – he sarcastic and mocking, I unimpressed. Truly, they don't correspond to his personality. This studied naivety and simplicity, and he the most complex of characters. I would like to tell him so – but fear he might be insulted.
I look forward to Monday.

Sunday 1 December
Sang through the Mahler songs all morning. I'm beginning to like some of them. It's pretty dour stuff.
Midday: Philharmonic concert
P.M. Mahler songs. Nice afternoon! Alone, undisturbed, left to my own devices. —30

Although Alma considered Mahler a mediocre composer at the most, he occupied a leading position in the musical life of Vienna: a life at his side would be one of splendour and excitement, and Alma would enter the ranks of Viennese high society as a grande dame. In her diary she wrote:

Monday 2 December
In the afternoon: Mahler.
He told me that he loved me – we kissed each other. He played me his pieces – my lips are sealed . . . His caresses are tender & agreeable. If only I knew! He or – the other.
I must gradually get Alex off my mind. I'm terribly sorry. If it weren't for all that, I would have got engaged today. But I couldn't respond to his caresses. Someone was standing between us . . . I told him so – without mentioning names. I <u>had</u> to tell him . . . If only he had come three years earlier! An unsullied mouth!

Tuesday 3 December
I'm on the horns of a <u>terrible</u> dilemma. I keep repeating the words 'my beloved' and follow them with 'Alex'. <u>Can</u> I really love Mahler as he

* Marie Henneberg, for whom Alma had invented the nickname 'Auntie Mie'.

46

deserves, and as I am really able? Shall I ever understand his art, & he mine!?
With Alex the sympathy is mutual. He loves every <u>note</u> of me.
Mahler just said: This is really serious. This I didn't expect!
How shall I break it to Alex? – I'm on first-name terms with Mahler now. He
told me how much he loved me and I could give him no reply.
Do I really love him? – I have no idea. Sometimes I actually think not.
So <u>much</u> irritates me:
<u>his smell,</u>
<u>the way he sings,</u>
<u>the way he speaks</u> «can't roll his rrrr's».
And longing? How <u>madly</u> I longed for Alex – when we first met . . . every
minute, every second – & now: well, I long for him, but no longer with the
<u>same</u> fire. Maybe I cannot love anyone <u>like that</u> a third time. He's a stranger to
me. Our tastes differ.
He said to me:
Alma, think it over – carefully – if ever I disappoint you, you must tell me.
At present I can live it down, though it's not easy – but in four months maybe
it will no longer be possible.
And I don't know what to think, how to think – whether I love him or not –
whether I love the director of the Opera, the wonderful conductor – or the
man . . . Whether, when I subtract the one, anything is left of the other. And
his art leaves me cold, so <u>dreadfully</u> cold. In plain words: I don't believe in
him as a composer. And I'm expected to bind my life to this person . . . I felt
nearer to him from a distance than from close by.
I shudder.
But if today I were to say 'no' – a long-cherished dream would dissolve!
We kissed – «drunk greedily from each other.» Although his hands are
expressive, I don't love them as much as Alex's. You can get used to a lot of
things – given time . . . but <u>patience</u> is not Mahler's strong point. –
What should I do?
And what if Alex were to become famous? – In my letter I wrote that I hadn't
the <u>slightest idea</u> what was going through my mind.
This morning I played music from Act I.* I feel so much sympathy for it.
One question <u>plagues</u> me: whether Mahler will inspire me to compose –
whether he will support my artistic striving – whether he will love me as Alex
does. Because <u>he</u> loves me completely and utterly.[31]

---

* i.e. from the ballet *Der Triumph der Zeit*, to a scenario by Hofmannsthal, which had been
the object of controversy at Alma's first meeting with Mahler. Zemlinsky planned to dedicate
the work to Alma; at this time he had lent her his rough draft of Act I.

Alma was unwilling to relegate Zemlinsky to second place, above all because he took her seriously as a composer. Instinctively she knew that she could hardly expect as much of Mahler; this was what troubled her most. 'I never showed Gustav Mahler a note of my music,' she wrote. [32] *Until nine years later it never even occurred to him to ask her about it.*

On 4 December Mahler sent three tickets for a performance of Hoffmann, *which he was to conduct that evening. In his accompanying letter he informed Alma that on 16 December he would be leaving for Germany to conduct the Berlin première of his* Fourth Symphony, *then travel on to Dresden to attend a performance of his* Second Symphony *on 20 December, conducted by Ernst von Schuch.*

4   [Vienna, 4 December 1901]
                                           Wednesday evening

My dear friend,
Here are your three tickets for 'The Tales of Hoffmann'. At the same time I bring you the sad news (all the sadder in that it concerns myself) that I shall have to leave for Berlin on Monday <night>, as the first rehearsal for my Symphony is scheduled for the Tuesday. For the same reason I can neither conduct 'Tristan' on Tuesday, nor can I visit you next Monday, an event to which I had been look-ing forward with great pleasure. As I shall be away for about ten days, which saddens me greatly, I fear that the war I waged yesterday on earthenware house-hold gods was all in vain. Nothing remains but the wounds I sustained in the process. It was most unkind of you to resign yourself to my fate by consenting to my banishment for a whole week. In that respect, Hero was quite different. 'Come back tomorrow,' she said. Well, instead of swimming across the Hellespont, I, a latter-day Leander, shall steam down from Berlin to Döbling per express night train, and doubtless I shall arrive, after all the exertions and night vigils, in a state of total 'decadence'. – Many greetings to your dear Mama. Tomorrow I hope to catch a passing glimpse of you, which I can take with me as comfort and nourishment on my journey.   Pyrrhus, the defeated victor

The references to 'earthenware household gods' (the lares *and* penates *of ancient Rome) and the signature, with its implication of a Pyrrhic victory, suggest that Mahler had tried to persuade the whole family to accompany him on his journey. In the event, Carl Moll travelled with him as far as Berlin, where he made a few business calls.*

Of her night at the opera Alma gives the following account in her diary:

Wednesday 4 December
This evening: Opera
The Tales of Hoffmann
<u>My</u> Gustav conducted. At every curtain he looked round – so sweet. If only
he were here <u>now</u>. –
If only I had already spoken to <u>Alex</u>. My thoughts are always with the other.
Muhr was sitting in our row – my God!
If he doesn't call before his departure, I shall go to him. –[33]

5   [Vienna, 5 December 1901]

Dearest friend,
I trust that yesterday's 'Hoffmann' gave you at least some pleasure, even
though the spirit had departed, 'leaving only phlegm in its place'. Schoder*
managed to bring something of our beloved poet to the surface (in the whole
work, regrettably, there is little but surface to be saved), but the triviality of
dear Schrödter[†] and his son-in-law[‡] were too much lead weight for the suffering Psyche.
Usually I conduct Acts 1 and 2 only with great reluctance. But yesterday I
was glad to do so, since it was for you. Act 3 is more felicitous, for it has
enough to offer – if one adds one's own creative energy – to come close to the
demonic element of its literary model. If you are interested to see how much
has been lost, you should read Hoffmann's novella 'Rath Krespel'. Schoder
was very touching, and her intentions were substantially in accord with my
own. But in some details she let me down, particularly when her tendency to
realism got the better of her. Antonia does not simply die of consumption, as
suggested by that accursed coughing, popular as it may be in theatrical circles. No, she forfeits her life to the demonic principle of art, a principle
which, once it has taken hold of a person, invariably constrains them to
abandon their individuality. Indeed, if a person is prone to spiritualization, it
possesses them to the point of physical collapse. One could say that Antonia
forfeits not her soul but her body. Or to apply a favourite analogy of yours,
she follows a path into the 'realm of darkest night', from which she finds no
means of escape. – But this is merely the outer shell of a powerful drama,
whose dark underground pathways need illuminating in horrific colours by
a music of genius. This is what I felt and wished for at yesterday's performance, in the hope that you too might be moved.

* The soprano Marie Gutheil-Schoder.
† Orig.: 'Schröter' (the tenor Fritz Schrödter).
‡ The baritone Wilhelm Hesch.

49

If you were to devote a little of your time to the works of Hoffmann, you would gain entirely new insights into the unique relationship between music – that eternally mysterious, totally unfathomable art which can penetrate like lightning into the deepest recesses of our thoughts and feelings – and reality. You would perceive that the only true reality on earth is our inner self, and that for those who have understood this the real world is nothing but a contour, a worthless shadow. – But please, I ask you <u>not</u> to view this as a 'poetic' allegory, but as an insight whose validity can never be refuted, not even by the sober voice of common sense. Soon, when I have returned, we must discuss this further! I have written in some detail today, because the concept is intimately related to my fond ambition to replace your 'earthenware gods' with my vision of the divine, even if this may strike you at present as mere sophistry. Much to my regret, I cannot come on Saturday. In due course, when I have returned from Berlin, I shall explain why. But since I have no time for polite excuses, for the time being please accept this laconically negative response to your kind invitation, untypical as it may be of myself.

During the past days, making conversation with you has become a favourite pastime of mine – whether arguing fiercely or simply sitting together in silence. So much so that before my departure I would like to voice a fond wish: dear comrade, remain true to your role, and do all you can to hold me to mine. Just think of our two favourite characters: Eva – and Hans Sachs. Auf Wiedersehen!   G.

One wonders whether Alma was able to identify the quotation from Schiller which Mahler here introduces as his opening ploy. Taken from the poem 'Kastraten und Männer' ('Eunuchs and Men', later retitled 'Männerwürde' – 'The Dignity of Men'), it runs:

> Zum Teufel ist der Spiritus
> Das Phlegma ist geblieben

(The spirit's to the devil, / only apathy remains.)

Schiller's metaphor refers to the distillation of alcohol, a process which leaves as residue an insipid fluid, formerly known as phlegma.

Reading the closing lines of this letter, Alma was aghast. She was stunned by the fact that Mahler had compared their relationship to that of Eva and Hans Sachs (in Wagner's Meistersinger), and baffled by his cancellation for the following Saturday. According to her diary entries for 4 and 5 December, she seems to have thought that Mahler was beating a retreat.

Thursday 5 December

In the evening: this letter. – I could weep! I think I have lost him – and in spirit he was already mine – what a fate! I feel quite wretched. I must see him before he leaves, must see him. –

He doesn't want me! He's written me off. That last sentence – that terrible last sentence! – Now I can feel how dear he is to me – suddenly I feel so empty. Tomorrow I must go to him. My longing is boundless.

Eva and Hans Sachs – a feeble excuse. It can't be true. –

Friday 6 December

He loves me no longer – I'm unhappy. Today I shall go to him and won't find him at home. I'd like to weep on his breast. Eva and Hans Sachs – I wasn't prepared for that.[34]

Why Mahler intended to cancel his Saturday visit is unclear. Whatever the case, Alma seems to have fulfilled her intention of going to him and persuading him to change his mind. As her diary reveals, he did indeed come to see her on the Saturday:

Saturday 7 December

Gustav was here. –

We kissed each other countless times. In his embrace I feel so warm. If only he still loved me as much – but I consider him fickle, dreadfully fickle. He tried to convert me, in many senses.

I shan't be seeing him for nineteen days. On Monday he's going to Berlin. I don't know what else I should write, but my feelings are for him & against Alex.

Never before have I watched the clock as avidly as today. I couldn't work for sheer longing.

At the thought of next Tuesday I tremble. «My poor Alex.» I'm convinced he knows everything . . . feels everything . . . Constantly I see Gustav's eyes before me, so kind and sweet – & always questioning. His lovely hands somewhat disfigured by nail-biting. He will write to me from B[erlin]. Never in my life have I met anyone as alien as he. How alien «and yet so close!» I cannot say. Maybe that's one of the things that attracts me to him. But he should let me be as I am. Already I am aware of changes in myself, due to him. He is taking much away from me and giving me much in return. If this process continues, he will make a new person of me. A better person? I don't know. I don't know at all. –

More than ever, a huge question mark hangs over my future. Everything is up to him. Today he confessed everything to me, all his sins – I even confessed some of mine.

He guessed Alex's name & was <u>appalled</u> – <u>couldn't</u> understand it.
Enough now – for both of us – and <u>no</u> concern for the mysteries of 'tomorrow'.
Today <u>is real</u> at least, and is <u>beautiful</u>, yes – beautiful.
«He is the <u>purest</u> person I ever met – because my love affairs were few and, thank God, just mechanical experiences.»
We were playing piano duets and he said:
There's a crotchet missing here. But I'll grant it you – I'll even grant you a minim. Yes – I'll grant you everything.*35

But even with a 'question mark' over it, Alma's future was to be a beautiful one. Mahler sent her a vocal score of Das klagende Lied, *describing it as 'a legend of earlier days'. And the same evening he conducted a performance of* Die Zauberflöte.

6 Two postcards   [Vienna, 8 December 1901]

Dearest Almschi,
Here is a 'legend of earlier days'. Yesterday you really delighted me! You listened to me so sweetly and replied so sweetly too. How brief is such an afternoon, and the coda in the evening was almost gloomy. – Today I look forward to the evening, when we shall be sitting close together, united in the profoundest sense of the word. In every bar I shall be thinking of you and conducting for you. It will be just like yesterday at the piano, when I was so glad to talk and open my heart to you. <But what of the days that follow? Everything within us will fade away, your every facial expression, your every word.> And sometimes I shall pause for thought with that 'distrustful' look on my face that so often surprises you. It isn't <u>mistrust</u> in the usual sense of the word, but <u>uncertainty</u> with regard to yourself and the future. My dearest, <u>learn to reply</u>! It's not at all easy, for one has to have weighed oneself in the balance, one has to know oneself. And <u>asking</u> is even harder. It can be learnt only in the light of a complete and intimate relationship with one's partner. My dearest dear, <u>learn to ask</u>!
Yesterday you made a completely changed impression and appeared far more mature. I can sense that the past few days have opened you up, have revealed you. – And after my return, what then? – Then I shall ask: Do you <u>love</u> me? <u>More than yesterday</u>? Did you know me then, and do you recognize me now? And now, my love, my comrade, addio!   Your Gustav

Alma recalled the performance many years later with the following words:

* Untranslatable pun on *Viertel* (quarter note), *Halbe* (half note) and *Ganze* (whole note).

Once, during the earliest days of our secret liaison, Mahler conducted 'The Magic Flute' just for me. He sent a ticket for his staff box. His sister, who had always enjoyed sole access to these seats, didn't know what to think when she was suddenly informed that they were unavailable. But Mahler said nothing, and she didn't dare to ask. After each act Mahler remained at the rostrum for quite a while, chatting uninhibitedly with his concertmaster R[osé], so that we could look at each other longer. At his request I wrote him a letter with my impressions of the performance.[36]

Immediately after the performance, she wrote in her diary:

Sunday 8 December
I have the feeling my world is in chaos. Everything is collapsing and growing anew. A new outlook on life – new belief. If only I can live up to his love. He is capable of giving infinitely. I am quite incapable of working. I don't know why. Alex had already given me <u>everything</u> – and I had absorbed so much from him. But now I have to discard so much in order to take in new things, better things.
At noon he sent me 'Das klagende Lied'. The text is excellent, the melody a little impoverished, but the structure firm and effective. I can imagine some passages sounding quite passable.
P.M. at the Opera: 'Die Zauberflöte'. Heavenly performance. Only now do I realize the true greatness and beauty of this work.
Then I looked over to Gustav and had to smile as if transfigured. At the end of each act he gave me such a touching smile – particularly at the end – as if casting me a line.
Then we drove past him «on the street». He was walking with his sister and Lechner[*] and didn't see me. My dearest Gustav – think, just think of me![37]

Mahler's next letter to Alma was written in Vienna, and not, as Alma states in AMM1, from 'Berlin-Dresden'.[38] Mahler had already got into the habit of writing to her from the Hofoper or the railway station before setting out on a journey.

7   [Vienna, 9 December 1901]

Dearest,
Many greetings to you! How lovely it would be if a few lines from you were waiting for me on arrival in Berlin – Palast Hotel will suffice as address. For

---

[*] Natalie Bauer-Lechner.

a few moments they would make me feel at home in that unfamiliar place. From now on, wherever you are is my abiding city, even the faintest reminder of your dear presence helps me forget for a while the pain of separation.

Write to me about The Magic Flute as well. I can imagine that such a work will not as yet have become clear to you, for it is still all too much a piece of yourself! For a long time I had similar experiences with those works which you describe as 'naive'. But I value and revere everything you can tell me about yourself, even the merest trifle. Please don't take too much trouble over your letters. Write everything just as it comes to you, and while writing, imagine I'm sitting next to you and you are chattering away about all and sundry.

But I'd also like to hear about the life you are leading – every detail! <One thing, though, my Alma: write clearly.>

So on Wednesday you'll be meeting my sister. I fondly hope you get on well together. Maybe you will discover something of myself in her, indeed some of her characteristics may seem familiar to you. – Hoorah! Your letter has just arrived, and I shall read it before carrying on.

Now I feel strengthened! I was longing for news from you, but scarcely dared hope you would write. My dearest love, I have to admit that if it hadn't arrived I would have left the house with considerable misgivings. You write such dear things about my sister, and I must tell you something I recently withheld so as not to prejudice you: she is completely in the picture and has already taken you into her heart. Yesterday we talked until far into the night about you and our future (we were alone, as we went home together immediately after dinner). She understands everything, and will be a true friend. – It's most unfortunate that I have to go away at this very time. I feel so unhappy, and yet it's almost like a call from the Master, from the Teacher (I put it like this to avoid saying 'God', because we haven't yet touched on that topic, and if we were to exchange but one phrase, I couldn't bear it). The voice calls out: 'Remain steadfast, resign yourself, have patience!' You see, my dearest, we remain in need of these words for the rest of our lives, indeed the voice <of the Teacher> can also be heard in the thunder, it should sound clearly to us at all times. – O God, I can write no more. There's so much noise around me, I can scarcely hear myself talk. I hear nothing but this one voice, stronger than all else. May it never fall silent – in my heart. A voice that knows but one word and one note: I love you, my Alma! As soon as I arrive in Berlin, I shall write again. All my unvoiced thoughts, the ones only you can hear and understand. Mine, mine!   Your Gustav

The same day Mahler sent a letter to Anna Moll (letter 9 includes a reference to it), accompanied by a box of pralines:

54

My journey begins this evening. Much to my regret, it will take me longer than I thought, because I have received an urgent request to attend the rehearsals for my Second Symphony, which is due to be performed in Dresden on 20 December. So I shall see you all again in a fortnight. I have to confess that for me this separation is a very long one, and that it affects me deeply. May I add that in these few days I feel I have grown close and sense a true solidarity towards you and your dear family. This confession comes all the more easily because I know you will take it in the same spirit in which it was made, and that you no longer regard me as a stranger. Farewell for now, and think well of me! Yours sincerely   Gustav Mahler

Following hallowed tradition, the contents of the enclosed package are to be divided equally between mother and daughter.[39]

Alma's diary echoes Mahler's letter:

Monday 9 December
I simply can't work – I pace around the room, go over to his picture, re-read his last letter – I love him!
At midday he sent me a big box of pralines and this dear, sweet letter. I believe I shall become a better person, he purifies me. My <u>desire</u> for him is unbroken.
This afternoon Muhr called. We made a lot of music together. Finally he asked again how things stood. I had no choice but to tell him the truth, no matter how <u>hard</u> it was. He was standing before me, pale and trembling:
    Fräulein, if you turn me down I shall kill myself.
I felt so sorry for him. I do like him very much – as a friend – and am convinced that I wouldn't be doing badly if I accepted him. But some things lie beyond our control.
My love and longing is boundless – Gustav, my dearest, my love . . . I have but one wish, one dream: to be yours alone . . .
Today Muhr informed me that a doctor had told him Gustav was suffering from an incurable disease and was weakening perceptibly. – Dear God, I shall nurse him like a child. I will not be the cause of his downfall. I shall restrain my longing and my passion – I want to cure him – let him recover through my strength and youthfulness.
My beloved Master . . .[40]

It seems strange that Alma should receive an admirer on the very day of Mahler's departure. Even stranger is the credence she gives to rumours passed on by Muhr from the Hofoper concerning Mahler's health (in those days, 'incurable disease' was a customary euphemism for tuberculosis).

In the space of a month her attitude towards Mahler had grown from mere interest to passionate involvement; this now was their first period of separation. Mahler had arranged that during his absence Alma should make the acquaintance of his sister Justine – a necessary and important step for the future. As Alma records in her diary:

Tuesday 10 December
I didn't get a wink of sleep all night – tossed and turned in my bed – thinking of my uncertain prospects, of Gustav's ill health, of his sister whom I already have taken into my heart – and of him, of him – you, my beloved.
Today Alex is due to call – that will be difficult for me.
And yet another morning has passed. To no effect, fruitlessly. I am simply incapable – my dear, sweet Gustav.
Grete sent me reviews from the Stuttgart daily papers* – of Gustav's 3rd symphony. <u>Dreadfully</u> rude. It robbed me of some – not all – but some of my faith in him. Why is he not here now, at this difficult time?
«What will Muhr do?
Another poor devil – Zemlinsky – when he arrives, will approach me with <u>pride</u> and bluntness. <u>I know him well</u>.»
I'm still waiting for Alex «Zem.» with fear in my heart. He is due at any moment. If he doesn't come, I'll write to him – but it would be better to talk. And my Gustav? In Berlin, amongst strangers. When shall I receive his first letter? What hasn't all been going through my mind this past fortnight! «I have grown so old!»
This evening 'Tristan' – in every note, in every bar my thoughts were with him.[41]

On 10 December Mahler met the conductor Ernst von Schuch in Dresden to discuss points of interpretation in his Second Symphony. Then he travelled on to Berlin. In Dresden there was no time to write the 'first letter' that Alma so longed for. Meanwhile, she and Justine had met for the first time.

Wednesday 11 December
P.M. at the Zuckerkandls'. Gustav had asked me to go, as his sister would be there. Although she has a slightly deflected look «in plain language, a squint», she feels a deep sympathy for me – I can recognize him in her. We got on quite well together. I only hope I can feel something for her. I really don't understand why Grete doesn't cultivate an affection for Wilhelm's sisters. I found them <u>immediately</u> sympathetic. Well, I only hope she likes me. I <u>fervently</u> hope so.

---

* Grete Legler was living in Stuttgart, where her husband was Professor of Art at the School of Art.

On Saturday I shall call on her at home. – What are we going to talk about? How are we going to face up to each other under these uncertain circumstances?[42]

In Berlin, a performance of Mahler's Fourth Symphony *had been announced with the Tonkünstler Orchester (soloist: Thila Plaichinger) conducted by Richard Strauss. In the event Mahler stepped in, and Strauss conducted the rest of the programme.*

8   Berlin [11 December 1901]
                                                              Palast Hotel
                                                       Wednesday morning

My dear, sweet girl,
In frightful haste between arrival and first rehearsal, let me quickly send you fondest greetings and a cry from the heart. Your dear letter of last Sunday accompanied me on my journey. I studied it like the New Testament. It has taught me the past and the future. Later today, if I can find time, I shall write an account of everything that has happened since that letter arrived (for me it is a kind of 'Hegyra', the starting point of the Muslim calendar[*]). – My new life begins here too. From now on I can live, breathe and exist only if I think of you. –
In Berlin I shall be conducting my composition myself. If only you were here! Others seek in my music the key to my being. But you, my Alma, if you take me, the entirety of here and now, as your point of departure, you will acquire the clairvoyance of love, the omniscience of yourself as me, of myself as you. To identify a star, astronomers have to analyze the particles it radiates (with this method, known as spectral analysis, they can detect any element known on Earth, but elements unique to any particular star defy analysis; here science is left in the dark) – but what do the inhabitants of that star care for the particles it emits? Admittedly, the metaphor isn't quite appropriate, but at present it comes closest to expressing all that I feel, all that comforts and enchants me.
When you have come to share your whole being with me, and I mine with you, when this powerful, agonized longing, coupled with so much anxiety and disquiet, is finally stilled, and each of us, separately and together, knows everything of the other, and we can love, can penetrate with blithe unconcern to the core of one another – what then? (But please don't misunderstand

[*] From the Arabic *hijrah*, or *hijra* ('flight' or 'emigration'). AD 622, the date of Mohammed's migration from Mecca to Medina, represents the starting point of the Muslim calendar.

what I wrote earlier: what I am experiencing on your account I will <u>not</u> share with you – not even the pain and the pressure.) Now I have to leave for rehearsal. If the notes, the sound waves were as powerful as the tremors of my love for you, you would feel them resounding all morning. They are yours, they are for you – all that dwells within me!

My beloved Alma   Your Gustav

[at top of page:] Extremely urgent

Meanwhile, Alma was struggling to gain control of her feelings:

Thursday 12 December

I feel <u>really</u> sorry for him. Who knows, perhaps it might be – what the hell! But his love is so <u>touching</u>. His immense ardour frightens me – my Saviour! This evening: 'Meistersinger'. [. . .] Although the piece is so wonderful, I must admit that I was dead tired. It took five hours. I haven't been feeling well for two days now – etc. On the other hand «in the same row sat the young Dr Adler, whom I find tremendously attractive. I made eyes at him outrageously. Finally we exchanged smiles. And suddenly I realized to my horror that Muhr was sitting next to him and had probably been observing the entire manoeuvre. I felt ashamed of myself, utterly ashamed. All the same, I noticed that M. was looking the other way, so I quickly turned my head in his direction and we exchanged a voluptuous glance – for a long, wonderful moment – regardless of onlookers. Such a glance can be stunningly sensual – and he's the very picture of a man, his eyes are black pools and . . . in short a face I find appealing. There's good stock for you. Mahler can't compete with that.» But otherwise I retain my independence and at heart I remain faithful to Gustav. My bold glances didn't come from deep inside.

I've written to Alex – he will be furious, will <u>never</u> forgive me. I wrote:

> Alex,
>
> You haven't called because you know everything. You know all that has happened. You can read even my most secret thoughts. For me, the last weeks have been torture.
>
> You know how <u>very</u> much I loved you. You fulfilled me <u>completely</u>. Just as suddenly as this love came, it has vanished – been cast aside. And befallen me with renewed power!
>
> On my knees I beg your forgiveness for the evil hours I have given you. Some things are beyond our powers. Maybe you have an explanation for that. You – you know me better than I know myself.

I shall <u>never</u> forget the joyous hours you have given me – don't <u>you</u> forget them either. One thing, though: don't desert me! If you are the man I think you are, then you will come here on Monday, give me your hand – and our first kiss of friendship.

Be a dear fellow, Alex. If you so wish, our friendship could be really meaningful. We could stick together, like old comrades.

Above all, answer me at once and without reserve – Mama will not read the letter.

Once again: forgive me – I no longer know myself.

Your Alma.[43]

When she edited the following letter for publication, Alma abridged it radically. As transpires from the passages she omitted, she had spoken to Mahler of her experiences with Muhr and Zemlinsky.

9   Berlin [12 December 1901]
                                                                   Palast Hotel
                                                              Thursday evening

<My dearest,
I have just returned from a trip to Weimar, where I spent a few hours on a surprise call to my married younger sister.* – The journey was long, and I found it terribly exhausting. The appalling boredom of sitting in a railway carriage (which I endure with all the grace of a caged beast) takes the pleasure out of travelling. I couldn't help thinking how it would be, my Alma, if you were sitting beside me, especially since I know you enjoy train journeys, probably because for you they are still a rare event. So clearly did I feel your presence that I almost started talking to you. Your last letter was my travelling companion, and I read it many times!

Oh Almschi (is that how it's spelt?), if only you would write a little more clearly! Believe me! I would gladly spend hours poring over your dear hieroglyphics. But in the process – and this is what torments me – all directness of utterance is lost. Instead of hearing your voice, as it were, instead of sensing your presence, I find myself constantly and painfully interrupted; time and again I have to stop to decipher and construe each letter in turn. Often, moreover, for all my efforts, there are some words I simply cannot make out. Dearest girl, do try to write clearly. Separate the letters more clearly and shape the consonants more precisely. Why don't you use <u>German</u> script, as I do?

* Emma Rosé.

You write that you spent a difficult afternoon with a handsome, rich, well-educated and musical young gentleman.* Almschl, Almschl! Just think! My God, what kind of a substitute would that be? I can't lay claim to half these fine attributes! – So there he stood, pale and trembling, and was even prepared to kill himself on your account! I would never dream of that! How I would love to run my fingers through your dear tresses – even though I prefer you without them, with just a simple hairstyle.

Here in Berlin a whole entourage of people is hovering perpetually around me. If only they would give me a moment's peace and quiet. There's so much I have to tell you. Secretly I had been hoping to find a letter from you on my return. A day that passes without feeling your breath: for me that is a lost day. I can scarcely wait for Saturday the 21st (the day on which I hope to arrive home). I turn into the Steinfeldgasse – no, I run; I ring the doorbell and the housemaid opens: 'Fräulein Alma is in the salon.' I rush upstairs, open the door – – –! Just read these hieroglyphics. You can decipher them quickly, can't you? If we want to make sensible conversation, we'll have to take a short walk after high tea. You haven't yet told me how your Mama reacted to my last letter. It was pretty clearly worded and left room for no doubt about my hopes and fears.>

The main rehearsals begin tomorrow. How would it be if you were there? Recently, since all my thoughts began centring on you, I have found myself guilty of a vulgar ambition, one entirely inappropriate to people of my rank. What I now strive for is success, for fame and all those trivial, insignificant things (insignificant in the truest sense of the word) that go with it. I would like to do you the honour! When I speak of ambition, don't get me wrong. I have always been ambitious, but I was never covetous of the honours that my neighbours and contemporaries could have heaped upon me. What I have always striven for was the understanding and respect of my colleagues, even if such a goal should elude me for the rest of my days (and in pursuit of such a goal time and place are indeed of no consequence). From now on this will be my greatest ambition! And for that, my beloved, I need your support. As you know, to win this reward, this wreath of honour, one has to forego the applause of the masses, indeed even of better, higher ranking people (for they too will not always concur). Until now I have gladly suffered the insults of Philistines, inarticulate scorn and hatred. Indeed, I am only too well aware that the scant respect I have earned may be based upon misunderstanding, and is at any rate only a vague indication of something higher, something

---

* i.e. Felix Muhr (cf. pp. 37 and 55).

beyond my reach. – Of course, this does not apply to my activities as 'director' and conductor, for in the final analysis these are talents and achievements of a lower order. – Please tell me if you understand what I mean and whether you <can> follow me. Alma! Could you stand by me and take all these burdens upon yourself – even to the point of humiliation – could you happily bear this cross with me? If this letter is to go off today, I must close now. I could commune with you like this for ever!

A thousand greetings, my dear, beloved Alma. I shall return over and over to the assent you gave me in the postscript at the end of your last letter.

Yours, dear girl   Gustav

Years later, when Alma edited these letters for publication, she was evidently still annoyed with Mahler for asking whether she 'could' follow him. Otherwise she would not have changed the wording to 'whether you can' to 'whether you will'. It was no mistake. In the next letter, dated 14 December, she made the same alteration. A further change, from 'beyond reach' (unzugänglich) to 'inadequate' (unzulänglich), was probably a transcription error.

The same day, Mahler wrote to his sister Justine:

[Berlin, 12 December 1901]

Dear Justi,

I've just got back from Weimar. [. . .] I can't wait to hear what you have to report about last Wednesday. It's still much too soon for you to start raising the dust or looking for somewhere else to live. Please, my dearest, be of good cheer. There's no need for haste. I still have many tests to complete. The dear girl herself is in quite a state, finding herself in a completely unfamiliar situation, to which I have to open both her eyes and my own. As I recently realized, she will have to mature considerably before I can consider taking such a momentous decision. – You, on the other hand, you hold your future entirely in your own hands. And whatever the outcome, you and I will remain lifetime allies. I want you to be happy and to help you in everything you need for clear vision and peace of mind. Don't worry about apartments and such details. There's plenty of time for that. For now, I see I must ensure that everyone keeps a level head. – I've just decided that you should arrive for the concert on Monday morning already. Maybe you will derive some pleasure from being here. The orchestra is on its best behaviour. Then on Tuesday we can travel to Dresden and spend a few days on our own together. Do you agree? If so, cable your arrival time straight away. I beg you, take a good look at Alma with your cool, feminine eye. I value your judgement very highly. Greetings and kisses from your   Gustav[44]

Two days later, Mahler wrote to his sister again. Meanwhile, she had reported back to him on her meeting with Alma in the presence of the Zuckerkandls.

[Berlin, 14 December]

Dear Justi,

You can imagine how I laughed and smiled at your letter. It went exactly as I thought it would, and your few allusions give the impression of great warmth and serenity. How wonderful it will be for both of us if everything ends as it appears to be shaping up. – I beg you, take A. really to heart, for then I shall be doubly happy. She's still so very young. When I think of the age difference I lose heart. – Keep calm if you can, and test her, or rather help me to test her. The matter is anything but trivial, and intentions may not be the father of ideas. – I'm still waiting for news from her. What you have to tell me about Saturday afternoon* will be doubly valuable to me. [. . .] Today I received a letter from Schuch,† who tells me that the King of Saxony wishes to attend the concert on Friday‡ and that I should send him a short pro-gramme note for his private use, as he is so interested in my work. I have assembled a few allusions, which I include here in rough copy, i.e. what one could justifiably describe as 'ad usum Delphini'. Naturally it's intended for a naive reader, one that doesn't delve too deeply. If you like, you can show it to Alma, so she can get at least some idea of the general outline. It's all still so unfamiliar to her, and here, as in everything that concerns my life and my existence, you must be my envoy.[45]

As implied by the reaction in her diary to Mahler's letter of 12 December, Alma regretted having written to him about Muhr and Zemlinsky.

Saturday 14 December

Today's letter is cooler. – I knew it before I had even read it, because it's all my fault. I answered at once. Now I'm waiting for Alex's reply – which I'm dreading . . .

---

* i.e. the same day, 14 December, on which Alma was due to call on Justine at home.
† Ernst von Schuch, Generalmusikdirektor of the Hofoper in Dresden.
‡ i.e. 20 December.

Sinfonie in C-moll.

<u>1. Satz</u>. Wir stehen an dem Sarge eines geliebten Menschen. Sein Leben, Kämpfen, Leiden und Wollen zieht noch einmal, zum letzten Male an unserem geistigen Auge vorüber. — Und nun in diesem ernsten und so tief erschütternden Augenblick, wo wir alles Verwirrende und herabziehende des Alltags wie eine dichte abstreifen greift eine fürchterlich ernste Stimme an unser Herz, die wir im betäubenden Treiben des Tages stets überhören: Was nun? Was ist dieses Leben — und dieser Tod? Gibt es für uns ein Fortdauer? Ist dieß Alles nur ein wüster Traum, oder hat dieses Leben und dieser Tod einen Sinn? — Und diese Frage müssen wir beantworten, wenn wir weiter leben sollen. —

Die nächsten 3 Sätze sind als Inter-mezzi gedacht.

<u>2. Satz</u> — <u>Andante</u>: am seligen Augen, blick aus dem Leben dieses theueren

First page of Mahler's programme note on his *Second Symphony*, written for King Albert of Saxony and enclosed in a letter to his sister Justine on 14 December 1901

P.M. at Justine's. She was uncommonly kind and courteous to me. I went into his room – stood in front of his desk, greeted his bed, his books, his surroundings. The apartment is decorated in pseudo-modern style, but <u>tastefully</u> and unostentatiously.

While I was there, a letter arrived for her, which also included something for me, namely the programme of his 2nd symphony in C minor.[46]

Justine did indeed give these pages to Alma, who preserved them in her diary.

<u>First Movement.</u> We are standing at the grave of a well-loved man. We contemplate his whole life, his struggles, his sufferings and his intentions on earth. And now, in this solemn and deeply stirring moment, when the confusion and distractions of everyday life are lifted like a hood from our eyes, a voice of awe-inspiring solemnity chills our heart, a voice that, blinded by the mirage of everyday life, we usually ignore: 'What next?' it says. 'What is life and what is death? Will we live on eternally? Is it all an empty dream or do our life and death have a meaning?' And we must answer this question, if we are to go on living.

The next three movements are conceived as intermezzi.

<u>Second Movement: Andante.</u> A blissful moment in the life of the dear departed and a sad recollection of his youth and lost innocence.

<u>Third Movement: Scherzo.</u> A spirit of disbelief and negation has seized him. He is bewildered by the bustle of appearances and he loses his perception of childhood and the profound strength that love alone can give. He despairs both of himself and of God. The world and life begin to seem unreal. Utter disgust for every form of existence and evolution seizes him in an iron grasp, torments him until he utters a cry of despair.

<u>Fourth Movement: Urlicht (alto solo).</u> The stirring words of simple faith sound in his ears: 'I am from God and will return to God! The dear God will give me a light, will light me to eternal, blessed life.'

<u>Fifth Movement.</u> «It begins with the 'cry of despair'.» Once more we are confronted with terrifying questions, and the atmosphere is the same as at the end of the third movement. The voice of the Caller is heard. The end of every living thing has come, the last judgement is at hand and the horror of the day of days has come upon us. The earth trembles, the graves burst open, the dead arise and march forth in endless procession. The great and the lowly of this earth, kings and beggars, the just and the godless, all press forward – «an endless procession of shuddering, expectant people». The cry for mercy and forgiveness sounds fearful in our ears. The wailing becomes gradually more terrible – our senses desert us, all consciousness dies as the Eternal

Spirit approaches. The 'last trump' sounds; the trumpets of the Apocalypse call out «to all flesh and all spirit». In the eerie silence that follows, we can just barely make out a distant nightingale, a last tremulous echo of earthly life. The gentle sound of a chorus of saints and heavenly hosts is then heard: 'Rise again, yes, rise again thou wilt!' Then God in all His glory comes into sight. A wondrously mild light strikes us to the heart. All is calm and bliss. And lo: there is no judgement – there are no sinners – no just men – no great – and no small – there is no punishment and no reward!

A feeling of overwhelming love imbues us with the bliss of knowing and being.*

10   Berlin [14 December 1901]
                                                        Palast Hotel
                                                    Saturday afternoon
                                                 after throwing everyone
                                                 out to be with you alone

My dearest girl,

I had been longing for a letter from you! And now, today, it has arrived and made my day radiant and beautiful. If only you could have seen the look on my face as I walked through the streets of Berlin! For then you would have known what a Blessed Spirit looks like. I believe everyone could read it in my facial expression, for everyone was looking at me with astonishment (or am I imagining things?). – So perhaps we need to rewrite Goethe slightly (and I know that you, as an expert in counterpoint, will appreciate this): 'People are amazed to see my darling's dear, sweet eyes a-shining!'† I always had a presentiment, always hoped you were like that, my Alma, my source of warmth and light, but until now I was never quite certain. All my life I never dreamt I would experience the bliss of loving someone who returned my love in equal measure. Time and again, whenever one of the fairer sex joined me on life's journey, I was forced to the painful realization that the bliss of dreams does not stand up to the inadequacies of reality. I always blamed myself for this, and deep inside me I had abandoned all hope.

Young as you are, Alma, you have made your own experiences, and you will

---

* Translation based on the version in Henry-Louis de La Grange, *Mahler, A Biography*, London, 1974, 785–6.
† Orig.: 'Über meines Liebchens Äuglein / Stehn verwundert alle Leute' (from Goethe's poem 'Geheimes' in *Ushk Nameh: Buch der Liebe, West-Östlicher Divan*). Mahler's 'slight' alteration is in the fourth word: Goethe writes 'Äugeln' (casting secret glances), while 'Äuglein' is simply a diminutive of 'Auge' (eye).

understand me when I tell you that my heartfelt, deeply lived emotions seem stronger and more blissful than ever. I can also admit to you that this is the first time I have truly loved.

Even now I simply cannot suppress my fear and concern at the thought that so beautiful, so sweet a dream could slip through my fingers, and I can scarcely wait for the moment when the taste of your lips, the savour of your sweet breath again convinces me that my ship has weathered every storm and safely reached its haven. – Since we were last together, I feel we have been drawn truly close together, and that our present separation actually serves to draw us even closer.

You see, my dearest, I read all this into your last letter. Alma, why aren't you here with me now? I clearly remember your telling me how much you loved to travel. And often I persuade myself that you are indeed here with me, that we are conversing together. And from the look on your face I can see how much you are relishing it, how eagerly you are letting yourself be assailed by all that is new and unaccustomed. Having observed your partiality for fruits and cakes (which used to be one of my own failings, by the way), whenever they serve me my dessert I feel like passing it across the table to you. Whenever I think of you (and you are constantly on my mind), life becomes worth living again.

Justi told me about your meeting. She has really fallen for you. – I for my part can no longer say the same, for I simply cannot find the words to express what you now mean to me, nor to describe this extraordinary, profoundly blissful union between us. I am greatly relieved to hear that you got on so well with my sister [one line obliterated] and have taken her into your heart. Nothing makes it easier to recognize and assess your love for me than this, for the same applies to myself: whatever is close to your heart will always be close to mine. From now on, everything I possess is yours too, and by the same reckoning I embrace everything that is yours with heart and soul. Dear God, I so long for you, I feel so anxious about you, light of my life, that today I'm talking like Walter von Stolzing and have completely forgotten his counterpart, poor old Hans Sachs, who is far more deserving of your love.

You know, my darling: sometimes it makes me almost sad to think that the finest things in life can never be earned or procured, <and that such things can be obtained only as gifts.> You have given me so much, my Alma! It was so sweet of you to confess how much you wished to mean to me. And if I consider how much I wish to (and shall) mean to you, I feel almost overawed. So strongly and profoundly do I sense my obligation – which is also my greatest bliss – that I would not dare to make any promise or vow for fear of tempting fate. I believe you feel just as I do: we are fulfilled and united by a power that is beyond and above us. It will be our holy duty tacitly to respect that power. When at such a moment I speak the name of God out loud, the omnipotent sense of your love and of mine will make you realize that this is a power that prevails over both of us and hence holds us in its grasp <u>as one</u>.

Please, dear Alma, let me know what you have to say about what I have written. I want to know whether you have fully understood me and whether you <can> follow me! Not a single word may stand between us. If you were to look at all this merely as beautiful phrases or an interesting 'style of correspondence', that would indeed be the case. But I beg you: <u>do not force anything upon yourself</u>.

<u>Never</u> believe that I would be less fond of you, that my love for you would be diminished, if you were to see things differently or if your opinions differed from mine. Should you be unable to understand my thoughts and feelings, I shall make every effort to assimilate yours. I would also like to hear your opinion of what I wrote in my last letter on the subject of <u>ambition</u>.

What I shall always love about you is your <u>sincerity</u>, your lack of <u>sophistication</u>. I cannot imagine you resorting to empty phrases. For that is a cardinal sin against the Holy Spirit. To deceive others is to deceive oneself! Do you remember our first conversation, when Burckhard was with us? What I said was spoken entirely to <u>you</u>. Already then, it was God's will that we should be <u>united</u>. You may have been unaware of it, but I had already experienced my baptism by fire.

O Alma, dearest, sweetest of girls, I would gladly go on writing about my innermost feelings, but then I would never find time to tell you about the outside world. And that I must. We have to share everything together. –

At present it's still rather hard for me, because I don't quite know where to begin. – It's all so strange to you still. You don't yet know how to see things in perspective, and therefore you cannot judge what is of value for my life and yours, and what is not (how sweet to think that everything henceforth will be meaningful for both of us – or for neither). It's rather like a modern novel: we begin in medias res, and not until the second chapter are we informed about the story so far. Yesterday I wrote to my sister and sent her something I was commissioned to write for my concert in Dresden by a very high ranking person. – By my reckoning, that letter should reach you roughly when you and she are due to meet. How I envy her for that! I have asked Justi to pass those pages on to you. (Actually, they were intended for you in the first place. To be honest, I'm so distracted and confused right now that I wouldn't have managed to put a single word to paper, not even for the King, unless it had something to do with you.) On Tuesday morning I'll be leaving for Dresden. So from Sunday on please write to me there at <u>Hotel Bellevue</u>. <I almost forgot: it looks as if some of my letters have not been reaching you. In future please confirm the arrival of each one. Did you receive my last letter (on the subject of ambition)?

Carl called on me at my hotel this morning. I would have fallen round his neck, were it not for the presence of Hofrat Wiener,* who strikes me as being particularly 'prim and proper'. I can well imagine that it was hard for you to write that letter to Zemlinsky. Quite different from the situation with that other young gentleman who is blessed, as you say, with so many virtues and talents, but whose name I couldn't decipher.>

I've arranged to meet Carl here and am expecting him any minute. I hope he can stay for the concert, for then at least a reflection of my beloved sunshine will be here to cheer me.

Many, many greetings from me to your dear Mama. I've grown so accustomed to thinking of her as my own that I shall probably soon find myself addressing her as 'Mama' outright.

<And now I must make haste to post this letter, so that it reaches you tomorrow. I would rather not send it by registered post, because tomorrow is a Sunday, which means you wouldn't get it until the following day.> Don't forget, Alma: for me every day is lost if I don't receive at least a couple of lines in your fair hand, my beloved, and I kiss it with fervour.

Love and kisses from me, my dearest one. Just think how blissful it is for me to be able to call you <u>my own</u>.   Gustav

The following day Alma attended a concert of the Vienna Philharmonic, and in the afternoon she met Burckhard. Her diary includes an account of their conversation:

Sunday 15 December

He advised me against Gustav, saying that when two strong personalities come together, they usually fight until one of them is forced into submission. And that would probably be me – which he would regret. Must <u>I</u> be subdued? I can and will not. And yet I feel that I stand at a far <u>lower</u> level – and it would do me no harm to be drawn up to his.[47]

---

* Dr Karl Ritter von Wiener, councillor at the Austrian Ministry of Education. He was a close friend of Carl and Anna Moll.

As can be seen from the next entry in Alma's diary, Mahler's letter did not in fact arrive until the Monday. He could scarcely have imagined the reassuring effect it had on her.

Monday 16 December 1901
My longing is indescribable. And my poor Alex – he's fuming, ignores me, hates me – with some justification. I could weep that I have caused him such sorrow – the poor, poor fellow. My love for him is «was» boundless.
P.M. – being inexplicably tired, I'd only just got out of bed – suddenly I could feel something special in the air. I went to the door and – in came Alex. I was speechless. He came into the room, paler than usual and very quiet – I went to him, drew his head against my breast, and kissed his hair. I felt so strange. Then we sat down and talked seriously, only of matters that concerned us both – side by side – we two, «whose bodies had coiled in love's wildest embrace.» He a little sarcastic, as ever, but otherwise kind, touchingly kind. My eyes kept filling with tears. But my will stood firm . . .
Today I buried a beautiful love «feeling». Gustav, you'll have to do much to replace it for me.
Although I told him that I no longer loved him – and that it was actually he who should be shamefaced – it was I who felt it more deeply. He seemed so noble, so pure, stood so high above me! Had he uttered just one angry or accusing word, I would never have begun to feel that way. Alex, I respect you – my respect for you is endless.
[...] But then in the evening Gustav's letter arrived and helped me over the worst. «My poor Alex» – I could see the suffering on his face. You noble man!
Tonight Gustav's 4th symphony is to be performed in Berlin. Those curs will cause a rumpus once again. Never mind.
The trials and tribulations of the past week have made me physically ill.[48]

11   Berlin [15 December 1901]
                                                      Palast Hotel
                                                      Sunday evening

My dearest,
Now comes the loveliest moment of my day, when I can sit down and commune with you. As I was expecting to receive at least a brief letter, I've been pestering the hotel porter since the early morning. I lived in hope all day, and now – I hope for tomorrow morning. Yes, in the space of just eight days I have grown so avid, so demanding, that I can no longer bear to go even for a single day without a letter. And to think that just a week ago I was perfectly

satisfied by the mere sight of that dear handwriting and the blue ink (at that time, your writing was so much larger).

You began your first letter with the words: Dear Herr Direktor. Ugh, how hideous! In the second letter you were already much less formal, but still very indecisive and hesitant: no opening gambit at all, and at the close merely: Alma. But then came your third letter! Now you had become my Alma – and now that you are mine, I shall never let you go. I scarcely had time to register the change before I left. It almost seems to me that I went away without saying goodbye, for since you wrote that letter I have neither had the chance to see you nor to speak to you in person. On Saturday, when I can at last clasp your dear hand in mine, I know you will be offering it to me for ever. This too, like everything else we have experienced, came almost completely out of the blue. –

Today was the public dress rehearsal, which in Berlin counts for as much as the concert itself. Immodest as it may seem, I am delighted to say that it went extremely well. I kept saying to myself: if only my dearest was in the audience. Mine! How proudly I would have looked down at her! If all goes as well tomorrow evening, Berlin will indeed be at my feet. And next time I am here, perhaps you will be with me – but of course! After all, everything is happening so quickly for us, isn't it? And surely the wings of love beat more rapidly than 'The Wings of Song'.*

Sometimes, when I manage to suppress my lack of courage (you know what I mean), my heart rejoices and I can – hope! Carl and I spent some time together yesterday, but unfortunately Wiener was there too, so I kept my silence. It would have meant so much to me to be able to talk about you to C., even on the most mundane of topics. He is indeed staying for the concert, and will then leave on the night train. Heavens, what if he doesn't care for my symphony after all, and starts to conspire with you against me? From this letter it will be clear to you how distracted I am. It's more than I can stand. Here in the writing room, where I have taken refuge, guests and waiters are rushing around and doing their damnedest to disturb me.

How very remarkable that you should have just discovered Hölderlin! Did you know that he's one of my favourites, both as a poet and as a human being? <If there's anything you don't understand in him, you must ask me.> My dearest, he is one of the very greatest.

How lovely it will be to browse through your library and put some order into it. Heavens, the very thought that I shall soon be within the same four

---

* Allusion to Mendelssohn's song 'Auf Flügeln des Gesanges', op. 34, no. 2.

walls as you, and in the same room, makes me so wildly impatient that I feel like setting off right away! If I am to stay the course here, I mustn't even think about it.

Sometimes it seems as if until now we had only exchanged letters, and would soon be meeting and getting to know each other for the first time.

Actually, that is just how the matter stands! Don't forget: even the last time I saw you we were still strangers, despite everything. In these last eight days everything has taken such a wonderful turn. The letter you sent me immediately after Die Zauberflöte brought everything onto a different plane. Until then it was merely a kind of 'conversation' between us. That letter burst the bounds of polite behaviour etc., in that you, my beloved, sounded for the first time that note which is destined to shape the course of our lives. If only I had your picture! I regret not having simply stolen the little photograph you showed me last time. Have your picture taken, Alma (facing the camera, so that you're looking at me). –

<In your last letter (I've been meaning to tell you this too) either you wrote far more clearly or I have meanwhile learnt to read your writing more effortlessly. In your most recent cards the writing has changed, and I must confess that I find them much easier to read. I'd love to know why you changed your handwriting from one page to the next. Just imagine: I'm vain enough to ascribe the change entirely to respect for me.>

Also this, my Alma, I beg you: write every day, even if it's just one page. Otherwise I wait all day, and when nothing arrives I go to bed frustrated. <The address: Hotel Bellevue, Dresden.> Write your last letter on Thursday, but don't send it off too late; be sure it reaches the post office in Vienna by the afternoon, in good time for the night train to Dresden, where it will reach me on Friday. The concert is on Friday evening <and I'll be leaving at 11.00 p.m.> On Saturday at 4.00 p.m. I shall suddenly appear in the Steinfeldgasse. As for the rest, I outlined the scenario to you recently, and since then I have been going over it in my mind every hour of every day. Warmest greetings – and other things I'd prefer not to mention for fear of dying of sheer desire. My beloved, my friend, my Alma!   Your Gustav

On the same day, Mahler wrote to his sister Justine, who was celebrating her thirty-third birthday:

Berlin [15 December 1901]

Dearest Justi,

Don't worry about the expense of your journey [to Dresden]. Remember, it's

my birthday present to you. [. . .] I can't wait to hear what you'll have to say about Alma! Yesterday she sent me a very sweet letter, which has dispersed all remaining doubts about her warmth and sincerity. On that score I believe everything is in order. Only one thing still worries me: whether a person on the threshold of middle age has the right to so much youthfulness and vigour, whether that person has the right to tether the spring to the autumn, to force his partner to forego the summer. I know I have much to offer, but that is no fair exchange for the right to be young. If Beethoven, Wagner and Goethe were to return to life today, the young at heart would kneel down and worship them; but flowers can only sprout and blossom when the spring comes. For me, that is the big question. For a while, of course, everything would be plain sailing. But what will happen when the autumn of my fruitfulness yields to winter? You understand? I was overjoyed by what she wrote about you and how she expressed herself. She calls you her 'sister', and is as delighted with you as you are with her. She recognized the family likeness, and the sound of your voice reminded her of mine. You can well imagine how this all draws me to her. It couldn't have worked out better, for this guarantees us all a secure future. [. . .] Fondest greetings and kisses   Your Gustav
Please also pass on my best wishes to Arnold.*⁴⁹

12   Berlin [16 December 1901]
                                                     Palast Hotel
                                                     Monday morning

<My dear, sweet Almschi,
Your dear letter has just arrived – in reply to the one in which I extemporized about that 'pasty young man'. – How deeply you have cheered and strengthened me. I can sense that love has made you perceptive, and that to your eyes 'all is now clear'!
As for my (last) letter, from my tone of voice you realized with unbelievable sensitivity that your letter, to which mine was the reply, had got me – how can I put it – had me needled. – Perhaps I hadn't read it properly. But in one point you misunderstood me: I hadn't the slightest notion that for you there was any choice in the matter. And the passage beginning 'Almschi, Almschi' – I remember it well – was written in my flippant tone, which was new to you. Had I spoken the same words to you, I would have been laughing and would have tweaked your ear as I did so. I just wanted to 'educate' you. –

---

* Arnold Rosé, first concertmaster of the Vienna Philharmonic, was Justine Mahler's fiancé. They celebrated their wedding one day after Mahler and Alma, on 10 March 1902.

You know, dear girl, I was longing for a word from you, and then, when you did write, it was to extol the virtues of some young man. Above all, I don't understand how I could have taken it all <u>so personally</u>. Is that what is meant by dissipating one's energies? At that moment I became painfully aware of our age difference which, since we began exchanging letters, had otherwise ceased to affect me – to my great joy, I should add. Nevertheless, I did all I could to get over it <u>at once</u> – and that, my Alma, is something we have to strive for for the rest of our days: <u>touchiness</u> should <u>never</u> get the better of you. But I had to be honest and write to you from the depth of my soul. – It should be clear to you that not an atom of my disgruntlement now remains. Since then you have also imparted to me so much calm and confidence. – I feel you have already become my helpmate, in every sense of the word, and hence I fear nothing and nobody!>

Dearest Almschi, don't throw out the baby with the bathwater. If a single composition of mine is to be understood, above all in Vienna, where people feel entitled to empirical opinions about my person, you should never let them influence your own, nor let them cause you to distrust my music; the same goes for those who approach it with incomprehension or ill will. I have spent the past fifteen years battling against superficiality and incomprehension, bringing down on me all the troubles, indeed all the miseries of the trail-blazer. – The main thing is that you should never let yourself be swayed by public opinion, that you should go your way unwaveringly, in life as in art, allowing yourself to be distracted neither by failure nor acclaim. – For it seems to me that what I once disseminated is now beginning to take root. Whatever the case, I am truly delighted that it is happening just <u>now</u>, and that you, dear heart, will no longer have to feel the agony of the goads. Likewise, if I am to remain true to myself (and that also means remaining true to you, for you and I will soon be one and the same), I shall never spare you that pain. In face of all things superficial, let us remain calm and aloof. To that end we shall support and encourage each other in life: this is the highest honour we can crave for!

<What do you mean when you write that on Saturday I should come to you straight away, as soon as I have arrived? I intend to come at 4 p.m. as usual, firstly so that I can spend the whole afternoon and evening with you (if I were to come in the morning, I would have to leave within a few hours), secondly because first I must hurry to the theatre, where I have a pile of urgent administrative duties to attend to.* Only then can heart and mind be clear for that blissful hour.>

* These included signing the contract with Richard Strauss and his publisher for the opera *Feuersnot*, which was to be staged the following year at the Hofoper.

Listen: in the first hour we shall surely be unable to talk – for we have <u>much</u> to discuss. Your Mama already knows everything, doesn't she? Tell her everything before I arrive; the only way I can now come to her is as her son – and I would like to be spared the customary 'asking for a daughter's hand' and other such formalities. Tell her everything. As you know, I wanted to speak to her myself – but that was at a time when I myself was still uncertain (to say nothing of you). – It would have been more like asking her advice, since she knows you so well. But now everything between us is so clear and indissoluble – I wouldn't know what to say other than: give me what is mine – enable me to breathe, to live – for your love has become as much a prerequisite for my existence as my own pulse and heartbeat. To me it seems ever more significant and fundamental for our entire future that these golden days should unite us not physically, but only spiritually. Hence we will establish a close spiritual union (golden days: this is the true meaning of the word 'Hochzeit', the time when two souls who have 'found' each other unite to become one). It could have taken us months to speak so intensively, to understand each other so profoundly as we have done during those two (infinitely protracted) weeks! – It fills me with joy to think that in this brief span of time a sunshine stronger than the brightest of stars in the heavens has matured and ripened us. Where nature takes a whole summer, we have come to fruition in just two weeks. – This would certainly never have happened if I had not been obliged to leave at the very moment when you resolved to give yourself, to make a gift of yourself to me. – In future we should number our letters, to ensure that none of them goes astray. – Yesterday I suddenly went down with a cold and general catarrh, the likes of which I can't remember. My goodness, what a fright! What if it had come on on Saturday – or if I were to have a relapse? – Then I wouldn't be able to come to you – in which case I would have to force the most terrible of <u>privations</u> upon myself (you see, Almschi, this is my 'flippant' tone). Of course I would come, even if I were at death's door. I wouldn't be able to kiss you, but, as you can imagine, merely <u>seeing you, hearing your voice</u>, holding your hand would be enough to cure me. If I were to die, I have the feeling you could bring me back to life. But heavens, now I must take great care of myself. When I travel, I am always so distracted and careless. At home, Justi always looks after me. – How did you get on together last Saturday? I really would love to know. You were in my room! And now, when I enter it again, what a warm, joyous feeling it will be! And now I have to leave! My dearest – I find it hard to find the words. They are all so shallow. In the mouths of the apathetic and the weak at heart they have lost all meaning! But you, my one and only, you know what it means when I say, 'My dearest dear! My Alma!' Take good care of yourself! All blessings on you! Oh, that I should enter your life as a blessing. For from now on your being is the soil in which I take root and from which I hope to germinate.

My beloved!   Your Gustav

<From now on I shall send my letters by registered post. Although it takes longer, at least I can be certain that they arrive.>

Alma was evidently still in two minds about Mahler:

Tuesday 17 December
A shopping spree. Then home, where I found this letter. He is such a dear man. How I look forward to his return. How kindly and nicely he writes . . . And Alex – if only I knew what he's feeling – «my poor devil.»
Strange though: yesterday I was calm and remained so, looked at him and suddenly felt, with a shudder, just how ugly he is, how strongly he smells etc. «Midsummer Night's Dream!» All things I had never noticed before. That is strange. «?!» Is there really some extrinsic force that controls us? Sometimes I believe so. These last weeks will remain rooted in my memory.[50]

From the next diary entry it transpires that Mahler wrote to Alma on 17 December, but the letter has not survived. This was also the day on which he had arranged to meet his sister Emma. Twice Alma remarks that the letter had her 'foxed'. In no uncertain terms she also criticizes Mahler's remarks about her attitude towards his sister Justine.

Wednesday 18 December
I must say, the letter has me foxed. I take the greatest pains to make friends with Justine, and she observes me with an eagle eye – every word, movement and sensation – and promptly passes on her fears to Gustav . . .
That annoys me because, if she perseveres in observing me so closely, it could become dangerous «unpleasant». What, for instance, if she should come to realize «believe» that I am heartless and unloving – things that I confide, but discretely, to my diary – that I am incapable of warmth, that everything in me is mere calculation, cold-blooded calculation? «All untrue!»
No – he's a sick man, his position is insecure, he's a Jew, no longer young, and as a composer . . . «deeply in debt». So where's the calculation on my part? Is it then all just folly? No, for there is something which draws me to him – without a doubt!
But if Justi intrigues against me and his interest wanes, I shall – not die. «I love him and shall stand by him!»

75

I can hardly say how much Gustav's letter has me foxed . . . and how his cooling off annoys me. I must be fond of him! My Gustav! – I long for him <u>disgracefully</u>.

This evening: 'Walküre'. I scarcely listened, have <u>absolutely</u> no ears for music right now. During the second act I stayed at the back of the box and took a break, chatted with Pollack. Anyway, the performance was mediocre.

But I am inexplicably restless. I have a feeling that Justi is poisoning his love.[51]

13   Dresden [18 December 1901]
Hotel Bellevue
Wednesday morning

My dearest love,

So, this is the last call on my journey (this time it has been a veritable via dolorosa)! Physically speaking, I am closer to you again. My longing for you is unabated! On Saturday, when I hold you in my arms, I know it will be the happiest moment of my life! – Today is the performance of my Second Symphony. My Almschi, didn't Justi explain that my programme was written for a shallow, oafish person (you know who I mean), and that it deals only with the extraneous, purely superficial aspects of the work – as in the final analysis does any programme for a musical work of art. All the more so in the case of this one, which is a rounded, unified whole and is no easier to explain than the world itself. – I am convinced, namely, that if God were asked to expound the programme of the 'world' He created, He would be just as incapable of doing so! – At most it would be some kind of a 'Revelation', which would reveal just as little about the nature of God and life as my feeble concoction tells us about my C-minor Symphony! Indeed, like all revelatory beliefs, it would inevitably lead to misunderstanding, incomprehension, oversimplification or coarsening, until finally the work and its creator grew distorted beyond recognition. – In Berlin I had a very earnest talk with Strauss, in which I tried to show him the futility of his position.[*] Unfortunately he didn't really understand me. He's such a dear fellow, and he takes a really touching attitude towards me. But where I have a clear view of him, all he can see of me is the pedestal on which I stand – hence he can make nothing of me. He'll be coming to Vienna soon. Maybe I'll bring him along with me when I call on you. [Two and a half lines obliterated]. Once again we talked until the dead of night. For me it is such a delight, so strangely touching, to contemplate and plan out the details of our future life

---

[*] Orig.: 'ihm seine Sackgasse zeigen' (lit. 'to show him his cul-de-sac').

together – always with you at the centre of my very being. I keep restarting and returning to my point of departure – during the day, during my waking hours, before going to bed, when I wake up at night or first thing in the morning! At present, due to a malady that often assails me when I travel, I am sleeping poorly and insufficiently. But even this is not unwelcome, for my thoughts immediately turn to you. – How deeply I regret that you cannot be here for my C-minor Symphony. On the piano it sounds nothing like the same. And it really is essential that you should hear it, for my Fourth Symphony will appear utterly foreign to you. Here all is <u>humour</u> – 'naivety' etc., you know: that part of me which <deep <u>inside</u> yourself> you understand least of all, and which only a <u>handful</u> of people will ever understand. But for you, my Alma, love will be your guide and lighten your way towards the obscurest corners. I greet you, my beloved, in my longing and loving, in my hopes and beliefs. Eternally yours   Your Gustav

In her diary Alma makes no mention of this letter. Her attention had been diverted:

Thursday 19 December
«Yesterday again I flirted madly with Louis Adler. The fellow is so damned good-looking. And Muhr was watching . . . If only Muhr was as handsome – there's a captivating fellow. He knew it too, kept looking over his shoulder. Unfortunately I was sitting rather far away. The music gave me no pleasure. My ears were shut, my eyes incapable of seeing. – » [. . .]
In the evening Pollack. We talked a lot about Gustav. I managed to talk my rage away. I had to make a clean breast of everything seething within me. If it ever comes to my marrying him, I must do everything <u>now</u> to stake <u>my</u> rightful claim . . . particularly in <u>artistic</u> questions. He thinks <u>nothing</u> of my art – and much of his own. And <u>I</u> think <u>nothing</u> of <u>his</u> art and much of my own. – That's how it is!
Now he talks unceasingly of safeguarding <u>his</u> art. I <u>can't</u> do that. With Zemlinsky it would have been possible, because I have sympathy for his art – he's such a brilliant fellow. But Gustav is so poor – so <u>dreadfully</u> poor. If he knew <u>just</u> how poor he was – he would cover his face in shame . . . And <u>I</u> am supposed to lie, lie for the rest of my life. And he – that's all right – but Justi, that woman! I have the feeling she's spying on me everywhere . . . And I simply <u>must</u> have my freedom![52]

Mahler's repeated efforts to express and explain his thoughts and feelings for Alma appear to have provoked little reaction from her, indeed perhaps none at all. Several times he begs her: 'Do write and tell me whether you under-

stand what I mean.' Not only did she pay no heed to such requests, in later years she was still offended that he should have expressed himself in such terms. Mahler appears to have taken her flirtations in his stride, just as he followed her 'rearguard action' against the erotic offensive of Felix Muhr with evident lack of concern.

Alma's aspirations as a composer were another matter. To her mind, her creative drive constituted a threat to Mahler's self-esteem. In AMM4 she recalls:

Mahler suggested in one of his later letters that I myself should ask my mother for his hand in marriage [letter 12], so that when he returned she would immediately accept him as her son-in-law. Shortly before his return, the first major conflicts arose. In one of my letters I had written 'I must stop now, because I have work to do', implying that I wanted to compose, an activity that had always meant the world to me. He was furious that anything at all could be more important than writing to him. So he sent me a long letter in which he forbade me to compose. What a dreadful thing to do! [. . .] At the time it signified the end of my fondest dream. Perhaps it was for the best. Instead I was able to instil my creative gifts in minds greater than my own. But inside me it inflicted a deep wound, which to this day has never quite ceased to ache.[53]

The letter to which Alma refers is Mahler's longest. With impressive clarity and complete honesty he outlines his expectations for their future partnership.

14   Dresden [19 December 1901]
                                                              Hotel Bellevue

My dearest Almschi,
Today, my beloved Alma, it is with a heavy heart that I set out to write this letter. I know that I must hurt you, but I have no choice. For I must give voice to everything in your last letter that aggravated me. If we are to be happy together, there is one particular aspect of our relationship that we must discuss and clarify for now and ever more, for it is the very basis of our bond.
Admittedly I am reading between the lines of yesterday's letter (for once again, dear Almschi, the lines themselves could be deciphered only with great difficulty). Between this letter and the one you sent me after The Magic Flute I perceive a profound contradiction. – At the time, you wrote: I want to be all you <u>need</u> and <u>wish for</u>. Those words made me profoundly happy, they filled

me with blissful trust. But now, perhaps without realizing it, you have revoked them. – Let me take the points in your last letter one by one. Firstly your conversation with Burckhard. What do you mean by 'individuality'. Do you see yourself as being 'individual'? As you will recall, I once told you that every human being possesses certain qualities that can be explained neither by their parentage nor by external circumstances. This is what makes every human being a person in their own right. In this sense each of us is 'individual'. But what Burckhard means (and you with him) is something quite different. – This kind of individuality can be attained only through a long process of struggle, anguish and experience, and then only by those capable of profound and vigorous development. On this earth such individuals are extremely rare. As yet, you cannot have reached such a state of fully reasoned, intrinsic being which, regardless of the circumstances, serves to evolve an individual, unalterable character, and then to maintain and safeguard it against all external, destructive forces; for in you everything is still nascent, latent and undeveloped. Young, sympathetic and boundlessly delightful as you are, unsullied in body and soul, richly gifted, open-hearted and precociously self-assured, all this still makes no true individual of you. What you are for me, my Alma, what you could perhaps one day be for me – the highest and dearest part of my life, a faithful, valiant partner, who understands me and spurs me on to higher things, an unassailable fortress, who shields me from all my intrinsic and extrinsic enemies, a haven, a heaven, in which I can always submerge, retrieve and reconstitute myself – all this is so indescribably noble and beautiful – so much and so great – in a word: MY WIFE – but even this is still no individuality in the sense of those superior beings who determine the course of their own existence as well as that of all mankind, and who alone bear that name. But now you should be aware of the following: if you wish to acquire – or to be – 'individual' in this way, will-power on its own will be of absolutely no use to you. – Goldmark once told me (with pride) that he deliberately avoids listening to new music or reading new scores, so as not to lose his individuality. – You see, my Alma-child, in my eyes that was symptomatic of his complete lack of individuality! It's as if someone were to abstain from eating beef for fear they might become an ox. Let me assure you, my Alma, that everything you absorb, everything that nurtures you, can influence your development in a positive or negative way. The most important thing is that such nourishment is appropriate and beneficial, and that your organism is capable of digesting it. – All these Burckhards, Zemlinskys etc. possess no true individuality. Each of them has their own particular sphere – an unusual place to live in, illegible handwriting (I mean this only in a metaphorical sense

– naturally it is not a matter of such trifles) – and to preserve their originality they defend these spheres with little sense of personal independence, always concerned to guard over their 'nourishment'. But a genuinely individual person is like a vigorous organism that seeks suitable nourishment with instinctive assurance, ingests it and decisively rejects all that is inappropriate. How fortunate are those whose early development is not hindered or even destroyed by harmful forces. Maybe the reason why the healthiest of organisms sometimes later grow weak or infirm is that during their early development they are made to ingest things inappropriate or damaging to them. And now – after this somewhat lengthy introduction – to you!

Look, my Alma! You have spent your entire youth – your whole life, in other words – in danger of being stifled by certain friends who have accompanied you, taken you by the hand and misled you, people who seek false paths in murky, troubled waters, who smother all inner life with raucous calls, and who continually confuse cause with effect. And all the while you believed yourself to be a free agent. These people have never ceased to flatter you, not because your contributions were of any benefit to them, but because you all expressed yourselves in momentous words (though they do not care for true opposition, they value the use of strong, persuasive rhetoric). I am speaking here of Burckhard and the likes of Zemlinsky (whom I do not know, but consider to be of greater value, though still vague and lacking in self-determination). You use portentous words (though you consider yourselves 'enlightened', you shutter up the windows and worship your beloved gaslight as if it were the sun) and – because you are good-looking and men are attracted to you, for <u>that</u> reason they are glad to pay tribute to you. Consider what it would be like if you were ugly. My Alma – you have grown vain (this may sound hard, but you must forgive me, for my love for you is <u>true</u> and already everlasting), your vanity is a result of what these people think they see in you or would like to see in you (i.e. you would, in fact, like to be what they think you are). But, thank the Lord, all this, as you yourself wrote in your dear letter, is merely <u>superficial</u>. – And these people are mutual admirers, who involuntarily reject superior beings as something disruptive, something that makes demands on them which they cannot fulfil. With your charm, you serve such people as an uncommonly delightful, <u>agreeable</u> adversary, and one, moreover, who lacks the force of factual argument. Thus, in the belief that you are mutually benefiting mankind, you move together in ever-diminishing circles – 'what you don't touch lies leagues afar'.* The

* Goethe, *Faust II*, 5008: '[Daran erkenn' ich den gelehrten Herrn!] / Was ihr nicht tastet steht euch meilenfern.'

<u>immodesty</u> of these people, who perceive the role of intellect solely as reeling off tangled skeins of thought within a diminutive and highly restricted circle, this is something, my Almschi, to which you yourself are also prone. – Remarks such as this: 'That we do not <u>agree</u> on certain questions, ideas etc. is proof thereof and of other things too' (not that I would take issue on this, because I know it is merely a façon de parler – but even this is conventional thinking). But dear child! It is in <u>our love</u>, in our hearts that we should agree! But to agree on ideas? My Alma! Where are your ideas? Schopenhauer's writings on womanhood, Nietzsche's utterly false and brazenly arrogant theories of masculine supremacy, the gut-rotting, murky fuddle of Maeterlinck, the public-house rhetoric of Bierbaum and co. etc., etc.? – These are not your ideas, <u>thank God</u>, but those of others. Surely this is no idea of yours, that the wonderful, profoundly unfathomable world we live in is nothing but a practical joke played on us by some numbskull, some stupid 'natural force', which knows nothing either of itself or of us (and hence stands not even as high as the human beings you so deride), a bubble that one day will simply burst – that my heart, which can fill me with unspeakable joy or torment, is no miracle but merely a lump of flesh with two valves, that my brain is nothing but blood-filled arteries and capillaries in a craftily 'meandering' mass of jelly etc. etc. This is surely no idea of your own, but merely general knowledge. As it is, now that famous scientists (truly great men, and men, moreover, who never looked on life as a mere arithmetical puzzle) have ascertained these facts in the course of laborious, <u>silent</u>, and totally selfless research, people have an easy time of it. – Poor me! I, who lie awake at night for the sheer bliss of having found <u>her</u>, who <u>from the outset</u> agrees profoundly with me about everything, who has become a very part of me, my other self, who herself wrote she felt she could do no other and no better than to come to terms with my world and enter into it, who believes in me so completely that she now instinctively senses she can share in my religion – because she loves me etc. etc.

And now I have to ask myself again: what kind of idée fixe has entered this head that I love so unutterably and so dearly, that she feels compelled to remain true to herself – and what form will this idée fixe assume when the first passion is spent (which happens very quickly) and our relationship has become one of friendship, of living (not dwelling, but existing) and of loving together? – And now I come to what is actually my prime cause of concern, the focus of all my fears and doubts, the reason why every detail pointing in this direction has acquired so much significance for me. In your letter, you write of 'your' music and 'my' music. <u>Forgive me, but I cannot remain silent</u>!

81

On this point, my Alma, we must set things straight, and I mean <u>right now</u>, before we meet again! And here, unfortunately, I must come back to you, for I find myself in the curious position of having to compare <u>my</u> music – in a certain sense – with yours. I have to defend my music, which you actually do not know and certainly do not yet understand, against yours, and show it in its true light. Surely, Alma, you will not consider me <u>vain</u>, and believe me, this is the first time I have ever discussed my music with someone who had not found the right approach to it. From now on, would you be able to regard <u>my</u> music as if it were <u>your own</u>? For the moment I would prefer not to talk specifically of 'your' music – let me return to that later. Let me speak in general terms. A husband and wife who are both composers: how do you envisage that? Such a strange relationship between rivals: do you have any idea how ridiculous it would appear, can you imagine the loss of self-respect it would later cause us both? If, at a time when you should be attending to household duties or fetching me something I urgently needed, or if, as you wrote, you wish to relieve me of life's trivia – if at such a moment you were befallen by 'inspiration': what then? Don't get me wrong! I don't want you to believe that I take that philistine view of marital relationships which sees a woman as some sort of diversion, with additional duties as her husband's housekeeper. Surely you wouldn't expect me to feel or think that way? But one thing is certain: if we are to be happy together, you will have to be 'as I need you' – not my colleague, but my wife! If you were to abandon <u>your</u> music in order to take possession of mine, and also to be mine: would this signify the end of life as you know it, and if you did so, would you feel you were renouncing a higher existence?

Before we can think of forging a bond for life, we <u>must</u> agree on this question. What do you mean when you write: 'I haven't worked any more – since then!' 'Now I have to return to my work' etc. etc.? What kind of work is this? Composition? Do you compose for your own pleasure or for the benefit of mankind?

You also write: 'I feel it my sole duty now to penetrate your world – I am playing through your songs, reading your letters etc.' I understood these words and took them into my heart as if they were the Gospel! But at a time like this (our golden days, as I call them) I simply cannot understand you plaguing your conscience for having neglected your studies of form and counterpoint! As I said, this has nothing to do with your compositions, for I don't even know them; this is about your attitude towards me and its essence, which will determine the future of our life together. – I have to go now, for there's <u>work</u> to do (you see – I really <u>must</u>, for a whole team of three hundred people is waiting for me). This afternoon I shall continue with this letter – probably the most important one I ever had to write!

* * *

So, the rehearsal is over and I am back, rather tired and actually rather saddened. I have re-read my letter up to this point. Since it must reach you by tomorrow, I have written it in great haste, and fear it will not be particularly easy to read. If so, don't punish me with my own words, for this is merely the outcome of that haste to which my profession forces me. But from now on you have only <u>one</u> profession: <u>to make me happy</u>! Do you understand, Alma? I do realize that if you are to make me happy, you yourself must be happy (on my account). But in this drama, which could develop equally well into a comedy or a tragedy (both of which would be inappropriate), the roles must be correctly cast. The role of the 'composer', the 'bread-winner', is mine; yours is that of the loving partner, the sympathetic comrade. Are you satisfied with it? – I am asking <u>much</u> of you, <u>very much</u> – but I can and must do so, because I also know what I have to offer (and shall offer) in return.

I simply cannot understand your cold-hearted attitude towards Zemlinsky! Did you love him? Is it then fair to relegate him to the sad role of teacher? Evidently you consider it manly and magnanimous of you to let him sit silent and courteous before you – the cause of his suffering – and simply take everything in his stride. If you really believe you loved him, could you still accept such a situation? And what kind of a figure would I cut if I were sitting next to you – and just imagine me there, sitting beside you! – Is your life not governed by other natural laws now? Has the disruption been so slight that you already can and wish to return to your former round – studying musical forms (character of the violin? that's how I construed it, but I don't understand), attending Philharmonic Concerts under Hellmesberger[*] (!) etc.? – How could you engage in 'small talk' with my sister, whose heart was reaching out for you, and who was only too eager to give wholeheartedly of herself? How could you sit there all afternoon without finding affectionate words for me and about me?

Almschi, Almschi – I don't understand any of this. What conventions could still come between us? What new fourth amendment[†] can I still expect of you? What is all this 'defiance' and 'pride'? And this to me, who in all humility is offering you his whole heart, who from the outset has consecrated his life to you (and I know that kind only too well: pretty, rich, well-educated, young etc. – whether still a girl or already a young woman).

[*] The popular composer, conductor and violinist Josef Hellmesberger Jr. He had been a Kapellmeister at the Vienna Hofoper since 1889.
[†] Orig.: '4. Fall' (literally: accusative case).

Almschi, I beg you, read this letter carefully. Our relationship must not degenerate into a mere flirt. Before we speak again, we must have clarified everything, you must know what I demand and expect of you, and what I can give in return – <u>what you must</u> be for me. You must 'renounce' (your word) everything <u>superficial</u> and <u>conventional,</u> all vanity and outward show (concerning your individuality and your work) – you must surrender yourself to me <u>unconditionally,</u> make every detail of your future life completely dependent on my needs, in return you must wish for nothing except my <u>love</u>! And what that is, Alma, I cannot tell you – I have already spoken too much about it. But let me tell you just this: for someone I love the way I would love you if you were to become my wife, I can forfeit all my life and all my happiness.

Today I have had to express myself without measure or restraint (to you this letter must appear immodest). And Alma, before I arrive on Saturday I must have your reply. This letter will reach you tomorrow, Friday. You can reply straight away, and if my judgement does not deceive me, you will feel <u>compelled</u> to do so <u>at once</u>, in which case your letter will reach me by Saturday afternoon. Better still, I shall send a servant to your apartment on Saturday morning to collect it. Almschi, my beloved, be strict with yourself, regard me <u>not</u> as the object of your love (though that is what I otherwise particularly delight in), but imagine you are writing to a stranger who will then send me his report. Write with utter candour, tell me all you have to say and all you know. Rather than living in self-deception, I would prefer for us to part at once. – Otherwise, being the way I am, I know it would end in a catastrophe for both of us.

This letter will come as a dreadful shock to you – I know it, Alma, and even if this is only cold comfort, you can well imagine that I am suffering just as much. I call to God, though aware that you have not yet made His acquaintance, to guide your hand, my love, in writing the truth and not letting yourself be led astray by ostentation. – For this is a moment of great importance, these are decisions that will weld two people together for eternity. I bless you, my dearest, my love, no matter how you react. – I shall not write tomorrow, but wait instead for your letter on Saturday. A servant will be sent round and kept waiting in readiness. Many tender kisses, my Alma. And I beg you: be truthful!   Your Gustav

Mahler's 'letter of agreement' caused Alma considerable consternation:

Friday 20 December
In town early in the morning. Shopping with Else L[egler] in an open fiacre.

A.M. at home – <u>this letter</u>. My heart missed a beat . . . give up my music – abandon what until now has been my life. My <u>first</u> reaction was – to pass him up. I had to weep – for then I realized that I loved him. Half-crazed with grief, I got into my finery and drove to 'Siegfried' – in tears! I told Pollack, and he was incensed – he would <u>never</u> have thought it possible. I feel as if a cold hand has torn the heart from my breast.

Mama & I talked it over till late at night. She had read the letter . . .! I was dumbfounded. I find his behaviour so ill-considered, so inept. It might have come all of its own . . . quite gently . . . But like this it will leave an indelible scar . . .[54]

Although this letter was of radical importance, Alma never published it. In AML she summarized it as follows:

Gustav Mahler wrote to me, demanding that I abandon my music forthwith and live only for his. He considered Robert and Clara Schumann's marriage, for instance, to have been 'ridiculous', and demanded that I declare my resolve then and there. Self-imposed asceticism is right and proper; but this asceticism forced upon me, as it was when I married Gustav Mahler, provoked me almost beyond endurance.[55]

After Mahler's death, Alma built up the 'composition ban' into a sentimental legend, perpetuating the myth of her having been smothered by Mahler's genius. In Mahler's letter there is nothing to suggest that he was comparing their relationship to that of Robert and Clara Schumann. Nor did Mahler imply that he wished to force Alma into marrying him. There can be no doubt that he gave her complete freedom of choice.

   Later she drew on passages from this letter for her own writings. Mahler writes that Goldmark was like someone who would 'abstain from eating beef for fear he might become an ox.' In AML, this humorous attempt to illustrate the notion of individuality undergoes a remarkable metamorphosis:

One day, after a rehearsal at the Hofoper, Mahler bumped into the composer Carl Goldmark on the Ringstrasse. That evening there was a performance of Tristan, and Mahler offered Goldmark a seat in his box for it. But the latter refused, explaining that he was anxious to avoid the influence of Wagner, and could already sense a dangerous tendency in himself . . . 'Even if you eat beef,' Mahler replied, 'it won't make an ox of you.'[56]

Mahler was here referring to an idea from one of his favourite books, Johann Peter Eckermann's Gespräche mit Goethe in den letzten Jahren seines Lebens. *Eckermann suggests that it was common in literary circles to cast doubt upon the originality of famous authors, and that 'one attempts to trace the source' from which such writers 'draw their culture'; Goethe replies: 'How very foolish. One might just as well ask a well-fed man how many oxen, sheep and pigs he has eaten, and if he owes his girth to them.'*[57]

In AMM4, Alma simplifies the problems outlined in this letter to the following:

Shortly after our secret engagement, Mahler left for Dresden. Unable to sleep, he lay in bed in a state of nervous excitement, and suddenly a thought occurred to him: 'What if I were too old for her?' And from that moment this anxiety never left him. By the time he returned to Vienna, he had changed completely. Pale and nervous.[58]

Her diary entry for the following day presents a striking contrast.

Saturday 21 December
I <u>forced</u> myself to sleep the night through. This morning I read his letter again – and suddenly I felt such warmth. What if I were to <u>renounce</u> «my music» <u>out of love</u> for him? Just forget all about it! I must admit that scarcely any music interests me now except for his.
Yes – he's right. I must live <u>entirely</u> for him, to make him happy. And now I have a strange feeling that my love for him is deep & genuine. For how long? I don't know, but already <u>that</u> is quite something. I long for him <u>boundlessly</u>. This morning Mama called on Klimt. That doesn't worry me at all.
Before lunch I went shopping in Döbling – just to get out of the house. My heart trembled in anticipation. On the way I met his servant. I read his letter on the street. How right he is about everything.
I love him!

This is the letter that Alma read on the street:

15   [Vienna, 21 December 1901]

My beloved Alma,
Here in my home town, where we can breathe the same air, I greet you from the heart! I had scarcely entered my room (how nice that you have already seen it!), when I espied that sweet, familiar handwriting, and I was not unmoved to read your dear words, which must have been written before you received my last letter. – During the past two days, the thought of the initial impression it must have made on you has been dampening my spirits. My wish for both of us is that my letter will communicate nothing but my love and fidelity, and that you come to see now how strong and deep they are.

You do realize, don't you, how hard and uncompromisingly truthful I can be when I love someone? Before I take you in my arms, we must be clear about everything – for this afternoon I would no longer possess the necessary strength and self-control to speak about the many things that have to be discussed. Never have I so desired or feared a letter from you as the one that my servant is now on his way to collect. What will you tell me?

But don't get me wrong. It's not what you say that will be decisive, but what you are. At this moment we have to disregard the passion that currently holds sway over us (which is only possible when we are not together – and that explains why I have communicated with you as long as possible in writing). Only then will we have found the inner calm and loving certainty to forge that bond which will bind us indissolubly, to our last breath.

> Let those who would be married prove themselves . . .
> For with the veil and bridal gown
> Delusion fair is torn asunder!*

And now no more – for at the very thought of seeing you again, my heart overflows! I shall come as soon as possible, but have no idea how long I shall be kept busy at the theatre. Today I must also go to the Obersthofmeister, who often keeps me until three o'clock in the afternoon. Farewell my dearest dear!   Your Gustav

Alma left only a brief record of succeeding events that Saturday afternoon:

Saturday 21 December
He arrived – as kind and loving as ever. Our kisses were hot. I am wax in his hands . . . I want to give him everything. My soul is his. If only everything were clear! –59

By the following morning her attitude had grown more positive:

Sunday 22 December
How lovely it was yesterday!
My longing for him is indescribable. Everything about him is loveable & familiar, his breath so sweet . . . I have the feeling: I could live . . . exist for him alone. If we marry, it will be in the spring, just as I thought.
I long to bear his child. If he has the strength. He hopes so.
Nothing, absolutely nothing – but to obey him.

---

* Orig.: 'Es prüfe, wer sich ewig bindet . . . / und mit dem Gürtel, mit dem Schleier / reißt der schöne Wahn entzwei!' (Friedrich Schiller, *Das Lied der Glocke*; in the original, the passage begins 'Drum prüfe . . .')

P.M. at Justi's. Initially we were somewhat inhibited. But then Gustav arrived and as a trio we were quite happy. Whenever Justi went out, he kissed me. They brought me home in the cab – we held hands.

My thoughts are continually of him. No work gives me pleasure. My beloved Gustav – my thoughts are only of him. [. . .]

This morning Carl came up to talk to me . . . kindly & seriously. – He explained all the possible eventualities. I know everything. He is sick, my poor dear, weighs only 63 kilos – far too little. I shall care for him like a child. My love for him is infinitely touching. – What a shame he can't pronounce an 'r'. And strangely enough, he would like me to call myself Maria, because he loves the strong r in the middle of the name. Strange and . . .!

Today Justi spoke of Arnold «Rosé», who also gave her «a lovely ring . . .»

I am so afraid his health will let me down – I can scarcely say. I can just see him lying in a pool of blood. –

He's right. On the one hand he could be satisfied, he said, because he believed «the affair with» Gustav wouldn't last much longer . . . But in my case he thinks quite differently.

I have no heart «? too much» & feel so warmly for him. And I have the feeling that he elevates me, while Burckhard's company brings out the frivolity in me. When Gustav is listening, I feel ashamed of my loose tongue – and can scarcely find words for all my thoughts. Is one happier when one lives frivolously, unscrupulously, or when one acquires a beautiful, sublime outlook on life? . . . Freer in the former case, happier. «In the latter case» better – purer. Does that not hinder one's path to freedom? Yes, yes a hundred times over, I tell you – stand firm!

He's right – we make a good match – like fire and water – outwardly and inwardly. For sure! But must one of us be subordinate? Isn't it possible – with the help of love – to merge two fundamentally opposing points of view into – one?[60]

And the next day her resolve stood firm:

Monday 23 December

I'm waiting – waiting – for Gustav & Justi! How I detest having to wait. It's torture – an eternity. He does me wrong.

Well, they came and this evening I got engaged – officially, in the presence of Carl and Mama. From now on only he shall have a place in my heart – only he. Never more shall I cast my roving eye on a good-looking young man. I shall give him everything – my husband «!». Our bond is already so close, it can scarcely grow closer. If my relationship with A.Z. was wild and carnal, then with Mahler I feel imbued with the holiest feelings. Once I told Z. I wanted to be the mother of his children. I was not speaking sincerely. I then believed I could never feel anything so profoundly beautiful – today I said nothing: but I could feel it. When we sit there, cuddled together, I feel him as my body. Nothing remotely foreign – so unbelievably dear . . . I can scarcely wait to see him again tomorrow. –[61]

On the afternoon of Christmas Eve Mahler brought Alma a gift and a letter:

16   [Vienna, 24 December 1901]

My Alma,

For the first time I send you greetings on Christmas Eve – also for the last time; for in future, my dear girl, we shall always spend Christmas together. – <Somebody kindly told me that you wished for some kind of a brooch (I myself would never have thought of such a thing) – from now on I shall read your every wish from your eyes.> Just imagine, Alma, soon, as I hope, we shall be united and have no further need of intermediaries! When I am in my room, I can already imagine you close by me. My fortune, our fortune seems to me like a fruit that has swiftly ripened in the warm sunshine of a love still unproven but full of optimism and trust, and is soon to fall to the ground at our feet. Even if we had never met, let us celebrate this day, which unites us, just as it unites all people in the joyous belief of children, as an everlasting token that we, for whom love has brought unity and happiness, should always open our hearts to our fellow men. (For the bond that unites us has been forged in the name of a love that surpasses understanding, divine love as we could call it, and this bond unites us indissolubly with all living creatures.) On this day, a day dedicated to children, a day on which the seed of love both earthly and divine takes root according to how it has been sown, I bless you, my dear heart. May your life bring blessings upon you and your family, may you rise above our earthly love – which shall be sanctified – to recognize divine love and grow capable of 'silently honouring the unfathomable'.[*] (Above all, we cannot count ourselves entirely fortunate as long as there are others on this earth who are unfortunate.) Please understand, my Alma, that today I can say nothing more. Nothing perhaps could prove more clearly the boundlessness and sanctity of my love for you than my wish – at a time when I am so close to the fulfilment of my fondest dream, and when I feel such joy within me – to lead us both into those higher regions where we can sense the presence of the Eternal and Divine. In this sense I wish to be yours, and you to be mine! My one and only!   Your Gustav

[*] Orig.: '[Das schönste Glück des denkenden Menschen ist, das Erforschliche erforscht zu haben und] das Unerforschliche still [ruhig] zu verehren' (Goethe, *Sinn- und Denksprüche*).

<Please send a reply – no 'finely worded' letter though, but just a few lines to let me know whether you have understood me, and if so, what you make of it.>

Once Mahler's visit was over, he spent Christmas Eve with his sister Justine. Meanwhile, Alma was host to her usual circle of friends. Mahler's desire to engage in a more serious discussion with Alma, as voiced in the postscript to this letter, seems once again to have remained unfulfilled. That evening Alma wrote in her diary:

Tuesday 24 December
I can't entirely let my joy overcome me. For fear of the gods, who cannot bear to contemplate pure joy.
I await him <u>eagerly</u> – today.
Gustav doesn't want it to be known, for fear of the newspapers – of crazy gossips.
I can neither think nor act clearly. Everything begins and ends with Gustav. My longing is infinite. I would give everything for him – my music – <u>everything</u> – so powerful is my longing! <u>That's</u> how I want to be his – I am <u>already</u> his – I belong to him and Justi, whom I love, because she's of the same blood.
Justi told Mama that Gustav kept saying:
Isn't it a crime that I – the autumn – should bind myself to the spring? She will forego her summer.
No, my Gustav, no!
Christmas Eve. And this year I couldn't give a damn.
Gustav was with me up here. We felt our blood pounding – followed our instincts and were happy. As to the presents, I shall write about them tomorrow – the day after – they mean nothing to me. Only one shall I mention – a diamond-edged pin from <u>my</u> Gustav.
In the evening: Burckhard and [Kolo] Moser. Burckhard is suspicious of everything – Moser is like a child. B. is edgy & imprudent. He teased me about my waning enthusiasm for Nietzsche. In Gustav's presence. What do I care. Only to him will I give myself.

Wednesday 25 December
Wieners, Burckhard, Moser etc.
P.M. at Gustav's. He was already waiting. I sat on his knee the whole time. I love him more than I can say. We melt into one another.
He had to conduct – 'Tannhäuser'. I stayed with Justi. I'm fond of her.

Thursday 26 December
Gustav called.

In the afternoon: Mama Moll. Gustav met me at the station and we drove home in a hansom cab.[62]

Due to an indiscretion, Mahler's engagement was announced in the evening edition of the Neue Freie Presse *on 27 December. It may have been Max Burckhard who leaked the information to the press, for he was a regular contributor to this paper. In her diary Alma records:*

Friday 27 December
This evening the bomb dropped. In big, bold letters it stood in the papers:
Director Mahler engaged
etc. etc. etc.
He was very put out. For fear of the personnel at the Opera.[63]

In Vienna the news spread like wildfire. The following morning the same paper published a longer announcement:
    'Engagement of Director Mahler. In yesterday's evening edition we announced the engagement of Director Mahler to Fräulein Alma Schindler, daughter of the renowned landscape painter Emil Schindler, who died young several years ago. In Vienna the news has aroused widespread interest and sympathy, and has surprised even the couple's closest friends. For the entire staff of the Hofoper and in Viennese musical circles this was the news of the day. As is well known, the painter Schindler died in 1892, and his widow subsequently married the painter Moll. – The date of Director Mahler's wedding is not yet known.'[64]
    The following evening Alma noted in her diary:

Saturday 28 December
Mrs Hellmann sent me a wonderful ostrich-feather fan. Gretl [Hellmann], who called yesterday, is half crazed.[*] Letters, telegrams, flowers – & the papers. Everywhere my beauty, my youth – & my musical talent are stressed. The 'Fremdenblatt' writes that <u>I am brilliant</u>. O Lord – and whatever else! P.M. Ilse and Erica.[†]
In the evening with Gustav. Drank a toast of brotherhood with A. Rosé – but otherwise mostly alone with G. in his room. We stood a long time in the dark corridor and were happy. <u>That</u> is my only wish, to make him happy. He deserves it![65]

---

[*] The industrialist Paul Hellmann and his wife Lina were close friends of the Molls. They had two children: Gretl (mentioned here) and Paul.
[†] Ilse and Erica Conrat (see footnote on p. 29 about the Conrat family).

Before the engagement was made public, Mahler broke the news to a few close friends, including the musicologist Guido Adler:

I am engaged to be married! It is still a secret, and I am informing only my most intimate friends. My fiancée's name is Alma Schindler. If you know her, you will know all; if not, I would have to overstep the boundaries of art, and paint with words. [. . .] Please understand that I can speak today of nothing else. Remain my valued friend during this 'transition to a new life'.[66]

Mahler's assistant at the Hofoper, Bruno Walter, summarized his thoughts and feelings in a letter to his parents dated 30 December 1901. No doubt his remarks reflect the opinion of many who were not directly involved:

'Well, *what do you say to Mahler's engagement? What a surprise, eh? Justi's engagement to our concertmaster Rosé was already on the stocks; but they wouldn't have felt the need to get married if Mahler himself hadn't got engaged; Justi would never have left her brother to fend for himself. The engagement came to us all as a complete surprise; even the Lipiners* and the Spieglers† first read about it in the daily papers; we too, of course. Even Justi knew nothing about it until two days beforehand, when they met his future father-in-law on the street. She was surprised how well her brother seemed to know this man, and told him so, whereupon he said: 'Well, I'd better tell you that I have just got engaged to his daughter.' His fiancée, Alma Schindler, [. . .] is twenty-two years old [sic], tall, slim and dazzlingly good-looking, the most beautiful girl in Vienna; she comes of good family and is very rich. – But we, his friends, are very concerned about all this; he is forty-one years old, she twenty-two; she is accustomed to moving in high society, he is tied up with himself, fond of isolation; so there is good cause for misgivings. He himself feels very awkward and uneasy in his role as bridegroom, and when people congratulate him he gets annoyed. [. . .] He greeted me with the words: "What do say to that? The newspapers have got me engaged! Actually it's true, I really am engaged to be married; but please don't congratulate me or – just speak a few quick words, that's right – and now let's forget the whole thing." A curious bridegroom, eh? But they are said to be deeply in love. The wedding is planned for the end of March; Justi will be marrying in four weeks' time; after all, they've waited long enough and they really make a well-matched couple.'[67]*

---

* The writer Siegfried Lipiner and his wife Clementine. La Grange characterizes Lipiner as 'a mystical and spiritualist, a *"raté"* genius to whom Mahler remained attached all his life, and for whom he had a quite unjustified admiration' (*Mahler*, Vol. I, London, 1974, p. 68).
† The doctor Albert Spiegler and his wife Nina, both of them close friends of Mahler since the 1880s.

On 29 December, when Mahler conducted Otto Nicolai's Merry Wives of Windsor *at the Hofoper, he was applauded more enthusiastically than usual, and at the close he was called before the curtain several times. In her diary Alma wrote:*

Sunday 29 December
This evening: at the Opera. For the first time in the Director's box – Mama, Justi and I.
Then to [Restaurant] Hartmann. Gustav & I walked alone for a while. We resolved to get married in mid-February. – Let's hope it works out.
My appearance in the box was a veritable début. Every opera-glass was trained on me – every single one. I felt offended & withdrew. Mildenburg came down to meet me – <u>awfully</u> sweet.
And he was sitting down there – so far, so far away from me![68]

Alma's diary entries for the following days, from 30 December 1901 to 4 January 1902, include many intimate details:

Wednesday 30 December
P.M. rendezvous with G. We failed to meet, & he got so angry that I had difficulty in calming him down.
Today we all but joined in wedlock. He let me feel his masculinity – his vigour – & it was a pure, holy sensation, such as I would <u>never</u> have expected. He must be suffering <u>dreadfully</u>. I can gauge his frustration by mine. Nobody knows how I long for him. And yet – I cannot imagine giving myself to him before the appointed time. A sense of injustice & shame would degrade the whole, holy mystery. My lover – in God.
When I'm on my own, I feel the emptiness – the missing other half.
We could scarcely bring ourselves to part. Why these <u>dreadful</u> conventions? Why can't I simply move in with him? <u>Without</u> a church wedding. We are consumed with longing, are dissipating our strongest desires. He bared his breast and I put my hand on his heart. I have the feeling: his body is <u>mine</u> – <u>he</u> and I are <u>one</u>. I love every part of him in turn – nobody exists other than he. No other thought!
I'm wearing my hair loose now – he loves it that way – and our bodies cried out for union. Oh – to bear his child!
My body
His soul
When shall I be his! Another ninety nights!

New Year's Eve
At midday I was with him.
P.M. at Zierers'.
In the evening he, Justi and Arnold «Rosé» called on us. Very, very nice!
More than that – O God. Once I was upon the point of giving myself to him.
Then I thought how awful if he had to leave straight after – and I remained
alone with my torment. No, no. His beloved hand explored my body, and
mine his. We clasped each other tightly. No – I want to give myself freely,
without constraint, with no fear of disturbance. I love him. I have only one
wish. May the New Year not shatter my dream. I love him – & so I close. My
life is his, he shares my joys, I his sorrows.
Amen![69]

1902

The year opened with perhaps the most distressing entry in Alma's entire diary:

New Year's Day 1902
What I have to write today is terribly sad. I called on Gustav – in the afternoon we were alone in his room. He gave me his body – & I let him touch me with his hand. Stiff and upright stood his vigour. He carried me to the sofa, laid me gently down and swung himself over me. Then – just as I felt him penetrate, he lost all strength. He laid his head on my breast, shattered – and almost wept for shame. Distraught as I was, I comforted him.
We drove home, dismayed and dejected. He grew a little more cheerful. Then I broke down, had to weep, weep on his breast. What if he were to lose – that! My poor, poor husband!
I can scarcely say how aggravating it all was. First his intimate caresses, so close – and then no satisfaction. Words cannot express what I today have undeservedly suffered. And then to observe his torment – his unbelievable torment! My beloved!

Friday 3 January
«Bliss and rapture.»

The following memorandum also dates from the first week of 1902. Mahler sent it as a covering note together with the piano-duet arrangement of his Fourth Symphony, *which had just been published by Ludwig Doblinger Verlag (in AMM1 Alma recalls receiving at this juncture the score of Mahler's 'first' composition,* Das klagende Lied[1]*).*

17   [Vienna, 3 January 1902]

Dearest Lux!*
Just arrived. Please accept this first copy. May it sound in your heart as it flowed from mine! Yesterday I was in fifth or sixth heaven! The seventh is still in store for us – do you know when? – <u>Your</u> Gustav

---

*Mahler's choice of 'Lux' as a nickname for Alma may have been influenced by Richard Dehmel, whose cycle of poems 'Zwei Menschen' is the tale of two lovers, Lea and Lux. However, where Dehmel gives the name Lux (an abbreviation of Lukas) to his male figure,

Saturday 4 January
Rapture without end.[2]

Two days later, Mahler invited relatives and friends to his apartment in the Auernbruggasse, in order to introduce them to Alma. The evening was a fiasco, from which the marriage never entirely recovered. Of the occasion Alma wrote in her diary:

Sunday 5 January
This evening: at Gustav's. His friends . . . all conspicuously Jewish. I could find no bond . . . amused myself by stunning them with unprecedented impudence, said I didn't care for Gustav's music etc. On the way home we laughed and laughed. It was so dreary.[3]

In AMM4 Alma writes at some length about her attitude towards Mahler's friends, and concludes: 'His friends could never be mine.'[4] Many years later she recalled the occasion as follows:

And now came the evening when I was put on parade. The guest list consisted of Lipiner [. . .] with his first wife, second wife and current mistress (Mahler's former girlfriend M.), his first wife's second husband (Lipiner's closest friend), Justine's friend R.,[*] my mother and Kolo Moser. I shall never forget the solemn grandeur of the occasion. Nobody spoke, but malicious, hostile eyes followed my every movement. 'What is your attitude to Gustav's music?' M[ildenburg] asked me. 'I haven't heard much,' I replied irately, 'but what I have heard I didn't like.' Mahler laughed out loud, but the others hung their heads. My mother was ashamed of my bad behaviour, and the atmosphere grew intolerable. Then Mahler took me by the arm and led me into Justine's little room. 'It was horrid in there,' he said, 'let's stay here alone for a while.' And now we were there for each other again, happy and carefree, while in the next room they were plotting my downfall.[5]

The occasion caused a deep rift between Mahler and his friends.

Monday 6 January
A wonderful afternoon.
Yesterday he sent me his Fourth Symphony – today we played it through together. It really moved me – pleased me very, very much.

Mahler appears to have relished the dual connotation of the word in connection with Alma as a combination of 'lux' (Latin, 'light') and Luchs (German, 'lynx'): the light of his life, but also a wildcat.
[*] i.e. Nina Spiegler, Clementine Lipiner, Anna Mildenburg, Albert Spiegler, Arnold Rosé.

And my poor Gustav is under doctors' orders. An inflammation – ice-bags, hot baths etc. etc. All because I withstood him so long – he has to suffer![6]

At this time Mahler evidently tried once again to explain his view of personal relationships in a way that Alma might understand. In AML, she recalled:

5 November 1927 – Vienna
Another evening at Arthur Schnitzler's. I remarked how strange it was that marriage often causes women to renounce their ego, something unheard of for the average man. I told Schnitzler that making conversation with Mahler was wonderful, but only at the time when our meetings were still clandestine. The moment our relationship became common knowledge and the day for the wedding had been announced, I found I could no longer understand him. For hours I would walk with him in the gardens of the Belvedere (our daily stroll) without saying a word, and one day I recall him expressing surprise at my silence. 'You were talking Chinese,' I replied, 'and I couldn't understand you.'[7]

Alma's diary entry for 6 January is followed by ten days of silence. The next entry was the last she wrote before the wedding:

Thursday 16 January
For a long time I have been truly happy, and therefore I haven't written anything down. But in the last few days everything has changed. He wants me different, completely different. And that's what I want as well. As long as I am with him, I succeed – but when I'm on my own, my other, vain self rises to the surface and desires to be let free. I let myself go. My eyes shine with frivolity – my mouth utters lies, streams of lies. And he senses it, knows it. Only now do I understand. I <u>must rise to meet him</u>. «For I live only in him.» Yesterday afternoon . . . he begged me to talk – and I couldn't find <u>one</u> word of warmth. <u>Not one</u>.
I wept. That was the end . . .
To be like him – my <u>only</u> wish.
I have two souls: I know it. –
Only one – which is my true soul? If I lie, will I not make us both unhappy? – And am I a liar? When he looks at me so happily, what a profound feeling of ecstasy. Is that a lie too? No, no. I must cast out my other soul. The one which has ruled so far must be banished. I must strive to become a real person, let everything <u>happen of its own accord</u>.[8]

Mahler's Fourth Symphony *received its Viennese première on 12 January.**

* A second performance followed eight days later.

The reviews were as hostile as those in Berlin four weeks previously. Max Kalbeck, for instance, considered the thematic material scarcely sufficient for a dance pantomime, and he described the work as a fierce battle between folk song and art song.

A further significant event in Viennese musical life was the première of Richard Strauss's opera Feuersnot *on 29 January. The composer was well satisfied with Mahler's musical preparation. This was the first of several occasions on which he and his wife Pauline came into contact with the Mahlers. Alma later found vivid if not exactly cordial words to describe their first meeting:*

On the first night Pauline Strauss sat with us in our box. She fumed all evening, saying nobody could possibly take pleasure in such rubbish; if we said we liked it, we were not telling the truth, for we knew just as well as she did that there wasn't <u>a single note</u> of music in it, that everything was stolen from Wagner and others, including Max von Schillings ('Maxi' as she called him), whose music she far preferred to her husband's anyway. In a word, she was livid. We pulled all kinds of faces, but took care to say nothing, let alone agree with her, for with her temperament this woman was capable of turning anything around and putting words into other people's mouths. – After the performance, which Mahler did not conduct, because he detested the work,[*] we were supposed to dine at Restaurant Hartmann. But there was a delay. Having taken an endless succession of curtain-calls, Strauss came to our box, visibly elated. 'Well, Pauksl, what d'you say to my success?' She didn't mince her words. 'You thief,' she cried, jumping at him like a wildcat, 'how dare you show your face here? I'm not going anywhere with you, you're just too bad.' That was enough for Mahler. He pushed the two of them into his office, while the rest of us stood in the anteroom waiting for the altercation to end. We heard wild cries, and before things became too unpleasant for Mahler, he knocked at the door and called inside to say we didn't want to wait any longer and would go on ahead to the restaurant. Thereupon the door flew open and Strauss stumbled out, followed by Pauline. 'You can go now,' she shouted. 'I'm going back to the hotel to spend the evening on my own.' 'Won't you even let me accompany you?' Strauss pleaded. 'Only if you walk ten paces behind me.' And off she went, with Strauss following at a respectful distance. We set off for dinner in silence. Strauss arrived soon afterwards, visibly exhausted, took his seat beside me and said: 'My wife's pretty grumpy, y'know, but I need it.' Those were his very words. That

---

[*] Mahler did indeed conduct the performance.

evening I got to see the other side of him too. The whole evening he had only one thought on his mind: money. He constantly pestered Mahler about the royalties he would earn on a large or medium-sized box office, and throughout the meal he held a pencil in his hand, occasionally sticking it behind his ear, as if in jest. In short, he behaved like a travelling salesman. Franz Schalk, the conductor, whispered to me: 'The sad part of it is: he isn't even joking, for him it's dead earnest.' – Everywhere Strauss played his stakes; he was a speculator, an exploiter of opera, an unashamed materialist. Over the years it got even worse. I see Pfitzner and Schoenberg to his right and left, like saints on pedestals, with Strauss between them as a mere figure of clay.[9]

When Strauss read AMM1, he added pencilled comments in the margin.[10] Of the passage quoted above he wrote: 'Completely implausible. At any rate an utter fabrication, and at least improbable. Where did she find the material for such a story? After all, my wife was particularly fond of Feuersnot.' Of the line beginning 'Well Pauksl' he writes: 'I would never have said anything of the sort.'

Several further passages are underlined. Over the words 'Won't you even let me accompany you?', which according to Alma she addressed to his wife, Strauss writes, 'All swindle.' Alma's description of him as a 'travelling salesman' is marked 'Unbelievable!', and at the end of the passage he writes: 'Terrific!' On the fly-leaf, Strauss sums up his impressions as follows:

'A biography written by a demi-mondaine dilettante. The inferiority complexes of a dissolute woman. Fabrications, falsifications and untruths about a faithful, respectable wife; as such, self-defeating. Many friends in Vienna, notably Ludwig Karpath, warned my wife against hobnobbing with Mahler's widow. What surprises me personally about this book, which does not even depict Mahler himself in particularly glowing colours, is that Mahler, whom I held in high esteem as an artist and towards whom I took a very friendly personal attitude, appears to have felt not the slightest gratitude that I paved the way for his public career. I conducted the world première of Titan in Weimar in 1894, in 1895 the first three movements of the Second Symphony with the Berlin Philharmonic (the finale was still incomplete). In 1902 I included the world première of the Fourth Symphony, conducted by Mahler, in my Novelty Concert series. Later at the [Vienna] Staatsoper I repeated his First Symphony and promoted the Viennese première of Das Lied von der Erde. I was also responsible for programming the premières of the Third and Fourth Symphonies at the Tonkünstler Festivals in Basle and Elberfeld. All this deserves at least mentioning.'

Strauss did indeed help disseminate the music of Mahler. Nevertheless, his claims, as outlined above, are not entirely accurate. His performance of

Mahler's First Symphony ('Titan') in Weimar was already the third, follow-ing Budapest (1889) and Hamburg (1893), and in Weimar Mahler himself conducted; again, it was he who conducted the first three movements of the Second Symphony in Berlin, and his 1901 performance of the Fourth Symphony in Berlin was not the world première. The first complete per-formance of the Third Symphony was given in Krefeld, and the world pre-mière of the Sixth in Essen. The performance in Basle to which Strauss refers was of the Second Symphony (1903), not the Third, and at the Tonkünstler Festival in Elberfeld no work of Mahler's was performed at all.

Mahler was in two minds about Strauss. Even though he admired him greatly as a composer, he viewed his colleague's commercial attitude to music with disapproval. Two days after the Feuersnot première he wrote to Alma from Semmering bei Wien, where he was taking a short break from his duties at the Hofoper.

18   [Semmering, 31 January 1902]

Beloved,

Your dear letter has just arrived, at breakfast time, and brought me immense joy. I too had been aching to hear from you. It wasn't just the farewell: I found the whole evening disappointing. Strauss has such a sobering influ-ence; in his world one scarcely recognizes oneself. If those are the fruits that hang from the tree, how can one love such a tree? Your judgement hits the nail on the head. And I feel <quite> proud of you for spontaneously arriving at such an assessment. Rather live in poverty and walk the path of the enlightened than surrender oneself to Mammon, don't you agree? One day people will separate the wheat from the chaff – and when his time has passed, my day will come. Would that I could live to see it at your side! But you, my Lux, will certainly live to see it, I hope, and you will remember the time when you had not yet learnt to distinguish the sun through the mist. Do you remember, in the Stadtpark, when everyone saw the sun as a hideous red stain? – [Four and a half lines obliterated.] All I now wish for is good health, so I can dedicate myself entirely to you. Already now, after a night of deep, peaceful sleep, I feel invigorated. Can I still hope for you to visit me here? On Saturday afternoon? On Sunday we could then return to Vienna together. But it's entirely up to your Mama. Don't make her feel obliged! Otherwise I shall simply wait a day longer and see you on the Sunday evening. Now it's time to go hiking. I'll finish the letter this evening. My Alma child, do at least try to write a plain, legible address. Have mercy on the poor postmen des-perately struggling to decipher your scrawl. I would take immense pleasure in it. By now you will have yourself found the answer to your remark of the night before last – 'You aren't contributing anything to the conversation.' At so intense a moment – and after all, such a performance unleashes my own creative energy too – what could I have contributed to that coffee-house prattle? Such a performance should serve to <u>liberate</u> you from the daily round, not drag you back into the swamp of royalties and capital gains (these, as always, are Strauss's fondest dreams – all but inseparable from his enthusiasm).

A thousand kisses from me – despite Strasser!* He just told me that I'm suffering from a dilation of the veins, caused by weeks of high blood pressure – same as last time. But don't worry. Fortunately I noticed it in good time, and soon I should be restored to health.   Your Gustav.

From the next letter we learn that the date for the wedding had finally been decided, also that the bridal couple were to leave immediately afterwards for their honeymoon, a trip to St Petersburg, where Mahler had been invited to conduct at the Hall of the Nobility on 17, 22 and 27 March.

19   [Semmering, 1 February 1902]

Almschi, dearest,

I've just got back from the station, where I was half expecting you. The snow is falling thick and fast, and everything is clad in white – you'd love it as much as I do. I'm completely over the moon about it – but I miss <u>you</u> all the same. I can imagine your dear face popping up all over the place. I've had a glorious idea: on Monday I could join you for lunch at home – as early as possible, I mean. I'd hope to be there by one o'clock, so there'd be time for a short walk. Then I could stay until 5.30, you could accompany me as far as Zögernitz, and from there I'd take the tram to the theatre, where I have a dreary performance to conduct. Is that all right with you? That way we could see more of each other than if you came to us. I feel fresher and healthier than ever! I knew it: up here I immediately feel better. So <u>10 March</u> is the day. Almschi, let's hope we can head off right away. The snow here has whetted my appetite for St Petersburg. And I know you'd like it there! For me that's the best part of it all. Lux! Do you miss me a little? I can hardly wait to see you again. <u>Believe me</u>, I'm only staying here 'for health reasons', because I can feel how much good it does to my system and my nerves. Almschi, d'you still love me?

As ever, your Gustav

* Mahler's physician, Dr Alois Strasser.

The 'dreary performance' on Monday 3 February was The Tales of Hoffmann.
It was Mahler's last performance of the work.

20[U]   [Vienna, 10 February 1902]
                                                          (8.00 p.m.)

Dearest Almschi,
So! I shan't be conducting tonight after all – but even so I can't see you today! I'm
wildly undecided. – For the past two hours I've been wanting to 'take off' to visit
you at home, but then I thought better of it, mostly because of certain scruples,
as I'm not sure if everything is 'in order'. And now it's too late, so I'll just write
these few words of heartfelt greeting, which should reach you tomorrow morning. I wonder if everything will be 'in order' by then! If so, <u>stay home</u> and <u>wire</u>
me at the Opera or call me by telephone at my private number, and I'll come out
to see you immediately after lunch. If not, we'll be expecting you at one o'clock
for lunch with us. Your letter this morning was so, so sweet! The address too,
which I read with such a broad grin that Hassinger[*] started grinning too.
A thousand greetings – and till <u>soon</u>.
Your Gustav

21[U]   [Vienna, February 1902]

Dearest Almschi,
Just look how considerate I am! This evening Hassinger will have a ticket for
Bertha[†] (a very good one), so she can see you home afterwards. I'm always
uneasy about putting your life in the hands of some cabby. And <u>how is your</u>
<u>dear throat</u>? I quite forgot to recommend <u>gargling</u> (at least with salt water)
and, if possible, a Priessnitz poultice.[‡] It occurred to me the moment I got
home. Considering that you yourself are an ear, nose and throat specialist
and GP rolled into one – for <u>me</u> – I hope it occurred to you too. At five
o'clock I shall check the state of that little neck of yours with my own hands
– and tongue.[§] Until then, dear, sweet girl,
Addio!   Your Gustav

[*] Carl Hassinger, Mahler's clerk at the Hofoper. His name features frequently in these letters,
for he was Mahler's factotum, did the shopping, delivered messages and attended to the more
tedious chores. As transpires from letter 78, Mahler had a private contractual arrangement
with him.
[†] The Molls' chambermaid.
[‡] A poultice named after its inventor, Vincenz Priessnitz, made from several layers of cold,
damp linen wrapped in a flannel or dry woollen cloth.
[§] Orig.: untranslatable pun on 'eigenhändig' and 'eingenzüngig'.

There can be no doubt that Mahler's concern for Alma – and later for the entire family, including her parents – was genuine. As can be seen from this letter, he even spared a thought for the Molls' domestic staff.

In AMM4 Alma recalls the wedding day as follows:

On 9 March 1902 Mahler and I were married; on 10 March, the day of our departure, followed the wedding of Justine and Arnold Rosé. It was raining heavily, so Mahler walked to the church in galoshes; my mother, Mahler's sister and I took a cab. Apart from the witnesses, Moll and Rosé, we had the Karlskirche to ourselves. It was early in the day. When the moment came for us to kneel, Mahler didn't see the hassock and slipped onto the stone-flagged floor; being small, he had to stand up, then kneel down all over again. Everyone smiled, including the vicar. When it was over, we all went for lunch, which was a rather taciturn affair; then we bade farewell to our guests, packed our bags on our own and drove to the station. The wedding had been announced for the evening, and later in the day, they say, the church was full of people hoping to catch a glimpse of us.[11]

Alma's recollections of St Petersburg make dramatic reading: temperatures of –30°C, with Mahler suffering from chilblains, a high temperature, a sore throat and a cough; but she also mentions Mahler's triumphant reception in the concert hall. An unpublished letter from Mahler to his sister Justine tells a different story. He complains about the exhausting train journey, adding that it had caused him a severe migraine, but his letter opens with the words, 'We arrived here in high spirits, and are staying in a delightful little apartment, where we can pass our two weeks most agreeably.' Evidently it was Alma who was feeling under the weather, for Mahler adds, 'Today we are invited to a breakfast party at the Austrian Embassy. So far Alma has had to cancel all engagements, but today I hope she'll come with me.' Nor can Alma's 'temperatures of –30°' be taken literally. 'It isn't at all cold here,' writes Mahler; 'we are managing very well with the clothes we brought with us.' In another letter to his sister he adds, 'Incidentally, Alma has decided not to buy herself a fur coat; instead I gave her a lovely fresh pineapple.'

Looking back on the long years spent in the company of his sister, Mahler adds, 'Isn't it strange: I feel no difference between then and now. I hope you feel the same about it.' And in another letter to Justine he writes, 'I'm in excellent health. It seems that marriage is doing me good.'[12]

Not until 20 January 1903 did Mahler again have occasion to write to Alma. By this time the contrast between their widely differing personalities had grown more palpable.

On returning from St Petersburg, Mahler was drawn into a series of alter-
cations with the orchestra and soloists' ensemble of the Hofoper. The 14th
Secessionist Exhibition, which opened at the Vienna Secession on 15 April
1902, presented two new masterpieces of representative art, Max Klinger's
Beethoven Monument *and Gustav Klimt's* Beethoven Frieze. *To mark the*
occasion, Mahler had planned to conduct a performance of the 'Choral'
Symphony. *However, a series of intrigues forced him to abandon the idea,*
and in its stead he conducted the 'Seid umschlungen' chorus from the finale
in an arrangement for an ensemble of six trombones, at a reception given in
Klinger's honour at the Secession on 14 April.

Mahler's involvement with this most progressive of Viennese art groups was a
direct outcome of his marriage to Alma. In 1898 his father-in-law Carl Moll had
joined with Gustav Klimt, Koloman Moser, Joseph Olbrich and other (mostly
younger) artists to found the Vienna Secession. Their aim was to counteract the
imperialist-reactionary tendencies that prevailed in official Austrian art circles,
to which end they published an art journal, Ver sacrum, *as a vehicle for their*
ideas and ideals. The First Secessionist Exhibition, which opened in March 1898,
was a huge success. In the autumn of 1898 followed the inauguration of the rev-
olutionary Secession building, designed by Olbrich (and lovingly restored in
1985–6). Since then, with a regular stream of influential exhibitions, the group
had remained at the forefront of the European avant-garde.

It was through the Secession that Mahler made the acquaintance of a
young artist named Alfred Roller. As a painter he stood in the shadow of
Klimt, Moser and Moll, but as a stage designer he developed a distinctive
style. Together with Mahler he was responsible for productions of Mozart,
Beethoven and Wagner that placed the Vienna Hofoper at the centre of
developments in contemporary music-theatre.

Six years had passed since Mahler completed his Third Symphony, *but so*
far only single movements had been performed in public. Towards the end of
May 1902 he and Alma travelled to Krefeld, where the combined forces of
the Gürzenich Orchestra (Cologne) and the Städtische Kapelle Krefeld were
to give the world première of the complete work. The concert was scheduled
for 9 June, and rehearsals, which were held in Cologne, began almost a week
in advance. On 3 June Mahler wrote to his sister Justine:

Today, at the first rehearsal, I tried through the 1st movement, later also the
4th and 5th – i.e. the ones we haven't yet heard. Really splendid, to my surprise. I don't have to make a single alteration, and am very satisfied. – Alma
very sickly and unwell. [. . .] Greetings to Arnold. We shall see you in Krefeld
– don't <u>fail to be there</u>.[13]

The performance, given at the 38th Composers Festival (Tonkünstlerfest) of
the Allgemeine Deutsche Musikverein, *was a huge success. At the end of the*
first movement Strauss left his seat and walked through the hall to offer
Mahler his congratulations. As Alma recalls:

Richard Strauss walked right up to the stage and applauded demonstratively, thus instantly sealing the movement's success. As further movements followed, the audience seemed even more deeply moved. Indeed, as the performance came to a close, a veritable frenzy of enthusiasm broke loose, with people leaping to their feet and pushing their way forwards towards the platform. Strauss took a progressively passive part in the proceedings, and by the close he was nowhere to be seen. [. . .] During the course of the evening it became clear just how cold-hearted he was. After the concert we all went for dinner at a small guest-house. Strauss walked in, shook hands patronisingly with each of us in turn, then moved on. He paid no heed to Mahler's dreadful agitation, and exchanged not a single word with him. Mahler took it very badly, and sat for some time in stony silence. His public success had paled into insignificance.[14]

The critics were unanimously effusive in their praise of Mahler's new work.
For the first time his stature as a composer was seen as matching his achieve-
ment as a performing artist. In later years Mahler often recalled the per-
formance in Krefeld with great joy and satisfaction. It marked the beginning
of a new phase in his creative career.

Soon afterwards the Hofoper closed for the summer vacation. Mahler and
his wife now settled into their holiday home at Maiernigg on the Wörthersee,
where Mahler was able to concentrate on the composition of his Fifth
Symphony. *Though only recently married, he evidently saw little reason to*
change his established lifestyle. Meals, work periods and free time were
organized according to a strict daily schedule which Alma, who was expect-
ing her first child, was expected to accept without demur.

For Alma, this first summer of married life appears to have been a partic-
ularly difficult time. Her diary entries for July and August 1902 reveal that
she was torn by doubts as to whether she had done the right thing in marry-
ing Mahler.

---

* Richard Strauss had been elected President of the Allgemeine Deutsche Musikverein the previous year. Almost all composers of stature in Austro-Germany belonged to the ADM (founded in 1859 by Franz Liszt and disbanded by the Nazis in 1937), whose annual *Tonkünstlerfest* offered a first-class opportunity for the propagation of new music. As a rule, the choice of works was decided by committee.

10 July 1902. Maiernigg

I don't know where to begin. I am plagued by an enormous inner conflict! And a pitiful longing for someone who thinks of me, who can help me find myself. Here I am no more than a housekeeper! I have just come out of Gustav's room. On his desk lay a thick book on philosophy, and it occurred to me: why couldn't he share it with me, let me read it with him, instead of poring over it on his own? I sit at the piano and feel an upsurge – but I have lost my way, I can no longer find the bridge to the other side. Someone has taken me roughly by the arm and led me far away – from myself. And I long to return to where I used to be. An unproductive winter, mindlessly hectic existence, the abandonment of all self-contemplation, finally the loss of all my friends – and the gain of a friend who does not know me.

12 July 1902

Today I see things differently. Yesterday morning we had a bitter exchange of words – I told him everything. And he – infinitely dear – tried to find some way of helping me. And I do understand that at the present time – he simply cannot! He is totally absorbed in his creative work. –

I shall use the summer to move forward in every possible way. I shall do my best to study, for I am in a position to find myself, to fulfil myself!

Yesterday I made my Gustav happy – for I restored his peace of mind. He thanked me unceasingly and said I would not regret it. And that makes me feel better.

I no longer feel so empty. And I have but one goal, one purpose in life: to sacrifice my happiness for his – and to grow happy for having done so!

13 July 1902

I spent the morning and afternoon on my own. And when Gustav came down [from the shack] – still full of his work – I couldn't share in his happiness, and tears came to my eyes again. He grew serious, my Gustav, terribly serious. And now he doubts whether I love him! – And how often have I doubted it myself.

One moment I pine for his love, the next I feel nothing – nothing at all! When I love him, I can accept everything without difficulty; when I don't, it's impossible.

And yet I'm constantly aware that I never ever felt so close to anyone as to him. If only I could find my inner balance! Yesterday he told me he had never worked with such ease and fluency as now, and that really cheered me.

If I know that my suffering is his bliss, how could I hesitate for a moment! From now on I don't want him to notice my inner struggles. [. . .] It's just my face, my eyes, that betray me. And these tears that keep flowing. Never before have I cried as much as now, at a time when I have everything that I – as a woman – could strive for.[15]

Alma's evident change of heart at Maiernigg that summer prompted Mahler to a very special declaration of love:

Yesterday my beloved sang me a song. He wrote it some days ago and slipped the manuscript into my vocal score of 'Siegfried', in the hope I would play the opera again and find it there myself. It's his first love song. 'Something very intimate, just for you,' he said. To a poem by Rückert: 'Liebst du um Schönheit'. The last line, 'Liebe mich immer, immerdar', is so moving. Looking at it recently, for the first time in many days, I was almost overwhelmed by emotion. Compared with his endless riches, how insignificant I often appear.[16]

Later that summer she wrote: 'My pregnancy is something of a hindrance, but I can surmount every weakness [. . .] My mission, to remove every obstacle from the path of this genius, is profoundly fulfilling.'[17]
    Some weeks after returning to Vienna, Alma gave birth to her first child, Maria ('Putzi').

25 November
I left my childbed a week ago. My infant saw the light of day on 3 November. To bring her into the world cost me incredible pain. I don't yet feel real love for her. All, all of me belongs to my beloved Gustav. I love him so dearly that everything other than him is dead to me. And I cannot find the words to tell him.

The resounding success of the Third Symphony *in Krefeld resulted in further performances of the work in Elberfeld, Barmen and Nuremberg. A performance was also scheduled for 23 January 1903 at a Kurhaus concert in Wiesbaden, but at the last moment the management decided to substitute the* Fourth Symphony, *with Mahler himself conducting. After poor receptions in Munich, Berlin and Vienna, this was the first time the work met with approval.*

1903

Twelve days before she received the next letter from Mahler, Alma entered the following in her diary:

8 January 1903
Just returned from the Opera. Blocking rehearsal! Euryanthe! Nice rehearsal! Gustav let that WHORE drink from his glass! I stand SO in dread of her that I fear his coming home. When he is with Mildenburg or Weidt,* his manner grows sweet and teasing, and he coos over them like a young love-bird – my God, may he NEVER come home! May I no longer have to live with him! I'm so upset, I can hardly write!

22ᵁ   [in the train to Wiesbaden, 20 January 1903]

Beloved Almscherl,
Sheer delight! For the past two hours I've been sitting in a carriage with panorama windows. Everywhere, as far as the eye can see, the ground is covered with magnificent white snow, and the sun is shining down brilliantly, almost warmly on it. I keep thinking: if only you were here – how you would enjoy it.
Heavens! When I started this letter, I had no idea that the wobbly ride would make it impossible to write, let alone think. I'll have to stop. But what a shame that one can't get out and wander around outside.
Station! So the wobbling has stopped! Now at least I can tell you what my pencil couldn't put on paper previously, due to all the buffeting, namely that I miss you very, very much and that I can't take real pleasure in anything, because you're not here.
Rrrrrr! On we go! Looking out of the window, I've just noticed that we're in Passau. And how picturesque this little old town looks, nestled into the folds of the Danube. Last time we passed through here it was night-time and we were <u>together</u> (on our way to Krefeld).

8.00 p.m. Nuremberg. I've been unwell for the past five hours! Evidently I can no longer cope with train travel. I let myself be talked into having

---

* The dramatic soprano Lucie Weidt. She had joined Mahler's ensemble in September 1902.

dinner* in the restaurant car, and although I ate only a modest meal, it gave me a stomach ache. – I shan't have anything else today, and hope that will save me for the night. In the station I heard that Kapellmeister Bruch† (who recently conducted my Third Symphony) had come to look for me in my compartment, but that I was pacing up and down the corridor at the time, as usual.

So, at the next stop I shall get this letter posted.

Good night my dearest. I hope you aren't worrying about things!

O‡ Your old Gustav

Mahler spent the night in Frankfurt. The following morning he sent Alma a telegram:

23^U Telegram   Frankfurt, 21 January [1903]
                                                            9.40 a.m.

arrived here in reasonable shape   slept well   carrying straight on to Wiesbaden   thousand greetings gustav

On arrival in Wiesbaden he wrote at once to Alma:

24   Wiesbaden, 21 January 1903
                                     Victoria-Hotel & Badehaus

So, my dearest, here I am again, just for a change, in a hotel room (and a hideous one at that) and I'm writing to you as before. How much has changed since then! – Again, curiously enough, after a rehearsal of my Fourth! Yesterday in the train I felt really <u>awful</u>! I sent you a few lines, and wonder whether they will reach you. We got to Frankfurt at 1.00 a.m. Unfortunately the heating was on in my hotel room, and despite all my efforts at ventilation I couldn't get it cool. As a result, I woke up with a slight headache. At 10.00 a.m. I went on to Wiesbaden, where I drove straight to the rehearsal. – I was greeted by the manager (I nearly wrote: by white-clad virgins), and began the rehearsal without further ado. – My thoughts were with you <u>constantly</u>, and I deeply regretted that a few lousy florins have kept you home and prevented you from being here. – You would have heard my work with different ears. Having forgotten all about it for so long, now I am

---

* Orig.: 'dejeuner'.
† Wilhelm Bruch conducted Mahler's *Third Symphony* in Nuremberg on 2 December 1902, with Paula Jensen as soloist.
‡ Mahler's symbol for 'kisses'.

totally absorbed in it again. – Dear God, how long will it take people to come to grips with it? – It makes you want to run a mile! And yet there's so much to relish in this work, so much to <u>linger</u> over! And such an abundance of <u>love</u>! In the Adagio I could just imagine you gazing at me with your dear blue eyes and <so – not 'worried' in the least (I can't bear them when you're like that), but> with that sweet look they assume when you love me and you're certain that I love you just as much. – If only you were here! Then you would have heard my work, and now, having eaten a revolting lunch, the likes of which only the Germans can dish up, we could walk away into the beautiful world, on which the sun has been shining so brightly these last few days! – This morning, before going to the station, I took a short stroll through the streets of Frankfurt. – All the people, all the shops, all the houses look identical. Everything has the same air about it: orderly, hugely trust-worthy, oppressively uniform. I was particularly struck by one shop, which had a sign over the door that sounded promising: sale of <u>artistic objects</u>. That really made me smile to myself (but I also felt rather sickened by it). That's the way! I couldn't think of a better word for what these Philistines expect from a theatre, a concert hall, an art gallery. – Ha! What will they say to the 'artistic object' I'll be presenting to them on Saturday? Brrrr! Would that we were spared such an ordeal! Or at least, if only <u>you</u> were here, my Almschi, so that I at last had someone by me – my <u>own</u>, the <u>very</u> one who now embodies all I belong to and all that belongs to me. – It's so sweet to have a home of one's own. Such a home can only be another human being – and for me that is you! My dear one! And now let me go outside and run around, as long as the nausea of these 'boorish' (respectable)[*] people doesn't drive me back inside. I embrace and kiss you, my Almscherl, with all my heart.   Your Gustav

[top of second page, upside down:] I wonder what you'll have to tell me in your next letter! Although I actually know and can guess everything! – You see, I'm replying in advance – in a word: <u>I love you</u>!

25[U] Telegram   Wiesbaden, 23 January [1903]
                                                                  10.11 a.m.

warmest greetings   returning by night train as arranged   already greatly looking forward gustav

In just four days Mahler had sent Alma two letters and two telegrams.

[*] Untranslatable pun on 'ordinär' and 'ordentlich'.

*Contacting her on a daily basis was a custom to which he adhered, with few
exceptions, for the rest of his life.*

Since the highly successful performance of his Third Symphony *in Krefeld,
Mahler had begun to win acclaim not only as conductor and stage director,
but also as a composer of some repute. This boost to his self-confidence is
confirmed in a letter to the impresario Norbert Salter, written early in 1903,
in which Mahler agreed to accept all guest engagements, provided at least
one of his own works was included in the programme and his fee was no
lower than 1,000 marks (approximately 2,000 Austrian crowns).*

*The following note from Mahler to Alma might have concerned the ques-
tion of his fee, which in turn prompted him to consider setting off on a journey together with her. If this letter fits into the overall chronology at all, then
only at this point.*

26^U [Vienna, 1903(?)]^E

Dearest,
Please read the enclosed letter! What do you say? Wouldn't you like to come
with me after all? It would be too sweet. Just like in Krefeld! We can send
Putzerl to stay with Mama!

*The highlight of the winter season at the Hofoper, indeed one of the land-
marks in the history of opera production, was Mahler's new* Tristan und
Isolde, *his first collaboration with Alfred Roller, which opened on 21
February 1903. On 24 March followed a much acclaimed production of
Gustave Charpentier's* Louise, *after which Mahler again found a little free
time for performances of his own music, this time in Lemberg (Lviv, which
at that time was still part of the Hapsburg Empire). The 460-mile train journey from Vienna via Krakow took thirteen hours.*

27^U [in the train to Lemberg, 30 March 1903]^E

My dearest,
Rail travel is the bane of my life. – I've been feeling sick all the way! And it
really is too tedious, sitting there hour after hour, deprived of all freedom
and smothered by the stench of burning coal. If only we had reached a point
at which I had no further need to travel for my art. Once again I am finding
it very hard to write. I'm writing these lines at <u>one o'clock</u>.* Frightful! I have
to sit here for another <u>seven hours</u>! I feel like jumping out of the window and

---

* i.e. in the afternoon.

throwing myself under the wheels! – Next to me in the compartment is a little girl, something like our Putzerl. I wonder what the poor child thinks about this eternal bumping and banging. Next time the train stops, I'll pop this little note unstamped into the nearest postbox. Let me know if it arrives. I'd like you to have something from me by tomorrow.

Many, many kisses from your   very unhappy Gustl

By the time this reaches you, I shall no longer be sitting in the train – thank Heaven.

On arrival in Lemberg, Mahler sent Alma the following cable (the original, as dispatched, included three spelling mistakes):

28 Telegram   Lemberg, 31 March 1903
                                                                       9.53

arrived with migraine   slept excellently feeling well today   fondest greetings gustav

Mahler had been invited by the Philharmonic Society of Lemberg to conduct the two last concerts of the regular season, on 2 and 4 April. The first programme included his First Symphony *and three overtures:* Leonore *no. 3 (Beethoven),* Roman Carnival *(Berlioz) and* Tannhäuser *(Wagner).*

29   Lemberg [31 March 1903]
                                                                  Hotel George

My dear Luxerl (otherwise known as Luchserl),
Here is my diary. – During the course of the journey I was assailed by the inevitable migraine with accompanying restlessness. I got out of the train and was on the point of 'throwing up' when the committee of the Philharmonic Society arrived, clad in white, four of them in all: the director, principal conductor, concertmaster and secretary – magnificent! – and tried to coax me into a posh landau. I resisted valiantly (grunting and rolling my eyes in agony) – but nobody said a word, and they offered to walk with me instead. I struck out at a brisk pace, with all four following in my path. – Since the railway station is some way out of town, it took us about three quarters of an hour. –
Having reached the hotel, I hastily took my leave and went straight to bed. Then it really came on – you remember what it was like in Russia. Poldi*

---

* According to Alma, Poldi was one of her serving maids (AMM1, 285).

had thoughtfully packed the aspirin away (instead of putting it into a side-flap) where I couldn't find it. – Finally I went off to sleep, groaning to myself (when I next see you, I'll tell you the adventure I went through beforehand). – The following morning I woke up fit as a fiddle and feeling hungry. First I sent you a cable, then I went down to breakfast. – The rehearsal began at ten o'clock. As I mounted the rostrum, the orchestra greeted me with a fanfare of trumpets and drums. – You can imagine the face I pulled: like a cat in a thunderstorm. Then I read through my First Symphony with the orchestra, which was on its best behaviour and had evidently been well prepared. Once or twice the music sent a shiver down my spine. Heavens above, people must be deaf and heartless if they don't understand <u>that</u>! The second rehearsal is at four o'clock this afternoon, and in the evening I'm going to the Italian opera – Puccini's <u>Tosca</u>. I'm in a good mood today and feel very refreshed. Life here has an aspect all of its own. The most endearing part of it are the Polish Jews that roam the streets here just like stray dogs in other places. – It's highly amusing to observe them! My God, are these supposed to be my kith and kin?! In the face of such evidence, all theories of racial origin appear more ludicrous than I can tell you! So far my leg has run away with me only once (actually one should write: 'run away with <u>Dauthage</u>'), namely just a moment ago, on my way from the restaurant back to my hotel, where I'm writing this letter. – A small boy was staring at my legs with such astonishment that I noticed it right away, and a voice inside me said: 'Dauthage!'* The room is <u>very</u> expensive – 11 crowns – but everything else here is cheap, so I should be able to keep to my budget. I gather that audiences here thirst for good music and take it more seriously than in Vienna. Otherwise they could scarcely support an organization that's just given its <u>hundredth orchestral</u> concert of the season! I'll be interested to see how they react. –

Almscherl, are you being a good girl and not overdoing it? – Take advantage of my absence to have a good rest! As for Abbazia, I wonder what you've come up with. By the way, it's most amusing to observe how well-known I am. In the train, even in an unfamiliar place like this, wherever I go, people address me as 'Herr Direktor' and are so deferent and obliging that it often puts me to shame.

<Warmest wishes to Mama & Carl.> I'm already looking forward to <u>Monday</u>! You know, I really wouldn't mind if we spent Easter hiking around in the Wienerwald and Hinterbrühl instead of paying high prices for rooms

---

* Probably references to Max Dauthage, a double-bass player in the orchestra of the Vienna Hofoper.

at Abbazia* and on the Semmering. But perhaps it would <u>do you</u> good. At any rate, ask Mama's advice.

A thousand kisses <and some big smoochy ones> from   Your Gustav

[diagonally across top of first page:] <This time my thoughts are often with Putzerl. Did you receive my unstamped letter from the station?>

Of Mahler's nervous tic, for which he and Alma devised the word 'geto-tascheln', Alfred Roller wrote a detailed account:

'No description of Mahler's appearance would be complete without mentioning a popular topic of conversation, his 'twitchy foot'. As a child he is said to have suffered from a malady that caused involuntary movements of the extremities. Left untreated, this condition, which is particularly common in mentally hyperactive children, can develop into the illness known as "St Vitus' Dance"; as a rule, appropriate physiological and psychological treatment, combined with the process of natural growth, leads in adulthood to complete recovery. Unfortunately Mahler never entirely succeeded in ridding himself of an involuntary twitch in his right leg. He never discussed it with me, so I presume it was a source of considerable embarrassment. When he walked, it became apparent in the form of a short sequence of abrupt, irregular paces; and when he stood still, he sometimes stamped his foot lightly, as if running on the spot. Thanks to his incomparably strong will power, he was usually able to suppress this nervous tic completely. But if he was somehow diverted or his defences were lowered, his right leg invariably began to twitch in this curious way. Any surprising occurrence, whether annoying or amusing, had the identical effect. Hence it would be wrong to interpret his stamping – as people often did – as a sign of impatience or mounting anger. It happened just as frequently, and often more noticeably, when he laughed. And Mahler laughed as often and as heartily as a child, so much so that tears often came to his eyes. His glasses would then steam up, and he would take them off to clean them; at the same time, wherever he happened to be standing, he would stamp out a veritable dance of joy.'[1]

In Mahler's absence, Alma had evidently returned to her old 'earthenware gods', as Mahler described them, including Nietzsche and Maeterlinck. In the opening section of his next letter to Alma, he expresses his displeasure at this new development.

---

* Alma evidently wished to visit the popular holiday resort of Abbazia (Opatija) on the coast of Istria. She got her way; indeed, she and her husband spent their Easter holidays there every year until 1906.

30   Lemberg [1 April 1903]
                                                                          Hotel George

My dear Almscherl,

I enclose Justi's card, at your request, also a cutting from the Berliner
Tagblatt, which reflects the opinion of <u>Helmholtz</u>* <concerning a matter that
has been troubling Frau Perrin† of late (she used to be much more sensible).>
One could scarcely write more aptly or more concisely about this balderdash
(Maeterlinck etc.) and all that goes with it. – These stupid fools – every one
of them – they look for hidden meanings in the world ('There are more
things in heaven and earth, Horatio, than are dreamt of in your philosophy'‡
etc.) as if they were searching for lice. – Another word they like to bandy
about is 'occultism' <(from occultus: concealed, secret, dark etc.).> <u>What</u>, in
a metaphysical sense, is <u>not</u> dark and secret? Flatheads, twisters the lot of
them! I'm convinced they gobble up all of Nietzsche for breakfast and
Maeterlinck for supper, but otherwise not a word of sense – whatever else
they may have read.

Yesterday evening I went to the Opera, where I saw Puccini's 'Tosca'. – A
truly remarkable performance in every sense.§ I was astonished to witness
anything like it in the Austrian provinces. But the work itself! Act 1: a Papal
procession, accompanied by an interminable ding-dong of bells (which had
to be specially imported from Italy). In Act 2 a <u>torture</u> scene with hideous
screams, after which a man is stabbed to death with a sharp-pointed bread-
knife. Act 3: panoramic view from a citadel over the city of Rome, to a
gigantic bim-bam-bum with another bevy of bells – and an execution by firing squad. Before the shooting started, I got up and left. I need scarcely add
that the score is a masterly sham; nowadays every shoemaker's apprentice is
an orchestrator of genius.**

---

* The physicist and physiologist Hermann von Helmholtz, author of *Die Lehre von den
Tonempfindungen* (*Sensations of Tone*), Berlin, 1862. Mahler was probably also influenced by
his writings on theory of knowledge.
† Jenny Perrin (née Feld), daughter of an insurance salesman from Budapest. In 1878 the
Perrin family settled in Vienna, where Jenny and her two sisters took piano lessons with
Mahler. Their friendship is all but undocumented, but since Mahler writes of her here in the
present tense, it may be assumed that they were still in contact. Ten years earlier, he had pre-
sented her with the manuscript of his *First Symphony*.
‡ Shakespeare, *The Tragedy of Hamlet*, I/v.
§ The performance was conducted by Francesco Spetrino, whom Mahler promptly engaged as
conductor for the Italian repertoire at the Hofoper.
** Despite his lifelong aversion to *Tosca*, Mahler genuinely admired *La Bohème*; in 1907 he
added *Madame Butterfly* to the repertoire of the Vienna Hofoper.

Incidentally, I sat with the white-clad Director in his private box; and on Friday I'm invited to wolf down a dinner with him as well. – <u>Despite</u> the orchestra's poor discipline, rehearsals are going well, and the musicians are extremely <u>willing</u>, <which keeps my spirits up. But to endure such guest appearances one needs the stomach of an ostrich,[*]> and this time the menu is ovation-provoking[†] too. To judge by the rehearsals, the Leonore overture is a novelty here! Why did you weigh Putzi again after just four days?

Listen, Almschi, on Monday evening I'll probably have to stay in Vienna and won't get away until Tuesday night. It's all the fault of Freifrau von Bielitz,[‡] who is cutting capers again. <The weather today is simply dreadful, and I left my umbrella in Café Imperial. Did Hassinger remember to go and ask for it?> And now I greet you, dearest heart – <u>look after yourself!</u>

Best wishes to Mama, Carl and Justi.   Your Gustav

31   Lemberg [2 April 1903]
                                                              Hotel George

Dearest,

<Whatever do you mean by these new, mysterious insinuations – what is troubling you – what are these 'inconsequential matters' that have become of such 'consequence' to you? Can't you ever relax?

By the way, your conversation with Ernst Moll appears to have been exceptionally enlightening. Take my advice and steer <u>well clear</u> of this revolting fellow. I'm certain Carl would take your side.[§]

What <u>Hammerschlag</u>^{**} has to say about your condition is far more important. I take it you really did ask him to call?>

Here my life is devoted partly to intense contemplation and partly to worldly tumult (rehearsals under the most primitive of conditions). Betweenwhiles I have avidly been reading <u>Zend-Avesta</u>, a book like an

---

[*] Orig.: '"Straussen"-magen'. An allusion to Richard Strauss, who had a reputation for never turning down a guest engagement, irrespective of the venue or artistic merit.

[†]Orig.: 'applaustreibend' (a favourite expression of Strauss's). Alma notes in her memoirs that the Viennese critic Gustav Schönaich described Hans Richter's long red beard as 'ovation-provoking' (AMM1, 393).

[‡] Sarcastic allusion to the soprano Selma Kurz, who was born in Bielitz (Bielsko-Biala, Galicia).

[§] Ernst Moll, younger brother of Alma's stepfather, was a businessman by profession. Obliged to leave Austria due to a speculation scandal, in the 1920s he settled in Argentina.

^{**} Alma's gynaecologist, Dr Albert Hammerschlag.

old, cherished friend, that brings one face to face with many things one has oneself seen and experienced.*

Fechner's world is strangely like Rückert's; the two are closely related, and one side of me is deeply in accord with both of them. How few people know anything of <u>those</u> two! <When you come to understand them, it will be a great step forward. Then you will be able to rid yourself of certain trivial ideas that are obscuring your vision and blinding you to reality. From your letters I can feel how inhibited you are, and how much torment and turmoil this causes you. How little you have yet learned from following my example! What use are Paulsen and all the prophets,† if you persistently get bogged down with them?> Tonight is my first concert. Sometimes it strikes me as inappropriate to present my First Symphony to an audience in Lemberg. But the die is cast, and I shall do what I can. Who knows, the experience might even prove fruitful! Anyway, it will earn me 1,000 fl. and bring me one small step closer to independence.‡ Actually, independence is merely an empty phrase if one lacks <u>inner freedom</u>. But this is something one has to achieve without the help of others. So do what you can to help me <and learn something in the process!> Today I took a splendid long walk, during which I had the strangest of experiences (with regard to landscape and psychology <– in case you get other ideas into your head>). I'll tell you about them when I see you. But in the end I returned to the prevailing mood of the traveller: sic transit gloria mundi! <u>What</u> a <u>filthy</u> place Lemberg is. Except for when I'm in the hotel, I take care not to lay my hands on anything. It's all so unsavoury. And one couldn't imagine anything dirtier than the Polish Jews here.

Unfortunately the weather is very bad, pouring incessantly, so I had to buy a new umbrella <(6 fl.)>. My hotel room is fine for sleeping – spacious and airy – but otherwise utterly cheerless. And I have to admit that it's costing me quite an effort to look on the brighter side. What bliss it will be to arrive at the Nordbahnhof at half past three on Sunday, to clamber into a cab <(but

---

* Gustav Theodor Fechner, *Zend-Avesta, or Concerning All Things in Heaven and the Beyond*, Leipzig, 1851 (3rd edn. 1901). For many years Fechner taught physics and psychology at the University of Leipzig. In contrast to classical metaphysics, his findings are based on the empirical research methods of a natural scientist, though also imbued with an awareness that the visible world is filled with symbols of the invisible. Both Fechner and Rückert were influenced by Oriental philosophies.

† The German philosopher Friedrich Paulsen, author of a best-seller entitled *Einleitung in die Philosophie*, Berlin, 1892 (Engl. trans. 1895).

‡ For the building of his villa in Maiernigg, Mahler borrowed money from his sister Justine, which he had arranged to pay back in instalments. The 'independence' of which he writes probably refers to these repayments (cf. letter 133).

first, apart from more enjoyable things, I shall have to tear you off a strip for being such a naughty girl)> and drive home with you. Then I shall wish for nothing more than a hot bath and a good lunch.

I hope you've received all my letters. Since arriving, I've been writing every day. A thousand kisses, my dear Almscherl. Your faithful Gustav

At Mahler's first concert his First Symphony *was such a success that the management asked him to repeat it on 4 April in place of the* Fourth Symphony. *The second concert also included Beethoven's* Seventh Symphony *and the* Preludes *to* Tristan *and* Die Meistersinger.

32   Lemberg [3 April 1903]
                                                              Hotel George

My dearest Almscherl,

Thank God it's nearly over. It's turned frightfully cold and miserable here, and I could do with my winter clothes. I'm chilled to the marrow. Yesterday was my symphony: it made a very powerful effect, and everyone is asking for a repeat performance, so I'll play it again at tomorrow's concert. That's what I call success! You would have loved the audience, which listened with rapt attention and in total silence. Today I dined with the Director – such a curious fellow – and his wife: the epitome of a provincial theatre director, and wealthy enough to hide his inner poverty with riches. He lives in a disused theatre, of which the foyer has been turned into a living room. Every column and alcove is gaudily decorated with fans, photographs, laurel wreathes and other trophies, all in exaggerated profusion such as I had never witnessed. His wife insisted on auditioning for me; I believe he's set his hopes on future business dealings, which was presumably the reason for the invitation and the presentation coram publico of a silver laurel wreath (or perhaps it was a golden one, I have no idea). You can imagine what a face I made.

The audience behaved very well and with the greatest <u>respect</u> (though initially their reaction was somewhat reserved). I was very worried yesterday, Almscherl, because there was <u>no</u> letter from you. I was on the point of sending a cable.

<The arrangements for Frau Stägemann* are perfectly justified; I hope you sorted everything out properly. It would be a faux pas on my part if I failed to return her hospitality.

* The soprano Helene Stägemann, daughter of Max Stägemann, Mahler's Intendant in Leipzig from 1886 to 1888. On 4 April 1903 Helene Stägemann gave a Lieder recital in Vienna. Mahler's remarks seem to imply that he organized accommodation for her.

So you think my letters are too jovial?

Do you expect me to put a gloomy face on everything, like you? Shame on you, my rascal! One has to make the best of everything and set aside Weltschmerz for the real sufferings of the world. If I didn't, I would hang around all day with my tail between my legs, and come home skinny as a rake. But like this I can potter around happily enough, do my studies, look forward to Sunday and all that. It's no fun drifting around in the world a whole week for the sake of a few pence, not even knowing where to find a little warmth (even the pubs and coffee houses are cold here, as is the hotel restaurant). Mark my words, Luxi, that's how to put up with the inevitable. Justi sent me the enclosed letter. I imagine it will make interesting reading for you.* >

Yesterday evening was my Second Symphony in Dusseldorf.† I wonder how it went down? And now another 1,000 kisses and, just to put your mind at rest, 100,000 more (you haven't sent me anything of the kind, merely 'I embrace you' – but that doesn't worry me). No more letters from me, thank heaven. Instead, I'll be there myself at 3.45 on Sunday at the Nordbahnhof. Very well: I embrace you etc. etc.. Your old Gustl

Mahler left Lemberg on the night train and arrived in Vienna the following afternoon. At 7.00 that same evening he conducted a performance of Charpentier's Louise *at the Hofoper.*

As transpires from letter 29, Mahler would have been content to spend the Easter vacation near Vienna. It was probably Alma who decided that they should travel instead to the fashionable Adriatic resort of Abbazia. They left Vienna on 7 April, and remained in Abbazia for six days.

Together with Alma and her parents, Mahler spent 19 and 20 May at Göding (Hodonin, in Moravia) as guests of Fritz Redlich, an old friend of the Molls.‡ Mahler returned home on his own and wrote at once to Alma.

33   [Vienna, 21 May 1903]

My beloved Almscherl,

I've just got up (five o'clock) – with a migraine. It came on as soon as I left, and by one o'clock it had got so bad – with all the familiar side-effects – that

---

* The enclosure has not been preserved.

† The performance, on 2 April, was conducted by Julius Buths.

‡ Fritz Redlich, owner of a sugar refinery as well as other businesses and industries in the region of Göding. His son Hans Ferdinand was later well-known as a Bruckner and Mahler specialist.

I ran home post-haste, tried various remedies, took some aspirin and lay down on the sofa. I couldn't stand it there for long, for my organism suddenly felt the urge for fresh air.[*] I leapt to my feet, and to the accompaniment of Elise's[†] tears and Poldi's cool but courteous commiserations, off I went. Much to the amusement of some bright young serving girls, I rushed about in the Schwarzenberg Garden for an hour. And now I feel considerably better. I was afraid I wouldn't be able to write to you, and that by tomorrow at the latest you would be utterly convinced that I no longer loved you and that you were born for a life of misery. Because of all this, I haven't yet said hello to Putzerl, and so far haven't even had a bite of food. Shall go early to bed, and tomorrow I'll take myself off to the Hohe Warte. By the way, in the Schwarzenberg Garden I suddenly felt a yearning for you, just as I was beginning to feel a little better. I didn't leave <u>any</u> tips – completely forgot – so please make due amends. I've been living very frugally; in fact, I haven't spent anything at all; in that respect at least, a migraine has its virtues.

I'm greatly looking forward to tomorrow evening. By the way, the novel I took with me was a sorry affair, and I soon set it aside. I was wrong to take it in the first place; the Grabbe would certainly have been more amusing. Even so, I wouldn't have been able to read it, because I was feeling so dreadful. Something at breakfast seems to have disagreed with me.

So, my dear Almscherl, a thousand kisses and a gentle rap on the knuckles – you know what for. Kindest regards to Mama and Carl, and pass on warmest greetings to Mr and Mrs Redlich.

Addio, my beloved!   Your Gustav

As soon as the theatre season had ended, preparations began for an event which was further to enhance Mahler's reputation as a composer: a performance of his Second Symphony *in Basle Cathedral at the 39th Tonkünstler Festival. Accompanied by Alma, he set out for Basle on 6 June. A few days before the concert, Mahler wrote to his sister Justine:*

My three rehearsals are already over. Everything extremely well prepared, with a <u>wonderful</u> chorus, so I hope for a satisfactory performance. The church is atmospheric. Today we want to look around town: Böcklin, Holbein etc. So far we've had little time to see anything. Kittel[‡] has already arrived, and sings 'Urlicht' magnificently. I don't yet know who is to sing the

---

[*] Mahler makes an untranslatable pun here on 'laufen' (to walk) and 'Lauffen' (name of a village near Bad Ischl).

[†] Elise was Mahler's cook. She had been in service with him since his Hamburg years.

[‡] Hermine Kittel, mezzo-soprano at the Vienna Hofoper.

soprano part.* What a pity you're not here. Arnold would have gained a far more positive impression of the work than in Munich. The orchestra is considerably better, and although they still sit there like stuffed dummies, they are on their best behaviour. None of our friends has yet arrived. Alma is feeling reasonably well, but still has problems with her stomach.[2]

Soon afterwards, Mahler's friends began to arrive. One of these, the physicist Arnold Berliner, whose researches were of relevance to Einstein's relativity theory, had befriended Mahler in Hamburg. Sitting with him in the hotel lobby, Mahler wrote the following note to Alma:

34U

Basle [mid-June 1903]
Hôtel des Trois Rois

My dearest,
I'm still sitting downstairs with Berliner. Almscherli, why don't you come down and join us? We're waiting for you! Your Gustav

The Second Symphony *was at least as jubilantly received in Basle as the* Third Symphony *in Krefeld the previous summer. Richard Strauss, Max von Schillings, Frederick Delius, Max Reger and Ernest Bloch were amongst the composers whose music was performed at the festival, but amongst Mahler's colleagues it was generally agreed that the* Second Symphony *took pride of place, and that the concert had been one of the greatest triumphs in his career to date. The reviews were equally affirmative, with the notable exception of the anti-Semite Rudolf Louis, whose own composition* Proteus, *a fantasy for organ and orchestra, was also included in the festival programme. Louis wrote two separate reviews for the* Münchner Neueste Nachrichten. *In the first, he questioned Mahler's right to include his symphony in the programme at all, since it left no room for masterpieces such as Friedrich Klose's symphony* Das Leben ein Traum. *In the second, Louis conceded that Mahler had dominated the festival – but as a conductor, not a composer. His praise went above all to the two Basle choirs, which 'had surpassed themselves'.[3]*

Thus, Mahler's remarkably successful season as conductor and stage director at the Vienna Hofoper was crowned by his triumph in Basle. The price for such renown was total physical and mental exhaustion, and now he wished for nothing more than calm and seclusion. To this end he travelled to Maiernigg, taking Alma and Putzi with him. But he could find no rest, and on arrival he immediately started work on his Sixth Symphony. *During the sum-*

---

* The soprano part was sung by Marie Knüpfer-Egli.

mer of 1903 he completed the second and third movements, and sketched out at least part of the first. Towards the end of July he took a break and set out via the Pustertal for the Dolomites, with a book by Helmholtz in his pack. Alma, who was in no mood for hiking, swimming or cycling, stayed behind in Maiernigg. On the road to Toblach, Mahler sent her a jovial postcard:

35^U Postcard: Greetings from Altprags [Tirol]   Toblach [21 July 1903]

Dearest Almscherl,
Arrived here (really here!) after a very amusing journey (Helmholtz had much to tell me). Just to be sure you hear something from me by tomorrow, I'm writing this at the station before taking the train to Schluderbach. Am feeling very well. I'll probably sleep like a log tonight and be furious about it! What a <u>shame</u> I <u>don't have</u> my bicycle with me. It would have been so useful! Best wishes etc.   G.

By the time Mahler reached Dölsach (near Lienz), the weather had deteriorated:

36^U Postcard: Greetings from Dölsach   Dölsach, 24 July 1903^P
[top third of card, above the houses:]
!!!!!! It's raining !!!!!!!
here! here! here! here! here!
[bottom third of card:]

D.A. My face is as long as the letters on the card! I'm in the village inn, surrounded by a swarm of carefree flies. I'll try to get at least as far as Winklern. But if by tomorrow the rain hasn't stopped, I'll turn back. I've been unlucky this time. Many greetings my A.
Your G.

Alma's second summer with Mahler in Maiernigg was not entirely carefree. AML includes accounts of several dreams that she recorded in her diary at this time. And she was still tormented by the problem of artistic fulfilment:

I played through my compositions again, my piano sonata, my many Lieder. I feel again: this is what I want. I long for creativity. My present life is a delusion. I need my art! Everything I played today was so profoundly familiar to me. If only Zemlinsky were here to work with me. But I can't ignore Gustav Mahler's utterly unfounded jealousy. And so I have nobody. I don't feel inwardly unhappy. Not at all. But I wouldn't be averse to a few more visible or palpable signs of Gustav's love.[4]

On 27 August Mahler returned to Vienna, leaving his family in Maiernigg. While waiting for the train at Klagenfurt, he wrote twice to Alma.

37^U Postcard   Klagenfurt, 28 August 1903[P]

D.A. After a very pleasant stroll I'm sitting here in Café Schiberth[*] and have already read all the daily papers, even the small ads. I haven't yet told you how moved I was to see the finished copy, so complete and so beautifully written.[†] – In the Wiener Tagblatt some schmock (probably Karpath) has taken a snipe at me. You'll find it in today's edition. The <u>watchmaker's</u> address is: Josef Meiringer, Obstplatz. I hope you're already dreaming sweetly. <u>Look after yourself</u> during the next few days, so we can enjoy a fine shopping spree in Vienna. I'm already looking forward to it. A thousand hugs and kisses.   Your G.

The bone of contention with Ludwig Karpath and other critics in Vienna was Mahler's decision to lower the orchestra pit at the Hofoper, in emulation of the Festspielhaus at Bayreuth. Once the new season had opened, on 18 August, Karpath was able to convince himself that the alteration had no adverse effect on the orchestral sound, but warned that further lowering of the pit would impair the acoustics of the entire building. Several other critics and orchestral players supported him, if only for the sake of launching further attacks on Mahler, and the issue continued to be debated for several months. Mahler took all this in his stride. The problem was finally solved in April 1905 with the installation of hydraulic machinery with which the pit could be raised or lowered at will.

38^U Postcard   Klagenfurt, 28 August 1903[P]
                                                 No. 2!

D.A. I've just weighed myself. Was so astounded by the result that I must send a second card and tell you. I weigh <u>70 kilos</u>! More then ever before. I was so taken aback that I trod on the toe of some fellow passenger, and he's still moaning about it. By the way, the train is three quarters of an hour late – so far. I have the pleasure of sitting here for another one and a half hours! Another thousand of the same.   Your G.

---

[*] Orig.: 'Schubert'. Café Schiberth (Bahnhofstrasse 16).
[†] During her stay at Maiernigg Alma had copied out the score of Mahler's *Fifth Symphony*. Her manuscript is preserved in the Astor, Lennox and Tilden Foundation collection, New York Public Library.

Tomorrow I start my 'Schweninger cure'.*

39 Postcard   Vienna, 29 August 1903[P]

D.A. I can't write a letter today. Here's a card instead, so at least tomorrow you'll hear something from me.
Splendid journey, thinking of my seventy kilos – a rattling railway carriage. Straight to the theatre. Change of clothes, then rushed around, impressed, also a hasty word with Arnold [Rosé] and [Bruno] Walter. Lunch with [Kolo] Moser at Leidinger's, coffee with [Alfred] Roller, then he walked with me to Kahlenberg[†] via Leopoldsberg. Terrible thirst. Tea and peaches. Wasp sting. Quickly sucked it clean and Roller bandaged it with gauze. Walked back to the theatre to check the orchestra sound, then cycled back here in 9 $^1/_2$ minutes. Very lovely room (have only looked at it through the window, for lack of time). Many heartfelt – – – Now off with Roller! Your G.

40   [Vienna, 30 August 1903]

My dearest Almscherl,
Firstly: I'm in despair. All the shops are shut, and even if they weren't, I still wouldn't know what to buy you for your birthday. So I can only hope you will be happy with my heartfelt wishes for tomorrow instead of an expensive present.
What more can one give, when one has already given oneself? If you join me for one of our beloved afternoon sprees on the Kärntnerstrasse, we can find something nice for you. Is that all right? I'm already looking forward to it. – Now it's time to catch up on the news. I'll have to make a big effort not to forget anything.
Yesterday, once Roller had swathed my hand in Billroth plaster,[‡] I wrote your card from the Kahlenberg, then we took the path you and I have so often trod, my Almscherl, through the Hohe Warte to the tram stop, and from there to the Opera. Soon I had satisfied myself that all the to-do about bad acoustics was nothing but a silly newspaper story (and I have reason to believe that the Rt. Hon. Schalk[§] is chiefly to blame for launching and nurturing it). Pollak came to the performance and imperiously commanded me to stay with him.

---

* A special diet, named after the dermatologist Ernst Schweninger.
† Mahler's apartment in the Auenbruggasse was redecorated every summer. On this occasion, he stayed at Hotel Kahlenberg until work was completed.
‡ Named after Brahms's surgeon friend, Dr Theodor Billroth.
§ Orig.: 'Ehren-Schalk' (honourable rogue), joking reference to Franz Schalk, 1st Kapellmeister at the Hofoper.

However, I pacified his agitated heart and took him to my box, where he joined in the adjudication and found just as little fault with the sound as the rest of us. At the end of the first act I went on stage, where I gave Schalk and Wondra* a piece of my mind and swore at a few bystanders. Afterwards I accompanied Pollak to Hotel Imperial, and ate a beefsteak and a highly sophisticated slice of plum cake. By nine o'clock I was sitting in the Stadtbahn, and I reached Kahlenberg at 10.30. There I went straight to my quarters: two rooms appropriately furnished with filthy, plush-upholstered settees. Through the window there's an unbelievably beautiful view of the lights of Vienna, framed by the superb, sombre colours of the Vienna Woods. Dead tired, I got undressed, taking care not to touch the fixtures and fittings,† and slept through till half past seven. Got out of bed and breakfasted (fully dressed, of course), surrounded by Viennese petit-bourgeoisie, then on foot via the Wildgrube and the Hohe Warte to the tram stop, and from there to the Opera, where everything is closed, because it's Sunday. 11.30: the Obersthofmeister, who gave me a warm welcome and agreed to everything <including my demand that the block‡ should be eliminated>, then lunch with Pollak. <An excellent repast, and now I'm sitting at my desk smoking a cigar and writing this letter.
I haven't yet seen Justi, but am invited to dine with her tomorrow.>
This evening was Meistersinger with a guest.§ After the first act I returned happily to Kahlenberg, which really was a splendid idea of your Mama. <All the same, I had quite a bone to pick with Pollak about it.>
As for yesterday, I should add that I wasn't alone with Moser for lunch, but that Hoffmann** was also there, together with three other gentlemen I didn't know. For me, of course, that was none too edifying.
Latest news: when I went to sign my pay-slip today, I was told that from now on I have to pay 15 fl. stamp duty – as opposed to the 5 fl. previously. I shall receive my salary tomorrow morning and forward it to you right away. By then, I hope, you will have written, for already now I'm simply longing to hear from you. I hope you won't be surprised to hear that I miss you, and that my thoughts are always of you. <I'm sending the enclosed papers so we can find them again next year.>
If only you had already written – just a few lines!

* Hubert Wondra, secretary and chorus-master at the Hofoper.
† Orig.: 'Möblemang' ('ameublement' in comic pseudo-French).
‡ Work on lowering the orchestra pit at the Hofoper had started in the summer, but was interrupted because of the surrounding wall (*Gurte*), which was feared might collapse. Later it was ascertained that the masonry in question had no structural function.
§ Peter Lordmann, from Cologne, who sang the role of Beckmesser.
** The celebrated architect and interior designer Josef Hoffmann.

<As I'm getting plenty of exercise (which is not the least advantage of staying in Kahlenberg), my bowels are in splendid order – and I'm not taking anything for it.> Dear heart, it's a terrible nuisance not being able to write to you from the Opera, and when I'm on the move it's scarcely possible. Don't forget that I'm commuting between Kahlenberg and the city, sometimes even twice a day. A thousand hugs and kisses, my dear Luxi, and don't forget to write.
Your Gustav

The following two letters were both written on Alma's birthday.

41   [Vienna, 31 August 1903]

Dearest,
Your dear, sweet letter arrived here yesterday evening.
Even if your choice of words was rather strange, we seem to be of one mind about your birthday 'surprise'. Sadly, today is the last time I can travel out (to Kahlenberg), and I'd like to make the most of it. As from tomorrow I have to attend four complete performances in succession,* and since there are no more trains to Kahlenberg after nine o'clock, it would be absurd to retain my room. Even so, I've been using it every afternoon. I'm moving in with <u>Pollak</u> for a few days.† The poor chap has to forfeit his bed and sleep on the sofa. He absolutely insisted on it, but I can't impose myself on him for long. I'll try to move back into my own bedroom, and shall ask Justi to lend me a sheet and a pillow (from the loft). If the serving maid can tidy it up, it will be perfectly all right. But first I'll try to find a nice room in Hietzing. Under present circumstances, that's what I'd prefer. I'll keep you informed.
Dearest Almscherl, where are my <u>suits</u>? I can't find them, and my wardrobe seems to have been cleared out. – I'm enclosing the letter from <u>Chelius</u> – you know, the one I have to answer very soon.‡
It would be best if you sent me a telegram with the address, and let me know where I can find my clothes. – My dear, I miss you dreadfully and can scarcely wait for your return. But <u>please</u>, stay as long as you can and take advantage of this splendid weather to restore your <u>health</u>. And don't forget little Putzi!

---

* Gala performances ('Théâtre paré') to mark the state visit of the King of England, Edward VII. It was originally planned that Mahler should conduct *Figaro* on 3 September, but in the event he delegated the performance to Schalk.
† Theodor Pollak had recently moved to Schleifmühlgasse 4 in the 4th precinct.
‡ Oscar von Chelius, major-general and composer in Berlin. Nothing is known of Mahler's contact with him. The letter mentioned here may have been associated with the ADM, of which Chelius was a member.

Why didn't you mention her in your letter?

I haven't yet seen Mildenburg, but they say she's hopping mad (I'm sure she'll collect her pay on the 1st, all the same). There are several others I haven't yet encountered, but I feel no particular urge to see them. So today I'll be dining with Justi. [Half a line obliterated.]

I'll be getting the money today, and shall send it on immediately; I hope it arrives with the same post as this letter.

A thousand hugs and kisses, dear heart, from your   Gustav

42   [Vienna, 31 August 1903]

Dearest Luxerl,

Just a quick note this evening. Earlier today I was in Hietzing, where I took a very pleasant, quiet room on the third floor of the Hietzinger Hof. I can breakfast at the Tivoli, which you and I have frequented on several occasions. Hietzing is readily accessible by train, and even late in the evening I can still get home. <I paid Kohn[*] today, and enclose the bill.>

Today I had lunch with the Rosés. They were very kind and steered clear of all awkward questions. Your letter and last conversation with them seem to have appeased them completely.

Fredi[†] was as 'charming' as ever. I feasted my eyes on his 'intelligent' appearance and remained for quite some time in rapturous contemplation. Afterwards we went for a stroll – they accompanied me back to Hietzing – and their 'little treasure' was our main topic of conversation. I took care not to give the game away – didn't move a muscle. Tickets for tomorrow night's gala are in great demand. <I've given ours to Pollak, and he in turn wishes to give Frau Gallia[‡] the honour. Is that all right with you? Frau Zehelbauer[§] wrote the enclosed card, to which I replied with great warmth.>

Please, my dearest Almscherl, send your letters from now on to Hietzing:
   Hietzinger Hof

Pollak will be shattered, but it would be too cruel to make the fellow stretch out on a Secessionist sofa for nights on end. If he makes too much fuss, I shall accept his hospitality after <u>Figaro</u> on Thursday.

1,000 kisses, my dear Almscherl, from your Gustav

[*] Bernhard Kohn, Viennese firm of piano dealers.
[†] Alfred Rosé, Mahler's nephew, born in 1901. Later he was a conductor and Professor of Music at the University of Western Ontario, Canada.
[‡] Hermine Gallia, daughter of the industrialist Karl Wittgenstein. She later modelled for Gustav Klimt.
[§] Identity unknown.

43   [Vienna, 1 September 1903]

My dearest Almscherl,

My latest news is that the hotel director in Kahlenberg won't let me leave and has offered me the use of his automobile after performances. As it's so wonderful up here, I hastily shook hands on the bargain. Today I took my breakfast on the veranda. There's nothing like it on earth. Luckily, nobody else gets up early, and I can enjoy the beauty of the moment in glorious isolation. The same when I go to bed: the view from my window is so magnificent that I don't feel the least desire to put out the light and lie down. – And the air is absolutely pure.

<Bowels tip-top.> So, I shall stay here as long as I can. I've also thought up a good plan. Sunday and Monday are free, so I'll spend those two days in Edlach* and wait for you at the station in Payerbach. Then we can travel home together, like last year. Is that all right with you?

I was very pleased to read your account of your lonely existence, also that you are again within reach of the Castalian fountain† <and that you're in good form!> Every human being needs frequent, intensive periods of isolation. Here on my mountain I relish the stillness and am delighted about the wonderful weather, which must also be doing you good. And then the best part of it all: our rendezvous in Payerbach and all that will follow etc. At the Opera I have no commitments, so I can stay home.

Berliner is really too kind. I'm enclosing the autograph. Just imagine, I'm exempted from stamp duty, as it transpires (because I was engaged not on a contractual basis, but by decree), and my 10 fl. is to be reimbursed. And now, my dearest, I shall return to my mountain retreat <(I'm writing this after lunch in Café Imperial), on my own this time.> This evening is théâtre paré, for which I have to return in full evening dress.

Afterwards I shall have a quick bite of supper, then to Kahlenberg by car. Heavens – if only you could be with me! How lovely it would be, and what fun you would have!

Adieu, my dearest. Many kisses, also for Putzi. You make no mention of her, strangely enough, except in your last letter, where you wrote that 'normally you were so fond of her'.   Your Gustav

---

* A popular mountain resort to the south of Vienna, near Mürzzuschlag.
† A spring sacred to Apollo and the Muses at Delphi; its waters were reputed to impart poetic inspiration. The remark implies that Alma had written to Mahler of her renewed 'longing for creativity'.

44^U Postcard   Vienna, 1 September 1903^P

D. A., Both your telegrams have just arrived. By now you must also have received my letter, in which I told you that I'll be staying at Kahlenberg until you return. I'm astonished at what you wrote today, that you have received only postcards from me. Except for the first day, I've been sending two letters every day. Perhaps one of them has gone astray. So far I have had lunch with Justi just once. As soon as this card arrives, cable me to confirm that you really want to come back on Thursday. Actually, it would be silly, because the apartment is still in a dreadful state. Think it over, Almscherl! Fondest greetings, your Gustav.

45   [Vienna-Kahlenberg, 2 September 1903]

My dearest Almscherl,
I'm sitting here on the terrace of Hotel am Kahlenberg. After lunch (at Café Imperial – entirely on my own, as usual) I came up here with the rack railway, half hoping to find news from you after waiting in vain at the theatre for a telegram or some other reply to yesterday's cable. I asked you to write to me at the Opera, mainly because I don't receive post from you up here until shortly before bed-time. As I hear, Poldi has already arrived and says you'll be coming on Sunday or Monday. Your telegram yesterday was presumably written in a passing moment of autumnal gloom. As I entered the hotel, just imagine whom I chanced upon, smoking, whistling, elegantly dressed in a white suit, and beaming from ear to ear? Ernst Moll, who's spending a few days here to recover from his exertions.
I exchanged a few words with him, then made off with a friendly laugh. Now I'm going to walk into town via Hermannskogel, Hameau and Dornbach, where we have a guest (Lordmann) at the Opera this evening.*
Tomorrow I conduct Figaro,† and the following day there is a very important guest appearance of the tenor Bazelli as Faust.‡ That's why I asked you not to come here before Friday under any circumstances, because it would be too sad if you had to spend the evening on your own. – The weather is simply wonderful. I particularly enjoy breakfast on the veranda, followed by my morning walk, usually through Grinzing, to the tram stop. How lovely it would be if you could be here too.

---

* Peter Lordmann, who sang the role of Colas Pariset in Ignaz Brüll's *Das goldene Kreuz*; the conductor was Schalk.
† The performance was actually conducted by Schalk (cf. footnote on p. 127).
‡ Giorgio Bazelli sang the title role in Gounod's *Faust*; the conductor was Hellmesberger.

We simply must take that walk together some time. I hope you'll arrive feeling fit and thoroughly refreshed.

I enclose the royalty statement for my Lieder from <u>Schott</u>.[*]
From now on I shall request exactly the same of Stritzko.[†] I'll save up the 18 Marks until you arrive. – Driving up here after the performance in the hotel manager's car is actually quite fun. I'm very glad that you haven't yet returned. In town it's so close and oppressive, you certainly wouldn't be able to sleep. If only I knew the exact time of the train for which I'm to reserve seats for you. I much regret your feeling so isolated, and that Grete hasn't been to see you.

It won't be long now before we are reunited, thank heaven. I'm really longing for it.

Love and kisses, my dear Almscherl, from   Your Gustav

46[U]   [Vienna, 4 September 1903]

My dearest Almscherl,

At last your letter. I'd been waiting for it for three days – but perhaps you didn't realize. If it weren't for yesterday's telegram, I would have been very anxious. Yesterday was not my day, I'm afraid: <u>migraine</u> and restlessness. You know all about that, don't you.

That's why I didn't write, and today you'll probably be very fidgety. Justi came over in the evening and took good care of me. Today I had lunch with her (for the second time). I have absolutely nothing to report. We talked about everything under the sun – orchestras, quartets – then I lay down and slept.

Now for the main news. Pollak has reserved seats for you, and I'm pretty sure you'll have a compartment to yourselves. Unfortunately the train doesn't stop in Payerbach, so I'll walk up the Semmering and wait for you at the station. Better still, if anything. I can hardly wait! Already now I'm very worried about you and Putzerl. Poldi will have finished clearing up the apartment, and soon we'll be back in our cosy little nest.

I've already moved out of Kahlenberg. For four days they had the nerve to charge me <u>30 fl.</u>

At home I'm sleeping quite well, and it's much cheaper too.

---

[*] In February 1892 B. Schott's Söhne in Mainz had published Mahler's fourteen early *Lieder und Gesänge* in three volumes.

[†] Josef Stritzko, director of Waldheim-Eberle, the firm that printed the first editions of Mahler's *First*, *Second*, *Third* and *Fourth Symphonies*, *Das klagende Lied* and the *Knaben Wunderhorn* songs.

Today we have our guest tenor, and tomorrow morning I'll walk up the Semmering. Roller is there too. He might call on me at the hotel. And the day after! What a joy it will be, Almscherl!

I was very angry with you for not writing these last three days, and simply couldn't explain it. But your letter this morning makes up for everything.

What gave you the idea that Mildenburg was staying with me at the Hietzinger Hof? Surely you know that she moved to Gumpendorfstrasse a year ago, over the road from the Lipiners? So there really was no need to make such a fuss! Hell's bells!* And now adieu till the day after tomorrow, my sweet Almscherl, my crazy little pork pie. Fondest kisses.

Your Gustav

Although this was a time of strife at the Hofoper, the tensions in Mahler's vita activa *had little effect on his* vita contemplativa. *In October 1903 he completed the revised score of his* Fifth Symphony, *which he dedicated 'To my dear Almscherl, the brave and valued supporter of all my endeavours.'*

His music was now also beginning to attract the interest of musicians abroad. On 21 October 1903 Henry Wood gave the British première of the First Symphony, *and the autumn of 1903 marked several performances of Mahler's music in Holland. Amongst the many who had enthusiastically applauded the* Third Symphony *in Krefeld were Willem Mengelberg (musical director of the Concertgebouw Orchestra in Amsterdam), Martin Heuckeroth (principal conductor of the Arnheim Symphony Orchestra) and Henri Viotta (director of the Conservatory in The Hague and editor of the Dutch periodical* Caecilia). *Heuckeroth conducted the* Third Symphony *on 17 October at a music festival in Arnheim; the following week, on 22 and 23 October, Mahler himself conducted the same work in Amsterdam; and on 25 October followed the Dutch première of his* First Symphony, *also in Amsterdam.*

Mahler travelled alone to Holland. During a stopover in Frankfurt he sent a postcard to Alma, who was then staying with her parents:

47[U] Postcard: Goethe with his parents   Frankfurt, 19 October 1903[P]

Dearest Almscherl,

I'm simply beside myself that you aren't here! A magnificent train – from here to Amsterdam an <u>express</u>[†] with endless servings of canapés and sherry.

---

* Orig.: 'Himmelherrgottkreuztausenddonnerundhagelsappermentnocheinmal!'
† Orig.: 'D-Zug'.

1 Gustav Mahler at the age of five or six (1865)

2 Alma Schindler at the age of ten (1889)

3 Mahler's parents: (a) Marie Mahler (née Hermann, 1837–1889); (b) Bernard Mahler
   (1827–1889)

4 The Schindler family with Carl Moll in the park at Schloss Plankenberg
(l. to r.): (standing) Grete, Emil Jakob Schindler, Carl Moll, Anna Schindler (née Bergen);
(sitting) Alma, Alexandra Nepalleck, [unidentified]

5 Anna Schindler
with her daughters
Alma and Grete

6 Alma's stepfather,
Carl Moll

7 Mahler in Iglau (1878)

8 Alma and Grete Schindler (c. 1897)

9 Gustav Mahler with his sister Justine in Vienna (1899)

10 Four sopranos at the Vienna Hofoper:
(a) Anna von Mildenburg; (b) Selma Kurz;
(c) Rita Michalek; (d) Marie Gutheil-Schoder

11 Gustav Klimt

12 Alexander Zemlinsky (1897)

13 Gustav Mahler with the violinist Alfred Rosé (1899)

14 Bertha Zuckerkandl

15 The Vienna Hofoper

16 Villa Mahler at Maiernigg
on the Wörthersee

17 Gustav Mahler, 1905   18 Alma Mahler, 1904

19 The house at Auernbruggergasse 2. Mahler and his family lived here
from 1902 to 1907 (right wing, top right-hand corner)

20 Alma Mahler with her daughter Maria ('Putzi') (1903)

21 Alma Mahler (1904)

22 Gustav and Alma Mahler in Basle (1903)

23 Mahler with his daughter
Maria at the Wörthersee (1906)

24 Alma Mahler with her daughters
Maria ('Putzi') and Anna ('Gucki')

25 Richard Strauss and Gustav Mahler at the Austrian première of *Salome* in Graz (16 May 1906)

26 Gustav Mahler (1905)

27 Mahler with his wife and children (1905)

28 Otto Klemperer (1905)

29 Gustav Mahler with Oskar Fried in Berlin (1905)

30 Richard Strauss with his wife Pauline and his son Franz

31 In the garden of Carl Moll's villa (l. to r.): Max Reinhardt, Gustav Mahler, Carl Moll, Hans Pfitzner (1905)

32 Gustav Mahler (1907), photograph by Moritz Nähr

Marvellous weather. This is a journey you really must experience. Many greetings to all. Your Gustav

[top of card:] Am dining at the same table as last time with you. Shall soon see the Rhein!*

48 [Amsterdam, 20 October 1903]

My dearest Almscherl,

Well, I'm staying with Mengelberg. He was so adamant about it that I simply couldn't refuse, and I cancelled my other booking (which was much finer). And now let me tell you the story from the very beginning. – I shared a train with the King of Belgium.† As I took my seat, I was astonished to observe a terrific tumult of servants and officials, with carpets rolled out and a whole bevy of uniforms and shakos. The passengers were hustled into the train like cattle, passports and papers were inspected and stamped in brutish haste. The news spread like wildfire, and everyone leaned eagerly out of the carriage windows. I kept my seat, of course, and witnessed the uplifting event only in the form of a sudden surge of noise (probably the heartbeats of His Majesty's devoted subjects). But then I made a fine fool of myself. Shortly afterwards, believing the danger to have passed, I was sitting there minding my own business, when an imposing fellow walked past our compartment and fixed his piercing gaze on me through the window. Later, as I realized, it was His Royal Highness in person! And for the first time I regretted that my Almscherl wasn't with me, for she would certainly have found it all quite enthralling. And now, at least every half hour, I feel pangs of fresh regret. The journey itself wasn't too bad. Every couple of hours I took out my lunch packet and wolfed something down. The journey seemed to take an age, and I was shivering with cold. At ten o'clock we finally arrived, and I was surrounded by hoardes of people who had come to meet me.‡

Half an hour later I was already sitting at Mengelberg's fireside nibbling at a piece of Edam. I haven't yet seen anything of the city, because I'm staying in the smart area, close to the Concertgebouw, where I spent this morning rehearsing. – You know, I just couldn't believe my eyes or ears when they started on the Third Symphony. It was utterly breathtaking. The orchestra is

---

* A reference to the trip to Krefeld in 1902, when Alma had travelled with him.
† Leopold II, under whose reign Belgium colonized the Congo. His wife, Maria Henriette, was of Hapsburg descent.
‡ Orig.: 'da gieng der edle Wettstreit um meinen Leichnam an' (then began the worthy tussle for my corpse).

superb and very well rehearsed. I can't wait to hear the chorus, which is said to be even better. – After lunch I crept away to write to you, my dearest; then we're going for a walk. My host is already waiting for me. I miss you terribly! <Next time, when you're here (they want to perform all my symphonies), we'll stay in a hotel. It's all well and good, but all this hospitality restricts one's freedom, and we don't want to put up with that again.> So now I'm off to see the canals, where I'm certain to bump into Mynheer Droogstoppel.[*]

A thousand kisses, my dear Almscherl, and take <u>good care</u> of <u>yourself</u>! Greetings to Mama and Carl.   Your old Gustav

49   [Amsterdam, 21 October 1903]

My dearest Almschili,

I can't tell you how much effort it has cost me to write this letter. I virtually had to sneak away.

Yesterday my host led me up and down the Grachts and Straats etc. all afternoon. In many respects it reminds me of Hamburg, except that everything there is more grandiose, more spacious etc. <You know, we thought we might settle in Holland when we retire – not a good idea. I'd hoped to meet a few Havelaars, but so far they've all been Droogstoppels. Strange faces! A unique combination of lethargy and determination.> Mengelberg is very kind, and he and his wife <(a descendant of the Droogstoppels and Kannitverstahns,[†] by the way)> are doing everything to make life – I almost wrote 'the world' – tolerable for me. The worst part of it is the eternal round of commitments. In that respect Lemberg was far more agreeable, for I was always on my own. Yesterday evening I was by myself <at home>, thank heaven, and I thumbed through a huge pile of scores by Dutch, Belgian and French composers. How extraordinary they all are, and yet how sterile! – This morning we continued with our rehearsals. The orchestra went wild about the music. It's so beautiful, one could die for it.[‡] I can't tell you what all goes through my head when I hear that music. The only sad part of it, dear heart, is that you're not here.

The performance promises to be superb. Better than Krefeld. This evening is the dress rehearsal. Now I'm going to take a look at the harbour. And

---

[*] In ELM Alma explains that she spent several evenings reading to Mahler from the novel *Max Havelaar* by Multatuli (i.e. Eduard Douwes Dekker), published in Berlin, in 1875. In this satire on foreign affairs, Max Havelaar represents the powerful face of colonialism, while Mynheer Droogstoppel is the subjugated simpleton.

[†] Literally: Can't-Understand.

[‡] Orig.: 'zum Erschiessen schön'.

tomorrow morning, which is free, we're going to the museum.

On Sunday, as has now been decided, I shall conduct <u>only</u> my First Symphony. A noble gesture, don't you think? Mengelberg will conduct the rest of the programme. Bringing back ham and cheese will be a problem, though. I'm so terribly inept, and if I were to ask my hosts, they'd take it as an avis au lecteur,* which I would find very embarrassing, since they've already overreached themselves. Today they even offered me a glass of <u>Asti</u>. Lord knows where they got it from. I'd rather bring the fee back with me, Almscherl, then we can go for a spree one afternoon and buy something nice for you and Putzi. In the final analysis, all this travelling around is a terrible sacrifice in the name of one's own works. I'm not cut out for this kind of life, Almscherl. <I couldn't read your latest letter (no. 1). Do write more clearly!> Many kisses, my beloved, and a fond embrace.   Your Gustl

<Greetings to Mama and Carl.> Yesterday I took a look at the <u>Stock Exchange</u>. Very impressive.† But the people here don't seem to think much of it – just like in Vienna!

Despite Mahler's ironical remarks about his host, this visit to Amsterdam was to lay the foundations for a lifelong friendship between the Mengelbergs and the Mahlers. This in turn gave rise to a particularly strong Mahler tradition in Holland, which remains unbroken to this day.

On the morning of the concert Mahler made an excursion to Zaandam. In order to give Alma a clear impression of the scenery, which he found particularly impressive, he sent her a series of nine picture postcards, arranged so as to culminate with a portrait of Tsar Peter the Great.

50 Nine postcards of Zaandam   Zaandam, 22 October 1903

I Kalf, near Zaandam
Dearest,
Took a boat this morning and sailed around the harbour, then to <u>Zaandam</u>, where it's <u>wonderful</u>! I'm sending you a few picture postcards, including one of the house in which Peter the Great lived.‡ I am really

---

* Orig.: 'avis en lecture'.
† In AMM1 (p. 288) Alma writes of the Amsterdam Stock Exchange: 'A modern building designed by [Hendrik Petrus] Berlage. My circle and I had drawn Mahler's attention to it.'
‡ Peter the Great lived incognito in Zaandam from 1697 to 1698, with the intention of acquiring insights into Western techniques of ship-building. He also attended anatomy classes in Amsterdam, and studied medicine at Leiden. The situation forms the basis of Albert Lortzing's comic opera *Zar und Zimmermann*.

II Kalf near Zaandam
sad that you aren't experiencing this with me. One can understand why so many painters make their home here! The colourful houses, the meadows and cows, windmills and waterways as far as the eye can see, flying and swimming

III Zaandam: Noordervaldeur lock – East side
gulls, the ships and a forest of masts – and above all the wonderful, hazy light in which everything is bathed. One could feast one's eyes on it for weeks on end. And then the people – so very unusual.

IV Rozengeecht
It often makes me think of Carl, who has taught me something about the art of 'seeing'. Mama would be in her element too. I'm really <u>worried</u> about her. One day we should come here together, all four of us. Yesterday's

V Planstdam
dress rehearsal was wonderful. <u>Two hundred</u> schoolboys, watched over by their teachers (six of them), belted out the bim-bam, also an excellent women's chorus of 330! The orchestra <u>wonderful</u>. Far better than in Krefeld – the violins sound just as beautiful as in Vienna.

VI Tsar Peter's house
The performers applauded and waved unceasingly. What a shame you aren't here! After all the walking and sailing, I've just sat down to lunch (very hungry). My hosts are delightful, and they're content to leave me to my own devices. I've made the acquaintance of a very interesting Dutch musician by the name of Diepenbrock, who composes highly original church music.*
The musical culture in this country is <u>stupendous</u>. These people really know how to <u>listen</u>! <Today I received your letter with the news of Ernst etc. But Almschi!

VII Bedroom in Tsar Peter's house
[blank]

VIII Entrance to Tsar Peter's house
And suddenly I thought of the wishy-wishy* and that sly, self-important look

---

* Alphons Diepenbrock, whose *Te Deum* aroused the interest of Mengelberg at its world première in 1902. In his *Hymnen an die Nacht* to texts by Novalis (1899), Diepenbrock gave the orchestral part priority over the vocal line, thus anticipating a structural principle of *Das Lied von der Erde*. Mahler advised Schalk to include the *Te Deum* in a concert of the Gesellschaft der Musikfreunde, but his recommendation went unheeded.
† According to ELM: little Putzi's incoherent babblings.

of hers – and almost laughed out loud.> A thousand kisses to you, my sweet, incor-

IX Portrait of Tsar Peter
rigible Almschi <and warmest greetings to Mama and Carl. I remain> your old Gustl

51   [Amsterdam, 23 October 1903]

My dear Almschili,
I don't understand why you haven't received a letter from me in four days. I've been writing every day! – Here I haven't been wasting an hour. This morning I took a splendid walk in the country. Dutch meadowlands! Criss-crossed with delightful pathways (paved and tree-lined) and long, straight canals converging from all directions and bathed in silvery light, ivy-clad cottages beneath grey-blue clouds, innumerable swarms of birds. Superb. How happy I am to know that you can enjoy all this with me next year (they want to perform my Second and Fourth Symphonies). There is much talk of you here – your beauty is renowned throughout the land, and everyone is dying to meet you. Now that I know them better, I find the people here splendid, very kind-hearted and hospitable. Actually, I'm glad to be staying with the Mengelbergs, for it obliges me to organize my time carefully and not to waste a single hour. Whatever I do, my thoughts are always with you all.
And now let me tell you about yesterday evening. It was marvellous. The initial reaction was somewhat reserved, but it grew warmer with every movement and, as on previous occasions, from the entry of the alto solo to the close, the emotion and tension rose steadily (I didn't tell you that our Dutch contralto was indisposed, and that Kittel was called in and sang very well[*]). The final chord was greeted with jubilation mixed with something more imposing. Everyone here tells me it was completely unprecedented, and that I now rank far higher than Richard Strauss, who's very much in vogue here. This evening is the second performance (completely sold out). This morning was the first rehearsal of my First Symphony. The orchestra was bowled over. How sorry I am that you aren't here.

This afternoon we're off to the museum to see the Rembrandts. Tomorrow The Hague and Scheveningen, and the following day, Sunday morning, the seaside near Haarlem. Then, at 6.30 on Monday morning, I take my leave and return to you, my Luxerl!

[*] Hermine Kittel substituted at short notice for Pauline de Haan-Manifarges.

137

<I'm delighted to hear that you're reading Fechner. Altogether I can sense a gradual widening of your horizons – what you write bears witness to an introspection, a desire to reach the 'heights'.

The air here has done me a power of good. For me these eight days have been a veritable convalescence. And now, my Almscherl, I kiss you and squeeze your hand. Take care of yourself! Best wishes to your people (who are also my people),[*] and kiss Putzerl for me!>

Your old Gustav

Mahler was now in considerable demand as interpreter of his own works. Performances of the Fifth Symphony *were scheduled for the 1903/4 concert season in Heidelberg, Mannheim, Köln and Prague. And his colleague Ludwig Rottenberg invited him to conduct a performance of the* Third Symphony *in Frankfurt on 2 December 1903. Before setting out on his journey, Mahler sent Alma a greeting from the Westbahnhof.*

52[U] Postcard   [Vienna], 28 November [1903][P]

D.A. I have a little time on my hands, and since I happen to be standing in front of a kiosk and there's a letter-box close by, let me at least send you this farewell greeting from the railway station. It should reach you in bed tomorrow morning. – Stay in bed, Almscherl, as long as you can.[†]

Fondly your Gustav

53[U]   Frankfurt [30 November 1903]
                                                              Hotel Imperial

My dearest Almschili,

Let me quickly follow up my telegram[‡] with a brief account of the journey. I slept soundly until nine o'clock, then coffee for breakfast. In the train I chanced upon Herr <u>Lothar</u>[§] from Vienna, who interviewed me. Gave him a precise account of my plans regarding Marienbad tablets and liquorice powder, and some useful tips on the nature of haemorrhoids.

Arrived here at midday, and Rottenburg met me at the station. Having just devoured a hearty lunch, I'm writing these few hasty lines which I'll take to the station myself, in time for the four o'clock train.

---

[*] Orig.: 'Grüsse die Deinen (die auch die meinen sind).'
[†] Alma was expecting her second child.
[‡] The telegram has not been preserved.
[§] Rudolf Lothar, staff journalist and reporter on cultural affairs for the *Neue Freie Presse*.

At the Westbahnhof I bumped into Kapellmeister <u>Rösch</u>,* who travelled on the same train as far as Munich. He was very agreeable, and we had a very good conversation.

A thousand kisses, my dearest Almschili. At 4.30 I have a rehearsal with the principal trombone and the flugelhorn.† Fondly, your Gustl

54   Frankfurt [1 December 1903]
                                                                                    Hotel Imperial

My dearest Almscherl,

<Could I ask you to forward the enclosed to Dr Horn. If you read it, you'll gather what it's all about.‡>

Now on with my report. As I told you in my cable, I'm staying at Hotel Imperial, directly opposite the Opera House, which is where I'm giving the concert. I have a splendid room on the fourth floor, with an adjoining bathroom and closet, telephone and all conceivable amenities; unfortunately I have no use for it all, as I'm never there. <It costs <u>7 marks</u> a day (8 marks as a double room). I'm afraid you forgot to pack my comb, nightshirt and slippers. I'll buy myself a comb here.> This morning we started rehearsing. Oh dear! What misery – going back to square one time and time again. If it goes on like this, I'll soon be sick and tired of my Third Symphony. But one thing is already certain: with this orchestra I wouldn't dream of conducting my Fifth! They're pretty short-tempered, rather like the Konzertverein orchestra in Vienna. I sigh from dawn to dusk under these wretched circumstances, and my longing for you knows no bounds. – I trust you're taking care of yourself and spending plenty of time lying down, my beloved Almscherl, so that you'll feel fit as a fiddle by the time I get home. – Farewell for today, dear heart. Write to me if you can.§ Also from Putzi! Fond embraces, your old Gustl

---

* Friedrich Rösch studied not only music but also law. Having worked briefly as Kapellmeister in St Petersburg, he specialized in copyright law, joining with Richard Strauss in founding the Genossenschaft Deutscher Tonsetzer. In 1919 he succeeded Strauss as president of the ADM.
† The *Third Symphony* includes important solos for both these instruments (trombone in the first movement, flugelhorn in the fourth).
‡ The enclosure was a newscutting from Cologne on 'Matter, Ether and Electricity'. Mahler's letter to the Viennese lawyer Richard Horn is included in GMB (pp. 318–9), but dated 'January 1907' instead of December 1903.
§ Orig.: 'schreibe mir, wenn Du kommst!' (write and tell me when you're coming); evidently a slip of the pen.

55   Frankfurt [1 December 1903]
                                                     Café Goethe-Eck

Look, my dearest Almscherl,
This is the cosy corner to which I retreat after my (very tiring) rehearsals
(from 9.30 to 11.30) and a very frugal meal at the Bierhaus. Here I can sip
my coffee* and commune with you for a quarter of an hour. Then I'll take the
letter to the Central Station to make sure it leaves with the 4.30 train and
reaches you the following morning while you're still in bed.
By the time you read this letter, I shall be conducting the (public) dress
rehearsal. Today it already went far better. The orchestra has meanwhile got
the hang of it and is evidently finding it very interesting. The Opera chorus
makes a good job of it (there isn't a single 'belle' amongst them, so when
you've finished reading this letter you can safely go back to sleep) and the
contralto† (who is not only an <u>alto</u> but also an <u>oldie</u>‡) is perfectly satisfactory. So I hope for a good performance tomorrow evening, followed by a
pleasant journey, which will end, thank heaven, in your arms. I'll be arriving
at the Westbahnhof at 5.25 (Thursday). Your dear letter arrived yesterday,
and today I hope for the same – but longer. I'm in excellent health, a change
of air always does me good. It hasn't stopped raining here, but I haven't let
it deter me, and in my free moments I've been splashing about quite happily.
So far I've spent every evening at the Opera, but haven't heard anything
worth mentioning. Even the stars that I've engaged shine pretty weakly, with
neither a Mars nor a Venus in their midst.§
And now off to the station with your letter. On my way there I'll be thinking
of you so hard that your ears will start to burn. Fondest kisses to you <and
kind regards to Mama and Carl, when you see them.> Say 'ay-ay' and 'goo-
goo'** to Putzi as often as you can.
Your faithful Gustl

* Orig.: 'Cäffeh'.
† Clara Weber.
‡ Orig.: pun on 'Alt' (alto voice) and 'alt' (old).
§ Mahler attended the following performances: 30 November: Lortzing *Der Waffenschmied*; 1
December: Leoncavallo *I Pagliacci* and Mascagni *Cavalleria rusticana*. His disappointment is
explained by the fact that some of the artists had been engaged, on the recommendation of
Schalk and Bruno Walter, to sing at the Vienna Hofoper.
** Orig.: 'Ei, ei' and 'brav, brav'.

56   Frankfurt [2 December 1903]
                                          Café Goethe-Eck

My beloved Almschi,
This is my last letter from here. In truth, it seems hard to believe that Goethe
was born in this place, for apart from the sign over the door of the coffee
house, which bears his name, there's absolutely nothing to remind you of it.
– I hope this letter arrives in the morning, as before, and then in the afternoon, at a few minutes past five o'clock, we shall meet again. –
Today was the final rehearsal. All in all, everyone did quite well. Due to
their lack of refinement, I have to admit that the first movement sounded
a little too massive, but the last three movements will make their effect. I
took absolutely no notice of the audience, and when someone timidly
attempted to applaud, I muttered something under my breath to the
orchestra.
When I next see you, I'll tell you how it went. – The last of your two dear letters arrived simultaneously. They are <u>very sweet</u>.
<I beg you not to torment yourself with 'sexual' problems. – My outlook
with regard to 'les femmes' is really of no consequence.> For me, my
Almscherl, you will always be the same! And I am indeed happy to be returning to you and Putzi.
Auf Wiedersehen, my dearest.   Your old Gustl

<Now I'm off to the station again, to post this letter.>

Encouraged by the success of Mahler's Second Symphony *in Basle, Oskar
Nedbal decided to perform the work on 18 December in Prague with the
Czech Philharmonic Orchestra. Mahler's commitments at the Hofoper prevented him from attending the performance. Therefore Alma attended the
concert in his place, accompanied by her mother. The success was so great
that Nedbal decided to repeat the performance ten days later. Mahler wrote
to Alma in Prague:*

57[U]   Vienna, 18 December 1903[P]

My Almscherl,
By the time I write these lines, I hope your ghastly journey will have ended.
What a pity the weather's so dreadful. You'd be well advised not to venture
out of doors. – I've already attended to Mama's message; at 9.30 Hassinger
left post-haste for Favoritenstrasse no. 47, as Mama had said. An hour later
he returned, out of breath, having searched the length and breadth of the

street without finding a trace of Xandi.* But evidently he'd checked only the odd-numbered houses, for on consulting 'Lehmann'† it transpired that the correct number was 44. Off he went again, and this time he found the right 'gnädige Frau'. So I hope Mama will have the pleasure on Sunday.

In all the confusion, I forgot to wire to the <u>Blauer Stern</u>.‡ I hope you're feeling comfortable, all the same. From here, I don't really know how to help you with seats for the return journey from Prague. In the hope that Nedbal has the necessary connections, I've written to him per express. After all (as you have now seen for yourselves), he's a Czech national hero. See you soon, my dears.   Your Gustl

Roller came to lunch as arranged, and now (at 4.30) I'm home again, this time for about an hour. On both occasions Putzi was in high spirits, almost wild. She kept calling for Mama and turning her little head expectantly towards the door. Having been woken so early this morning, she took her nap at eleven o'clock, and by the time I returned, at 1.30, she was already wide awake. Now I'm off for high tea, then I'll call on Carl at the Secession.

* Alexandrine Nepalleck ('Aunt Xandi'), half-sister of Alma's father.
† *Lehmann's allgemeiner Wohnungs-Anzeiger*, the official address book for the city of Vienna.
‡ Mahler's favourite hotel in Prague.

1904

Mahler's triumphal reception at Krefeld proved remarkably fruitful: apart from performances of the Third Symphony *in January in Munich (under Bernhard Stavenhagen) and Zurich (under Volkmar Andreae), early in 1904 he himself conducted the work at the fifth subscription concert of the Heidelberg Bachverein (soloist: Betty Kofler), and the following day he repeated the concert in the Rosengarten Museum Hall, Mannheim. Once again he travelled alone, as Alma was expecting her second child. Before leaving Vienna he sent her a greeting from the station.*

58[U] Postcard   Vienna, 27 January 1904[P]

Dearest Almschili,
To my great delight I can send you a second greeting, which should reach you tomorrow morning before you get out of bed. I shall still be trundling along on this awful journey, tapping my feet impatiently. Please don't forget to write to Nanna[*] and Frau Wolff.[†] A thousand greetings   Your Gustav

Having spent the night in a sleeping car, he wrote to her again during an interim stop in Munich.

59[U] Postcard: Gallery Schack, Munich   Munich, 28 January 1904[P]

Dearest,
Slept quite well (detailed report to follow). Here at the station 6.30 a.m. for breakfast. Just ordered a ham roll and a cup of tea. A thousand greetings. Your Gustl

And the following day he sent his detailed report, as promised.

---

[*] i.e. Nina Spiegler.
[†] The impresario Louise Wolff, head of the concert agency founded by her husband, Hermann Wolff. After his death in 1902 she succeeded him as managing director. The agency soon grew to become the most influential in the whole of Germany. In 1933 it was closed by the Nazis.

60   Mannheim, 29 January 1904[P]
                                                        Park Hotel

My dearest Almschili,
Following my two postcards, which I hope have now reached you, here's a
brief report of my journey. – At the Westbahnhof I bumped into my brother,
the writer and chief bookkeeper.[*] The poor fellow looked rather sheepish,
half shy, half inquisitive. It was more moving for us both than I had
expected. – I was only afraid it would end with him travelling in the same
compartment; I even had visions of us sharing a sleeping car. Well, I was
spared that – instead I had the pleasure of being cooped up with somebody
else. Unfortunately there was no choice, as the carriage was fully booked. –
It wasn't too bad though: he didn't snore too much, didn't make too much
noise, and wasn't at all smelly. All the same, in such cramped quarters it's no
pleasure to breathe the same air as a stranger. I went to bed fully dressed, and
got a reasonable night's sleep. How lovely it would have been if you had
been lying there. At last the journey was over. I took advantage of every stop
to take a »walk«, and here at the station I was met by Kapellmeister
Kaehler,[†] who was due to take an orchestral rehearsal of my symphony the
same evening. I opted for an evening in the theatre, where a performance of
Romeo and Juliet – bungled as it was – opened my eyes once again to the
greatest of all writers and perhaps of all human beings: Shakespeare, and
again it helped me to new insights. – In a sense I prefer a <u>bad</u> performance of
such a work to a half-good one, for it stimulates the imagination. The truth
is that 'the inadequate here does become an "achievement"';[‡] everything is
elevated to the level of a sign or symbol.
Afterwards I enjoyed a glass of Bavarian beer with our two 'Hofkapellmeis-
ters', and we talked shop until midnight. At today's rehearsal, by all
accounts, I should find everything in pretty good shape.
How nice it would be if you were sitting in the audience, and I had someone for whom I could do everything in my power. But what's 'Hecuba' to
me?[§]
Since there's no late-evening connection between Heidelberg and Mannheim,

---

[*] Mahler's brother Alois, seven years his junior, was considered the black sheep of the family.
Later he adopted the forenames Hans Christian, as they sounded less Jewish. He emigrated to
America, and eventually settled in Chicago where he worked as a stockbroker. He lived there
from 1910 until his death on 14 April 1931.
[†] Willibald Kaehler, 1st Kapellmeister at the Nationaltheater in Mannheim.
[‡] Goethe, Faust II: 'Das Unzulängliche, / Hier wird's Ereignis.'
[§] cf. Hamlet II/ii: 'What's Hecuba to him, or he to Hecuba / That he should weep for her?'

I shall be staying at the Mannheim <u>hotel</u> throughout. So send all your letters to this address.

What is Putzerl up to? What progress is she making in those two converse regions of her existence: down below and up above – back and front? So far, it seems, she has found no happy medium!

A thousand greetings and kisses from your Gustl.

<Warmest greetings to Mama & Carl. Now I'm going to write to Grete.>

61^U Postcard   Mannheim, 30 January 1904[P]

D. A. This morning I had to be up and about at six o'clock, and the train to Heidelberg, where we are rehearsing today, leaves at 8.00. Hence the postcard. This afternoon I might manage a full letter. Yesterday's rehearsal was quite passable. I hope it will go really well. It's strange how my music alienates people at first hearing. It's the same wherever I take it. I sent a cable to Grete. We'll meet up in Heidelberg on Monday at 2.00.

Kindest regards.   Your Gust

62 Postcard   Mannheim, 31 January 1904[P]

My dear Almschli,

Today you'll have to make do with another card! This accursed commuting between Mannheim and Heidelberg is robbing me of all my time. I've never had a more hectic time. The second rehearsal was already pretty good. – This evening I'm going to see Die Rose vom Liebesgarten. – Yesterday Heidelberg – delightful little place – long walk to the famous castle. Really very fine. I've been turning down all invitations. – Tomorrow is the final rehearsal <and afterwards, at two o'clock, I'm expecting the Leglers, with whom I shall have lunch. Maybe also take a walk with them in the afternoon.> The Heidelberg boys choir is wonderful. The female voices in both towns sound pretty dull. The same kind of soloist as in Krefeld. – Mannheim is a hideous dump. This time, unfortunately, I don't even have time for a stroll. Neisser[*] has just been to call – I'll be attending his lecture. He's <u>staying</u> for <u>both</u> concerts; he's very upset that you're not here. If you had come, his wife would have accompanied him. No news from you today.

Warmest greetings   Your faithful[†] Gustl

---

[*] Albert Neisser, a dermatologist from Breslau and a cousin of Arnold Berliner (cf. p. 122). He was famous for having isolated the sources of gonorrhoea, meningitis and other related illnesses, known henceforth as the Neisseria bacteria.

[†] Orig.: 'Dein 3er' (i.e. 'Dein dreier', Saxon dialect pun on 'Dein treuer').

63   Heidelberg [1 February 1904]
                                                    Hôtel de l'Europe

My beloved,
Yesterday I heard Die Rose vom Liebesgarten. The performance was very
good, and fully confirmed my opinion of the work when I read the score. It
brought me no new insights. My opinion of Pfitzner remains unchanged. A
strong sense of atmosphere and very interesting range of orchestral colours.
But too shapeless and vague. A <perpetual> jelly and primeval slime, constantly calling for life but unable to gestate. It evolves only as far as the inver-
tebrates; vertebrates cannot follow. Like Kalchas in La belle Hélène, one
would like to call out, 'Flowers, nothing but flowers.'* The audience came
with the best of intentions, but in such a stifling atmosphere of smog and
mysticism, the interest waned.
Afterwards I dined with Kaehler and Wolfrum,† then travelled with the latter to Heidelberg, where I spent the night.
Nodnagel appeared out of the blue with an analysis of my Third Symphony.‡
Now it's time for the final rehearsal.
<The Leglers are coming at 2.00, and I want to stay with them.
Don't send the enclosed letter to Nanna, Almschili – it will only give rise
to further misunderstandings and, contrary to your belief, will do nothing
to 'clarify' the situation.> Neisser accompanied me everywhere, and will
be staying here until my departure. I like him much better now (he came
here solely for the purpose of hearing my symphony, and arranged his lecture to fit in with it). He takes an immense, warm-hearted interest in my
work and understands it remarkably well – knows the Third Symphony
by heart.
I only hope the Neckar will treat me as kindly as the Rhine. At any rate, all
signs are pointing in that direction. – There's tremendous interest here in all
circles, and both concerts are <u>sold out</u> (which doesn't happen even with
Strauss). But I can see how <u>important</u> it is for now that I am <u>present</u> at all
these performances – when I'm not in command, it's unbelievable what nonsense people make of my work. Strauss is absolutely right in conducting his
music everywhere in person.

* From Act I of Offenbach's *La belle Hélène*.
† Philipp Wolfrum, founder and director of the Heidelberg Bachverein and Akademischer
Gesangverein, which made Heidelberg at that time an important musical centre.
‡ Otto Nodnagel, essayist, composer and music critic of the *Berliner Tagblatt*. He studied with
Philipp Wolfrum and was later professor of music at Königsberg. His analysis of Mahler's
Third Symphony was published in Darmstadt in 1904.

And now I close with my warmest greetings, my dearest. (Yesterday I didn't hear from you all day, I hope you're well!) And what is my sweet little Putzi up to?
Your Gust

Mahler's quotation from La Belle Hélène *reveals the man of theatre whose working knowledge of well-known (and often less than well-known) works provided him with a store of quotations for almost any situation in life. This aspect of his character often becomes apparent in his letters. Mahler himself had conducted* La belle Hélène *in 1882, and evidently knew it well, as did Alma. On 23 August 1898, after seeing a performance in Franzensbad (Frantiskovy Lázně), she wrote: 'Why is the work so seldom played in Vienna? It's so melodious – delightful.'[1] And on 31 August 1900 we learn from her diary that she played selections from the work at the piano, implying that she had access to a vocal score. Certainly by the summer of 1910 there was a vocal score of* La belle Hélène *in the Mahler household, for the critic Oskar Bie observed Mahler playing from it at Toblach one evening, while Alma, 'whose Venetian delicacy could scarcely have been captured by Palma Vecchio',[2] added the vocal parts in the treble.*

The world première of Die Rose vom Liebesgarten *was given in Elberfeld in 1901. Pfitzner, who sent Mahler the score and the libretto, asked permission to play him the work as soon as possible. An opportunity presented itself, as Alma recalls, at the Tonkünstlerfest of 1902 in Krefeld:*

Mahler and I were sitting in our large bed-sitting room, which had an alcove with a massive double bed concealed behind a black curtain. A gentleman was announced. Mahler looked at the card, and asked me to sneak off into the alcove for a few minutes so that he could speak with him undisturbed. I did so, and drew the curtain behind me.
I heard a thin, high voice addressing Mahler in persistent tones. I would have loved to hear what was being said. Dreadful!
What I did hear sounded singularly pitiable and humiliating. Here was an artist begging for the performance of his work, 'Die Rose vom Liebesgarten'. And as soon as I heard him speak, I knew this was an artist. Mahler refused. Coolly, calmly and curtly.
He must have forgotten his own early years: 'No singers – the libretto simply too dreadful – all this symbolism: incomprehensible – too long, much too long –'. Betweenwhiles I heard the quivering voice of the supplicant: 'Just one try – one last chance – the only musician capable of understanding him, Mahler – he was in despair'.

The voices grew louder, then moved towards the door. I couldn't bear it any longer, I leaped up, opened the curtain, rushed towards Pfitzner and clasped his hand as a token of solidarity. I shall never forget the look he gave me. Then he went. Mahler was not angry. Strangely enough, he was not angry![3]

Later Mahler recommended Pfitzner's String Quartet op. 13 *to the Rosé Quartet. Then, in 1905, thanks to the advocacy of Bruno Walter, who was a great admirer of Pfitzner, he finally relented and agreed to stage* Die Rose vom Liebesgarten *at the Hofoper.*

Mahler spent the evening before the concert in the company of Wilhelm and Grete Legler, Philipp Wolfrum and Albert Neisser.

64[U] Postcard: courtyard of Heidelberg castle　　　　Heidelberg, 1 February
1904[P]

> In a little bar that's snug and fine,
> With Perrier[*] and Piesport wine,
> And almonds and sultanas,
> We raise our glass to Alma's.
> 　　　　Gust

(The Leglers are coming with us to Mannheim tomorrow, and the following day we shall all travel on to Stuttgart, where I have to break my journey for four hours.) See my separate letter![†]
[signed] A. Neisser
[written by W. Legler:] Warmest greetings Grete Wilhelm
[written by P. Wolfrum, edge of page:] Wolfrum, famulus

65　　　　　　　　　　　　　　　　　　Mannheim, 2 February 1904[P]
　　　　　　　　　　　　　　　　　　　　　　Park Hotel

Dearest Almschl,
Well, yesterday was Heidelberg! It went magnificently. First-class perform-ance – à la Krefeld. <Grete and Wilhelm were there and witnessed every-thing. Afterwards we dined in a public house, really most enjoyable.> Wolfrum behaved very generously, and I believe he is quite won over. <Late to bed.> This morning I travelled to Mannheim with Neisser (who won't let me out of his sight, and is very good company). Another rehearsal. Lunch with the Intendant. <Grete and Wilhelm stayed in Heidelberg, where they

---

[*] Orig.: 'Giesshübler', a sparkling water marketed by the firm of Mattoni (Carlsbad and Vienna).
[†] i.e. letter 63.

explored the town with a painter friend. Now I'm expecting them for tea. After the concert I'm invited to an 'off-licence' house, together with the Leglers and the Neissers.> And tomorrow, thank heaven, it's time to go home. I'm heartily sick of staying in strange hotels, and greatly look forward to seeing you again. This time I hope to have made another step forward. In this part of the world I have gained ground, repeat performances are scheduled for the near future in <u>both</u> towns, and next year I am to conduct the Second Symphony here.

How I loathe this life of a strolling player – but it <u>has</u> to be! That's quite clear to me.

The inevitable Nodnagel has written a hideous analysis and swoons like a young girl. <No need to be jealous.> I have been cultivating the society of conductors and musicologists (between you and me, I far prefer them to tedious females). I can quite imagine that you have been causing a furore. In your new outfit you must create as much of a stir as a good performance of my Third Symphony.

So I look forward to seeing you on Thursday morning (for you that means the following day, while I have to wait $1\frac{1}{2}$ days, worst luck.) Many, many greetings, my Almschili.   Your Gust

I can't wait to see Putzi again. Sh! Sh! Sh!

Audience and press reactions to the Heidelberg and Mannheim concerts were largely positive. Nevertheless, the repeat performances of which Mahler wrote never materialized (nor for that matter did that of the Second Symphony *the following season). Three weeks later he conducted a further performance of his* Third Symphony *in Prague, this time with Ottilie Fellwock as alto soloist; the orchestra was prepared by Leo Blech. The absence of letters to Alma from Prague implies that she travelled with him.*

On 23 March Mahler conducted his Fourth Symphony *in Mainz, at the invitation of Emil Steinbach, principal conductor of the Municipal Orchestra. The concert was given in the Liedertafel Hall, with Stefanie Becker as soloist.*

66[U] Postcard   Vienna, 20 March 1904[P]

Almschi my dearest,
Just time to scribble a quick addio. The train's about to leave!
1,000 X! Your Gustav

Mainz [21 March 1904]
Hof von Holland

My dearest Almschili,
Arrived in splendid shape. A fine dinner and a long walk along the Rhine.
The sunshine is so pleasant, the air smells so sweet, and I'm really upset that
you aren't here with me. I recall those lovely days by the Rhine in Basle, and
I do believe that you would feel happy here. – It's so warm that I've simply
folded my raincoat over my arm. – The hotel is pretty primitive; evidently
there isn't anything better, for it isn't at all cheap. For the same money one
would expect more agreeable accommodation.
I hope to have plenty of time to myself here, for so far nobody has put in an
appearance. Only Herr Hofrat Steinbach[*] has announced himself by phone
(everyone here is either a Hofrat or a Generalmusikdirektor) and sent his
orchestral attendant as envoy. God bless him! The Musikverein[†] has been
very much on my mind. Vederemo![‡] Now I shall dash off a postcard for Herr
Hofrat.[§] After that I have a rehearsal with my soprano soloist. And this
evening I'm going to the theatre (Undine).[**]
A thousand greetings my dearest from your   Gustl.

As from tomorrow I'll send your letters to Abbazia. Greetings to Mama and
Carl.

*Later the same day Mahler wrote to Alma again, this time on the subject of
their Easter vacation, which was due to begin shortly afterwards. As in
1903, she wished to travel to Abbazia. Mahler asked his secretary at the
Hofoper, Alois Przistaupinski, to make the necessary arrangements, and
suggested that Alma should contact her friend Pollak to organize the rail
tickets.*

---

[*] Emil Steinbach, an accredited Wagner specialist, was conductor of the Stadtkapelle in
Mainz. His younger brother Fritz succeeded Franz Wüllner as Generalmusikdirektor in
Cologne, where he was conductor of the Gürzenich Concerts and the Musik-Gesellschaft.
[†] Mahler was considering an offer by the Gesellschaft der Musikfreunde in Wien to succeed
Ferdinand Löwe as conductor of the *Gesellschaftskonzerte*. In the event he decided against it,
and the post was filled by Schalk (cf. letter 70).
[‡] Vederemo (Ladino): we shall see.
[§] i.e. Karl von Wiener, who was later appointed president of the Gesellschaft der
Musikfreunde in Wien.
[**] *Undine*, romantic magic opera in four acts by Lortzing.

68[U]   Mainz [21 March 1904]
                                                          Hof von Holland
                                                          No. 2

Motto: I must work this out craftily.*
My dearest,
Have just received a cable from Przistaupinski.
If you can book just a complete compartment (<u>but the booking must be
firm</u>), that would be quite enough. Mama (and perhaps also Fanni[†]) can sit
anywhere, then they can join you at St Peter,[‡] and from there the journey
lasts only two hours. Even if you can book only half a compartment, Fanni
could sit <u>next door</u> (even if other people are there), to be at hand when you
need her. If Mama travels in another carriage, she can join you later on.
Pollak must help. – If it can't be arranged <u>for certain</u>, dear Almschi, then be
sensible and go to <u>Edlach</u>, where it's really lovely and you will feel <u>perfectly</u>
happy. Easter is a difficult time everywhere. Even for Edlach, Hassinger or
Przistaupinski must <u>phone</u> and make a reservation.
A thousand kisses   Your G.

I fear the <u>return journey</u> will be even more difficult. – Dearest, take my
advice and settle for Edlach!

Between rehearsals for the Fourth Symphony *Mahler continued to send
instructions about the excursion to Abbazia.*

69   Mainz [22 March 1904]
                                                          Hof von Holland

My dearest Almschili,
Although I'm not quite sure whether this letter will reach you, or where, I'd
like to send a brief report on how I passed the day (or rather, yesterday).
Yesterday evening I went to a lousy performance of <u>Undine</u> – half-way
through Act 2 I got up and walked out. Steinbach hasn't left my side for an
instant – I rejoiced too soon – but he's very dear and kind-hearted <by the
way>. He heard my Fourth Symphony in Wiesbaden, and doesn't yet know
any other works of mine. All the same, he liked it so much that he immediately

---

* Orig.: 'Das muss ich schlau einfädeln': quotation (slightly altered) from Act II/iv of
Lortzing's opera *Der Waffenschmied*. Mahler had recently conducted a new production of the
work at the Hofoper, which opened on 4 January 1904.
† Putzi's nanny.
‡ Pivka, a railway junction on the line between Ljubljana and Trieste.

decided to schedule a performance of it here. The more he hears it, as he told me, the better he likes it. – This morning was the rehearsal. The orchestra is perfectly adequate and very willing. In four rehearsals Steinbach has made an excellent job of preparing it. The soprano soloist is first rate, with a clear timbre and a straightforward approach. – Having taken lunch with Steinbach, I went for another two-hour walk (alone). Tomorrow, after the concert, Steinbach has arranged a big binge in his house, probably to compensate for the drubbing I can expect from the audience by serving me a tasty supper.

Steinbach will probably come with me to Cologne, to hear my Third Symphony. If only I knew what you're going to do. Przistaupinski is keeping me informed, but all I can gather is that nothing has yet been decided. I trust in your common sense, dear Almschl, that you won't do anything that doesn't agree with you or Putzi. – I'm going to the theatre again this evening, this time to 'As you like it' <by Shakespeare>.

If only I had received a few lines from you. If you wrote yesterday, your letter might still arrive today. Warm and tender greetings to you, and kisses to you both.   Your Gustav

70   Mainz [23 March 1904]
                                                    Hof von Holland

My dearest Almschel,

<u>Przist</u>. cabled me yesterday evening to say that the train tickets had been attended to. – I imagine you will have received my express letter around 5.30 or soon after, i.e. shortly before leaving for Abbazia. While I put these lines to paper, you will already be sunning yourself on the beach, Putzi will be rolling her eyes and calling: Papa etc.

Unfortunately I <u>still</u> have no news from you whatsoever! Look, Almschel, you're always reminding me to write, and I always take the greatest of care to do so; why then do I regularly have to wait so long to hear from you?

Today was the final rehearsal. It's all going pretty well; the solo soprano is a concert singer, Fräulein Becker from Cologne, who is really excellent. It's been a pleasure to watch the enthusiasm growing from one rehearsal to the next. Steinbach was very buttoned up to begin with, but he's thawed out completely and has become so warm-hearted and affectionate that it's a joy to observe. – In him I have won another major and very important ally. – Let's hope things go as well for me in Cologne! – What a pity that you <and Mama> can't be here. You would understand and enjoy my work in a completely different light.

After all these exertions I can scarcely wait for the train to arrive at

Mattuglie* on Wednesday morning, and for you, my Almscherl, to collect me from the station in a smart two-seater (if not a brougham). And then for four whole days and nights I shall have nothing to do but relax and stroll around town with you and Mama.

I'm still not entirely certain about the Musikverein, but I do have some idea how it might be managed. We'll talk it all over in Abbazia.

<If only I had heard from you. Now I'll get some fresh air† and take an hour's walk. A thousand greetings and kisses, to Mama too, from Your Gustl

It must be delightful to see how Putzi reacts to all these new impressions. Do take good care of her though!>

The day after this concert, Mahler travelled on to Cologne to rehearse his Third Symphony. Having encountered Emil Steinbach in Mainz, he now made the acquaintance of his brother Fritz.

Meanwhile, the family had set off for Abbazia. After all the trouble Mahler had taken to organize the journey, Alma expressed her gratitude as follows: 'Mahler came on soon afterwards. As usual he travelled by sleeping car, whereas I had to make do with an ordinary seat in a compartment. I picked him up at Mattuglie.'[4]

71   Cologne [24 March 1904]
                                                        Hotel Disch

My dearest Almschi,

Yesterday went pretty well. The audience is said to have been very appreciative, but I'm no judge of that. In my view they seemed a little stupefied, but that's hardly surprising. Afterwards we had a very enjoyable time at Steinbach's. I got home late, but had to get up early. I've just arrived here, on a disgustingly slow train, and now I'm waiting for the Cologne Steinbach to take me to a sectional rehearsal for trombones and trumpets.

I'm pretty tired and would have loved to be with you right now. Here <at the hotel> everyone has delightful memories of the time we spent in Krefeld. I wish you were here!

I'm worried about Putzi, because of the unremittingly cold, rainy weather. Is it just as bad in Abbazia? Many greetings, my Almschili. Your first dear letter arrived here yesterday. I was glad to have heard from you at last.

Write and tell me exactly how your journey was, and how you are feeling.

Fondly, your Gustav

* Last stop on the railway line to Abbazia.
† Orig.: 'auf die Luft' (Bohemian dialect for 'in die [frische] Luft').

72   Cologne [25 March 1904]
                                                              Hotel Disch

My dearest Almschl,
First of all: Fritz (Steinbach) is really delighted with me.*
The orchestra is wonderful, a real joy. The chorus has also already been to
rehearsal: excellent! All that's missing so far is the alto solo; I'm rehearsing
now (at 6 o'clock). – The best of it all is that I've had to promise Steinbach
the world première of my Fifth Symphony. He'll rehearse it with the orchestra all summer, then I shall come to conduct the final rehearsals. The performance is scheduled for 14 (or 15) October. That would be really
wonderful. Who knows, here in Cologne I may have found an artistic habitat for myself. 'Am Rhein, am Rhein, da wachsen unsre Reben!'† Hurrah for
today.
I'm dead beat.‡
I'm taking all my meals at the Steinbachs'; they're very kind and won't let me
go. Tomorrow evening he's invited the critics. Very thoughtful of him.
But I can't wait to get to Mattuglie!
Fondest greetings   Your Gustav

<No news from you again today.>

73   Cologne [27 March 1904]
                                                              Hotel Disch

My Almschl,
This, thank heaven, is the last letter I shall be sending you before my journey.
– The final rehearsal went superbly. The orchestra is far better than in
Krefeld. The violins are almost as good as those of the Vienna Philharmonic.
The alto solo (a Frau Hertzer-Deppe) not exactly marvellous (a little too
'theatrical'), but musical and perfectly adequate. To my surprise, the chorus
was not quite as excellent as I would have expected in the Rhineland.
All in all I'm very satisfied, and now that my Third Symphony has roved so
far, I hope it has found a good resting place. It is now agreed that the Fifth
will be given at the first of next season's Gürzenich concerts. Just imagine,
Steinbach wanted to include it in the programme for the Cologne Musikfest
on 20 May, but out of consideration for your condition I rejected the pro-

* Orig.: 'der Fritze (Steinbach) ist nu ganz wech mit mir!' (Saxon dialect).
† 'The Rhine, the Rhine, that's where our vineyards flourish.' From Johann André's popular
Rheinweinlied (publ. 1776) to a poem by Matthias Claudius.
‡ Orig.: 'Ich bin schachmatt' (colloquial, lit. 'I am checkmated').

posal. – I'm quite exhausted. And Hotel Disch is none too comfortable – it's very draughty, and there's a dreadful din day and night.

I have been Steinbach's guest for every meal. <Fortunately he's leaving tonight.> Unless anything untoward should occur, I should be with you on Wednesday morning. If the weather is still so bad, <u>don't</u> come to the station to meet me, but stay in your room. Except for my first day here, which was beautiful, I haven't seen any sunshine at all. Most of the time it's been raining – enough to drive you to despair.

<Once again I was stupid enough not to bring any sensible shoes with me. And Almscherl, you also forgot my <u>cutlery</u>.>

What do you mean by the 'gaps in my letters'? They're at least three times as long as yours, yet you're still not satisfied!

I can just imagine how Putzi is.

But take good care of her.

<Best wishes to you and Mama.> Looking forward to seeing you soon, my Almscherl. Your Gustav

Mahler returned to Vienna the following day, 28 March.

74^U Telegram   Vienna, 29 March [1904]

cologne exceptionally good fifth symphony mid-october arrive tomorrow morning fondest greetings   gustav

Shortly after dispatching the above telegram Mahler set out on the thirteen-hour train journey to Abbazia. After the Easter weekend he returned home alone. Back in Vienna, he made arrangements for the family's return journey.

75^U   [Vienna, 5 April 1904]

My Almschili,

Now at last I can pull myself together and write a letter. Yesterday was a dreadful day. I didn't have a moment's rest. Wondra is ill, and over the past fortnight a pile of work has accumulated.

I had a very pleasant journey. The sleeping cars are very <u>comfortable,</u> and I came to the conclusion that you should take <u>three second-class sleepers.</u> Then you're entitled to a <u>whole second-class compartment</u> (which is just the same as first-class), which costs about 15–18 fl. – I discussed it with Pollak, and he agreed with me. From here it's <u>impossible</u> to be certain whether that ass of a station-master at <u>Mattuglie</u> will get a compartment for you. And surely you recall the confusion about seats last year. So go <u>at once</u> to the <u>travel agency</u> in

Hotel Stefanie and book a <u>complete</u> second-class compartment for Saturday evening. As I've discovered, you only need to pay for <u>three seats</u>. Fanni should <u>sit with you</u>, and when you arrive at St. Peter (at about <u>10 o'clock</u>) she should move to <u>any</u> one of the first-class carriages and keep her eyes open for a dashing young ticket inspector, coachman or something of the kind. That way you'll have a comfortable night, and our little one will be well cared for. – Otherwise I can try at least to <u>secure</u> a <u>half-compartment</u> for you. You, Almscherl, could travel in it on your own, or possibly <u>Mama</u>. – After all, I have you all to think of, and you'll see that I can take care of everything! But <u>whatever happens</u> reserve an entire second-class compartment; that will be the safest. Yesterday I was kept busy until 2.15 and had to put off Carl (unfortunately he didn't get my cable until three o'clock, so he waited here until after two), then I had lunch with Arnold [Rosé] at Hotel <u>Imperial</u>. He had much to tell me about Alfi. Later we took a careful look at the entire orchestral budget. Then he accompanied me to the Schottenring, and again he managed to bring the conversation round to Alfi. – From there I drove to Carl's, where I met Pollak. We went for a walk, had high tea, then I drove back to the theatre. Pollak sat in my box and wallowed in The Tales of Hoffmann, while I corrected my Fifth Symphony, which has to go back to Leipzig tomorrow so that everything will be ready in good time. This morning I sent off the travelling bag. It should serve you well on your journey. This afternoon I'm going to the Secession.* – Fritz† has just called, and I had lunch with him and Arnold at the Erzherzog Karl. – It's been a lovely day here, and I hope you're having good weather too. – Don't be silly, Almschl, take your open carriage in the afternoon, so you can get some fresh air in your lungs. The enclosed press cutting by Neitzel comes from the <u>Kölnische Zeitung</u>. I find his article makes pretty good sense.‡ How <u>tedious</u> life is here without you! I don't feel the least urge to sit at home. I'll send you the key to the travelling bag in a separate envelope. – I almost forgot, yesterday, once I had finished, I dined with Pollak at Hotel Imperial, and after the performance we were joined by Arnold [Rosé] and [Bruno] Walter (who's in very high spirits). – Once again

---

* The 20th Secessionist Exhibition, which opened on 25 March and ran until 12 June. Three artists were on display, Adolf Böhm, Kolo Moser and Carl Moll.
† The archaeologist Friedrich (Fritz) Löhr. Like many of Mahler's older friends, Alma could not abide him. After the death of Bernard and Marie Mahler in 1889, Löhr was appointed guardian of Otto Mahler and his sisters Justine and Emma.
‡ Neitzel had written of the *Third Symphony* that it was easy to discern not a programme, but underlying moods and changes of mood, *joie de vivre* and despair, 'scornful, satanic laughter' and 'cynical gnashing of teeth'; Mahler's titanic will knew to 'transpose the inspiration of an hour or a moment into art', his handling of themes and his masterful sense of colour were 'universally uplifting and ennobling'.

there was much talk of Alfi, but later also of other things, e.g. the <u>moderne Vereinigung</u>* in Vienna.

Greetings from Walter, Arnold, Fritz etc. I hear that Justi will be arriving on Thursday. A thousand kisses, my Almscherl.   Your Gustav

76^U   [Vienna, 6 April 1904]

My dearest,

Maybe Pollak has managed to reserve a <u>compartment</u> for you after all. He was here this morning and explained everything to me. If he can manage it today, he'll cable you this afternoon. In that case the so-called 'cours coupé' in the <u>sleeping car</u> would be kept for you. It's an ordinary <u>full-size compartment</u> (albeit a very comfortable one) in the sleeping car, and normally it's available for officials only. It would cost you <u>nothing</u>, all you need is regular train tickets. – I would advise you to let Mama, Fanni and the children use it. – But Almscherl, you should also book <u>two</u> first-class <u>sleepers</u> (half-compartment), so that you're provided for, whatever happens. If need be you could sleep in this <u>half-compartment</u> on your own, and the others would still be taken care of.

I can't wait for you all to get back. This return journey is a confounded nuisance.

No doubt you've already read in the papers about our bad luck with Wondra. Some lunatic took a pot shot at him, now he's <u>in hospital</u>, and I have to take care of the mountains of paperwork on my own.

Your second letter was so sweet, my Almscherl – once again, considerable progress in every sense.

Yesterday I had dinner with Carl and Arnold at the Spatenbräu.

Today I had lunch with Arnold at the Erzherzog Karl. I've been wandering through the streets of Vienna like a lost soul,[†] and I'll be absolutely thrilled to see you back.

There's absolutely no news. I'm hard at work rehearsing Falstaff. The third set of proofs[‡] is going off today.

Write and tell me exactly what you want to do about your return journey.

Many kisses to you and Putzl, and (seeing as you set so much store by it) I remain your true[§]   Gustl

---

* The *Vereinigung schaffender Tonkünstler in Wien* (Society of Creative Composers in Vienna) was inaugurated a few days later, on 23 April. Zemlinsky was appointed president, Schoenberg vice-president, and at the suggestion of Guido Adler, Mahler was invited to assume the honorary presidency.

† Orig.: 'verlassenes Waserl' (Viennese dialect: abandoned orphan).

‡ i.e. for the score of the *Fifth Symphony*.

§ Orig.: '3er' (cf. footnote on p. 145).

77^U [Vienna, 7 April 1904]

My dearest Almscherl,

I hope all is now in order, and that I shall take delivery of you, safe and well, on Saturday. Did you receive my two telegrams yesterday? To my previous letter I should add that yesterday I drove out to see <u>G. Adler</u>, who was so thrilled that he almost fainted. I spent an hour with him, then he accompanied me part of the way back. Just as I was leaving, Frau Mimose[*] arrived and promptly pursed her mouth into a line like this ‿. Justi arrived today, and I had lunch with her. She'd brought all kinds of Hamburg gossip with her – only agreeable things, fortunately. Nobody has taken my marriage 'amiss', and that's quite something.

Rumours of your many talents are already legion in Hamburg, and next season, when you make your first appearance with me, you'll be greeted as a Wonder of the Seas.[†]

Unfortunately I'm overburdened with work, and tomorrow, to crown it all, I also have to conduct Tristan.

Tomorrow I'll have lunch at home, so I can have a good rest in the afternoon. I've invited Justi and Arnold to join me. I'm really very concerned about you. I can scarcely eat for worry! But I'd rather make a bit of a fool of myself than rush around like a lost sheep. All this time Ernestine[‡] has been very kind and attentive.

I've also spent a good deal of time with Carl. He won't be at all pleased that you're arriving home tomorrow, because he has to spend the evening at the Lanckoroński's.[§] Mama will probably have dinner with us, and then Carl will simply come and collect her.

<u>No</u> letter from you today! What's this, my lazybones? You could at least have sent a card.

An embrace and a big kiss to you, my Almschi, and many greetings to Mama from your Gustav

Mahler's second daughter, Anna Justine ('Gucki'), was born on 15 June. It was no easy birth, and subsequently Alma remained in confinement for three weeks.

On 21 June Mahler set off for Maiernigg, where he evidently wished to work undisturbed on his Sixth Symphony, leaving Alma and the children in

---

[*] Guido Adler's wife Betty (née Bergen). Her nickname 'Mimose' implies a hypersensitive character.
[†] In the event, Alma did not join Mahler on his trip to Hamburg the following year (cf. letters 128–131).
[‡] Orig.: 'Ern.' : a housemaid.
[§] Karl Graf Lanckoroński, a noted Viennese patron of the arts.

*the care of Anna Moll. After the exertions of the previous season he was in a
state of exhaustion. Before leaving Vienna he sent Alma his customary card
from the railway station.*

78^U Postcard   Vienna, 21 June 1904^P

My beloved A.,
Had a leisurely dinner, bought tickets. Luggage <u>had</u> to be deposited, but cost
only 4 fl. altogether. I'm already worried! Don't mention Albi* to our 'suburban' sort† – no point in provoking resentment shortly before departure.
After the holidays we'll sort it all out. I found time to pay Hassinger everything I owed him. A thousand kisses. <u>Take care of yourself</u>, my Almschi!
Your Gustl

79^U Telegram   Klagenfurt, 22 June 1904^E

arrived happily   warmest greetings gustav

80^U Postcard   Klagenfurt, 22 June 1904^P

My dear A.,
Just arrived, sent Elise ahead to Maiernigg, had breakfast in Café Schiberth
(no longer as salubrious as before, it seems), had a haircut, and now home
per pedes via Loretto, where Anton is expecting me.‡ The weather has
improved; I'm told it rained yesterday. I had a <u>lousy</u> journey. You really must
insist that <u>Wittek</u>§ gets you a <u>whole compartment</u> in a <u>new</u> carriage. The <u>old</u>
ones are real boneshakers. Many greetings to you all!
Your old Gustl

*Mahler's state of mind can well be imagined. On the one hand his profession
forced him to limit his work 'for the benefit of mankind' (letter 14) to the
summer months, on the other he was head of a family that called for his
affection and attention. Before setting to work on a new composition, he
arranged for the building of a small playground for his children.*

* Albine Adler, a friend of Justine's, whom Mahler had known since his early days in Iglau.
† According to Alma (ELM I), '"Suburban sort" (Vorstadtnatur) was Mahler's way of referring to his sister J[ustine].'
‡ From the railway station in Klagenfurt to Maria Loretto on the Wörthersee (a spot favoured
by sightseers) is a distance of about one and a half miles. From there Mahler was rowed across
the lake to his villa by Anton, the caretaker.
§ Heinrich Ritter von Wittek, Austrian Minister of Railways, an old friend of the Molls.

81 [Maiernigg, 23 June 1904]

My dearest Almschili,

Yesterday I went to bed dog-tired at 9.30 and slept through until 8 o'clock. Then I had my first breakfast in the 'Häuschen'. – It's strange: every time I come here the climate seems to get me down. The moment I reach Maiernigg I lose all energy and joie de vivre, and it usually takes two or three weeks to get back to normal. – You experienced the same thing during your last two summers here. It's no different this time, except that I miss you and have to slink about on my own all day. Heaven knows how long I'll need to pull myself together.

I haven't felt so muted* for a long time. The only consolation is that the climate will do the children a power of good, so at least they will benefit from it. But I'd really prefer to put the villa up for sale.[†]

In my upstairs room it smells awful, something like mouldy paste. They say it comes from the <u>paint</u>, which they had to use after repairing the cracks in the plasterwork. – For this reason I'm spending most of my time in the Böcklin salon, but I have to sleep upstairs, and only hope it won't do me any harm. You might ask Carl if he has an idea what substances these 'painters' use, and what it is that's causing such a smell.

I've given a great deal of thought to the question of the fence. The place we had in mind for it turns out to be <u>far too small</u>; Putzi could hardly swing a cat there. But there's a place further down which would be ideal. I've taken a close look at it, and Theuer[‡] has advised me too. I want to have it completely <u>fenced in</u> and put down <u>10 fl.</u> worth of fine sand. – In future years it will give the children a little area where they can play <under supervision>. If you agree, I'll have it done. It's the place where we keep the bench, table and two chairs <(the wooden ones)>:

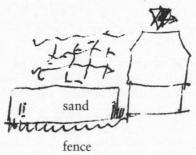

fence

* Orig.: 'sordinirt'.
[†] Mahler sold his Maiernigg villa, after the death of his daughter Maria (Putzi), in 1908.
[‡] Alfred Theuer, who supervised the building of Mahler's villa, lived nearby, at Villa Schwarzenfels.

Snakes can get in there just as well as they can down here, but anyway the children should never play without someone to supervise them. (Besides, not all water-snakes are poisonous; in fact, poisonous animals are only found in particularly hot, dry places. Ask any doctor.) – There's no other way of doing it. So please write and tell me what you think. At any rate, the area in front of the house, which we had initially envisaged, is impossible because it's too small.

Just to be sure, I'll have all the steeper slopes in front of the house fenced off. – At last the hail and thunder has stopped, and I'll try to get this letter posted right away.

Warmest greetings and kisses from   your Gustav

<Dearest Mama,
Warmest greetings and (Almschel, look the other way) a kiss to you too. Write and tell me about everything.
Do talk Almschl out of her silly fear of snakes (after all, you can meet up with them anywhere, in Plankenberg too). It's just that in the countryside children need taking particular care of.>

82   [Krumpendorf, 24 June 1904]

My dearest Almschili,
The first day (the first whole day) is over. Simply dreadful! Apart from the musty smell of paint in the bedroom, I struggled vainly to assemble the frag-ments of my inner self (how long will it take to pull myself together?). Then meetings with Theuer <(who has already worked everything out and is now waiting for your verdict),> then I took a bath and ate my lunch. I spent the whole day thumbing through Wagner's correspondence with the Wesendoncks.* These insights into probably the most important chapter in the life of this unique and cherished great figure: I found them truly uplifting. After that I had intended to go out into the woods, but a hailstorm broke loose and raged on into the night, ruining all my plans. To divert myself I played the piano – chamber music by Brahms, some of which, I regret to say, is sterile note-spinning. Had I not suddenly chanced on a delightful Sextet in B-flat major, I would have lost all the faith I ever placed in him,† as I have in myself

---

* Mahler was reading Wolfgang Golther's first edition of the *Briefwechsel zwischen Richard Wagner und Mathilde Wesendonck*, Rostock, 1904.
† Mahler's opinion of Brahms had always been ambivalent. During the course of his career he nevertheless conducted several of the major works, including the first three symphonies, the *Haydn Variations*, the *First Piano Concerto* and the *Violin Concerto*.

during the last few days. – Then more Wagner letters, which in this context acquired a demonic aspect high above all worldly affairs. I also read a few pages of Tolstoy's 'My Confession':* frightfully cheerless stuff, barbarously self-destructive, questioning, but in a distorted way that leads him unrelentingly to dismantle all nobility of heart and mind. Once or twice I ventured out into the rain, ordered a cup of coffee at Maiernigg, but it was mud-coloured, so I didn't touch it. I was surrounded by petit bourgeois – old hags with their knitting, and dotards eating cheese – who soon scared me away. And so at last the day was over and I fell into bed (smelly paste and all) and slept till 8.30. Today I was in slightly better spirits. Your card, above all, dear Almscherl <and Mama's dear letter> helped to dispel the monotony. Now I've taken the customary footpath to Klagenfurt, am sitting here in the café (Kaiser von Österreich, because the female staff at Café Schiberth have made the place intolerable) drinking coffee and chocolate and writing these lines. They delivered the rowing boat today as well. It looks like new – <I had to pay 24 crowns.> I've some shopping to do, then I'll walk to Loretto, where Anton will again fetch me with the boat. Keep your spirits up, my Almschi. I'm counting the days to your arrival. Does Putzi sometimes ask after me? Warmest greetings and kisses to you all from your   Gustl

<Emma's letter was perfectly pleasant, wasn't it?>
Almschi, on no account are you to write to me. It can't be good for you!

To emphasize this last point, Mahler addresses all but the first line of his next letter to his mother-in-law.

83^U Postcard   Krumpendorf, 25 June 1904^P

Dearest,
No news from you today, I'm afraid.
Dearest Mama,
Do write to me every day, even if it's only a concise bulletin on a postcard. I've been sleeping ten to eleven hours a day – like a stuffed dumpling. I don't understand why, as actually I'm not over-tired in the least. I'm sure it's the air, combined with the stench of painters' paste. Appalling! I've taken to mooching about on my own and have been taking a closer look at the locals. I'm certain there's no more stupid, useless a breed in the whole of Europe. Hopeless!
Best wishes   Your Gustav

* Leo Tolstoy, *Ispoved*, publ. 1884; Engl. trans. (*My Confession*) publ. 1887.

84   [Maiernigg, 26 June 1904]

My dearest Almschel,

I wonder if life is treating you as well as it's treating me. It's been raining all day, and I'm sitting around in the house; rather like when there's a storm on the ski slopes. – Jergitsch* came today, and tomorrow he'll send me the estimate. We'll take care to arrange everything to your satisfaction. You'll be happy, Almschel, when our little one can romp in the sand in this excellent air (and how I wish you were already here!). Tomorrow I'll go to Klagenfurt and buy a cot. – I've asked about the snakes too – they're just water-snakes. They live on the shore of the lake, and they're <u>not</u> poisonous. Poisonous snakes need a <u>dry</u>, <u>hot</u> climate, and don't go near water. Ask any zoologist! So there really is no need to worry. – I'm slowly getting accustomed to the isolation, just as with anything that's inevitable. But never in my life have I felt so <u>lonely</u>!

<I haven't called on the Theuers yet. I can't persuade myself to go. You really have no need to worry. Today she came to see Elise, and gave her a chicken for me (saying she had actually intended to invite me round, but didn't want to disturb me). That chicken has kept me fed all day. But Almschel, please send me <u>butter</u> right away and also two loaves of <u>Graham bread</u>, for that's the most important part of my diet, and the rolls are inedible.

At the end of the letter I've made a list of the other things you should bring for me.

Meanwhile, I've made myself comfortable in <u>your salon</u>, brought my books and sheet music downstairs (because of the paint smell in my room), and now I'm making your little room really cosy. I include a letter from Frau Neisser, which I'll leave you to reply to. After all, you owe her a letter.

Now the list of things to bring:

1) The blue blanket (the one Frau Binder was using)
2) The leather strop for sharpening my razors (I left it in the bedroom)
3) one of my old suits – I don't have any really warm ones here
4) another of my white caps (from Herrenhuter)
5) ink for my fountain pen

If anything else springs to mind, I'll mention it in my next letter.>

Meanwhile, I've read through almost all of Brahms. What a puny figure he cuts, and how narrow-minded. Good Lord, just think of the force with which the genius of Richard Wagner must have struck him. Brahms must

---

* Unidentified; evidently a craftsman or builders merchant in Klagenfurt.

have turned every penny in his pocket of ideas twice over, just to scrape by! But I wouldn't want to be unjust. His '<u>so-called development sections</u>' are the crux of the problem. Rarely does he know what to do with his themes, beautiful as they often are. Only Beethoven and Wagner were true masters of that art.

So farewell for now to you and our little Putzis <and even if you're more steady on your pins again, don't get on Mama's wick.*> And now (by the light of two candles) I'll turn my attention to Bach. After Brahms, one needs to come up for air.† Already longing to see you   Your Gustl

85ᵁ   [Maiernigg, 27 June 1904]

Dearest,

I have sent the Hellmanns a cable, as you requested. Today I also went to see Riedl about a cot. I sorted out the most suitable types, and am enclosing a catalogue of the available ones. I imagine you will want to choose between nos. 61, 62 and 64. It hasn't stopped raining here. As a result I have to spend all day reading etc. Not exactly good for my eyes. Amongst the works of Brahms I have at last discovered a Piano Quartet in G minor which I find entirely satisfactory. Being a conscientious chronicler, it's my duty to tell you so. – I'm very eager to hear what it was that [Guido] Adler had to tell you so urgently. No doubt it was something utterly trivial. Maybe he feels the need to rescue me once more! By now you must have at least some idea of when you'll be in a position to leave. Please let me know. Tomorrow our little girl will be two weeks old; with luck I can expect your arrival the following week. But don't overdo it! By the sound of it, the house is full of visitors right now. – I have to admit that I wouldn't mind being there myself some of the time. It's not exactly edifying to sit here amidst grazing herds with Elise the milkmaid as sole companion. And nothing but salads! While Anton was rowing me over, he filled me in on every mishap that has occurred in Carinthia during the past twelve months. The latest news is that an owl has made its nest in my wooden shack, and seeing that the bird refuses to take heed of the round opening, Anton feels obliged to pronounce the death sentence.‡

Heartfelt greetings   Your Gustav

---

* Orig.: 'und pisak' jetzt die arme Mama nicht, seitdem Du wieder Dein Schnoferl nach oben machst' (Austrian slang).
† Orig.: 'ein bischen auspusten'.
‡ The bird had evidently made its nest in the privy adjoining the shack.

86^U [Maiernigg, 27 June 1904]

Dearest,

In all haste I'm sending you the enclosed cutting from a Berlin paper. It appears that washing with boric acid* before breast-feeding is not quite as harmless as was thought. Think it over, I beg of you. If the worst comes to the worst, the lesser of two evils seems to be to wash the breasts not with boric acid, which is harmful, but with clear water or liniment (in the latter case, first make sure they're really dry). After three days of rain it's looking brighter this afternoon. I shall take the opportunity to take a cycle ride and give Herr Jergitsch a dig in the ribs (he still hasn't tendered an estimate). So you'll be out of confinement on <u>Saturday</u>? In that case it won't be long before you can leave. I'll call at Klagenfurt station today to ask about transit. Would you prefer a sedan or an open carriage?

Warmest greetings   Your Gustav

87 [Maiernigg, 28 June 1904]
Tuesday

Dearest Almschili,

After all that, I forgot to send the cutting yesterday, and maybe you'll be more eager about it than it's actually worth. So here it is (unless I forget it again after all).

Jergitsch's new estimate, as enclosed, is lower than the first one. Jergitsch would like to know what colour you'd like it <u>painted</u>. Please write straight away and tell me what you've decided. – It will be ready long before Tuesday (today week), and there will be sand in abundance – strewn all around, and with a special heap to play with. To prevent your having to burden yourself with useless items, I'll buy spades and things for Putzi in Klagenfurt.

In Klagenfurt I also managed to track down the finest of carriages, with rubber wheels and excellent suspension (it was bought specially for the Kaiser). If your doctor permits it, this is the vehicle in which you shall ride, like a princess, to your palace. I simply can't wait to hear your latest news.

So you'll be out of confinement on Saturday?

I just gave Elise 5 fl., because she wants to go shopping in Klagenfurt tomorrow. At the grocer's I found some splendid bottles of Bavarian beer, and I've been

---

* Boric acid or borax (hydrogen orthoborate), which possesses antiseptic properties, was formerly used in a borax and honey preparation given to teething infants on their soothers. Administered in larger doses, borax is mildly toxic; its use has been associated with skin, eye and respiratory irritation.

imbibing one every evening. – The weather is pretty lousy. Now and then, when it stops raining, I grab the chance to »walk« or »ride«[*] (on my bicycle). And so I'm fretting the time away until you arrive, and in emulation of the ancient philosophers (in contrast to those of today), or almost in the style of the most recent (the Dehmels of this world), I am making the best of things. My Almscherl, some time I shall send you off to the mountains[†] for a fortnight, so you can see what it's like. Even so, I can scarcely stoop to the duties you are currently obliged to perform. But I shall be as pleased as Punch when at last I have someone to talk to! I kiss you a thousand times, my dearest, and take good care of yourself, so I can hold you in my arms very soon.   Your Gustav

Warmest greetings to Mama and Carl.

I've discovered another piano quartet by Brahms, the one in C minor,[‡] which we played four-hands last year. The first two movements are wonderful. Unfortunately the other two are trivial by comparison. So far, the G minor quartet is the only one which meets completely with my approval.[§] <Then I'm reading Wilde's Picture of Dorian Gray, which I'm finding very stimulating. I'll be interested to see how the story develops.> I have put Tolstoy aside for the time being; one needs a break from him – but I'm speaking only of the prophetical writings. His short stories and novels are quite a different matter.

For reasons known only to herself, Alma published the postscript to letter 87 at the end of letter 135.

88[U]   [Wörthersee, June 1904]
                                          Hotel und Pension Hugelmann

No news from you so far, my Almschi. Today is the first nice day, and I'm taking advantage of it to cycle round the lake. I've just stopped for a break and a cup of coffee. The ship is about to leave and will take these greetings with it. I'll have to make haste, otherwise it won't reach you tomorrow. Warmest greetings   Your Gust

---

[*] Orig.: 'Rid'.
[†] Orig.: 'Alm' (mountain pasture); the pun is probably intended, also the ribald allusion to milking.
[‡] Brahms, *Piano Quartet in C minor*, op. 60.
[§] Orig.: Sentence order reversed. It is nevertheless clear that it was the C-minor Piano Quartet of which Mahler felt that the last two movements were 'trivial by comparison'.

89^U [Maiernigg, June 1904]

My love,

You'll have to make do without a letter today (or rather tomorrow). Riding along the forest paths, which are still appallingly muddy and bumpy after the heavy rains earlier this year, I lost my way, and won't be able to post this letter in time. I paid another visit to the Spintiker ponds,* which brought back fond memories. I found it hard to believe that you and I had once dallied there. Today I finally got round to calling on the Theuers. Heavens, what a business! Both the mothers-in-law were there, and Theuer was getting the feel of his motorcycle (his latest craze). He had propped it on its stand and was wobbling about on it, making the most awful stench. But the Theuers were very agreeable and not in the least offended. After quite some time, being uncertain whether to put my hands over my ears or hold my nose, I begged for mercy, whereupon Theuer dismounted, throttled down the motor and spent half an hour showing me exactly how it worked. Then the subject changed to the Grünwalds,† and finally he told me the latest gossip, namely that Mrs G. had given birth to a baby boy. The poor woman was in labour for forty hours, and in the end they had to give her an anaesthetic and deliver the child with forceps. Tomorrow I hope at last to hear what you have decided about the cot, painting the fence etc., so I can make all necessary arrangements. How much longer must I wait for you? I'm pining away. Your card about the changing-table arrived today. I'll look for one in town tomorrow.

For today, my dearest, a thousand kisses, and greetings to Mama. Putzi will probably read this letter herself.   Your Gustav

[top edge of first page:] My socks are in a bad way! They're all <u>darned</u> at the heels, which makes them very tight, and they're full of potatoes too. Bring some new ones with you!

90^U Postcard Klagenfurt, 1 July 1904^P

D. A. I'm writing this from town, where I've ordered the cot according to your instructions, and two <u>Thonet</u> children's stools.‡ The former cost 32 crowns, the latter 21 crowns. But you still haven't written to say <u>what colour</u>

---

* Ponds between Maiernigg and Keutschach.
† Unidentified friends of Mahler who lived in Krumpendorf, on the opposite shore of the Wörthersee.
‡ Thonet Bros., famous since 1830 for 'bentwood' furniture, which was practical and inexpensive.

they should paint the wire fence to keep out the snakes. Could my letter possibly have gone astray? So today you're on your feet for the first time. I'm writing this postcard to celebrate the event – standing up, as if proposing a toast. Three cheers for Alma! You won't have to bring the strop with you. I bought a new one here. Warmest greetings   G.

91   [Maiernigg, 3 July 1904]

My dear,

The rainfall is unremitting. Crashes of thunder, lightning: how I adore it. For me it's the most beautiful spectacle the lake has to offer. The raging storm outside, and here inside I'm sitting all snug and warm in your salon, with a lamp, books, sheet music, a piano and writing paper. But it's too late for today's post, so tomorrow there will be no letter for you. That's the disadvantage, but only for you. – How long will it go on like this? If only there were more possibilities here, if only the paths were firmer and more easily passable. I'm spending my time as it pleases me, in contemplation of the world – blissful, but also expectant. Unfortunately I'm beginning to run out of reading material. And as I can't follow the example of Quintus Fixlein, who wrote his own library piece by piece <(as soon as he found a new title in a learned journal, he promptly claimed its authorship for himself)>, I'll have to buy something when I next go to Klagenfurt.

Today, Sunday, these pests on the lake and in the streets are creating no end of a hubbub. As soon as one of these morons is fired by a sense of well-being – boom! The bubble has to burst, so the explosion of joy can be heard by all: Yeah, yeah! and all that. Tom, Dick and Harry[*] have to let it be known that they're feeling pleased with themselves. – <Warmest thanks to Mama for her kind letter, which arrived today. I was so glad to hear such full news of our little Putzis at last. Yes indeed, if only you were here. Why is Carl travelling to Carlsbad? Tomorrow I'll go to Klagenfurt and jolt Jergitsch into action. I certainly hope that all will be ready by the time you arrive.>

The Wilde is very exciting, but at the same time rather shallow. The idea itself isn't so bad, but it's spoiled by his arbitrary, rather amateurish treatment. It wouldn't be suitable reading for you. – Having worked through all of Brahms, I returned to Bruckner. A curiously mediocre figure. – The one spent too long 'in the ladle', the other was in need of that very treatment. Now I've come to rest with Beethoven. <u>Only he and Richard</u> [Wagner] are beyond reproach – and <u>nobody</u> else!! Mark my words! You can look for-

---

[*] Orig.: 'Hans Affe und Peter Viech' (Hans Ape and Peter Brute).

ward to reading his letters [to Mathilde Wesendock], <and so can Mama>. It was about time that someone put an end to this wretched wrangling between the hangers-on on both sides.

With love and kisses* Your Gustav

Mahler's reference to 'Quintus Fixlein' reflects his enthusiasm for the works of Jean Paul. Here, however, his memory fails him. The character 'who wrote his own library piece by piece' was not the hero of Jean Paul's Leben des Quintus Fixlein *(1796),† but the schoolmaster Maria Wuz in the idyll* Leben des vergnügten Schulmeisterlein Maria Wuz in Auenthal *(1793).*

In Mahler's comments on Brahms and Bruckner he alludes to a scene from Act V of Ibsen's Peer Gynt. *Here, shortly before his death, Peer meets with a transcendental character named the Button-Moulder, who addresses him with the words: 'Look, here it is written: Peer Gynt shalt thou summon. He has set at defiance his life's design; clap him into the ladle with other spoilt goods.'*

92ᵁ Postcard   [Maiernigg, 4 July 1904]

My Almschili,
I can well understand your impatience! Therefore I shall send you my copy of the [Wagner–Wesendonck] correspondence straight away. It's in such good condition, you should be able to swap it for anything you wish for. As long as the book doesn't excite you too much, I'm sure it will provide you with the finest reading matter for those long, tedious hours before your departure.
The sand has been delivered and is being set down. What a treat for Putzi! I'll close now, so I can take this card to be posted right away. I'll probably write again this afternoon; for now just a thousand kisses, my dearest. Already now, I'm frightfully worried about you all!
Your Gustav

93ᵁ   [Maiernigg, 4 July 1904]

Dearest,
Nothing but rain (with the usual intervals, when the sun burns rather than shines). But I'm not feeling irritable on that account. Sometimes one has to

---

* Orig.: 'Dich vielmals abbusselnd'.
† *Leben des Quintus Fixlein aus funfzehn Zettelkästen gezogen; nebst einem Mussteil und einigen Jus de tablette*, Bayreuth, 1796; publ. in English (transl. Thomas Carlyle) as *Quintus Fixlein*, London, 1827.

put one's own philosophy to the test. And if I had a few more books here like the volume of letters I sent you today, I'd be able to hold out quite a bit longer. – In view of the fact that the wretched weather is preventing me from going for rides, today I devised a new form of sport to compensate for the lack of exercise. (In weather like this Toblach would be no fun either. Whether I set off for at least a day's worth of mountain air depends on whether I can rid myself of my current physical depression by taking things particularly easy.) I have been filling wheelbarrows with sand, transporting it from the road, where it was delivered, to the playpen on the lakeside, then emptying it onto the ground and raking it smooth.

It's an exercise that leaves me dripping with perspiration.

Write and tell me whether my package has arrived. Tomorrow it will be three weeks since Guckerl was born and a fortnight since I moved into my hermitage here. – Within a week at the most, my Almschili, I hope to be holding you in my arms. I feel totally starved of your affection. I believe it's the longest we have ever been separated. Incidentally, I went around all day today in the belief that I'd been here for three weeks, until Elise pointed out that I was wrong – which amused me greatly.

I greet you from the bottom of my heart, my love.

Gustav

Tell me, is Mama offended that I haven't been replying directly to her dear letters? I know you're feeling very restless at the moment, and that your need for letters to take your mind off things is greater than hers. Does she read them too?

94[U] Postcard   [Maiernigg]* 5 July 1904[P]

M. d. A.,

I went to Klagenfurt today and cleared things up with Jergitsch, who promised to finish the job off <u>this</u> week. Is there really no chance of your arriving here on Sunday already? I wonder what Fleischmann[†] will have to say. – On the way back I was caught in one of those windy showers typical of the Wörthersee, and arrived home soaked to the skin (I swathed myself from head to foot in blankets, of course). It's still pouring even now. But that has actually been the tenor of every letter so far. People say they don't remember a higher water level. Fortunately the lie of the land rules out any possibility of flooding. Well, maybe we can expect fine weather soon, and perhaps even

* According to the postmark, the card was dispatched from Klagenfurt.
† Dr Carl Fleischmann, Alma's gynaecologist in Vienna.

– you, my Almschili. No news from you again today. Under the circumstances, I'm not surprised. Warmest greetings   Your G.

95^U   [Maiernigg, July 1904]

My Almschili,
This is really bad news. So you're coming a week later than I had expected?
In that case I shall change my programme, and before you arrive I'll take a
trip to the Dolomites. In fact, I'm rather in need of it, and one has to admit
that we adults find the air here decidedly <u>muggy</u>. However, it should do the
children a power of good. – If I do go, I think I shall set out early next week.
At any rate I'll let you know in advance and give you my address. It's more
practical at this time of year, as it happens, because the summer crush doesn't
begin until the end of July,[*] and some resorts are still quite empty.
I find the enclosed article delightful.[†] – What a shame! If your Papa had been
here, I could have gone with him, and we would both have profited from it.
No need to worry about my cycling either. I ride really slowly – and not very
often. In recent days, despite my extreme moderation, I've been constantly
unwell. Today I'm beginning to feel myself again.
I've given Elise another 5 fl.
What was Adler's big secret, what did he want?
And now it's time to set out again. It's such a nuisance here: on this side of
the lake everything is far less accessible. If one's in company, even the poor-
est of paths is easier to travel, and one doesn't even notice how often one
rides along the same road.
Don't forget to write every day, even if it's only a card.
Almschili, Addio:
Take good care of yourself.
The fact that your confinement obliges you to remain in Vienna at this time
of year is a dreadful sacrifice for us both, to say nothing of the poor children.
Your Gustav

*Alma's mammary inflammation had worsened to the extent that Dr
Fleischmann finally advised her to cancel her projected journey to Maiernigg
altogether. Mahler therefore had to come to terms with the idea of cutting
short his holiday and returning to Vienna.*

---

[*] Orig.: 'Juni' (June).
[†] The press cutting has not been preserved.

96^U Postcard [Maiernigg, July 1904]

My Almschel,

Your news fills me with dismay. Above all, don't be discouraged! If the worst comes to the worst, we'll simply agree to this minor (perfectly harmless) operation that Fleischmann is proposing. Above all, let us abide entirely by his instructions. With a patient as young and robust as yourself, nature often <u>works</u> (apparent) wonders. So, whatever the case, keep your chin up!

The point of this card is simply to ask you, sans façon, whether I should <u>come home</u>. If so, <u>send a cable</u>, and tomorrow I shall be with you. If not, please wire me anyway, because I shall be anxious to hear from you. I beg you, my dearest, if you think it necessary, don't hesitate to <u>summon</u> me. Otherwise I'd have no peace of mind. As it is, I couldn't sleep last night. So: a telegram please! Keep smiling, my love.   Your Gustav

97^U [Maiernigg, July 1904]

My Almschel,

Very well, I shall stay here. By my reckoning it's only another five days, I believe. Please send exact details of your arrival, as I have to order two carriages, one of which is the de luxe model with rubber wheels, which I have already checked over. For you, nothing could be more suitable! In Vienna one would never find anything quite as fine.

I've just taken delivery of the cot for dear little Putzi, as well as a sweet little table and two stools. – I didn't quite know where to put them, so I had them taken up to the children's room, just as they are, where they await your further instructions.

I've already had the beds changed round, as you requested, and this time dear Mama should sleep a little better, I'm sure. – I'm still occupied with the sand (having given Anton strict orders to leave it entirely to me), but the wire fencing still hasn't arrived. Tomorrow I'll go and give Jergitsch a piece of my mind such as he won't forget in a hurry. To avoid meeting you head-on with a radical change of appearance, I've been shaving from time to time. It's only a small moustache, and even by the time you arrive it won't be making too martial an impression. After that – vederemo. The <u>butter</u> – the Graham bread: have you seen to them? What are your doctors saying? [One line obliterated.] Is the operation really necessary?

Fondest kisses, as ever   Your Gustl

98 [Maiernigg, July 1904]

My dear Almschili,
Today the job was finished! You'll be astounded to see what a dear little playground we've set up for our Putzi. It's a real brainwave. One could still make a host of improvements, but for that I'll wait till you arrive. For the time being I myself have tried out a few ideas. – I can hardly wait for the moment when we inspect it and then bring Putzi along to have a look. She'll find all that the heart could desire. – I still don't know when to expect you. <Don't forget the <u>air cushion</u>.> Write <u>at once</u> and let me know when the doctor says you can leave. It must be dreadful in the apartment.
<Your letter, which arrived today, was so sweet, and truly it filled me with longing for you.> By my reckoning, you'll arrive on Wednesday at about 3.30 p.m. – If it happens to be raining, the luxury rubber-wheeler won't be suitable, because it's an <u>open</u> carriage. In that case I'd prefer them to hitch up a landau. What do you think? Don't forget to reply to this question. I'll be writing twice more, and then – you'll be with me, and there won't be any further need for letters. It's wonderful here, despite everything, and for the immediate future it will be just perfect for the children. But in the long run I can foresee that this mild air is <u>not</u> for us <and Pollak will have to do his best to put the villa on the market.>
A thousand kisses and the most gentle of squeezes from   Your Gustav

99 [Maiernigg, 9 July 1904]
Saturday night

My Almschel,
The sultry weather is beginning to get me down, so I've decided (on the spur of the moment, as I always prefer) to take a trip to the Dolomites. I'll be leaving early tomorrow morning (6.30) for Toblach, then I'll hike via Schluderbach to Misurina, where I can go for walks and spend the night. The following day (Monday) I'll return by the same route, reaching Maiernigg by the evening. <On Tuesday I'll buy all the things you've requested and> on Wednesday, God willing, I can expect you in Klagenfurt. Be sure to write and tell me your exact time of arrival. Your dear letter has just arrived, just before my departure, and I was overjoyed by the insights and affinities you have drawn from that wonderful book.*
Reading such letters, one always tends to draw analogies to oneself in one

---

* i.e. the Wagner–Wesendonck correspondence.

form or another, and that indeed is the great attraction of such a book. On the one hand, one feels capable of following the writers with understanding and sympathy, on the other one enjoys the deep satisfaction of discovering in such elevated circles fellow-sufferers, people whose destinies are just like yours and mine. No matter what course your life may take, this is something you will always experience. A select gathering of solitary individuals assembles in a region beyond time and place to intensify their lives by sharing in each other's company. And even if one discovers only a vague image of oneself, one still scrutinizes its outlines in search of that expression which one understands so well and which is unique to – people of such calibre. In my eyes, your ability to respond to such things is your most valuable contribution to your own life and to mine. Fondest greetings, my Almschi from   Your Gustav

Whenever he came to the end of a period of intensive creative activity, Mahler liked to spend a few days in the Dolomites. The fact that he did so at this juncture implies that he had just completed the second and fifth of his Kindertotenlieder. *In fact, he inferred as much when he wrote to Willem Mengelberg at the end of June: 'I am doing my utmost to pick up the traces of an older composition and, if possible, complete it.'*[5]

100[U] Postcard   [Schluderbach] 11 July 1904[P]

M.A. Yesterday started with a sweltering railway journey, followed by an equally sweltering coach-ride to Schluderbach; then there was a storm and a cloudburst. The heat and discomfort brought on a migraine, and as a result I decided to remain here. Today I'm feeling very well, and at least I can return home feeling refreshed. – One thing, above all: in the <u>middle drawer</u> of my <u>desk</u> (you have the key) are some <u>manuscripts</u> which you should bring with you. I most urgently need the second and third movements of the Sixth Symphony, which I forgot to bring with me. When I get back to Maiernigg, I very much hope to find a letter from you. I can't wait. Here in Schluderbach I bumped into Kapellmeister Weigmann,[*] whom you may remember from Krefeld. I like him very much, and he is – or appears to be – one of my faithful followers. He told me some very amusing anecdotes about Frankfurt. Warmest greetings to you all from   G.

On the return journey Mahler wrote twice to Alma.

---

[*] Orig.: 'Weidmann'. Karl Friedrich Weigmann, who was musical director at Graz.

101^U Postcard [Toblach, 11 July 1904]

Dearest,

Having partaken of a 'diner' (at which I made a point of refusing the soup, and left the other 'courses' untouched), I'm now waiting for the express train and have time to send another message of cordial greeting. Greetings also to Carl and Mama. Send news of Gucki.   Your G.

102^U Villach, 11 July 1904^P
Railway station

My Almischili,

I'll write to you again when I'm in the train. In Toblach I left a postcard addressed to you on the table where I had lunch. Unfortunately it included derogatory remarks about the hotel, so I doubt whether anyone will post it for me. I don't need to write any more, thank the Lord, because you'll soon be there in person. With such a heatwave in Vienna, you poor people must be suffering! It's on my mind all the time. Has everything been arranged for your train journey? All this hiking and biking gives me no pleasure without you. But I've thought out a splendid plan for the two of us. Shall tell you about it later.

Warmest greetings, my dear, for the very last time. I wonder what news I can expect when I get home.   Gustav

One of the Mahlers' house-guests at Maiernigg was Erica Conrat, the second of Hugo Conrat's three daughters. Later she compiled a dossier of letters from the summer of 1904 and presented it to Alma. The typescript, preserved in the Mahler-Werfel Collection in Philadelphia, bears the following comment in Alma's hand: 'Entrusted to me for publication by Frau Dr Erica Tietze,* a friend of my early years, whom we invited to stay with us at Maiernigg.' Here are two extracts from this document:

'The night was fine, and I was sitting alone on the flagstone terrace. [. . .] At 10.30 G.M. came out to join me, and recited verses from the West-Östliche Divan: "Das Lebendige will ich preisen, Das den Flammentod sich wählt – – – Und so lang Du dies nicht hast, Dieses: Stirb und werde! Bist Du nur ein trüber Gast auf dieser dunklen Erde."† Then he spoke of Goethe's

---

* Orig.: 'Tiedze'. Erica Conrat later married the art-historian Hans Tietze.
† Orig.: 'Fernöstliche Divan' (also three trifling misquotations). The poem is 'Selige Sehnsucht', from *Moganni Nameh: Buch des Sängers*: 'Let me praise those living things that choose to die by fire. [. . .] And as long as you lack this sense of "die to be", you are but a dull guest on this dark earth.'

life, saying it was actually a fragment, that he was a "beginner", in the elevated sense of the word: "a beginner in a sphere which I shall never live to attain." Then he spoke at some length, saying there was actually no difference between a rocket that shoots into the air then vanishes into the lake without a sound, and a sun that shines for a billion years. And yet it should be our aim to create works that outlive us, for posterity, we should always aim to better ourselves – but then! [. . .] He spoke of the intoxicating miracle a composer experiences when he hears his work for the first time – quite different from anything he had imagined in his head. Then he went into the house and played a number of short pieces by Bach. They were so clear and simple that one felt transported to Ancient Greece. I was sitting outside, contemplating the sky and the many stars, and far away, while I was listening, I saw rockets falling into the water . . .'

'This afternoon we rowed across to Krumpendorf. Alma took the helm, while G.M. and I worked the oars. G.M. gave the rhythm, and I felt like a whole opera orchestra, indeed I was trembling for fear of missing a beat. Disembarking and ordering high tea was like running the gauntlet: a beautiful woman and a famous man, known to all. [. . .] On the return journey I sat facing Alma. In the light of the setting sun her hair seemed like a halo of red flame, and she herself like some beautiful beast of prey.'

As the summer vacation drew to a close, Mahler set out on another trip to the Dolomites: sure indication that he had brought a further phase of creative activity to a successful conclusion.

103[U] Postcard Dölsach, 18 August 1904[P]

D. A. Have just reached Dölsach, where the weather is wonderful. This morning there was thick fog, and Anton had to tack across the lake in his boat. I'm writing this in the train, in the hope I can send you a further greeting later today, because a card from Heiligenbluth would probably not reach Maiernigg much before I do. I shall pop this one in the post at the station in Dölsach. Kind regards to Erica once again, and a thousand kisses to you. Your G.

O dear! It's just begun to cloud over. Vederemo!

As in the summer of 1901, when Mahler was working on his Fourth Symphony, the summer of 1904 had begun in a state of creative deadlock. In his letters to Alma, he had avoided mentioning the problem directly, for at this difficult time he had no intention of burdening her or the rest of the family with his problems. As the weeks passed, he seems gradually to have recovered from the stresses and strains of the Hofoper, as well as those accompanying the birth of his second child.

This period of relaxation was followed by a veritable frenzy of creative activity. First he completed the cycle of five Kindertotenlieder *(which were to receive their first performance at a concert of the Vereinigung schaffender Tonkünstler in Vienna on 29 January 1905); then, in the space of approximately six weeks, he composed the finale of his Sixth Symphony and the two 'Nachtmusik' movements of the Seventh.*

Following so soon after the birth of her second child, Alma was not at all happy that Mahler was setting poems about infant mortality to music: 'For heaven's sake, this is courting disaster,' she told him.[6] But otherwise she remembered the summer of 1904 as 'fine, undisturbed and happy'.[7]

In contrast to the summer of 1903, Alma had no cause to complain of lack of company. Not only did her parents come to Maiernigg, where they rented a nearby house, but the Mahlers also played host to several friends and acquaintances, including Pollak, Roller and Burckhard.

Alma recalls the following conversation between herself and Mahler while out walking:

I said to him, [. . .] 'The only thing I love about a man is what he achieves. The greater his achievement, the more I feel compelled to love him.'
Mahler: 'That makes it pretty dangerous for me. What if someone were to come along who was more than me –?'
'I would have to love him,' I replied.
'Then I'm not worried for now,' he replied, with a grin. 'I don't know anyone who's more than me.'
But even if we both denied it, we were jealous of one another. Often he would say, 'If you were suddenly to succumb to a disfiguring illness, smallpox for instance (his very words), and your face was so badly scarred that nobody found you attractive, that would be the moment when I could show you how much I really love you.'[8]

A few days before Alma's twenty-fifth birthday (31 August), the family returned to Vienna. As an exception to Mahler's general rule, they travelled together. He made his first conducting appearance of the new season on 6 September, with Tristan und Isolde, *and his celebrated new production of* Fidelio, *with sets by Alfred Roller, opened on 7 October.*

Less than a week later he left for Cologne to conduct the world première of his Fifth Symphony. Then he travelled on to Holland (his second visit to that country), where he conducted the Concertgebouw Orchestra in performances of his Fourth *and* Second Symphonies.

During his trip to Cologne, Mahler wrote to Alma at least once a day. The series of letters and cards opens with his customary farewell greeting from the station – though on this occasion Mahler almost missed the train.

104^U Postcard   Vienna, 12 October 1904^P

M. d. A.,

I leapt into the tram in great haste, but a power cut brought it to a standstill. Fortunately I was able to hail a cab[*] that just happened to be standing there, and so I got here in good time to send you a greeting for tomorrow morning. I'm already ravenous, and am looking forward to the departure of the train, so I can tuck into my packed supper. Once again, warmest, fondest greetings from   Your G.

While changing trains at Frankfurt, Mahler took advantage of the half-hour stopover to write again and remind Alma of the journey to Krefeld in 1902, on which she had accompanied him.

105^U Postcard   Frankfurt, 13 October 1904^P

My Almschi,

Have just got off the train in Frankfurt, wolfed down some roast beef and apple cake, and lit up a cigar. Very pleasant journey. I was on my own. Didn't need any aspirin or cola. Soon we'll be travelling on to Cologne. What a shame you're not sitting beside me, as before! – I would have ordered you a wonderful meal.
Warmest greetings   Your G.

106^U   Cologne [13 October 1904]
Dom Hotel
10.00 p.m.

My dearest Almschi,

Once I've finished this letter, I'll take it across to the station. By rights, it should leave with the special train and reach you tomorrow morning.
The room that [Fritz] Steinbach organized for me has two large beds side by side, is very nice and costs 6 marks. He came here soon after I arrived, and told me that several musical directors from other cities have announced themselves for the concert. He invited me to dine with him on Monday –

---

[*] Orig.: 'Comfortabel' (horse and carriage).

completely on our own! Naturally I accepted. I definitely expect you to
arrive on Sunday afternoon. The train stops at Frankfurt for half an hour,
and from there to Cologne there's a very pleasant dining car. Maybe you
could eat a <u>soup</u> at the station, then have lunch in the dining car to while
away the time.

The Dom Hotel is really far more pleasant and comfortable than Hotel
Disch. I'm looking forward to our revisiting the Mosel wine bars!

A thousand kisses, my love   Your Gustl

107   Cologne, 14 October 1904^P
                                                      Dom Hotel
                          Friday afternoon, after the first rehearsal

Motto:
  How blissful, how blissful
  a cobbler to be!*
                          (with variations)
Dearest Almschi,

If I take this letter across to the station right now, according to my calcula-
tions it should reach you tomorrow morning.

Well, today was the first rehearsal.

Everything went tolerably well. That scherzo is an accursed movement! It
will have a long tale of woe! For the next fifty years conductors will take it
too fast and make nonsense of it. And audiences – heavens! – how should
they react to this chaos, which is constantly giving birth to new worlds and
promptly destroying them again? What should they make of these primeval
noises, this rushing, roaring, raging sea, these dancing stars, these ebbing,
shimmering, gleaming waves? What can a herd of sheep answer to an
'ancient lay 'mid brother-spheres',† other than bleat?! How blissful, how
blissful a tailor to be! Would that I had been born an assistant procurer, or a
baritone in an opera house!‡ Would that I could perform my symphonies for
the first time fifty years after my death!

---

* Orig.: 'O selig, o selig, ein Schuster zu sein' – a variant of 'O selig, o selig, ein Kind noch zu
sein', the refrain of the song 'Sonst spielt' ich mit Zepter, mit Krone und Stern' from Act III/v
of Lortzing's opera *Zar und Zimmermann*. Further variants of the refrain appear in several of
Mahler's subsequent letters to Alma.
† Goethe, *Faust I*, Prologue in Heaven, opening words: 'Die Sonne tönt, nach alter Weise, in
Brudersphären Wettgesang' (The sun-orb sings, in emulation, / 'mid brother-spheres his
ancient lay).
‡ Allusion to Leopold Demuth, who worked as an assistant procurer before taking up singing.

Now I shall go to the Rhine, the only soul in Cologne that will calmly wend its way after the première and not assert that I'm a monster! If only I were 'just like Mama, just like Papa'.*
'How blissful, how blissful, a locksmith to be' – and then a tenor at the Vienna Opera![†]

This evening I have to go to hear a soprano. They're giving Fedora by Puccini.[‡]
Would that I were an Italian chestnut vendor!
Would that I were an informer for the Russian police!
Would that I were an alderman of Cologne, and had a box at the Stadttheater and another at the Gürzenich,[§] and could scoff at all this modern music!
Would that I were a university professor, and could give lectures on Wagner and publish them![**]
I'm banking on your presence on Sunday. Somebody has to be there who actually enjoys listening to my symphony. If you were here now, we'd be sitting in an automobile and driving along the Rhine; but since you're not, I wouldn't want to make you envious, so I'll walk. The weather is magnificent. Warmest greetings from your oh so 'blissful'   Gustl

Meanwhile, Alma had caught a cold, and sent a telegram cancelling her trip to Cologne.

108   Cologne, 15 October 1904[P]
                                                        Dom Hotel

This is really terrible! Almschl, my first impulse was to fly into a rage like a child, and I all but boxed the messenger boy's ears. But now that I've let off a bit of steam, I don't yet want to give up hope! Do all you can: sweat it out, drink quantities of cognac, swallow aspirins. You can get over your cold in two days, and if you set off on Monday <u>evening</u> you would still be here in time for the concert on Tuesday. I beg you, Almschili: do all you can. How

---

* Allusion to the popularity of Richard Strauss. Orig.: 'Ganz die Mama, ganz der Papa!' from Richard Sprecht's foreword to the score of the *Sinfonia Domestica,* which Mahler was scheduled to conduct in Vienna the following month.
[†] Allusion to Leo Slezak, who had learnt the craft of lock-making.
[‡] *Fedora* was composed not by Puccini but by Umberto Giordano. Mahler heard Frieda Felser sing the title role, on the strength of which he engaged her for a guest appearance at the Hofoper in December 1904.
[§] The concert-hall in Cologne from which the municipal orchestra took (and still takes) its name.
[**] Allusion to Guido Adler, whose book *Richard Wagner: Vorlesungen gehalten an der Universität in Wien* had just been published in Leipzig.

awful it would be if I were left on my own for my world première. Something like being a guest at one's own funeral.* – By the way, today's rehearsal was already much more satisfactory. <Today I received a package from Emma [Rosé], with the enclosed note. I'll post it you in Vienna.> The silly thing is that I'm also worried that you might be seriously ill. After all, Fleischmann wouldn't forbid you to travel unless he had his reasons.

Write <u>at once</u>! I won't give up hope. Warmest greetings. I'll take this letter to the station now and send it per express – maybe it will still reach you by tomorrow. Your speechless   Gust

In an unpublished letter to Emma Rosé in Weimar, Mahler confirmed that her package had arrived.⁹ En passant, his letter also reveals the nature of its contents: two slips for Alma. Rather than entrust this precious gift to the post, he took it with him to Amsterdam.

109ᵁ Telegram   Cologne, 18 October 1904
                                                              10.38 [a.m.]

final rehearsal very satisfactory   orchestra played well   audience attentive initially taken aback but finally enthusiastic   hinrichsen already offering for the sixth†   greetings gustav

As the telegram infers, Alma had indeed been unable to attend the concert. 'We wanted to travel to Cologne together for the rehearsals,' she recalls. 'But Nature is not to be played with. I had weaned my child too abruptly, and as a result I fell ill. We both hoped I would be able to travel at a later date, but this proved impossible. And so while the Fifth Symphony was receiving its first performance, I was lying in bed with a temperature. That work was the first one of which I experienced the entire genesis. I copied out the whole score; in fact, I did even more than that. Knowing that I was familiar with the part-writing, and because he had blind faith in me, Mahler often omitted whole lines.'¹⁰

---

* Orig.: 'Da kann Einen wirklich die Leich' nicht freuen.'
† Henri Hinrichsen, managing director of C. F. Peters. If he did in fact make an offer for the *Sixth Symphony*, he withdrew it immediately after the première.

110   Cologne [18 October 1904]
                                           Dom Hotel

Dearest Almschel,
Just briefly. I'm in a flap! Yesterday's dress rehearsal went very well, and musi-
cally it was outstanding. The audience was immensely engrossed and attentive – for all the displeasure that was shown after the opening movements.
After the Scherzo a few people even hissed. But the Adagietto and Rondo
seem to have made their effect. A crowd of musicians, conductors etc. had
come to Cologne to hear the work. Hinrichsen was very <u>enthusiastic</u>, and has
already given me a <u>solemn</u> promise for my Sixth. ('Please don't ask a higher
fee,' he added with a chuckle. And I certainly won't, because he's such a fine
fellow.) My two loyal followers [Bruno] Walter and [Arnold] Berliner are here
too. Walter arrived yesterday to hear the dress rehearsal – he'll tell you all
about it. Berliner got here only this morning. Now he's sitting here, bewailing
your absence. I do believe he came here only because of you.
Well, this evening is the concert. I'll cable you tomorrow, then I have to leave
at once for Amsterdam. <I can't give you the address until I get there.> To
begin with just write to:
    Concertgebouw
    Amsterdam
That will suffice.
Almschi, your not being here has cheated me of all the pleasure, and for me the
event has become almost meaningless. You would have so enjoyed hearing it!
Kiss our little angels for me. Make sure you all get well soon. Struth! *
Your old Gustl

<Greetings to Carl and Mama. Why didn't Mama come in your place? It
would have been such fun. – Justi and Arnold.>

111   Cologne, 19 October 1904[P]
                                           Dom Hotel

My Almschili,
Walter will call as soon as he gets back and fill you in with the details.
Hinrichsen is very enthusiastic and refuses to let my opponents impair his
judgement. I do believe the work made a very significant impression. I'm just
about to leave for Amsterdam, from where I'll write in greater detail. – I
missed you so sorely. For me it was all so half-boiled. What an irony of fate

---

* Orig.: 'Himmelherrgott noch einmal!'

that this should happen to me with my Fifth, of all things. If I see any reviews, I'll send them along. Nodnagel was there too and full of my praises. Ask Walter to tell you all about it. It's absorbing to see how opinions differ about the work. Every movement has its supporters and detractors. A thousand kisses to you and the children. I hope you are all well, or rather <u>get</u> well soon. My dearest   Your Gustl

Soon after arriving in Amsterdam, Mahler rehearsed with the soprano Alida Oldenboom-Lutkeman, who was to sing the solo part in his Fourth Symphony. *The following morning he wrote to Alma.*

112   Amsterdam [20 October 1904]
                                                        Van Eeghenstraat 107

Dear Almschl,
Well, I've arrived in Amsterdam. Mengelberg and his wife were waiting for me at the station, and would give me no rest until I agreed to stay with them. – So here I am again, like last year. Such kind, unpretentious people. – Already yesterday evening I rehearsed the solo music with the singer. A fat little woman, something like Cilli,* but she sings marvellously, and her voice is as clear as a bell. <Everything has been prepared with the greatest of care.> Why can't you be here? You would have benefited from it greatly.
I trust that Walter told you all about Cologne. I believe it was everything we could have hoped for. –
It's time to go to the first rehearsal (they start here at nine in the morning), and I'm hastily writing these lines to ensure that you hear something from me today. Write to me at the <u>Concertgebouw</u>. It's easier that way, and post is brought round as soon as it arrives.
A thousand kisses in haste   Your Gust

113   Amsterdam [21 October 1904]
                                                        Van Eeghenstraat 107

Dearest,
I'm enclosing the review from the Kölnische Zeitung, which was sent on to me here. As yet, I haven't seen any others. I can just imagine the twaddle they're all writing. Particularly the Neue Freie Presse is bound to surpass itself.
The people here are a real pleasure.

---

* In her memoirs Alma identifies Cilli, distantly, as 'a cook' (AMM1, 319). In fact, Cilli had been in service for several years as the Molls' own cook and housemaid.

Just imagine, the programme for Sunday is as follows:
1. Symphony no. IV by G. Mahler
   Interval
2. Symphony no. IV by G. Mahler.

What do you think of that?

They're playing my work twice in a row – after the interval we start all over again. I'll be interested to see whether the audience will react more warmly the second time.

In my opinion it's an ingenious idea for a new work. – At the rehearsal today the orchestra played my Fourth with wonderful polish <and great enthusiasm>. In Cologne too, my most fervent admirers (perhaps indeed the only ones) were members of the orchestra.

I have to leave for rehearsal. Warmest greetings, my dearest   Your Gustl

If some of the reviews are really scathing, don't take it to heart.

In AMM4 Alma writes that Mengelberg conducted the second of these performances; indeed, she even elaborates on the idea. 'Mahler took a seat in the stalls and listened to his work. Later, when he came home, he told me it had been as if he himself had conducted. Mengelberg had grasped his intentions down to the last nuance.'[11] These assertions are borne out neither by the printed programme nor by the reviews; indeed, Mahler's own remarks (in letter 117) prove beyond doubt that he himself conducted both performances.

114   Amsterdam [21 October 1904]
                                           Van Eeghenstraat 107

Well, my Almschl,

Life goes on here in a veritable whirl of rehearsals. Everything is wonderfully well prepared, and soon I believe I shall have carved out something of a musical niche for myself here. Now I look forward to hearing the chorus, with which I shall be rehearsing this evening. I have far less free time than last year, so I shan't have the pleasure of going for such nice excursions.

I'm overjoyed by your news. To be quite honest, as time went on I was growing more and more concerned about you. But I made a solemn pact with myself: by the time this 'cup' has passed us by, I shall be as brave as a hero of yesteryear.

Hanging around in strange places is a dreadful way of spending one's time, even if one is welcomed as warmly as here. After all, one is subject to disturbances from every quarter, and in the final analysis one does feel very much alone.

I wonder how the audience on Sunday will react to the repeat performance of my Fourth Symphony. <I'll pack the two slips in my suitcase and bring them with me.> – As I now realize, I forgot to give Walter the darned key to the safe.* Never mind, you don't have time to do any copying at present, and anyway you're not yet supposed to.†

A week today I'll be sitting in the train, homeward bound. Hoorah!

At present I really have no idea whether I shall have to hide my face in shame when I return to Vienna, or not.

Was it a setback – or a breakthrough?

Fondest greetings, my dearest. Let me have news of you as often as you can. After all, you have so much time to write <to me> about everything.   Your old Gustl

115   Amsterdam [22 October 1904]
Van Eeghenstraat 107

Dearest Almschl,

Enclosed with this letter is a 'photograph' of me, made by an 'admirer' at a concert.‡

---

* Orig.: 'Nun habe ich mit dem guten Walter doch die Kassaschlüssel verpudelt.' Mahler was in the habit of keeping his manuscripts in an iron strongbox.

† In her memoirs (AMM1, 326) Alma makes the outrageous claim: 'I made copies of all Mahler's works.' In the original typescript of the memoirs (ELM) she does not go quite so far, but explains: 'I was supposed to resume copying the Sixth Symphony. Mahler never kept any money in the strongbox, only his manuscripts.' It is unclear why she omitted this information from the printed edition.

‡ The identity of the artist is unknown.

I think it will probably amuse you, so I'm sending it along – as a snapshot of me at this moment in time (I'm just listening to Mengelberg conducting a superb performance of Schumann's D-minor Symphony). – Today is the final rehearsal of the Fourth. Yesterday evening I rehearsed the chorus for the Second. They sang magnificently – almost as well as in Basle.

How I wish it was already Friday and I was back in the train. I'm not made for all this travelling – were it not for the fact that it's so essential.

On these journeys, I only feel really in my element when I'm rehearsing. How I wish that conductors had already come to terms with my musical style. Then I'd be perfectly happy to potter about in Heiligenstadt.

Now I'm beginning to realize how foolish I was to agree to premièring a new work in Cologne, where the audience gave my Third Symphony such a frosty reception. Audience reactions always rub off on the critics, who are a weak-kneed breed and depend entirely on the opinions of others. All the strain and inconvenience of a long journey, just for that: what folly. I could have had the same in Vienna, and it would have cost me far less!

When it comes to the Sixth Symphony, I'll try to arrange things more prudently. Fondest greetings to you, my Almscherl. Make sure you're fit and well when I get home!

Your very frayed   Gustl

<Greetings to Mama, Carl
Justi and Arnold. –
What are our little Putzis up to?>

Mahler's regret at having decided to give the world première of his Fifth Symphony *in Cologne was founded on the fact that several other possibilities had been open to him, including Prague, Mannheim, Heidelberg and Berlin.*

116[U]   [Amsterdam, 22 October 1904][E]

Dearest Almschel,
The enclosed,[*] to which I have already replied, might amuse you and should make a worthy addition to your 'Shannon' collection.[†] A thousand <u>kisses</u>.
Your Gustl

---

[*] The enclosure has not been preserved.
[†] 'Shannon': brand name of a document filing system.

117[U] Postcard   Amsterdam [23 October 1904]*

Well, Almschl,
Now I'm off to the concert-hall to conduct my Fourth Symphony twice in a row. A tough endurance test for the stomachs of the burghers of Amsterdam, and one that could easily lead to dyspepsia. – If only you could have written to me at greater length! I have virtually no news of you at all. Here in Amsterdam my music seems to be very much in vogue. Maybe it's the fault of my affinity with the old Flemish master-musicians. I wonder what kind of a reception to expect this evening. Warmest greetings etc.   Your G.

118   Amsterdam [24 October 1904]
           Van Eeghenstraat 107

Dearest,
What an extraordinary concert! From the very beginning there was such concentration and rapport, and it grew warmer from one movement to the next. – Reactions were even more enthusiastic the second time round, and at the close there was a scene similar to that in Krefeld. The soprano sang her solo simply and movingly, and the orchestra accompanied like rays of sunshine. It was a picture on a background of gold. – Now I really believe I have found a musical habitat of the kind I was hoping for in silly old Cologne.
Today we have the first main rehearsal of the Second Symphony. Another tough nut to crack! Once again, the members of the orchestra have been so very friendly! Many kisses, my Almschi. <Greetings to Carl and Mama.>
Yours (in great haste)   Gustl

119[U] Postcard   Haarlem, 24 October 1904[P]

From an outing to Haarlem – where I regret to say that Frans Hals was no longer at home (closed). – Must quickly post this card!   Gustav

[Written by the individual signatories:]
Warmest greetings from
W. Mengelberg
A. Diepenbrock
Tilly Mengelberg

* Postmarked 24 October 1904.

Amsterdam [25 October 1904]
Van Eeghenstraat 107

Dearest,

Enclosed is a review (from the country's <u>leading</u> newspaper), translated for you by Mrs Mengelberg. It will give you a rough picture of the impression made by my Fourth Symphony. <u>Far</u> warmer than the Third. Mengelberg has already decided to perform it at his next concert and wants to conduct it on several other occasions too. The last movement with solo soprano made the <u>strongest</u> impression of all.

Now I'm busy rehearsing the Second Symphony, which is incredibly taxing. This evening is the final rehearsal.*

So far I haven't really been able to do any sightseeing, because all my mornings and evenings have been booked up.

Yesterday I went to Haarlem to look at <u>Hals,</u> but unfortunately the museum closes at three o'clock. I hope I can cancel the rehearsal tomorrow morning, in which case I'll go to Zandvoert on the North Sea (just an hour on the tram from here). On the way I'll stop off at Haarlem, and hope to have better luck.

And then, thank heaven, it will be time to go home. I'm leaving on Friday morning and should be with you around eight o'clock Saturday morning. <Please have a bath ready for me. Elise will probably be off duty at that time.>

You've been a poor correspondent this time, my Almschi. However, I ascribe it to your state of health, poor thing. But you could at least have managed a postcard a day. Please, Almschi, <u>read</u> the enclosed review, then pass it on to Mama. She's much more receptive for these things and absorbs them with greater sympathy.

Whatever one may think of it, it's a pleasure to read something written with so much insight and impartiality.

All the other reviews were in a similar vein. You haven't told me anything about the children. No doubt Putzi has already forgotten me, and little Gucki won't recognize me at all.

Fondest kisses to all three of you. <Greetings to Arnold and Justi, and also of course to Mama and Carl.> Your old   Gustl

---

* The soloists were Alida Oldenboom-Lutkeman and Martha Stapelfeld.

121
Amsterdam [26 October 1904]
Van Eeghenstraat 107

Dearest,
Here is yet another review (by the director of the Amsterdam Conservatory), translated by Diepenbrock (the remarkable composer, of whom I once told you). And therewith, thank heaven, this very <u>one-sided</u> correspondence comes to a close, for tomorrow evening I conduct my last concert, and the day after that I leave. – Though in excellent health, I'm sick and tired of all this trundling about, and look forward to tucking my feet under my own desk again. And how I miss my three little imps. Admittedly I'm <u>very</u> dissatisfied with the eldest: such a poor correspondent! Almschi! I'll just have to let it pass. The actual dressing-down will come on Saturday morning when I'm sitting in my bath.
Now it's time for the Second Symphony.
The final rehearsal yesterday went very well. The participants were unbelievably enthusiastic. A thousand kisses from   Your Gustav

122^U Postcard
Amsterdam, 27 October 1904^P

Dear Almschi,
Well, yesterday was the Second Symphony! It completely served its purpose. Same kind of physiognomy as in Basle and Krefeld.
This evening is the repeat performance, and then I'm off – to you! Auf Wiedersehen!   Gust

Mahler's last guest engagement for 1904 took him to Leipzig, where the conductor Hans Winderstein had invited him to conduct the Third Symphony *(soloist: Marie Hertzer-Deppe). He wrote as usual from the station, but with an unusual greeting – 'L. A.-li' in the original – to Alma.*

123^U Postcard
Vienna, 25 November 1904^P

Dear Almschli,
Well, I got here in time to send you my customary greeting for tomorrow morning – and I still have time to eat a ham roll. Unfortunately I've just heard that the sleeping car is full, and therefore I shall have to spend the night fully clothed. Not very cheering.
Thousands of everything! Your old [unsigned]

189

124[U]   Leipzig, 26 November 1904[P]
                                                         Hôtel de Prusse

Dear Almschli,

I'm suffering from a particularly nasty attack of lumbago, and as a result am feeling utterly wretched. So now, at two o'clock, I'm going to lie down for a rest before the chorus rehearsal at four. I breakfasted at six o'clock in Tetschen,* and upset my stomach with the disgusting swill they served me (coffee – they didn't have tea). But I've already managed to get over it. I was met here by the concertmaster, who's very agreeable. He told me the orchestra was very enthusiastic about my work, and that I would find them very well prepared. When I hear something like that it always cuts me to the quick, for it makes me think: damn it all, Almschi should have come along too. – Anyway, vederemo. – My first rehearsal is tomorrow morning at 10.30. After that I'll write again.

Tonight I'll wear my stomach-warmer again.

Warmest greetings. I'm feeling incredibly sleepy.

Your old Gustl

125   Leipzig [27 November 1904]
                                                         Hôtel de Prusse

Good morning, my beloved,

I put myself to bed at 9.30 last night, made myself a warm poultice with (I don't know what the stuff is called, it's a sort of vegetable paste; the hotel manager's wife recommended it and also prepared it for me), and then I slept until 8.00 a.m. Today I feel as fit as a fiddle – only a slight pain in the region of my left hip reminds me that if I don't behave myself the lumbago will come on again.[†]

I ate a hearty breakfast (raw ham) and now I'm just dashing off these few lines of greeting. – Your dear letter has just arrived, and I'll take it with me to rehearsal, where it will give me a boost if the woodwind play too coarsely or the violins sound too depressingly scratchy. – I hope I can write again this afternoon, though I have meetings with Peters, Staegemann and Nikisch.[‡]

Warmest greetings, my dear, good Almscherl. I'm so glad it won't take too long this time – only three days! Your   Gustl

* Today: Děčín in the Czech Republic.
† Orig.: 'dass [. . .] sofort wieder die Hexe schiessen wird' (that the witch will immediately shoot again) – untranslatable pun on the word 'Hexenschuss' (lumbago).
‡ Nikisch was scheduled to conduct the Berlin première of Mahler's *Fifth Symphony* on 20 February 1905.

126   Leipzig [28 November 1904]
                                                 Hôtel de Prusse

My Almschili,
The rehearsals are over, and now I'm sitting quietly – and utterly exhausted
– waiting for the performance. One thing, above all: where yesterday the
orchestra was little more than a wreckage of incoherent noises, today it
acquired a clear structure. The stones heard the song of Arion and willingly
let themselves be arrayed,* and so I look forward to this evening's performance with a certain sense of acquiescence.
The poor devils were extremely courteous. Yesterday and today they put up
with my scolding for four hours at a time, undeterred, and when it was over
they actually bade me an enthusiastic farewell.
My work is attracting immense interest here; the leading Leipzig critics
attended both rehearsals, and it is indeed fortunate that I came here to give
this performance. Now for the details.
At the first rehearsal yesterday I glanced around. And who did I espy, standing at the back like a devoted disciple? Herr Nodnagel!
At first I was beside myself, but later I found it rather touching. What a character! In the afternoon I called on the Staegemanns.† They were as welcoming
as ever, asked after you, and wanted to invite me to dinner, but I had to
refuse because I'd already accepted an invitation from Hinrichsen. When I
arrived (he'd phoned to ask if he could come and collect me), he was sitting
at the piano with a four-hands arrangement of a Bruckner symphony, swot-
ting up the secondo part.
I sat down and played the whole piece through with him, silently persuading
myself that this was a suitable peace-offering and a token of gratitude for his
generosity, and that in this way I was compensating the poor fellow at least
in part for all the money he invested in the fiasco of my Fifth Symphony.
Then we were joined by Musikdirektor Straube,‡ a very sympathetic and
excellent local musician, who happens to be a fervent supporter of mine.
<This morning Emma and Eduard [Rosé] were here – very unassuming.
They listened to the rehearsal and joined me for lunch, but I couldn't persuade them to let me foot the bill.
Emma accompanied me back to the hotel, where I gave her your gift of

---

* Mixed mythology: Arion was the minstrel (as Herodotus reports) who was saved from drown-
ing by a school of dolphins; the musician who moved stones with his song was Orpheus.
† It was Max Staegemann who in 1886 had offered Mahler his contract as Kapellmeister at
the Leipzig Stadt-Theater.
‡ Karl Straube, cantor of the Leipzig Thomaskirche as eleventh in succession to J. S. Bach.

Kugler pralines. She took them from me with an air of solemn devotion.>
I've just had a visit from a publisher (Kahnt),[*] who is eager to acquire my
new Lieder and ballads.[†] I'll send him the piano arrangements from Vienna,
then he'll make an offer.
And now addio, my Almschl.

Nikisch has invited me to dine with him tomorrow (per telegram, as he's
conducting in Berlin today), and afterwards I'm to play him my Fifth
Symphony, to give him a clear idea of my intentions. – In the evening I'll set
off home, and I should be with you the following morning (Wednesday). A
thousand kisses from   Your Gustl

Having conducted his Third Symphony *at almost every major musical centre
in Germany, Mahler was particularly concerned that the work should also
succeed in Leipzig, a city steeped in the tradition of Bach, Mendelssohn and
Schumann. However, circumstances surrounding the performance were anything but propitious. Henri Hinrichsen had warned Mahler about the poor
quality of the Winderstein Orchestra (augmented for the occasion by players
from the Band of the 107th Regiment), and alerted him to the fact that
Weingartner was conducting a rival concert the same evening. For all the
inconvenience, it was doubtless for these reasons that Mahler decided to
travel to Leipzig and conduct the performance himself.*

    *Before setting out on his homeward journey, he summed up the outcome
of his endeavours in a telegram to Alma.*

127[U] Telegram   Leipzig, 29 November 1904
                                                       1.36

complete success   greetings gustav

*Nevertheless, the reviews in the Leipzig press were devastating. Two weeks
later, on 13 December, Mahler again conducted his* Third Symphony, *this
time in the 'Golden Hall' of the Vienna Musikverein. On this occasion the
performance was so successful that it had to be repeated eight days later.
Schoenberg, Zemlinsky and some of their pupils attended the final rehearsal
on 12 December. So far they had summoned up little enthusiasm for*

---

[*] Mahler negotiated with Alfred Hoffmann, managing director of C. F. Kahnt since 1902. The
connection with Kahnt dated back to Mahler's Leipzig years, when the firm had published his
performing edition of Weber's *Die drei Pintos*.
[†] Ten Lieder to texts by Friedrich Rückert (the *Kindertotenlieder* and four separate songs) and
two songs from *Des Knaben Wunderhorn*. These were published by Kahnt in the summer of
1905, with the exception of *Liebst du um Schönheit*, which was published two years later.

Mahler's music (cf. Zemlinsky's remarks, as reported on p. 46), but now they found their reservations swept aside. The same day, Schoenberg sent Mahler a fervent letter of appreciation:

'I saw your soul naked, stripped bare. It lay before me like a wild, mysterious landscape with terrifying reefs and chasms; and at the next turning there were delightful, sunlit meadows, idyllic resting-places. [. . .] I saw the forces of good and evil locked in mortal combat, saw a man agonisedly striving for inner harmony, sensed a human being, a drama, the <u>truth</u>, the unrelenting truth.'[12]

Zemlinsky was too overawed to approach Mahler directly, and wrote instead to Alma:

'From start to finish I had the impression of a music that plumbed nature's most intimate depths. I tell you frankly that only in the music of the very greatest have I heard a power and profundity comparable, for example, to the first part of the first movement or the two final movements; only in Beethoven and Brahms (disregarding the pre-Beethovenian composers) have I heard themes so precisely and expressively shaped and developed. And the second movement: the essence of charm distilled into sound, grace in final perfection. [. . .] What I long suspected is now an absolute certainty, and yesterday I told my friends: this is one of the elect. I was so happy yesterday to have witnessed a major event in the history of music. –'[13]

'My children are sick,' wrote Alma later that year.

Maria is feeling better, but little Anna is very poorly. Sad as it may seem, this has helped me regain my own strength. The greater the demands one makes on oneself, the stronger one feels. [. . .] I feel uncommonly serene and jovial. Suddenly it became clear to me why I am alive: my children need me. And Gustav Mahler needs me. But I feel incapable of giving him all my warmth. Why, actually? Initially I found him remote, and in many respects this is still the case. There is much about him I do not understand – and if I do, it repulses me. But he has so many good qualities. I know that I really love him and that I could not live without him – now. For he has taken so much away from me that his presence is my sole support. Now I must try to benefit from everything else our short span of life can offer us. To benefit, as I understand it, means to be so virtuous, so useful, so calm, so self-sufficient that one feels fulfilled. But I am only a little over twenty years of age. My life is totally uneventful. The children – Gustav. Gustav – the children . . .![14]

1905

Fortified by the success of Tristan *in February 1903, Mahler and Roller began work on the first new production of Wagner's* Ring *since its Viennese première in 1879. Roller's innovative use of light and decorative elements have since made theatre history. At the time, his ideas met with considerable opposition, particularly from the technical staff of the Hofoper.*

For all the controversy surrounding it, the Rheingold *première on 23 January 1905 was a resounding success. Two days later, on 25 January, Mahler attended the first orchestral concert of the Vereinigung schaffender Tonkünstler. The programme consisted of three world premières: Zemlinsky's* Die Seejungfrau, *Oskar Posa's* Five Poems of Liliencron *for baritone and orchestra, and Schoenberg's* Pelleas und Melisande. *Mahler, who was honorary president of the Vereinigung, followed four days later with an 'orchestral song-recital', consisting of a group of* Wunderhorn *songs, followed by the world première of the* Kindertotenlieder *and four of the* Rückert-Lieder. *The concert was so successful that it had to be repeated on 3 February.*

A further event of particular interest to Alma was the Viennese première of Pfitzner's Rose vom Liebesgarten *on 6 April. Since their first meeting, Pfitzner had meanwhile dedicated his* String Quartet *op. 13 to her. Certainly, his late-Romantic ideals came closer to her own than those of the man she had chosen to marry.*

In letter 63 Mahler had expressed himself in no uncertain terms on the subject of Pfitzner and the score of his opera. Were it not for the intercessions of Alma and Bruno Walter, this new production at the Hofoper would scarcely have been possible. Needless to say, Mahler rehearsed it with the same care and attention he brought to everything else he conducted. In March 1905 Pfitzner came to Vienna to attend rehearsals at the Hofoper. One day he called on Mahler, but found only Alma at home, whereupon he presented her with a red rose. Her diary for 21 March gives an account of one of their subsequent meetings:

Yesterday, at Pfitzner's request, I played him some of my old Lieder. He liked them, and assured me with a smile that I had a gift for composition and a fine feeling for melody. 'I wouldn't mind teaching you,' he said. 'It's such a shame.' His words filled me with joy and melancholy. A brief moment of happiness.[1]

The following day she wrote:

Yesterday evening was rather spoilt by the presence of Pfitzner. In some respects his outlook is blinkered. The most profound and genuine aspect of Wagner, he said, was his Teutonic character. [Gerhart] Hauptmann and Gustav agreed that the greater an artist, the further he dissociates himself from nationalism. Pfitzner stood there like a worm, and went off soon afterwards with his tail between his legs. Later he was as if transformed. After a performance of Fidelio [on 25 March] he and I spent an evening at home, playing through his Lieder, and later also mine. We had arranged to meet up with Mahler and the Hauptmanns in the cellar restaurant of Meissl & Schadn, but were so carried away with our music that we lost track of the time. We arrived late, but nobody seems to have taken it amiss. Pfitzner played through each of his songs about ten times, or at least he kept repeating each one until I approved of it.[2]

Alma's unpublished diaries include her unabridged account of this meeting. Where in the published version she writes that Pfitzner had accompanied her to the restaurant, here the story ends quite differently:

Pfitzner was in love with me that night. Why it suddenly blew up and promptly died out again, I do not know. All I know is that he made intimate advances, touching me wherever he could, and finally begging me in a hoarse voice to give him my photograph (we were alone in the living room). I didn't resist – and enjoyed that tingling sensation I had not felt for so long. He preferred not to join Gustav and the Hauptmanns for dinner, and I had no regrets about letting him go. Yesterday morning I failed to show up at his rehearsal. He was very angry, as if transformed.[3]

On 7 March Mahler travelled to Hamburg to conduct two performances of his Fifth Symphony *for the Philharmonic Society. Having worked in Hamburg for six years as 1st Kapellmeister (1891–97), for him this was like a homecoming. As usual he sent Alma a greeting before boarding the train.*

128[U] Postcard   Vienna, 7 March [1905][P]

My dearest A,
Good morning! I've just been for a nice little stroll through town, and taken the opportunity to buy a pair of slippers and a necktie. I trust that Hassinger will bring the boxes home. And now a thousand O and be <u>good</u>.*
<u>Write</u>! Your G.

---

* Orig.: 'sei schön <u>bjav</u>' (Putzi, like her father, had difficulty pronouncing the r in 'brav').

[top corner:] Once again I lingered for quite a time by the 'Steffel'* and the 'Golden Fountain'.†
[bottom corner:] Kind regards from the 'Steffel'.

129[U] Postcard   Hamburg, 8 March 1905[P]

Dearest,
Once again I've been suffering all day from a migraine, just as I expected. In Berlin I spent three hours telling Berliner about Almscherl, then left for Hamburg, and here, <u>right</u> in front of the hotel, I bumped into old Mr and Mrs <u>Hertz</u>.‡ – Now my headache is beginning to go away. I shall sit in on two acts at the Opera (Carmen), then go to bed. The first rehearsal is tomorrow at nine. Shall write about it next time. And since this card will take two days to reach you, I'll wire you tomorrow morning. Write soon, and don't forget to send news of our dear Putzis.
Warmest greetings, your faithful G.

Instead of sending a telegram, Mahler found time the following morning to write a brief letter.

130   Hamburg [9 March 1905]
                                                         Streit's Hotel

My Almschi,
I'm just off to my first rehearsal. The headache wore off already yesterday evening. I watched two acts of Carmen. The singers taking curtain calls – Edel-Fleischer, Thyssen and Metzger – were all rejects from Vienna, but the public gave them a rousing reception. Then Demuth came on like a superstar, and I left. Brecher and Karl Wagner§ emerged, and I joined them for dinner. Brecher (who was conducting) has made <u>enormous</u> progress, and has become a really fine fellow. – <This afternoon I'm going to see Willy and Alma.**>

---

* i.e. St Stephen's Cathedral.
† Orig.: 'Goldene Brunnen' – conceivably the so-called Donner Brunnen on the Neuer Markt, of which the figures are cast in bronze.
‡ Helene Hertz was the mother of Mahler's first landlady in Hamburg, Adele Marcus. Both mother and daughter were staunch supporters and close friends of Mahler during his Hamburg years.
§ Karl Wagner, son of a well-known actor at the Vienna Burgtheater. Mahler knew him from Kassel. In Hamburg, where he played at the Deutsche Schauspielhaus, Wagner was so popular that he became known as the 'Hamburg Kainz'.
** Alma's maternal uncle and aunt, Willy and Alma Bergen.

What a pity you're not here! Hotel Streit is rather run-down, but the room costs 10 marks all the same. Maybe I'll move out.
Warmest greetings from   Your Gustl

<How's your cold? Send me a nice long letter, my love!>

Mahler's account of his evening at the opera implies that he waited until the opening of Act III before taking his seat in the auditorium.

The tenor who sang the role of Don José, Josef Thyssen, had appeared at the Vienna Hofoper as recently as 26 January, where he was cast in the title role of Gounod's Faust; the Carmen, Ottilie Metzger, sang in Vienna on 7, 10, 14 and 16 May 1901 (respectively) the roles of Berthe (Le Prophète), Amneris (Aida), Azucena (Il Trovatore) and Carmen; the Micaela, Katharina Fleischer-Edel, made equally unsuccessful trial appearances at the Hofoper as Elsa (Lohengrin) and Margarethe (Faust) on 27 and 29 August 1901. Evidently Mahler later revised his opinion of Metzger, for in 1910 she sang first alto solo and the part of Mulier Samaritana in the world premiere of his Eighth Symphony. Leopold Demuth was appearing in Hamburg as guest artist in the role of Escamillo. He had been a permanent member of Mahler's Hofoper ensemble since 1898.

It was on the recommendation of Richard Strauss that Mahler had engaged Gustav Brecher as 1st Kapellmeister at the Hofoper in 1901. 'Brecher is a splendid and delightful man,' wrote Mahler to Strauss in August 1901, 'but he lacks the necessary experience and manual dexterity. I shall attempt to find him an interim appointment for one or two seasons at some smaller municipal theatre.'⁴ In 1903, after one season at Olmütz (Olomouc), Brecher was appointed chief conductor of the Stadt-Theater in Hamburg. During his tenure, which lasted eight years, he was able to lay the foundations for a distinguished career.

131   Hamburg [9 March 1905]
                                                  Streit's Hotel

My Almschili,
Here are all the letters, and one extra one.
As far as Zemlinsky is concerned, there is nothing I can add. To be honest, I would have written exactly the same. How you react depends entirely on what you feel about it. But you should certainly approach Countess

Wydenbruck.* When I get back, I'll do what I can to help. Marschalk is a stupid fool.† It must have been the 'publisher' in him that wrote that letter. But I don't have the least desire to entrust my Lieder to him. – At rehearsal today, I kept saying to myself, 'How blissful, how blissful a cobbler to be.' This Fifth Symphony has a curse on it. Nobody understands it. Towards the end it was going a little better. Ah well, tomorrow will tell.

<Today I spent an hour trying to find your Uncle <u>Willy</u>. Unfortunately Mama had given me the wrong address. The correct house number isn't <u>188</u> but 80.‡ Just imagine, I found it by sheer chance (from a housemaid, who happened to be in the shop where I had gone to ask). – They were both out, worst luck, so I simply left my greetings and a visiting card. The distances are all so huge here! At any rate, I'll try to meet up with <u>Willy</u> and <u>Alma</u> and their respective other halves.>

It hasn't stopped raining. I'm utterly worn out.

Behn§ called on me, as kind-hearted as ever. We'll be spending some time together tomorrow. He was adamant that I should stay with him, but I'd rather not. For today I've arranged to meet Brecher, who has taken a turn for the better in every respect.

I also called on Mr and Mrs <u>Hertz</u> (at six o'clock) and joined them for supper. The old people were so touching. Her eyes were constantly welling up with tears!

By the way, everyone has been scolding me for not having brought you with me. How I wish you were here!

And now, my dearest, farewell. It was sweet of you to write so soon.

Kiss our little Putzis from me, also warmest greetings to <u>Mama</u>   Your Gustl

In view of the crippling cost of the two orchestral concerts of the Vereinigung in January, Zemlinsky had written to Alma, asking her to intercede with influential friends on his behalf: 'As "everyone" knows,' he wrote, 'you are on better terms than ever with Countess Wydenbruck. The Countess seems to be very well-connected, and a word from her could save the committee members of our Society from being scattered to the winds. [. . .] Would you do that for us? I beg you!'[5]

* Countess Misa Wydenbruck-Esterházy, patron of the arts and an indefatigable charity worker. She lived not far from Mahler, at Rennweg 1A, and had been on good terms with him since 1897.
† The critic and composer Max Marschalk, proprietor of Dreililien Verlag in Berlin and brother-in-law of Gerhart Hauptmann. Evidently he had entered into competition with Kahnt to acquire the rights of Mahler's new Lieder.
‡ Willy Bergen's address was Eppendorfer Landstrasse 80.
§ The composer-pianist Hermann Behn, who had been a friend of Mahler's since 1893. His two-piano arrangement of Mahler's *Second Symphony* was published by Hofmeister, Leipzig, in 1895. Later that same year, Mahler presented him with the autographed orchestral score of the *Lieder eines fahrenden Gesellen*.

132^U   Hamburg [10 March 1905]
                                                         Streit's Hotel

My dearest Almschili,

Well, today's rehearsal went splendidly. It's amazing how the orchestra has pulled itself together and warmed to the music. Behn has been fathering me most agreeably. I called on <u>Willi</u>, and after a most ardent discussion, which touched on social injustice, then turned abruptly to objets d'art, we went off to see Aunt Alma, whom we found at home in the company of her youngest son. I took an immediate liking to her, because she looks so like Mama. Later we were joined by Frau Bergen. They were very keen for me to come and dine with them, and indeed I would gladly do so, but fear there simply won't be time. Naturally I had to fill them in on all the news. In conversation, Willy said, 'When you make it back to Vienna,* send everyone our kind regards.'

There won't be time to call on Berth,† but I've persuaded the management to let me have five tickets for the final rehearsal and concert.

Behn will see to the Vierlanden doll‡ for little Putzi. I'm writing this letter in a tearing hurry, because I'm just off to <u>Berger's</u> theatre.§

I miss you sorely, my Almschi. All the same, I've been praising you <u>to the skies</u>. Particularly Alma wanted to know all about you.

Kisses and warmest greetings to you and the children. Why haven't you <u>written</u> anything about them?   Your old Gustl

Alma's comments on the first paragraph of this letter make strangely incoherent reading:

This Willy was a tedious old Philistine. Touching to observe [Mahler's] rapport with my mother's petit-bourgeois relatives. The whole paragraph has a facetious undertone. Immeasurably kind-hearted as he was, he took the trouble to call on all my mother's relatives in Hamburg.[6]

Mahler's final rehearsal was scheduled for 12 March, and his concert for the following day (repeated on 14 March). As a rule, he included detailed reports of such events in his letters to Alma. Their absence in this instance implies

---

* Orig.: 'Wenn sie mal wieder nach Wien zurückmachen' (Saxon dialect).
† Bertha Bergen, the younger sister of Alma's mother.
‡ Vierlanden: an outlying rural area to the south-east of Hamburg.
§ The Deutsche Schauspielhaus (director, Alfred von Berger), where Mahler saw a performance of Ludwig Anzengruber's play *Doppelselbstmord*. In Vienna Baron von Berger had lectured at the University on philosophy and aesthetics. He returned to Vienna in 1912 as director of the Burgtheater.

that one or two letters have gone astray. The fact that he appears also to have left no record of his meeting with Richard and Ida Dehmel supports this theory. Alma, who was particularly fond of Dehmel's verse, makes amends in AMM for the absence of letters by including a substantial extract from Ida Dehmel's diary, which gives a detailed account of the meeting:

'He was delighted by the reception of his symphony in Hamburg. The warmth of the applause after the rehearsal alone was a great satisfaction to him, and on the way to Berlin he told me more of what he felt about it. Travelling and particularly stopping in hotels was a martyrdom. "But you travel all the same – for the sake of your children, no doubt," I observed. "Do you mean my real children or my musical ones?" I had meant only his musical children. "I have to think of both. Actually, I would prefer to live only for my compositions, and, to tell the truth, I am beginning to neglect my operatic duties, but if I gave up my salary as Director of the Opera I should have to make it good in some other way, as a guest conductor perhaps. I doubt whether I shall ever make a penny from performances of my own works." [. . .]

'He asked my opinion of the settings of Dehmel's poems, and was obviously delighted when I said we found Fried promising. That was his opinion too. We also agreed about Pfitzner. Only the way composers search for librettos strikes him as ludicrous (in Pfitzner's case too). If a play was well-rounded, he said, music was superfluous; no playwright worthy of his profession would ever leave a work unfinished in such a way that a composer could add what he himself had omitted; and no music, however inspired, could transform a bad play into great art. Therefore, nobody who was not in command of both gifts, like Wagner, should even attempt it. [. . .]

'In my opinion, the human, all-too-human aspect of the man emerged when he spoke of Strauss and of the Strauss and Hauptmann marriages. He spoke of Strauss's music only very cursorily, but underlined the man's commercial attitude towards it. Strauss was first and foremost a businessman, he said, and an artist only in second place; when the two interests conflicted, it was always the businessman who won through. Here I detected a little envy of Strauss's success – in financial terms, that is. Of Strauss's marriage he spoke with contempt, even with disgust. He thought it verged on masochism.'[7]

As it happens, contact between Mahler and Strauss was more frequent and cordial at this time than ever before. Both musicians appeared at the first Festival of Alsace-Lorraine at Strasburg on 20–22 May. Accompanied by Alma, Mahler arrived in Strasburg on 13 May for rehearsals of his Fifth Symphony *and an all-Beethoven programme, to be given consecutively on 21 and 22 May. It was at this time that he first heard the music of Strauss's new opera,* Salome.

In AMM4 Alma includes an eye-witness account of the occasion:

He [Strauss] had succeeded in locating a piano showroom, so the three of us made our way into a large room packed with pianos. As it happened, the room was surrounded on all sides by tall, bright shop windows, and a constant stream of people passed by or simply stood and stared, their noses pressed to the glass in the hope of hearing something.

Strauss played and sang incomparably well. Mahler was spellbound. We got to the Dance [of the Seven Veils]. It was missing. 'I haven't written it yet,' Strauss explained, and after the gap he played on to the end. 'Isn't it risky,' Mahler asked, 'to leave out the dance and write it later, perhaps at a time when you are no longer in the same mood?' But Strauss laughed heedlessly: 'I'll manage.' But manage he did not: the Dance is the only weak link in the score – nothing more than a potpourri of the rest.[8]

Strauss and Mahler met again a few days later at the annual festival of the ADM, held this year from 31 May to 2 June in Graz. As Alma was quick to observe, relations between Mahler and other members of the ADM were not always cordial:

A good deal of the time we were left to our own devices; indeed, it was noticeable that some composers gave Mahler the cold shoulder. Schillings made a wan attempt to greet, but Rösch simply looked the other way. Anti-Semitism was already rampant, and for Mahler it was palpable. We took due note of the fact and, with no sense of envy, took our meals on our own.[9]

As president of the ADM, Strauss had arranged for Mahler to conduct a concert in Graz devoted entirely to his own orchestral songs (cf. facsimile of the programme on facing page). In turn, for the benefit of the international guests at the Festival, Mahler had organized a series of gala performances at the Vienna Hofoper on 5–7 June: a revival (Neueinstudierung) of Strauss's Feuersnot, *conducted by the composer, followed by Oskar Nedbal's ballet* Der faule Hans,* *conducted by the composer; Pfitzner's* Die Rose vom Liebesgarten, *conducted by Mahler; and finally Liszt's* Legend of St Elizabeth, *conducted by Schalk. Accordingly, Mahler returned to Vienna on 2 June, soon after his concert of orchestral Lieder. On this occasion he was the guest of his parents-in-law on the Hohe Warte. Meanwhile, Alma had travelled on from Graz to Maiernigg, where she rejoined her children.*

---

* Oskar Nedbal's ballet-pantomime *Der faule Hans*, op. 18. The work was premièred at the National Theater, Prague, in 1902, and chosen by Mahler the following year for the ballet repertoire of the Hofoper.

Allgemeiner Deutscher Musikverein.

Tonkünstlerfest in Graz.

Donnerstag, den 1. Juni, abends 6 Uhr
(Hauptprobe vormittags 10 Uhr)

Im Stephaniensaal

Erstes Orchesterkonzert.

Roderich v. Mojsisovics: Romantische Fantasie für die Orgel (op. 9), III. (letzter) Satz.
Herr Otto Burkert.

Guido Peters: Aus der Sinfonie No. 2, E-moll.
I. Satz. Frei rezitatorisch; mit Leidenschaft und großem Ausdruck; heroisch.
IV. (letzter) Satz. Möglichst rasch; feurig; trotzig; bachantisch.

Pause.

Gustav Mahler: Gesänge für eine Singstimme mit Orchester.

I.

1. Der Schildwache Nachtlied.
2. Das Irdische Leben.
3. Der Tamboursg'sell.
4. Ich bin der Welt abhanden gekommen.
Herr Friedrich Weidemann.

II.

1. Lied des Gefangenen im Turm.
2. Wo die schönen Trompeten blasen.
3. Des Antonius von Padua Fischpredigt.
Herr Anton Moser.

III.

1. Revelge.
Herr F. Schrödter.

2. Um Mitternacht.
Herr Erik Schmedes.

IV.

1. Nun will die Sonne so hell aufgeh'n.
2. Nun seh ich wohl.
3. Wenn dein Mütterlein.
4. Oft denk ich.
5. In diesem Wetter.
Herr Friedrich Weidemann.

Pause.

Paul Ertel: „Der Mensch".
Sinfonische Dichtung für großes Orchester und Orgel, nach dem gleichnamigen Triptychon von Lesser Ury, in Form eines Präludiums und einer Tripelfuge (op. 9).
Orgel: Herr Alois Kofler.

---

133   [Vienna, 3 June 1905]

My Almschl,

Why haven't you written to me yet? I was very disappointed this morning, when I saw you had sent Mama an eight-page letter, but hadn't even found time for a postcard for me. At least I now know that you all arrived safely.

Well, as from this morning I'm staying in what used to be your room and shall be sleeping in your bed, <in which I presume nobody except you has ever slept before.> Perhaps for me it will be like taking a sip from someone else's glass: then I can read your thoughts!

Graz was really quite amusing. Mama will write and tell you what happened. I did all I could to give her a good time. But whenever we took a ride in an open carriage etc. we were sorry you weren't with us.

The main news is that Kahnt has offered me 15,000 fl., and now I'm in a dilemma, because I don't know what to say to Peters. Let me sleep on it for a few nights. This is an unexpected windfall, and on no account do I want it to slip through my fingers.

Today I had lunch at Justi's, and afterwards we took high tea in the Volksgarten. <(She's still a grass widow, and Arnold is staying [in Graz] until Monday)>. Afterwards I paid for a cab to take her home. – That, I hope, will have appeased her. <This morning I sent you 1,000 crowns out of my fee, also

for Emma,	100 crowns		
I gave Justi	1,200	"	
also	40	"	for Emma
and	40	"	for the grave in Iglau>

I enclose the receipt for my fee.

Before leaving for Maiernigg I'll repay the rest of my debt to Justi, which will be a considerable step forward.

Strauss and I had a compartment to ourselves in the train from Vienna to Graz, and made very agreeable conversation, just like old times.* Unfortunately he had to leave the next day, due to the sudden death of his (84-year-old) father, so he didn't get to hear my Lieder.†

The other gentlemen spoke in those dulcet, over-refined, politely evasive tones we know only too well. It was the 'song of sour honey'!‡ But after the concert I went back to the hotel alone, just with Mama, Walter and Adler. In the company of the Mauthners and Moser§ we spent a very pleasant evening together and didn't bother about the Festival reception on the Schlossberg. – I shouldn't think anyone missed us.

And now I send you my greetings, Almschi, but I am a bit 'put out'. Your Gustl

Here, as elsewhere, Alma omits from AMM the passage about Mahler's finances. She gives a succinct account of the situation as she had found it:

When I took over the household it was in a state of chaos. Mahler had received a substantial reparation payment from Budapest, since when he had been earning good money wherever he went. But his brothers and sisters, with his eldest sister [Justine] to the fore, had squandered so much of it that in Hamburg he usually had to borrow from friends at the beginning of every

* During the journey, Mahler was also engaged in a conversation with the Styrian poet Peter Rosegger, of whom he was a great admirer. In his essay 'Stunden mit Mahler' (*Die Musik*, [Gustav Mahler-Heft], 2nd June vol. and August vol. , 1911, 352–6 and 143–53.) Ernst Decsey indeed recalls that Mahler spoke of Rosegger as 'the greatest poet of our time'.
† Franz Strauss died in Munich on 31 May. Mahler therefore took over the performance of *Feuersnot*, leaving Richard Strauss free to return to Munich for the funeral.
‡ Orig.: 'die sauere Honigweis' (parody on the names of the 'Prize-Master tones' in Wagner's *Meistersinger*).
§ Presumably Editha, wife of the industrialist Karl-Ferdinand Mauthner von Markhof, her daughter Editha and her future son-in-law, the painter and graphic designer Kolo Moser, who married Editha a month later, on 5 July.

month, because his own resources had run completely dry. He once showed me a letter to his sister in which he had written: 'Why can't you live more economically? For several months I've been wanting to get my shoes resoled, but I don't have the money.' And this was the 1st Kapellmeister of the Hamburg Stadt-Theater! When we got married, Mahler said, 'My sister never learnt how to manage the household. I was already resigned to the idea that I would never be able to pay off my debts. Now I want you to try.' I discovered he was in debt to the tune of 50,000 gold crowns, apart from which he still owed money to the builders for the house in Maiernigg. But first I had to reimburse his three sisters, who had lent him their share of the inheritance, having been brought up to live thriftily, I myself had no objection to economizing or even penny-pinching. On the contrary, it was my ambition that Mahler should be entirely free of debts. But he suffered, because we seemed unable to allow ourselves any extras at all – for five long years! Once I took Justine to task for her reckless extravagance, and she replied, 'Had we ever found ourselves completely high and dry, I would have gone begging with him.'[10]

Mahler had borrowed Justine's share of their father's inheritance to defray the cost of building the house at Maiernigg. As transpires from letter 138, it was Mahler himself who paid off the remainder of the loan to Justine in June 1905, not Alma, as she asserts in AMM. However, there can be no denying that Mahler was content to let Alma manage his household affairs (cf. his letter to Guido Adler, quoted on pp. 352–3), or that she did so with considerable skill. She herself left this further record of the financial problems that beset them:

Before we married, Mahler revealed to me the true extent of his debts and entrusted me with the task of repaying them, saying, 'I trust in "God and my Euryanthe"* that you shall soon accomplish the deed.' It was a heavy responsibility, and he left it to me to manage the household. Mahler's suits were made to measure by first-class tailors, and his innumerable pairs of shoes were made by the finest English shoemakers. Admittedly, I had to make do with the same dress for five or six years . . .[11]

134   [Vienna, 5 June 1905]

My Almscherl,
Today I had lunch at Justi's. Arnold was back from Graz, and we discussed

---

* Orig.: 'Ich bau auf Gott und mein Euryanth' (opening words of Adolar's first aria from Weber's *Euryanthe*).

a few 'orchestral matters'. It was very 'engaging'. Afterwards I undressed, settled on the settee and roasted for a while (the heat is simply murderous). Then I left and ordered a black coffee at Hotel Imperial. While I was waiting, I went to sleep. The waiter woke me up. What a shame! I had been dreaming so sweetly, though I no longer remember what it was. Now I'm sitting in my office and slowly working myself into a solemn mood for 'Feuersnot', which we are giving at seven o'clock this evening for the benefit of a thousand happy listeners.

<Mama and Carl are coming too, and afterwards we're going to the <u>Spaten</u>.> It's so stupid that the Shah won't be arriving until the 15th. Otherwise I could happily leave next Sunday!*

The children must be so sweet now. What a pity I can't be there to see Putzi discovering everything and marvelling at it all. Does she remember the house from last year?

Have they finished the railing?

Warmest greetings and embraces, my Almscherl   Gustav

That same evening in Maiernigg, Alma confided to her diary:

If only I were still capable – as I once was – of putting all my thoughts and feelings to paper . . . My two children are in the room, yet again I have just experienced that old feeling of spiritual freedom and fruitfulness. If only I were alone for longer – really isolated for a long time . . . [. . .] I have been working all day. Copying music for Gustav, minding the children, playing the piano. In the evening I finally managed to calm down. I walked to the village on my own – I was longing for Gustav and still am. Everywhere I saw his image: in the lake, in the forest, everywhere. Separation makes the heart grow sighted. Indeed I live ONLY in him.

I copy music for him, play the piano to impress him – I study, read books, all for the same reason . . . And when he's there I deprive myself of the pleasure – due to my irritability. My former pride, my domineering nature, my measureless ambition – my thirst for fame – they all raise their ugly heads – instead of striving to beautify «and mollify» ONLY HIS life. For that is my sole purpose in life, the only justification for my existence. And my dear little brats «children». I'm very worried. «I have heard nothing from him for several days.»[12]

---

* Mahler feared he would have to postpone his journey to Maiernigg, due to a state visit by the Shah of Persia.

135   [Vienna, 6 June 1905]

My beloved,
Your dear letter was truly refreshing for me. Now, as I see, you are on the
right path. When one spends longer periods on one's own, one comes to
forge a <u>unity</u> with <u>nature</u> – admittedly a more tranquil 'surrounding' than
the people to whom one is accustomed. This state of mind engenders a positive outlook (as opposed to our normal attitude, which is a quagmire of
negations) and, in the long run, a creative one. This is only normal. Isolation
hence helps us to find ourselves, and from there it is but a small step to God.
At present you are imbued with this spirit, which pleases me beyond measure, for I never doubted that you had it in you.
Our everyday existence, completely hampered as it is by fault-finding and
'criticisms', seems small-minded by comparison. You see, it's just the same
with your choice of reading matter: Shakespeare is <u>positive</u> and <u>productive</u>,
while Ibsen is nothing but analysis, negation, infecundity. – <The same contrast applies to you <u>as you are now</u> and to <u>you</u> as you are in Vienna, where
you get angry about 'theatre folk' and such things.>
Now you will understand why I attempt to isolate the <u>positive</u>, <u>productive</u>
voices from the chaotic counterpoint of everyday life, and why I take a
bird's-eye view of certain things <while you are caught up in the very midst
of them.> – If again you find yourself beset by negative attitudes <whether
due to physical depression or some passing aggravation> [several words
obliterated] and your view is momentarily obscured, don't be deterred.
Don't let yourself believe that life has no <u>affirmative</u> side, or that its positive
aspects are not of primary importance. – Just persuade yourself that the sun
is hiding behind the clouds, and at present all is dark, cold and unfriendly.
But: it <u>will shine</u> again!
Dearest, the heat here is unbearable. Yesterday was <u>Feuersnot</u>, which astonished the German critics and provoked the <u>envy</u> of the German opera composers. Der faule Hans came as a consolation to them all, and they wept for
joy and sorrow. –
<Mama has been following me wherever I go, and indeed leading the way. She
and Carl have been moving heaven and earth to make life comfortable for
me.> How I would <u>love</u> to be with you and the little ones already! This evening
I'll be dining with the festival committee, <u>Schillings</u> etc., at Hotel Sacher.
<This evening is Die Rose vom Liebesgarten!>*
A thousand kisses from   Your Gustl

* Orig.: 'Rose v. L.' Alma misconstrued Mahler's abbreviation in ELM as 'Rosé and Legler'.

<But this time you've been a good girl, my Almschili, and written to me, sweetly curbing the pangs of separation.>

136[U]   Vienna, 8 June 1905[P]

My dear Almschili,
Neither yesterday nor today did I have a free moment to write to you. The 'Tonkünstler' have been monopolizing my time. – All the same, some of these attentions are most welcome, e.g. I have made personal and really cordial contact with Schillings. Yesterday he and <u>Mengelberg</u> from Amsterdam joined me for lunch at Mama's. Tomorrow I have a little breathing space, and I'll write in greater detail. – Your letters are so sweet and refreshing for me. If only I were already with you. A thousand kisses, my Almschl.   Your Gustl

137   [Vienna, 10 June 1905]

My Almschili,
You'll have to forgive me. In the last few days I literally haven't had a minute to sit down and write. – I never experienced a more hectic time, not only because of the music festival but also due to end-of-season meetings, rehearsals etc. – One great danger has been averted. Just imagine, it almost looked as if I'd have to remain here until the 20th (!), because that's when the <Pig of>[*] Persia is due to arrive. All manner of crazy ideas went through my head until finally I hit on the solution of pleading doctor's orders. So now I have sick leave as from next Thursday. All going well, I can get away on Wednesday evening and join you for breakfast, my dearest, on Thursday morning. Now <u>there's</u> a breakfast that I'm madly[†] looking forward to.
Mengelberg is <still> here! <He's taking up a huge amount of my time, and of course it's also costing me a small fortune. But after all, somehow I have to return his hospitality.> Schillings and I have become really good friends. I have come to find him remarkably sympathetic. Mama has also taken a liking to him, and to Mengelberg too. Two days without a letter from you. I hope nothing has gone wrong! Your dear letters are always like a breath of fresh air. I'm really delighted to see that you're ' <u>lost to the world</u>'.[‡] It's at

---

[*] Orig.: 'Schwein' (instead of 'Schah'). In AMM1 (p. 341), Alma substitutes the word 'Herr'. Muzaffar ad-Din had been crowned Shah of Persia in 1896 and reigned until his death in 1907.
[†] Orig.: 'tamisch' (Styrian dialect: crazy).
[‡] Orig.: 'der Welt abhanden gekommen' (opening words of Mahler's eponymous Rückert-Song).

such times that one's true qualities come to the fore (assuming, naturally, that they were there in the first place, but hidden). – Be a dear and write me a nice long letter. And you could cheer me up by sending news of our dear little mites. I've already bought a bicycle (150 fl.).

A thousand kisses to you, my beloved Almschi   Your old Gustl

138[U] Postcard   Vienna, 11 June 1905[P]

My dearest,

Already three days and still no letter? Why on earth? Here it's as hectic as on a railway train. On Wednesday, thank heaven, I'm off to join you. Then I can take a little rest, and you will all be with me. Today I opened the strong-box in search of a couple of sketches I put away for the summer – but I couldn't find them. Did I perhaps leave them in Maiernigg? Yesterday we went to Minna von Barnhelm[*] (to be quite honest, I found it rather tedious).

I shall probably entrust the Sixth Symphony to Kahnt, because Peters refuses to pay more. And I simply can't turn down 5,000 fl., particularly since Kahnt is very much on the upsurge just now. More about this when I see you.[†]

Today I received my fee, and tomorrow I'm going to pay Justi the rest of her money. – Fondest greetings from   Your Gustav

During the summer of 1904 Mahler had composed or at least sketched out the two 'Nachtmusik' movements of his Seventh Symphony. *He may well have left them in Maiernigg, in which case Alma will have been able to put his mind at rest about them. In AMM4 she writes: 'Mahler wrote the Seventh Symphony in* one *sudden frenzy of activity during the summer of 1905. He had already prepared the "ground-plan", as he called it, in mid-summer of 1904. – His Nachtmusik movements were based on images inspired by Eichendorff: burbling fountains, German Romanticism. The rest of the symphony has no programme.'[13]*

Willem Mengelberg cites another source of inspiration for the Seventh Symphony, *Rembrandt's celebrated* Night Watch, *which Mahler saw at the Rijksmuseum during his visit to Amsterdam in the autumn of 1903.[14]*

---

[*] Guest appearance of Max Reinhardt's Kleines und Neues Theater from Berlin with Lessing's *Minna von Barnhelm* at the Theater an der Wien. Reinhardt not only directed but also played the role of Just (servant of Major von Tellheim).

[†] Mahler signed his contract for the *Sixth Symphony* with C. F. Kahnt on 15 July 1905. The fee amounted to 30,000 crowns (15,000 fl.).

139[U]   [Vienna, 12 June 1905]

Dearest,

I shudder to think that I may not be able to get away on Wednesday after all. The death has just been announced of Princess Kinsky, sister of Liechtenstein and mother-in-law of Montenuovo,* which means postponing a meeting at which my presence is essential. How awful that would be. I'm taking your 2,000 crowns' housekeeping money for July and August to have it broken down into new fifty-crown notes, so you won't have any 'frets' when it comes to changing them later this summer. At present you're saving money on me, I must say! I'm already looking forward to our first breakfast together. It will be wonderful. –

Whitsun was completely rained off here, but it didn't trouble me at all: going for walks no longer gives me any pleasure. I still hope to hear from you. Have you given our little Putzis the run of the garden? And the walking rail?[†] That must be an adorable sight!

Love and kisses, my dearest. Write!   Your Gustl

I miss you very much!

On 15 June Mahler was at last able to leave for Maiernigg.

140 Postcard   Vienna, 13 June 1905[P]

My Almschi,

<u>Hurray</u>! I'll be arriving the day after tomorrow. In other words, you can expect to see me wobbling down the path on my bicycle around 7.30 on <u>Thursday</u> morning. I'll be wanting a healthy breakfast. Then the first thing I want to do is take it easy. This drudgery is simply too stupid. Tomorrow I'll wire you, just to be certain. – Your story about the lamp gave us a nasty fright. Thank God no harm came of it.

Warmest   Your Gustl

Alma explains the 'story about the lamp' in AMM1:

I was working on the fair copy of the Sixth Symphony, and wanted to get a fresh sheet of manuscript paper out of the desk. But there was a petrol-lamp

---

* Princess Marie Kinsky, née Liechtenstein, who had died in the night of 11 June at her home near Prague. Her second daughter, Franziska, was married to 2nd Obersthofmeister Montenuovo; her younger brother, Rudolf von Liechtenstein, occupied the position of 1st Obersthofmeister at the imperial court.

† Orig.: 'Gehschule' (a railing with the aid of which small children could take their first steps).

half-perched on the lid, and it fell over, causing the carpet and the sofa to catch fire. I shouted through the open window, but by the time the servants arrived I had already managed to smother almost everything with cushions and blankets. My two children were sleeping in the rooms to the left and the right.[15]

When Mahler finally arrived on 15 June (Gucki's second birthday), he seems indeed to have 'taken it easy'. Contrary to his usual habit, he left again after only a few days for an excursion to the Dolomites. Writing of these events in letter 303, he recalls having spent a fortnight at Maiernigg before moving on. In fact, he stayed only six days, until 21 June.

141   Schluderbach, 23 June 1905[P]

My Almschili,
I was determined to stay in the train at Lienz, for fear of succumbing to the temptations of the station buffet. But a dull pain made me aware that I'd fallen victim to the inevitable migraine, and once I arrived here in Schluderbach it hit me with full force. I lay down, but that only made things worse, and finally it drove me from my couch and into the street. I walked right round the lake ($2\frac{1}{2}$ hours) and returned with a pretty clear head, so now I'm settling in here for the night. Already while taking my 'run' (through a forest of young pines) I thought to myself: if only Almschi were here! How she'd love it! What a shame! The area happens to be free of mischief-makers at present – though today, admittedly, the rafters have been echoing to the din of yokels and soldiers (from the fortress at Landro). But one only need step outside into the fresh air, and at once all the horrors fade away.
A thousand kisses   Your Gustl

<Tomorrow I'm off to Misurina.>

In letter 303 Mahler remembers feeling anxious that the summer of 1905 had been 'lost', and that when he returned to Maiernigg the sound of the oars of the boat ferrying him home had suddenly inspired him to the opening bars of the Seventh Symphony. *Having resumed work, he recalls that he completed the first, third and fifth movements 'in four weeks'. In fact, it took somewhat longer: after his return from the Dolomites, his vacation at Maiernigg lasted a further seven weeks.*
   The first to receive news of the symphony's completion was Guido Adler, to whom Mahler wrote (in Latin): 'Septima mea finita est. Credo hoc opus

fauste natum et bene gestum. Salutationes plurimas tibi et tuis etiam meae uxoris. G. M.'[16] *Four days later he informed Strauss, more concisely (and in German): 'My 7th is finished.'*[17]

In 1905 *there were fewer visitors than the previous year: Theobald Pollak travelled down from Vienna, as did Alfred Roller and his fiancée Milewa;*[†] *there were two guests from Graz, the critic Ernst Decsey*[‡] *and the conductor Julius Weis-Osborn; and in the second week of July Schoenberg and Zemlinsky interrupted their vacation on the Traunsee to spend three days in nearby Sekirn.*[§] *Such visits often helped relieve that feeling of frustration of which Alma had written in her diary (cf. p. 206), but on 6 July she again complained bitterly of her isolation:*

Today our friend Pollak arrived here. I'm so glad to have someone to talk to. With Gustav I often don't know what to say. Before he even opens his mouth, I already know exactly what to expect. The past weeks have been tremendously hot, and I haven't felt like doing anything. Neither reading nor working, nor anything else for that matter. I long for a husband – for I have NONE . . . But I feel too lethargic . . . even for that . . .[18]

Mahler was obliged to return to Vienna earlier than expected that summer, due to administrative problems at the Hofoper. For one thing, he found himself obliged to postpone his planned new production of Die Walküre; *for another, there was much to attend to in connection with the forthcoming Mozart anniversary season.*

While waiting for the annual renovation work in his apartment to be completed, Mahler booked into a hotel at Edlach. Before boarding the train at Klagenfurt on 21 August he had sent Alma his customary farewell greeting. Though mentioned in his first letter from Vienna, the card itself has not survived.

142   [Vienna, 23 August 1905]

My Almschili,
Yesterday was a delightful day! All that rowing about on the lake had given

---

* 'My Seventh is finished. I believe this work to be comely and well-born. Very many greetings to you and your family, also from my wife.'
† Milewa Stoisavljevic, Alfred Roller's Croatian-born wife and former pupil.
‡ Ernst Decsey, critic of the *Grazer Tagespost* and biographer of Hugo Wolf (see also footnote on p. 204). He first met Mahler in 1905, during the Graz Festival of the ADM later visited him in Maiernigg. In 'Stunden mit Mahler', Decsey published a full account of these and other encounters.
§ It was evidently at this time that Mahler entrusted Zemlinsky with the task of preparing for C. F. Kahnt a four-handed piano arrangement of the *Sixth Symphony*.

me quite an appetite, so I went to the <u>station</u> buffet and ate a plate of Palatschinken. – I hope you received my card. – Unfortunately I had to share a sleeping car, and hence got scarcely a wink of sleep. All the same, it is more pleasant if one can at least stretch out. Once I arrived here (where Hassinger was waiting), I went straight to the apartment, <gave Johanna the bag,> locked my Seventh Symphony in the strong-box, took clean clothes and fresh linen, and made my way to the theatre.

There, to my surprise, I found (apart from Wondra and Przistaupinski) only Roller, who was more affable than ever; I sorted out all my affairs, and now I'm off to lunch. Afterwards I'll drive out to <u>Edlach</u>, where I phoned to reserve a room. From there I shall probably wend my way slowly up the Schneeberg. <u>What</u> a shame you can't come with me.

Send your next letters to Edlach – Edlacherhof. If I decide to leave, I'll cable you right away.

Fondest kisses, my dearest!

Write and tell me what the children are up to   Your Gustl

In ELM, Alma comments on this letter as follows:

Mahler had to return to Vienna, because the Opera always re-opened on the Kaiser's birthday (18 August). I always stayed on [in Maiernigg] for another eight to ten days, set the house in order, packed, then travelled to Vienna to prepare our apartment for our return. Meanwhile, Mahler remained in the vicinity of Vienna, and drove out there every day as soon as he had finished at the office. Staying at a hotel would anyway have been too expensive, with two children and a bonne.[19]

143[U]   Edlach [24 August 1905]
                                                      Hotel Edlacherhof

My Almschi,

I'd only just posted yesterday's letter when Arnold arrived (he wasn't offended in the least, as one always hastens to add). – Justi is staying on at Aussee until 15 September. – He accompanied me to the Südbahnhof, where we had lunch together, then I took the train to Edlach and walked here from the station. Frau Horwitz[*] was sitting in the coffee-house. – I had scarcely sat down when along came Dr Sewald.[†] – It didn't take long before Frau Horwitz had minced over from her table, despite my looking the other way

---

[*] A friend of the Molls, often mentioned in AMD, though never by her first name.
[†] Orig.: 'Seewald' (consistently). Probably the barrister Dr Bernhard Sewald, another old friend of the Molls.

whenever she greeted me. So there I was, in the most entrancing company. She insisted on talking in a loud voice about Alma, Anna etc. There was an elderly gentleman sitting opposite us, who looked remarkably like your Papa, as Sewald also agreed. I did my best to make a bolt for it, then went out for a lovely walk. It's beautiful here, but the guests can go to the devil. This morning at breakfast I was promptly greeted by Herr Ludwig Grünfeld.[*] I'll do my best to keep a low profile, and shall probably move further up the Semmering. Tomorrow I want to climb the Rax.

What a dreadful shame you can't be here. It would have made it far more enjoyable for me. In future you should come out here with me more often. I intend to take two or three days' break after every opening night. Don't forget to write and tell me if Putzi has got over her tummy-ache. I'm rather concerned about it.

Now it's time for an outing.

Fondest kisses, my Almscherl   Your Gustl

Could you possibly post me my <u>Sixth</u> Symphony? I'd like to have the other movements copied, besides which you won't have to burden yourself with it. But make sure to send it by registered mail, won't you.

144   Edlach [25 August 1905]
                                                            Hotel Edlacherhof

Dearest,

Well, yesterday I came back here during quite a violent storm. I had brought <u>Fechner</u>'s <u>Aesthetics</u>[†] with me by way of reading material (highly interesting, you'll love it). It was the only book you had left on my desk. – Half-way through the first chapter, I realized that this was Part II – in other words, Part I was still in the packing case. However, in my desperation I just went on reading. But then I managed to leave the book in the train. I shall write to the Südbahn. I'm sure this is a book that can only fall into the hands of 'honest' finders.

Today it's still drizzling, so there's no chance of an outing on the Rax. Tomorrow, I hope. Today I'll wander around on the lower ground.

I shan't be conducting Fidelio. My intention is to 'take up the baton' for the first time with Tristan.[‡] – By that time you'll already be back, and maybe you'd

---

[*] The concert-agent Ludwig Grünfeld.

[†] Gustav Theodor Fechner, *Vorschule der Ästhetik*, 2 vols, Leipzig, 1876.

[‡] The performance of *Fidelio* on 24 August was conducted by Bruno Walter. Mahler made his first appearance of the season on 5 September, as in 1904, with *Tristan und Isolde*.

like to come and see it. – <Obviously I can't pass on your message about the fruit conserves to Johanna.* Maybe you'd better write and tell her yourself.> I miss you terribly. How lovely it would be for us to go hiking together. This is almost the only part of the season when I have neither worries nor duties. – I only hope this rain hasn't set in, for otherwise I'll have to return to town tomorrow. These three days have been uncommonly refreshing and relaxing. And now a thousand kisses, my treasure. Send news of the children!
Your Gustl

145   Edlach, 25 August 1905
                                                        Hotel Edlacherhof

My dearest,
Your sweet letter, addressed to the Hofoper, arrived here only today. I'm very glad to hear that your visitors arrived at such an opportune moment. I would probably have got bored with them, but it seems they have helped you escape the arduous monotony that has been plaguing you of late. All the same, don't let yourself be taken in by Rosthorn.† If you could see how relaxed and well I'm feeling already now, and if you knew how well I know my own physical limits, you would have no reason to worry. – People like this Rosthorn could never imagine an entelechy like mine. On the contrary, they have no idea how rapidly I would deteriorate if I were to stop working. – In recent years, indeed, I was far more worried about the dizzy spells I was having before going to bed. More recently I haven't experienced anything of the kind. In other words, this is clear evidence that I have indeed not been overstraining myself. – <Such problems as I experienced this summer were the fault of my sluggish digestion, and this has already improved markedly.>
Despite the continuous rainfall, today I went for another five-hour walk. – The food here is really the best I have ever been served at a restaurant. Nothing has disagreed with me at all. Unfortunately it's pouring again. If it doesn't stop, I'll return to Vienna tomorrow. But I give you my word, dear Almschel, to take it easy and go for short walks – or rather, as soon as the weather improves, I'll be off for another trip to the mountains.
Is there then no chance of your coming back a little sooner?
I feel terribly apprehensive; furthermore, I'm fed up with being alone and eating out.

---

* Johanna was the new housemaid. At this time she was responsible for overseeing the painting and decorating of Mahler's apartment.
† The gynaecologist Dr Alfred Rosthorn. Alma has left no record of the other friends who visited her in Maiernigg at this time.

Warmest greetings. <(I still haven't managed to climb the Rax.)>
Your Gustav

146[U]   [Vienna, 26 August 1905]

Dearest,
I slept at Pollak's last night, and the air was terrible. The poor fellow's quite
mad. At eight o'clock he's already sitting in his office, and he never finds
time to escape the stifling air of the city. – I'm just about to leave for
Schneeberg, and if nothing unforeseen occurs I'll stay there till the 31st,
then meet you at <u>Wiener</u> Neustadt and travel home with you. – Heavens, I
can't wait! – I don't much enjoy roving around on my own. Right now I
need you at my side. What's more, all this eating out is playing havoc with
my digestive system.
In that respect only <u>Edlach</u> filled the bill, and there it was superb. It
wasn't as much the bad weather that drove me away as a handful of
importunate people. The cuisine was almost like a health cure. In the
autumn or winter, when it's quiet, we really must go back there together.
– I went to see the apartment, and it's looking terrible. I only hope it will
be ready in time. –
According to Pollak, Banhans[*] is <u>certain</u> to reserve splendid seats for you –
but <u>write at once</u>, should you not already have done so, and tell him <u>exactly</u>
which train you'll be taking.   Your Gustl

147   Hochschneeberg [26 August 1905]
                                              Hotel Hochschneeberg

My Almschl,
Despite some rain and squally weather on the way up, I've now arrived.
Almschl, it's the most beautiful, magnificent scenery I ever saw! You really
<u>must</u> come here with me, at least for an afternoon. One can <u>drive</u> all the way
up and back down. You really must see it. – I just don't know how I could
have failed to notice it last time I was here. The only reason was that Arnold
was with me at the time, and he was obscuring my thoughts as if a thick
cloud was constricting my breathing and weighing down on me. What an ass
I have been! Why didn't I come here straight away, instead of going to
Edlach? But now I shall stay until I can collect you from the station in
<u>Payerbach</u>. Please write and tell me exactly when you'll be arriving. –

---

[*] Karl Freiherr von Banhans, a friend of the Molls. He was a privy councillor and later
Minister of Railways. Alma recalls in ELM: 'He always took care of my train reservations.'

<Hassinger assured me today, having had the matter out with Johanna (who is just as 'cool' as ever, by the way – make sure you don't get drawn into another argument with her), that we won't be able to move into the apartment until the 1st [September]. – However, I impressed upon her that you and the children would be arriving on the evening of the 31st. – I'm having problems with Kahnt. He claims he never received the revisions – you know, the <u>packet</u> you sent off to Leipzig at the time. Please, Almschl, see if you can find the <u>postal receipt</u>. It's very important. Or did you perhaps bungle it?[*]
You write that Mama won't be able to take the children off your hands, but I simply won't accept that. You really <u>must</u> look after yourself! Otherwise I shall neglect my own health by way of protest. Let's talk it over. If the weather stays fine, the Schneeberg would still be a possibility, and I could visit you there from time to time. – In September they lower the prices, by the way. Just in case, I'll choose a nice room with a balcony, either on the East or the South side. The best they could do for me was a poky little room. But even that doesn't diminish the pleasure. The food is <u>very good</u>, and cheaper than in Edlach. I believe full board and lodging costs about 6 or 7 fl. (it wasn't part of my arrangement).>
Many kisses, my beloved   Your Gustav

Mahler's enthusiasm for the Semmering region was understandable, not only because of the good air and wonderful scenery, but also due to its easy accessibility from Vienna. In 1910 he purchased a plot of land close by, at Breitenstein, with a view to building a new country retreat for himself. He never lived to carry out the plan, but shortly after his death Alma did indeed build a house there, which she retained until 1937.

148[U]   Hochschneeberg, 27 August 1905[P]

Dearest,
It's pouring today – with brief interruptions. Nevertheless, it's still wonderful. I remain undeterred, and shall hold the fort until you arrive. Walter came up to see me at midday, and kept me company all afternoon. Yes indeed, you'd love it here. Every time the sun comes out, I think of you. You really must come up here with me sometime. Unfortunately I haven't received any post from you since yesterday. It will probably have to make its way here via Edlach and Vienna. How was the tea? And did Hammerschlag[†] manage to

---

[*] The problem of the missing corrections for the *Sixth Symphony* appears to have been solved, for there is no further mention of it in this correspondence.
[†] 'Hammerschlag' could either have been Alma's gynaecologist, Dr Albert Hammerschlag, or his brother Paul Hammerschlag, director of the Credit-Anstalt (a major Austrian bank).

swim in the Wörthersee without having to be dragged out of the water half dead? But how lovely it will be when we can sit together at home of an evening, with me sipping my Bavarian beer at your side. Warmest greetings Your Gustav

149[U]   Hochschneeberg, 28 August 1905[P]

My dearest,
I'm sorry to say that I haven't heard from you in two days. Most likely it's my own fault because I should have cabled my new address to you. All the same, it makes me rather uneasy. I beg you, write well in advance or, better still, cable me your exact departure time on <u>Wednesday</u>. Depending on the weather, I'll either make the descent to Payerbach on foot, or if I have to leave here by train, I can wait for you either at <u>Payerbach</u> or Wiener Neustadt. When the train stops at the station, you'd better look out of the window. If you don't see me at either place, I'll be waiting for you at the Südbahnhof [in Vienna]. – It's indescribably beautiful here, and I'm really sad that you can't be with me. It would suit you down to the ground. However, it's been costing me a small <u>fortune</u>. The portions are immense and would be ample for both of us. But I have a double room (apart from my first, poky little room, nothing else was free) and I've had to pay the full rate. Even when the weather is really stormy, there's a wonderful covered walkway with the most magnificent panoramic views. Fondest greetings and kisses   Your Gustav

Alma returned to Vienna with her children on 30 August (one day before her twenty-sixth birthday). In mid-September the whole family spent a few days at Göding as guests of Fritz and Emma Redlich (cf. commentary, p. 120). As on the previous occasion, Mahler himself had to return home after a few days to attend to urgent business at the Hofoper, while Alma and the children stayed behind. The following letter must have been written shortly after Mahler's return, but neither this nor the two that followed can be dated exactly. However, since all three were sent to Göding, it seems likely that they all date from the second half of September.

150[U]   [Vienna, September 1905]

My dearest Almschili,
It was nice at Göding! As yet I haven't had a moment to catch my breath, due to the visit of <u>Fried</u> from Berlin and several cancellations (Slezak etc.). – Fried dined with me at home. Then we went through my Second Symphony. His ability inspires considerable confidence.

I consider this Berlin performance (8 Nov.) to be extremely important, and therefore I'm planning to go there and take you with me. – The maid has just arrived. Unfortunately we haven't been able to find a room at a hostel for her (the poor girl spent a whole morning trudging around in search of one), so I've suggested to Mama that we find her an inexpensive hotel room. I wouldn't want her living in until Johanna has left. – Write at once (send a telegram if necessary) and tell me whether I should give Johanna her references. The 15,000 fl.[*] have arrived.

I'm so glad to hear that you're having good weather. Stay there with the children as long as you can. – I'd like to return on Tuesday afternoon at five o'clock, and stay all day Wednesday. I'm feeling wonderfully relaxed. Thousands of kisses on the way. Write at once.

Your old Gustl

'The maid', as Alma explains, 'was a new nanny, who arrived earlier than expected.'[20] Evidently matters with Johanna had come to a head, and she had been given notice.

Oskar Fried, one of Mahler's finest and most dedicated interpreters, started life as a horn-player. Having studied with Humperdinck and Scharwenka, he began his career as a composer and arranger, but soon also made his mark as a conductor. Das trunkene Lied, a choral setting of a poem from Nietzsche's Also sprach Zarathustra, was his most successful work. It was well received in Berlin, where Karl Muck conducted the world première in 1904. In March 1905 followed the Viennese première, conducted by Schalk. Mahler attended the performance, at which he evidently met Fried for the first time.[†]

At the Hofoper Mahler was preparing a new production of Le donne curiose by Ermanno Wolf-Ferrari, which was to open on 4 October. His plan, as outlined in the following letter, was to return to Göding, as soon as his rehearsals were over, on Tuesday 19 September.

151[U]   [Vienna, September 1905]

My Almschili,

Just a brief greeting today (my rehearsal schedule is endless). As long as nothing untoward occurs, I'll be arriving on Tuesday (about five o'clock). Today I'm having lunch with Mama (Carl won't be there, but I fear that

---

[*] Orig.: '15 000 Spiesse' (i.e. the payment from C. F. Kahnt for the *Sixth Symphony*).
[†] Fried's oeuvre also includes a setting of Dehmel's *Verklärte Nacht* for two solo voices and orchestra, choral works to texts by Dehmel and Verhaeren, a Fantasy on Humperdinck's *Hänsel und Gretel*, and an unpublished opera, *Die vernarrte Prinzess*. In 1913 he abandoned composition for the sake of his conducting career.

Willy and Martha* will be). I'd be far happier if Mama were on her own! – I spent yesterday evening with Fried, who's an extremely witty and original individual. I foresee a great future for him, and believe he will be of great value to me. What a pity you can't meet him. But I simply <u>must</u> go to Berlin, and you <u>must</u> come with me.

Warmest greetings to the Redlichs. They're such wonderful people, and I'm very glad to know that they are taking care of you. What should I do about Johanna? Wire me if necessary. Warmest greetings   Your Gustav

152ᵁ   [Vienna, September 1905]

Dearest,

Yesterday was another of those hectic days: rehearsals, meetings with the Obersthofmeister in his office, administrative duties, cancellations and all the other things I love so dearly. A postal order arrived for you from Marakky,† but it can be cashed only by the recipient in person. Since you weren't here, I asked for the money to be returned to the sender. You'll have to recoup it from her when you get back. –

Fritz [Löhr] came round in the afternoon, and we went for a stroll together. We walked much of the way in silence and had quite a pleasant conversation. – In the evening I was visited in my office by <u>Hammerschlag</u>,‡ who asked after you. He may be a little too keen on socializing, but he was very charming and seems to be have taken to us both. – In the evening I had a cold supper with Roller at Café Imperial. Mama sat in my box, and I had a brief chat with her.

Let me know the exact time of your arrival. I can't tell you how much I'm looking forward to the end of this bachelor's existence, when we can at last sit together again of an evening.

And then you and I should take long walks together – like in our first year. Do you remember how lovely it was?

Today I have a long orchestral rehearsal. I probably won't get home till late. Could you perhaps phone me tomorrow? I'll await your call in the apartment at three o'clock in the afternoon.

Are our little monsters healthy and happy? It's such a stroke of luck that the three of you are having such a lovely holiday. The Redlichs are really delightful people; I've grown very fond of them. Warmest greetings and kisses, my Almschi, from   Your Gustav

* Willy and Martha Bergen, who were visiting Vienna.
† Identity unknown.
‡ Identity uncertain: either Alfred or Paul Hammerschlag (cf. footnote on p. 217).

As it transpired, Mahler was unable to return to Göding. He may simply have been hindered by pressure of work, as implied in his letters, but there were also pressing strategical reasons for him to remain in Vienna. On 20 September he was informed that the court censor, Emil Jettel von Ettenach, had banned the projected new production of Salome *at the Hofoper on moral grounds. According to his report to Mahler, dated 31 October, the libretto included passages calling for 'actions emanating from the realm of sexual pathology, which are unsuitable for portrayal on the stage of our Hoftheater'. The decision was final, and had been taken after a long series of meetings and letters of protest. This was a particularly severe blow to Mahler's self-esteem and a sure indication that people in high places were intriguing against him. At such a sensitive moment he will have felt obliged to stay at his post.*

He may have intended that Alma should travel with him to Berlin for the performance of his Second Symphony *(cf. letters 150 and 151), but in the event she stayed at home. Before boarding the train he sent her his customary greeting from the station.*

153^U Postcard   Vienna, 6 November 1905^P

My Almschili,
Top of the morning to you! What a shame you're still lying in bed instead of drinking a lovely cup of tea with me in Dresden. Kiss our little Putzis and send my best wishes to Berliner. A thousand more of the same from   Your Gust

154 Postcard   Berlin, 7 November 1905^P

Dearest Almschl,
<u>Motto</u>: How blissful, how blissful a cobbler to be! I'm writing this at the very table at which I sat when I wrote you all <u>those</u> letters from the Palast Hotel*
– at a time when I never dreamt I would ever come to envy the lot of a humble cobbler. – The breakfast was splendid (a ray of light on this murky day). (As you will have gathered, I've just returned from the final rehearsal.) This evening I'm invited to dine chez Strauss. Were it not for my obligations in Leipzig the day after tomorrow, I'd leave for home tonight! How blissful, how blissful a tenor to be!   Your Gustav

The main topic of conversation with Strauss on the evening of 7 November will certainly have been the controversy over Salome *at the Hofoper, and*

* Letters 8–12.

Mahler's attempts to mollify the censor or circumvent his ban. This was, after all, as much of an affront for Strauss as for Mahler, and for the composer it also signified a substantial loss of revenue. But it was not to be: the Austrian première of Salome was given not in Vienna but in Graz, on 16 May 1906 (cf. letter 165), and the first Viennese performance, on 25 May 1907, was given neither at the Hofoper nor at the Volksoper, but at the Deutsches Volkstheater by a theatre company from Breslau.

155   Berlin, 8 November 1905[P]
                                                      Palast Hotel

My dearest heart,
Once again I'm writing at the very table at which I sat about four years ago, bombarding you with daily letters. Since then, as I now realize, my feelings for you have not changed in the least. I think of you with the same love and joy, and it gives me as much pleasure as ever to tell you so. – Today I'm in a mad rush: I have to call on Ochs, Hülsen, Muck, G. Hauptmann and Fernow,[*] then rehearsals for the concert, post-mortems with Fried etc. etc. I had a very pleasant time with Strauss yesterday evening, but one cannot entirely disregard his offhanded, self-important attitude. Incidentally, he gave me a copy of his latest book (a spiced-up version of Berlioz's Treatise of Orchestration[†]). It should make very interesting reading for you; indeed, you could learn a lot from it. I shall present you with a copy for your library <(I believe it costs 50 marks)>. He also promised me a full score of Salome, which I shall also pass on to you. So, from now on, the envy of all creative composers[‡] will know no bounds.
But, as I said, instead of such gifts I would have preferred a little more warmth <(though I'm still very pleased on your behalf).> [Two lines obliterated.] This evening we're all invited to Frau Wolff's. – O God, what motto should I be mumbling? But Fried is very willing, and my broad hints[§] will perhaps be of value to him (they'll help me to assess his talent: yesterday everything was almost twice too fast).

[*] Siegfried Ochs, founder and conductor of the Philharmonischer Chor, reputed to have been the finest choir in Germany; Georg von Hülsen-Haesseler, Intendant of the Royal Theater; Karl Muck, 1st Kapellmeister at the Royal Opera; Gerhart Hauptmann, the celebrated playwright; Hermann Fernow, business manager of the Wolff concert agency.
[†] Orig.: 'mit neuem "Kren" dazu von ihm' (with new 'horseradish sauce' of his own). The book, published under the title *Instrumentationslehre von Hector Berlioz*, Leipzig, 1905, includes several references to Mahler's orchestration.
[‡] Orig.: 'aller schaffenden Tonkünstler' (allusion to the Vereinigung schaffender Tonkünstler).
[§] Orig.: 'Winke mit Zaunpfählen' (colloquial, ironical).

I'm still sitting here, drinking my tea. Soon I expect Berliner, with whom I also had lunch, and then we'll be off to the concert. Tomorrow I leave at 8 a.m. for Leipzig. The following day at eight o'clock: kisses all round, Putzi, Gucki, a hot bath and breakfast, then up and away and 'down to business'* – there's a vast amount to be done. Warmest greetings, dear Almschel, also to Mama.   Your Gustav

Alma has left a detailed account of Mahler's first meetings with Gerhart Hauptmann:

Hauptmann was in Vienna for the première of his 'Rose Bernd' (at the Burgtheater).† He felt a tender affection for Mahler, which was not entirely reciprocated. However, I could sense that Hauptmann's company would one day be beneficial to Mahler, so I arranged daily meetings between them, confronting Mahler each time with a fait accompli. And each time it was more beautiful. We were always on our own, just the four of us. The discussion turned to the subject of Christ. Soon afterwards Hauptmann wrote his Emanuel Quint.‡ There was a wondrous excitement in Mahler's voice, and Hauptmann listened with bated breath. Once, when Mahler had left the room (we were dining at Hotel Erzherzog Karl), Hauptmann said, 'Your husband finds clear words for everything that is still chaotic in my mind. Nobody has ever been of greater value to me.' Mahler grew fonder of Hauptmann, but sometimes he lacked the patience for the latter's deliberation and reserved manner of making conversation.[21]

Before returning to Vienna Mahler travelled to Leipzig where, on 9 November, he recorded four piano rolls for the firm of Welte-Mignon. His programme consisted of 'Das himmlische Leben' from the Fourth Symphony, *the opening movement of the* Fifth Symphony, *'Ging heut' morgen übers Feld' from the* Lieder eines fahrenden Gesellen *and 'Ich ging mit Lust durch einen grünen Wald' from the early* Lieder und Gesänge. *The Welte-Mignon technique set new standards of precision. Mahler acknowledged as much with his entry in the visitors' book: 'With astonishment and admiration I add my name to the list of previous signatories.'*

As the year drew to a close, Mahler's Fifth Symphony *received four perform-*

---

* Orig.: 'rin in's Jeschäft' (Berlin dialect).
† The first Viennese production of Hauptmann's five-act social drama opened on 11 February 1904.
‡ Gerhart Hauptmann, *Der Narr in Christo Emanuel Quint*, Berlin, 1910: an epic novel, once regarded as his most important work. Though not completed until 1910, he had in fact started work on it in 1901.

ances within the space of three weeks: at Trieste on 1 December, in a pro-
gramme that also included Beethoven's Coriolan *overture and Mozart's*
'Jupiter' Symphony; then the Viennese première at a Gesellschaftskonzert on
7 December; finally, on 19 and 20 December, Mahler conducted two per-
formances in Breslau.

The invitation to Trieste came from the manager of the Philharmonic
Society, Enrico (or Heinrich) Schott, who also took care of Mahler during his
brief stay. If Mahler sent his customary greeting to Alma from the station, it has
not survived. His first extant letter from Trieste was written after the first day
of rehearsal.

156   Trieste [30 November 1905]
                                                         Hôtel de la Ville

Dearest Almschi,
Well, the first day was a success. The orchestra is quite passable, excellently
prepared, ardent and enthusiastic. I hope for a good performance. The hall
is sold out. Unfortunately it's been raining all day, and I've been splashing
about as best I can, armed with an umbrella and a pair of galoshes.
This afternoon I went by coach to Miramare* (accompanied by H. Schott),
where we spent two hours looking around. I was really sorry you couldn't
come with me. It's a wonderful place to stay. Cypresses and laurel trees, all
still green, ponds with swans etc. etc. And a heavenly calm. The hotel is
ghastly (though it's the best in town) – noisy and disorderly. Rehearsals are
from twelve to two, and in the <u>evenings</u> from eight to eleven. – Very much
the Italian way of doing things. Likewise the concert, which doesn't begin
until 8.15.
All in all, I shall be heartily glad to get back to Vienna and my familiar
round: first to your bedside, then to the children, then a hot bath, and finally
an epicurean breakfast. Fondest kisses, my Almschi   Your Gustav

157   Trieste [1 December 1905]
                                                         Hôtel de la Ville

My Almscherl,
This ghastly hotel is making my stay something of an ordeal. I'm really glad
you aren't here. You'd be appalled by the piggery. And it's noisy all night.

---

* A castle with park and gardens on the sea-coast near Trieste. It was built in the 1850s for
Archduke Maximilian of Hapsburg, who later became Emperor of Mexico.

I've been getting five hours' sleep at the most. Today's the concert, thank heaven, and I'm leaving tomorrow. – The orchestra has been doing its <very> best, so as far as they're concerned it has been plain sailing.

People here are charming. Indeed, two of the committee members have taken it upon themselves to form an 'escort' and have been shepherding me around town (they haven't left me to myself for a moment – that would conflict with their idea of hospitality). This pen is entirely typical of the hotel: it's practically impossible to write with it. – Almscherl, why haven't you sent news of our little Putzis? I can only assume they're happy and well. When I get back on Sunday, let's try to organize a nice long walk. Warmest and fondest greetings   Your Gustav

According to the Triester Zeitung, *the audience applauded Mahler's conducting but responded less warmly to his music.*[22] *Seven days later the audience in Vienna reacted enthusiastically to the* Fifth Symphony, *but the reviews were devastating.*

Only one short letter survives from the trip to Breslau, where Mahler was a house guest of his old friends the Neissers. It was at this time that his portrait was painted by Fritz Erler, a friend of his hosts. Perhaps it was the long sittings that prevented Mahler from writing more frequently to Alma, or at greater length; it could be, of course, that he sent further letters, which have not survived.*

158   Breslau, 18 December 1905[P]

My dearest Almschili,

Only a few lines today. I'm being very well looked after. The Neissers are wonderful hosts, and their house is magnificent. – I've been rehearsing with a vengeance! After every meal I have been sitting for my portrait (I'm very taken with Erler, by the way – very serious and unaffected). – Berliner is with me constantly, and every tenth word that passes between us is about you.

There's bad news from the Opera, I'm afraid, which is taking all the pleasure out of life here. I'll tell you more about it when I get back. I've been going to

---

* The painter, interior decorator, graphic artist and stage designer Fritz Erler, born near Breslau. His decorations for the Neissers' music room were a classic example of *fin-de-siècle* art, ranging from frescos and chandeliers to music stands and door-knobs. He was also renowned for his portraits of musicians, notably of Pablo de Sarasate and Richard Strauss (1898). Later he used his portrait of Mahler as the basis for an engraving (see Frontispiece).

bed at eleven and getting up at eight. Altogether, my hosts have given me a princely welcome.

Warmest greetings, my Almschili. See you on Thursday morning.

Your Gustav

For Mahler, the forthcoming 150th anniversary of Mozart's birth was the ideal opportunity to fulfil his long-held ambition of presenting a cycle of Mozart's major operas in new productions. During his time as Hofoperndirektor this was arguably his finest achievement. The series had already been launched in November 1905, with Così fan Tutte; Don Giovanni *followed in December. Roller's sets for* Giovanni *were so striking and brilliantly conceived that they remained in use until the conflagration of 1945, when the Vienna State Opera was razed to the ground. At the time they were considered the last word in modernity, a typical product of Viennese Secessionist design. But in fact Roller's idea of combining a proscenium arch with fixed elements (in this case two pairs of towers) was inspired by Shakespearean theatre.*

The 'bad news from the opera' mentioned in letter 158 concerned the baritone Leopold Demuth (cf. p. 197, where Mahler mentions his pose of stardom). Demuth was double-cast in the title role of Don Giovanni *with his colleague Friedrich Weidemann. Being the more experienced of the two, Demuth expected to sing on the opening night, 21 December, but instead the honour went to Weidemann. Thereupon the aggrieved Demuth protested to Mahler and in due course withdrew from his contract at the Hofoper.*

1906

The new production of Die Entführung aus dem Serail *opened on 29 January, followed on 30 March by* Le Nozze di Figaro *(or rather,* Figaros Hochzeit, *for Mahler adhered to the Hofoper rule that all operas should be sung in German). He then completed the cycle with* Die Zauberflöte, *which opened on 1 June. Thus between 21 December 1905 and 8 June 1906 Mahler conducted no less than thirty-three evenings of Mozart. During this entire period he left Vienna only twice, at the beginning of March to conduct his* Fifth Symphony *in Antwerp and in Amsterdam, and at the end of May to conduct the world première of his* Sixth Symphony *at the annual festival of the ADM, held that year in Essen.*

159   Antwerp [3 March 1906]
                                                     Grand Hôtel

My dear Almschili,
That was a sweet idea of yours! I had to smile when I unpacked the picture, but I was also very pleased. I've put it on my bedside table, where I can engage in the most amiable of conversations with you and our little ones.*
I'm living here in style: a huge room with twin beds (what an irony of fate)! Next door I have a large, bright bathroom with hot water at the touch of a lever. I've been bathing for an hour every day – one of my greatest pleasures here. The other side of the coin in Antwerp, unfortunately, is the orchestra. Unspeakable! The performance is going to be sheer hell. – I would gladly do without my bath if the musicians would only play a little more cleanly. Van Dyck has kindly been doing me the honours. A really splendid fellow – if only he wouldn't insist on singing!
I have invitations to dinner every day; the people are easy-going, affluent but uncomplicated. – The journey was pleasant enough: I had a whole compartment to myself. What a pity you're not here with me. It would have been so comfortable this time.
For today, warmest greetings and a thousand kisses, my dearest. I hope you'll soon dip your pen into the ink. <Tell me how you got on with Engel –

---

* When Alma supervised the packing of Mahler's baggage, she was in the habit of secreting family photographs in his suitcase.

and with Rothschild.*> Greetings to Mama and Carl.   Your Gustav

On the programme of this concert, promoted by the Société des Nouveaux Concerts of Antwerp, Mahler's Fifth Symphony was followed by Liszt's transcription for piano and orchestra of Schubert's Wanderer Fantasy, with Eugen d'Albert as soloist; the concert ended with Weber's Freischütz overture.

Much of Mahler's spare time was taken up with seeing the sights of the town, with the Belgian tenor Ernest van Dyck as his guide. This was indeed 'doing the honours', for van Dyck could hardly have forgotten how badly Mahler had treated him at the Hofoper. In his heyday the tenor had enjoyed immense popularity, but Mahler disliked not only his singing and acting but also the repertoire in which he excelled, notably Massenet's Werther *and* Manon. *Unwilling to accept the singer's status as a 'star', Mahler therefore did all he could to discourage him. The result was that in September 1900 van Dyck withdrew from his contract. In 1903 he had been instrumental in founding the Société des Nouveaux Concerts in his home town, and doubtless it was he whom Mahler had to thank for this invitation.*

160   Antwerp [4 March 1906]
                                                              Grand Hôtel

My Almscherl,
Well, the dress rehearsal is over now. I think I can say the same as they said of <u>Bach</u>: 'He gave the boys a good thrashing, and afterwards it sounded terrible.' Yesterday <u>Clemenceau</u> and <u>Picquart</u>† travelled up from Paris (specially for the symphony), and over breakfast we all pined for you. Picquart shook his head sorrowfully for minutes on end (you know how he takes everything to heart), and Clemenceau assured me he was in love with you! I'm so glad you didn't subject yourself to this Breughel-out-of-hell. Otherwise the people are perfectly pleasant, and have done all they could.
If it's like this in Amsterdam, I'll beat a retreat. I hope to receive at least a few lines from you tomorrow. I've been spending a good deal of time on my own and avoiding people whenever I could. Tomorrow is free, so I'll do some sightseeing. Warmest greetings, my Luxi   Your old Gust

---

* The Hungarian writer Sandor (or Alexander) Engel; the banker Albert Rothschild.
† Paul Clemenceau, younger brother of the politician Georges Clemenceau, and Colonel Georges Picquart, who had been cashiered and imprisoned for his defence of Dreyfus.

Two of Mahler's French visitors were old friends whom he had first met in
Paris in 1900. The other two members of this 'dreyfusard' quartet, each of
whom was renowned for his liberalism and love of music, were Paul Painlevé
and Guillaume de Lallemand. They had already heard Mahler conduct his
Fifth Symphony *at the Strasbourg Festival in May 1905.*

From Antwerp Mahler travelled on to Amsterdam. This being his third
visit to Holland, he was immediately surrounded by devoted friends.
Mengelberg had again prepared the Concertgebouw Orchestra with meticu-
lous care. The programme of Mahler's first concert, on 8 March, again
included the Fifth Symphony, *followed by the* Kindertotenlieder *and the*
Rückert-Song Ich bin der Welt abhanden gekommen. *Friedrich Weidemann,*
who had sung the first performance of these songs in Vienna the previous
year, was engaged as soloist but had to cancel at the last minute due to indis-
position; his place was taken by the Dutch baritone Gerard Zalsman.

Mahler's second concert was devoted to just one work, Das klagende Lied,
which was receiving its Dutch première.

161   Amsterdam [6 March 1906]
                                                           Het Concertgebouw

My dearest,
I've settled in here now, and have already taken my first rehearsal. 'What a
different spirit'! The orchestra is <u>wonderfully</u> prepared and plays perhaps
even better than in Vienna. The choir (in Das klagende Lied) is well trained
and knows the work to a T. Mengelberg really is a splendid fellow, the only
one to whom I can entrust my works with complete confidence. – The sym-
phony will be given next week in <u>The Hague</u>, <u>Rotterdam</u>, <u>Haarlem</u>, <u>Utrecht</u>
and <u>Arnhem</u>, where Mengelberg is giving concerts with the orchestra from
Amsterdam. I'll be rehearsing the Kindertotenlieder later today. Haven't met
the singer yet. I wonder what he's like.
Antwerp was most definitely a 'success'. Splendid reviews. Your letter
reached me here. Putzi's drawing is simply incredible. <u>She has such an eye</u>!
I'll be home on <u>Monday</u> morning. Heavens, how I'm looking forward to it.
For today, my dear, warmest greetings. Everyone here is thoroughly <u>dis-</u>
<u>mayed</u> that you aren't here with me. By the way, the Mengelbergs didn't
want to let me stay at the hotel. They're such kind-hearted, straightforward
people, and he is so exceptionally <u>reliable</u>. Diepenbrock has already been to
see me. These people are real <u>friends</u>!   Your Gustl

162^U Postcard   Amsterdam, 8 March 1906^P

M.d.A.,

Today was very strenuous. Morning and afternoon rehearsals. Concert in
the evening. I'm particularly glad to hear you're 'living it up'. That means
you're feeling well! When I get back, I also hope to join in the high life a
bit. Don't forget: I'll be arriving on <u>Monday</u> morning. Warmest greetings
Your Gustl

Mahler had originally agreed to conduct a further performance of Das
klagende Lied *on 11 March, but in the event he decided to curtail his visit.
To this end, he contacted Alois Przistaupinski, and instructed him to send
a telegram 'approximately as follows: Generalintendant urgently requests
your presence due to important business.'¹ The ruse was successful, and
on 11 March the concert was therefore conducted by Mengelberg.*

163^U   Amsterdam [9 March 1906]
                                        Het Concertgebouw

My dearest Almschili,

I'm writing today despite your 'barbed' <second> letter, <since when I've
heard nothing more (so far I've written every day).>

Yesterday was the symphony & Kindertotenlieder – <u>magnificent</u> performance, except for the singer, who was too superficial.

This evening is the final rehearsal of Das klagende Lied, tomorrow is the
performance, and the following day I make an early departure. I'll be with
you all again on Monday, thank God. – Although these people are all very
kind and are taking the greatest pains, I feel totally abandoned. – Here in
Amsterdam I already have a staunch crowd of supporters, particularly
young people, who go quite wild about me. The audience was most
<u>respectful</u>, the press downright friendly.

Most important of all: Mengelberg performs my works regularly. In the next
two weeks, the Fifth will be heard in The Hague, Rotterdam, <Utrecht,
Haarlem> and Arnhem – what's more, it will also be given <u>here</u> on two further
occasions.

Meanwhile, there's something unpleasant brewing in Vienna between <u>Roller</u>
and the <u>chorus</u>. I'm worried that the consequences could be far-reaching. It
would be only too easy to drag me into the affair.

My little rogue, I wonder when <u>you</u> will find time to write to me again? Still

living it up till two in the morning?
So long* to you too.   Your Gust

The only cloud in an otherwise clear sky was the news from Vienna: shortly before Mahler left for Antwerp, the Hofoper had staged a new production of Lohengrin, *and Roller's chorus costumes were so elaborate that the singers refused to wear them (later it was ascertained that some of them weighed nearly forty-five pounds). Roller, who was no master of diplomacy, simply decided to exclude several of the more portly chorus members from the production, whereupon the offended parties complained to Prince Montenuovo and threatened strike action. The conflict remained unresolved until after Mahler's return.*

164[U] Postcard   Amsterdam, 10 March 1906[P]

M.d.A.,
The klagende Lied dress rehearsal went superbly. Today I have the morning free, so I'm going with Mengelberg to get some fresh air on the Zuider Zee. This eternal standing on one's feet at rehearsals and concerts is very strenuous. The weather today is magnificent – but I'll miss you on our outing. All I can do is say farewell. I'll be with you again on Monday morning.
Your G.

Back in Vienna, Mahler resumed work on his new production of Figaro. *The première, on 30 March, was hailed as a triumph of lucid staging and finely integrated ensemble work. Meanwhile, he was concentrating on the forthcoming world première of his Sixth Symphony in Essen; to this end, on 1 May he held a reading rehearsal of the work with the Vienna Philharmonic.*

Two weeks later he travelled to Graz for the Austrian première of Salome, *conducted by the composer in person. Mahler left a brief message for Alma in the hotel.*

165[U] Visiting card   [Graz, 15 or 16 May 1906]

Dearest Almscherl,
I couldn't wait any longer and have to leave right now. See you in the theatre. Yours [unsigned]

Have been cultivating Rich. Strauss, which has again made me very 'arrogant'.

---

* Orig.: 'Servus' (colloquial). With regard to Mahler's closing remark, Alma explains in ELM, 'I often used to sign off with that word'.

The world première of the Sixth Symphony, *in the Städtische Saalbau, Essen, was scheduled for 27 May. Mahler arrived eight days in advance, on the evening of 19 May, allowing himself enough time to correct the orchestral parts. Alma was supposed to join him on 24 May for the final rehearsals and concert, but in the event, she arrived a day later.*

166^U   Essen, [21] May 1906^E

Motto:
   How blissful, how blissful – a composer to be.
My Almschili,
Very satisfied with the <u>first rehearsal</u>. The orchestra is in fine form, and everything sounds as well I could have hoped for. This time I believe I've made a good job of it. – The journey was terribly dreary, and we arrived an hour late. The hotel is <u>splendid</u>. I have a first-floor room, so my Almschi won't have to climb too many stairs. Very attractive room and good food. Everything <u>spick and span</u>! Having arrived at seven, I corrected parts until eleven then ate a sandwich, and this morning I worked on from seven to nine. The first rehearsal was from 9.30 to 12.30. Now I've just had lunch, and at 4.30 I have my second rehearsal. So now I'm going to lie down for an hour and catch up on lost sleep. Your telegram was a great comfort to me. It was waiting for me on arrival. Will write again tomorrow morning.
Warmest greetings, my Almschl, and write soon. Your train leaves on Thursday at 8.30.
Your Gustav

Apart from Alma, several members of Mahler's inner circle were expected for the première, including Anna Moll, Theobald Pollak and Guillaume de Lallemand. Their number was swelled by several conductors and musicians, including Mahler's new assistant at the Hofoper, Klaus Pringsheim (brother-in-law of Thomas Mann), Willem Mengelberg, Oskar Fried (who, according to Alma, 'followed Mahler like his shadow'²) and the Russian pianist and conductor Ossip Gabrilovich, with whom Mahler and Alma were soon to cultivate individual, close friendships.*

167^U Telegram   Essen, 22 May 1906^E

very heavy day yesterday   no time to write   many corrections   your letters very sweet   expecting you at station on thursday   fondly gustav

---

* cf. footnote on p. 228 and commentary on p.229.

168   Essen [22 May 1906]^E
                                                                Essener Hof

My dearest Almschili,
Yesterday was quite a day. Five hours of rehearsal, seven hours correcting
parts. I'm feeling fine all the same. Your letters were very sweet. Let's talk it
all over. This morning I'm rehearsing again at nine. I'm writing these few
lines so that you receive at least some news. It's not at all easy to find
accommodation here. The Essener Hof is fully booked. I've done my utmost
to find something for Mama. <I'll try for Pollak today.> You'll love the hotel.
I'm very taken with a young Russian (the well-known pianist and conductor
Gabrilovich), who's been attending my rehearsals and joining me for meals
at the hotel. He told me about my followers amongst the younger generation
in St Petersburg.
I'm finding the rehearsals very satisfying. I hope I haven't miscalculated. So
far I've been working through the first three movements. Today we'll tackle
the finale. Your remarks on 'Salome' are very interesting. It's just as I predicted. But now you underestimate the work, which really is a very significant one, though 'virtuosic' in the negative sense, as you rightly discerned.
Wagner is something quite different. The further you develop in life, the
more clearly you will sense the difference between those few great, genuine
figures and the mere 'virtuosos'. I'm happy to see how quickly you're beginning to grasp such things. There's something cold about Strauss that has
nothing to do with his talent but with his character. You can sense it, and it
repels you.
What are our Putzis up to? Never forget to write about them. And now my
warmest greetings, my love, and see you on Friday. I hope it will give you
pleasure.
Your old   Gustl

169^U Telegram   Essen [24 May 1906]^E

have a good journey almscherli   am already very worried   gustav

*The publisher Kahnt had clumsily attempted to publicize the world première
by releasing a press notice in which the* Sixth Symphony *was said to demand
unprecedentedly lavish orchestral resources, including the largest percussion
section ever assembled for a symphony.*
*An eyewitness of the première, Klaus Pringsheim, wrote of Mahler's patho-
logical insecurity, even while conducting, of his constant alterations to the
score, and of his last-minute reversal of the order of the second and third*

movements.³ *Like the* Fifth, *at its world première the* Sixth *achieved no more than a* succès d'estime, *and the applause was mixed with whistles and catcalls.*

Two weeks after the opening night of Die Zauberflöte, *on 13 June, Mahler left Vienna for Maiernigg. Alma's memoirs provide surprisingly little information about the summer of 1906; however, four years later Mahler himself recalled the first days of his vacation (letter 303):* 'On the first morning [...] I went up to my shack, resolved to take things easy (at the time I was in dire need of it) and to gather new strength. – As I entered that all-too-familiar room, the creator spiritus took possession of me, held me in its clutches and chastised me for eight weeks, until the work was all but finished.'

Within a little over two months the short score of the Eighth Symphony *was finished, and on 12 or 13 August Mahler wrote to Mengelberg:* 'I have just completed my Eighth, my largest work to date. Its form and content are so unusual that I find it impossible to write about them. Imagine the universe itself beginning to resound. These are no longer human voices, but the sound of the planets and stars as they rotate.'⁴

As was his custom when a creative phase came to an end, Mahler now set off for a hike in the mountains. Alma, for whom physical exercise had lost its appeal, never accompanied him on these trips. Around 17 July he left for Toblach, but the following day he changed his mind (so, at least, it would appear) and made his way to Bleiberg, near Villach, from where he climbed the Dobratsch (2166 m). Instead of returning straight to Maiernigg, as he had planned, he travelled on by rail to Dölsach near Lienz, where the road starts off to the north towards the Grossglockner (3797 m).

170ᵁ Postcard   Bleiberg, 19 July 1906ᴾ

Dearest,
Marvellous weather, feeling extremely well. Right now I'm climbing the Dobratsch (three hours). Shall spend the night on the mountain, then probably return tomorrow, arriving in Krumpendorf around 6.15. Anton should wait for me. Warmest greetings.
Your G.

171ᵁ Postcard   Döllach, 19 July 1906ᴾ

Dearest,
My second card!
Döllach. On foot to <u>Winklern</u> (a sheer two-hour climb, rising to <u>1200 metres</u>) in very fine weather with a few clouds. From there a half-hour

descent. Before beginning the climb I ate two soft-boiled eggs in Dölsach. They must have been bad, for I felt awful and was struggling to suppress a migraine. But I held out bravely, and reached Winklern sweating but feeling <u>fine</u>. Had lunch (plain schnitzel with a compote of cranberries and blueberries). Then the heavens opened. Took a carriage to Heiligenblut,* where I called a <u>halt</u>. Meanwhile, the clouds had dispersed, so while the coachman had his lunch I walked on ahead. <u>What a pity</u> my Almschl isn't with me! G.

Back in Maiernigg, Mahler evidently played Alma part or even all of the Eighth Symphony before leaving for Salzburg. It was unusual for him to play a new work before completing it, but in this case there is concrete evidence that he did so: a scrap of manuscript paper in Alma's hand, with a quotation from the second movement. She had written it down from memory, a feat for which Mahler congratulated her in two successive letters (letter 173, 'Your musical jottings', and letter 175 facsimile).

In the middle of August Mahler was obliged to interrupt his work. The score of the new symphony was practically finished, but he had to leave for Salzburg, where he was scheduled to conduct two performances of Figaro *with his Hofoper ensemble, subsidized for the occasion by the Emperor. As was perhaps to have been expected, Mahler enjoyed neither Salzburg itself nor the hectic atmosphere of the festival.*

Since 1901 the artistic direction of the Salzburg Festival had been in the hands of the celebrated soprano Lilli Lehmann. For the Mozart celebrations of 1906 she had decided to present not only the Vienna production of Figaro *but also her own new production of* Don Giovanni, *sung in the original Italian, in which she was herself to assume the role of Donna Anna. The orchestra for both productions was the Vienna Philharmonic, which had also been engaged to play three concerts, with Felix Mottl and Karl Muck as conductors. In the event, Muck was unable to participate, and his place was taken at short notice by Richard Strauss.*

172   [Salzburg, 16 August 1906]

My Almschili,
The crush is hideous! I'm shattered. On arrival yesterday I was greeted by Roller, Stoll,† Hassinger, a festival official and a Hofrat from the festival

---

* Heiligenblut is at the foot of the Grossglockner.
† August Stoll, stage-manager at the Hofoper, who was responsible for the scenic realization of Mahler's new productions, and sometimes also conducted stage rehearsals. Mahler seems to have taken a dim view of him.

committee (there were no maidens in white muslin). I did my best to shake them off, except for Roller, who took me to the hotel and kept me company. Misurina* – or do I mean Kiurina, no, Milewa, had been visiting Burckhard <and Archduke Eugen.†> We took a stroll through the town. Then along came Strauss, who joined us. I had dinner with him, while Roller went to the station to collect Schluderbach – no, I mean Misurina. At 8.30 Strauss went off to the festival reception (which I had managed to shirk); meanwhile, Roller arrived back with Toblach – or do I mean Schluderbach – and we sat together for a while. Then Tre Croci went off to bed, and Strauss returned from the banquet in a merry mood, with some journalist in tow. We spoke about fees, royalties etc. for a further hour, then I went to bed. I couldn't sleep, the devil knows why. This morning I got up at six and ate a gigantic breakfast. Now I'm waiting for the impresario from Munich.‡ At 10.00 I have a rehearsal. Afterwards I'll make myself scarce and try to leap from a great height or pull off some other sensational stunt. Then perhaps they'll leave me in peace. The devil fetch the lot of them.

Strauss has already set some scenes from <u>Elektra</u> (Hofmannsthal), but he won't part with them for less than a 10 per cent royalty and a fee of 100,000 marks (however, I'm only guessing). Since he didn't bother to ask, I didn't tell him about the old-fashioned life I've been leading this summer. I don't think he'd be impressed if I told him about the old hat I've been playing with of late.§ – How blissful, how blissful – to be up-to-date!

A thousand kisses to you, my Alm. It would in fact have been better if you had come along. This evening I'll go up to my room at ten o'clock. <[Julius] Korngold has been asking after you.> I've already received twenty letters and fifty invitations. On Friday at 4.30 there's a <u>reception</u> at Archduke Eugen's. Every participating artist is invited (a thousand in all), and evening dress is obligatory. I don't yet know what I'll do.

Write soon   Your Gustav

---

* Mahler playfully confuses the name of Milewa (Stoisavljevic) with various place names around Cortina in the Ampezzo valley.
† Archduke Eugen of Hapsburg-Lorraine, a distinguished military commander, but also one of the few genuine music-lovers in the imperial family. He was Protektor of the Salzburg Mozarteum.
‡ Emil Gutmann, who had recently opened a concert agency in Munich and was later to organize the world première of Mahler's *Eighth Symphony*. Presumably this meeting was concerned with the forthcoming Munich performance of the *Sixth Symphony* (cf. letters 189 and 190).
§ i.e. the *Eighth Symphony*.

173   Salzburg [17 August 1906]

My Almschili,

That was a sweet letter today. Your musical jottings were quite correct, and I've adjusted only a few details (the 'voice-leading' wasn't quite 'clean'). What an amazing memory you have! – On with my report. I'm on my own at the hotel, thank God. Roller is staying in the annexe with Cortina <(today she's off to Graz for three days).> Roller would amaze you: he's been taking long walks with me; the two of them are perfectly nice to each other but otherwise non-committal, as they were before they married. [One line obliterated.] We've been taking all our meals together. Afterwards she goes up to her room, and he comes down to join me. Strauss is always with us too and has been very friendly to me, as he always is when he's alone with me. But I shall never come to terms with him as a person. I wonder whether the two of us would ever meet again on the same planet? The rehearsal went pretty well. I went straight into the orchestra pit and greeted my soloists from below.

<Today is the party, for which a tailor has lent me a frock-coat. Just imagine: Schoder is said to be pregnant.* It will of course upset my repertoire plans, but it's also very good news, because it will put her out of circulation for a few months. While strolling with Roller yesterday, we bumped into Hammerschlag (the director), who came along with us. He was really upset that you weren't here.> Yesterday Strauss and I went to see Don Giovanni (they'd reserved a box for you and me). The production is so appallingly bad that we left after scene two and had supper on our own at the hotel. <From the moment I arrived here my digestive system has been playing me up badly.> – Your news of Gucki was good, thank heaven.

Warmest greetings, my dearest. It won't be very long now.

Your Gustl.

<I've just received the enclosed letter from Picquart.>†

Alma's first quotation from the Eighth Symphony *corresponds to bars 1,116–1,125 ('Neige, neige, Du Ohnegleiche') from Part Two. This is, however, a very approximate version of the passage: neither the key signature nor the time signature is correct, and the text is misquoted. Mahler's corrections to the bass line are clearly visible in the facsimile. The second quotation*

---

* Before Mahler's marriage, it was speculated that he had a liaison with Gutheil-Schoder, even though she was married to the conductor Gustav Gutheil. In the spring of 1906 she had a disagreement with Mahler over his refusal to grant her leave of absence from the Hofoper.
† In Alma's edition of this letter, she replaced this line with words borrowed from letter 176 (first paragraph, last sentence): 'I say it again: I'm truly amazed by your musical memory!'

(*without text*) *corresponds to bars 825–830 of Part Two ('Wer zerreisst aus eig'ner Kraft der Gelüste Ketten'), but notated a semitone higher than in the score. Having deleted the last two bars, Mahler writes on the reverse side of the paper, 'There are many ways of prolonging the passage, but this is not one of them: this is just a banal sequence. The first time, it goes like this.' But he is uncertain, and writes, 'Heavens above, I can't remember it myself. The festive hubbub of Salzburg has robbed me of all my erotic senses.' The following day (letter 175) he remembers: 'Aha! Now I have it!', and writes down bars 825–830, but in F major, following Alma, instead of the original E major. In Alma's edition of this letter she omitted the musical quotation, making nonsense of the context.*

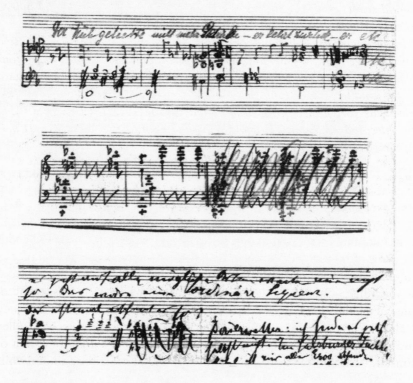

The title role in Lehmann's production of Don Giovanni *was sung by the Portuguese baritone Francesco d'Andrade, a singer well past his prime and evidently more concerned to ingratiate himself with the public than attend to the finer points of Mozartian style. A further problem was Lehmann's choice of the young composer Reynaldo Hahn, one of her protégés, as conductor. Reviewing the production for the* Neue Musikalische Presse, *Josef Reitler*

summed up Hahn's achievement with the words: 'Already the overture revealed a certain failing in the equipment of Herr Hahn from Paris, namely that he cannot conduct.'5

Mahler greatly admired Lilli Lehmann; indeed, he had often engaged her for guest appearances at the Hofoper. Of her abilities as a stage director, however, he remained unconvinced. But perhaps his judgement was not entirely unbiased. Alma records in AMM4 that he was heard to scoff at Lehmann (presumably in the interval) by misquoting the solemn words of Sarastro from Act I of Die Zauberflöte: *'Ein Mann muss eure Herzen leiten, / denn ohne ihn pflegt jede "Kuh" / aus seinem Wirkungskreis zu schreiten'.*6 This seems to conflict with his own report that he left the theatre after the second scene. However, his remarks in letter 175 imply that he did indeed commit an indiscretion of this order.*

In her memoirs, Lehmann complains that Mahler allowed her only two days of stage-time for Giovanni, while himself occupying the theatre for four days merely to adapt his meticulously prepared Vienna production of Figaro *to the smaller stage7 (and yet Mahler writes in letter 175 of the 'two rehearsals' for his own production). Whatever the case,* Figaro *was praised to the skies; indeed, Julius Korngold remembered it as the finest Mozart performance he had ever heard.*

174   Salzburg [18 August 1906]

My dear Almschili,
Yesterday the distinguishing feature of the day was a genuine 'Schnürlregen'.[†] In the morning I went to the concert (conducted by Rich. Strauss). To honour the name of Mozart they performed the Ninth Symphony of Bruckner (just as they had given Beethoven's Fifth the previous day). <The work is the last word in <u>absurdity</u>.> Salzburg was a-tremble with enthusiasm. It was a kind of musical midday snack in Bavarian style.[‡] <At any rate, once it was over a good deal of Stieglbräu was consumed.> Later I had lunch with Strauss and Roller, and during dessert Specht arrived, looking pale and rather uncertain of himself. – Strauss took his leave, and I sat and listened for an hour while

---

[*] Mahler substituted 'Kuh' (cow) for 'Weib' (woman): 'A cow [woman] needs a man to guide her. / If she should stray / without a man to show the way / then woe betide her' (English translation by Jeremy Sams).
[†] Persistent heavy rainfall, typical of the climate in Salzburg and surrounding areas.
[‡] Orig.: 'Frühschoppen-Rettich mit Salzstangel' (pre-lunch [sliced] radish with salt stick). In Southern Germany and Austria these two commodities are often served with a glass of white wine ('Schoppen').

Specht* held forth. Then I donned my borrowed frock-coat and proceeded to the reception. Once HM the Kaiser had singled me out for a word of greeting, I lurched excitedly to the buffet, drank a cup of something and wolfed down a sandwich, then made off for the theatre, where at six o'clock we sailed into a very successful dress rehearsal of Figaro (behind closed doors). – Later I dined at the hotel with the Hammerschlags, Dr Botstiber,† Roller and Specht. – Specht returned to Vienna, a happy man. Strauss (yes, Strauss) still insists I should write an opera. According to him, I possess all the necessary talent. <This morning I want to take a long walk with Roller. In the evening is the performance. – Both my sleep and my digestion leave a lot to be desired.> I'll be with you by Tuesday evening, hurrah! I wish I had never left! Warmest greetings from Your Gustl

<I take it my letters are reaching you? I've been writing every day after breakfast.>

175   Salzburg, 18 [August 1906]

Dearest,

I've been writing every day. The damned connection is to blame for the late arrival of my first letter. – <There's no need to worry about Gutheil-Schoder. I'm taking as little notice of her as of the others. During our two rehearsals and at the reception I kept my distance; in fact, I didn't even speak to her.> Now it's time for afternoon tea, then I'll get dressed and make my way to the performance. The author (Maxi)‡ has now arrived too, and will be doing us the honour.

I've just received the Redlichs' card. To hell with it! Who else should I insult? Anyway, that's what I'm known for ... You mention Lilli Lehmann, but it's too late now. My rude remarks about her have already gone the rounds. I haven't said anything about Strauss yet, because he's still here. Anyway, I should be more careful about what I say. I've already trodden on the toes of the Intendant, so there's little more to be expected from that quarter. – Tomorrow, if the weather is clement, I want to set out early to Hintersee, near Berchtesgaden, with Roller and Hammerschlag, who has arranged the

* Richard Specht had recently published a short biographical study entitled *Gustav Mahler* (Berlin, 1905).
† Orig.: 'Botstieber'. Hugo Botstiber, secretary of the Wiener Konzertverein and, as from 1905, administrative director of the Conservatory of the Gesellschaft der Musikfreunde in Wien.
‡ According to Alma, 'Maxi' was Max von Schillings. Since Schillings was a composer, not a writer, it seems more likely that this was Max Kalbeck, who at Mahler's request had prepared a new German translation of the *Figaro* libretto.

excursion. That's why I'm writing to you this evening, to make sure you won't be without a letter tomorrow.

Aha! Now I have it!

I've just had a visit from our benign friend Frischauer from Paris.* 'He was so looking forward to you.' I did <u>all I could</u> to help him file a flowery report from Paris for the dear Fatherland. He exudes a mixture of intellectual brilliance and perversity. Maybe Strauss will set him to music one day. For now he's working on Elektra.

Warmest greetings, my Almschi, and give the children a big wet kiss from me (but don't pinch the chambermaid by mistake).

Your Gustav

<I've ordered the [Mozart] Kugeln and [marzipan] potatoes; they'll be ready on Tuesday at ten, and I'm leaving at 11.30.>

176[U]   [Salzburg, 19 August 1906]

My Almschl,

It's pouring buckets – which is why our outing to Berchtesgaden has fallen through. – I'm gladder than ever that you aren't with me. You wouldn't have had anything out of it <u>at all</u>. Figaro yesterday evening was really wonderful. The audience was very earnest and as quiet as a mouse. No interruptions to applaud individual singers. Afterwards I returned to the hotel with Roller, the Hammerschlags and Dr Botstiber. I'll take this letter across to the station. I expect it to reach you on Tuesday. Yes, and by the evening I'll be with you. I'm truly amazed by your musical memory!

Today I'm going to see the Redlichs.

Your letter has just arrived. How sweet of you to write every day. – The personal news I'm sending you is reliable: whom I have been in touch with, what I've been up to. Outside the theatre, I haven't yet seen any theatre people.

* Otto Frischauer, Paris correspondent of the *Neues Wiener Tagblatt*.

Tomorrow is the last day, thank God. The day after that, I'll be off. I simply can't wait. I'm looking forward to a fortnight of nice, quiet working days, and in between you'll have to keep up with me.
Warmest greetings. I'll wire you my arrival time.
Your Gustav.

[top corner of first page]: I've just received the enclosed card (all of them Viennese critics).

Having fulfilled his Salzburg commitments, Mahler returned to Maiernigg where he spent the last two weeks of his vacation working on the orchestration of the Eighth Symphony. *When Julius Korngold came for a brief stay at the end of August, he found Mahler cordial and relaxed. On this occasion Korngold also discovered aspects of Mahler of which he had hitherto been unaware: the devoted husband, the loving father, the warm-hearted friend.*[8]
Before and after boarding the train on his way to Vienna, Mahler sent Alma his customary brief messages.

177[U] Postcard   Klagenfurt [3 September 1906]*

Dearest, a fifteen-minute delay permits me to wish you good night, though by the time you take delivery of this card it will already be tomorrow. Greetings to Mama too. Love and kisses   Your G.

178[U]   Vienna, 4 September 1906[P]

Dearest,
In all haste a word of greeting.
I enclose a cutting from 'Die Musik' and a telegram from <u>Wolff</u> – Berlin.[†]
Good news, don't you think? –
I couldn't get a <u>first-class compartment</u> and had to make do with a sleeping car. Be sure to write to Banhans at once. Freund was waiting for me at the station, so he sauntered over to the apartment with me, where I put my manuscript in the strong-box and gave him the deposit book. He can pay in only <u>400 crowns</u>, because I have 200 crowns of tax to pay (I found out about the increase when I arrived).[‡] I'll keep 100 crowns for myself, in case I run short.
– I haven't yet been to the Conrats, but I'm going over there now (10.30);

---

* Postmark: 4 September 1906.
† Louise Wolff was planning to promote a performance of Mahler's *Third Symphony* the following January (cf. letters 193 *et seq.*).
‡ Emil Freund was not only an old friend of Mahler's but also his legal and financial advisor.

I'm expected by 'Ida', who's just called me up on the telephone. I probably will go to <u>Dornbach</u> today after all, as we have marvellous weather here, and I don't have anything to do in town.

A thousand kisses. Write soon   Your Gustl

Stomach in perfect order and <u>no</u> winds.

[upper corner of the first page:] I've taken care to remove all the keys (everything is locked up all right) and shall keep them here in my office until Friday.

The first September issue of Die Musik *included a report on the previous concert season in Boston, Mass. 'The event of the year was the North American première of Mahler's* Fifth Symphony. *For me it was the most pleasing discovery I had made in years,' wrote the critic. 'How everything sings, glows and blooms! As if Schubert had been reborn. It was the first time that a work of Mahler's was played in Boston, and the performance was beyond praise. The solo trumpet (Mr Kloepfel) and solo horn (Max Hesse) were wonderful. Due to public demand, the symphony had to be repeated at the next concert.' The performance took place on 2 February 1906, with the Boston Symphony Orchestra conducted by Wilhelm Gericke.*

Mahler locked up the manuscript of the Eighth Symphony *in his strongbox. As he liked to escape the heat of the city at the beginning of each new season, he then spent a few days with Hugo and Ida Conrat, who at this time of the year commuted between their city apartment in the Walfischgasse and their villa at Dornbach, on the outskirts of Vienna.*

179[U]   [Vienna, 5 September 1906]

My Almschili,

So yesterday I met Carl at table (Imperial), and today he'll fetch me from the office to dine. Have heard nothing as yet from Justi and Arnold. Went out in the afternoon to the Conrats, took a two-hour walk with Horn. Excellent meal. Slept wonderfully. It's amazing how the Conrats manage to make everything so cosy and snug. It's touching to see how much trouble his wife (Ida) goes to. When you get back, we really should go and spend an afternoon with them. When the time comes for our annual redecorating, I think it will be our best way of relaxing. It's wonderful there on the veranda, in the garden, in the woods. The weather is wonderful too. –

This morning I managed to sacrifice to the gods without the aid of aeronautic instruments. –[*]

---

[*] A further allusion to Mahler's hypersensitive digestive system.

243

Am feeling really well. This evening: Tristan!* I'm dreading it. Have you sent off the letter to Kahnt? Are you receiving the daily papers?
Warmest greetings and kisses from   Your Gustav

The solicitor Richard Horn was a close friend of Hugo and Ida Conrat. In AMM4, Alma quotes a letter from him in which he recalled these idyllic days with Mahler: 'The guest we held in such awe was nothing like as fussy as expected. As long as he was served apples for breakfast, lunch and dinner, and as long as he could dip into volume one of Bielschowsky's Goethe biography† at Dornbach, or volume two in the Walfischgasse, he was perfectly happy. Goethe and apples were about the only things he seemed to consume on a regular basis.'[9]

180   [Vienna, 6 September 1906]

Dearest,
So yesterday before Tristan was the moment of truth. Arnold [Rosé] burst in, beaming from ear to ear (just like any other enthusiastic opera-goer) and greeted me as if nothing had ever come between us. But five minutes later we were going at each other like Titschi and Tatschi.‡ From what he said, it became clear that he saw Justi and himself as the very picture of innocence – I hadn't been expecting anything else – and us two as calculating, selfish devils.
Rather than risk doing myself harm before Tristan, I postponed this picking of bones for a more suitable time. He simply doesn't realize that his letters were so edgy, and is deeply offended that you never replied to him and Justi. And so it goes on! Yesterday I slept in town. Frau Conrat's hospitality is really touching. Today I'm returning to Dornbach, <where Horn makes very agreeable company,> and shall remain there.
Tomorrow I'm expecting the Prince [Montenuovo], and then the whole business resumes officially. <I've been dining with Carl every day.>
After work today I have to go to the dentist, I'm afraid to say, but there's no reason to lose my appetite on that account, for it's as huge as ever. The bread

---

* The new season at the Hofoper had opened as usual on the Kaiser's birthday, 18 August.
† Albert Bielschowsky, *Goethe – Sein Leben und seine Werke* (2 vols), Munich, 1895–1903, over 30 edns; Engl. transl. by William A. Cooper, New York/London, 1905–8. The book was completed after Bielschowsky's death by Theobald Ziegler. Chapter III, 'The naturalist', was written by Salomon Kalischer; a section on 'Goethe's poems set to music' was added by Max Friedlaender.
‡ Titschi and Tatschi: according to Alma (AMM1, 346) two dogs of a friend that were constantly scrapping with each other.

has arrived, and I'm gradually eating my way through it. As for the apples, I've left them at Freund's, where he'll be responsible for them. Woe to him if a single one goes bad.

When are you coming back, actually? I wouldn't blame you and the children if you were to stay away for quite a while yet. But I'd also be happy to get the whole business wound up. Warmest greetings to Mama.

A thousand kisses to you and the children   Your Gustav

Justine's relationship with Alma had sometimes been warm and occasionally even affectionate. Nevertheless, the two sisters-in-law still considered them-selves rivals for Mahler's affection. Justine could never forget that she had kept house for her brother for nine years and had moved out only at the time of her marriage to Arnold Rosé. Since then there had often been friction between the two couples, as shown, for instance, in an unpublished letter from Mahler to his sister, dating from January 1903:

It's been clear to me for quite a while that something is 'bugging' you. Whether you have a bone to pick with Alma or with me, I cannot tell. But I can sense that Arnold feels the same way, and I suspect you're egging each other on. For one thing, let me tell you that this is stupid, for another that it is not good. You can leave such touchiness to people of 'Jewish disposition'. And if your cause is in fact justified, then remember that each of us has his burden to shoulder, and that there should be no need to make it harder than it already is. [. . .] Lastly, you know very well that there is nothing I dislike more than people bearing personal grudges, and I hope my way of seeing such things has not lost its value for you. [. . .] So don't throw out the baby with the bath-water, and stop inciting each other.

181[U]   Vienna, 7 September 1906[P]

Dearest Almschi,

You seem to be wrong about Berlin. The performance of my Sixth Symphony on 8 October won't be affected at all. Apart from that, I'll be conducting my Third on 15 January. There's nothing in that which would offend Fried. As for this tax business, <u>Freund</u> is <u>not</u> to blame. He was act-ing on my behalf. So don't trouble yourself about it and don't be angry with him. I did the right thing, and it was a necessary precaution. My addi-tional income from royalty payments and concert tours cannot remain undisclosed, and if I hadn't asked to pay the higher rate of my own voli-tion, I could have got into dreadful trouble. So don't get angry, my little squabbler.

The enclosed letter from Mr Schroeder in St Petersburg* should bring back fond memories for you. I'll have to turn him down, of course, because my schedule is already too full, and anyway I'd prefer not to leave things in the air. – I'm still <u>greatly</u> enjoying Dornbach, and have decided to stay there a little longer. I'm sleeping marvellously, have no digestive problems, and everything else is taken care of. The Conrats are unbeatable. Kössler hasn't changed a bit (I used to be very fond of him) and seems to be slowly burying the hatchet.[†]

Warmest greetings, also to Mammerl. Now I'm off to see Montenuovo. – – Yesterday I went to the dentist. This evening I must listen to the new tenor,[‡] who's said to be <u>very poor</u>. Addio my darling.

Gustl

I was waiting for your letter with considerable impatience.

Mahler's next trip was to Berlin at the beginning of October, to attend Oskar Fried's performance of the Sixth Symphony *(with new retouchings). There he met two old friends, Arnold Berliner and Albert Neisser.*

182[U] Postcard   Berlin, 7 October 1906[P]

My dear Almischi,

Pretty miserable journey. This morning's rehearsal went surprisingly well. Fried is a splendid fellow. What a <u>shame</u> you're not here. It sounds wonderful. My retouchings work very well.

This card should reach you by tomorrow, I hope. The following day my train is due at the Nordbahnhof around 3.45 p.m. Both the <u>Neissers</u> are here for the symphony. Greetings to you from Berliner and all the others. Warmest greetings   Your Gustl

Shortly after his return from Berlin, Mahler gave a series of opera performances primarily for the benefit of his four 'dreyfusard' friends from Paris. The 'kleine Franzosenwoche' (little French festival), as he called it, opened on 9 October with Fidelio, *continued with* Le Nozze di Figaro, Die Entführung aus dem Serail *and* Die Zauberflöte, *and ended on 19 October with* Tristan und Isolde.

---

* The piano manufacturer and impresario C. M. Schröder, who was responsible for organizing the concerts of the Imperial Musical Society in St Petersburg. Mahler did eventually accept his invitation (cf. letters 233–46).

† The German composer Hans Kössler, a close friend of Brahms, whom Mahler had befriended in Budapest. The cause of Mahler's disagreement with him is not known.

‡ Carl Kurz-Stolzenberg. He had made his début on 2 September 1906 as Walter von Stolzing in *Die Meistersinger.*

On 21 October Mahler travelled to Breslau (Wroclaw) to conduct his Third Symphony (soloist: Toni Daeglau) and four of his orchestral songs (soloist: Friedrich Weidemann). As in 1905, he enjoyed the hospitality of Albert Neisser and his wife Toni.

183ᵁ Postcard   [Vienna, 20 October 1906]

Just another wake-up greeting, my dear Almschili. Did you sleep well?
Fondest greetings   Your G.

184ᵁ Telegram   Breslau, 21 October 1906

arrived safely   living very comfortably   coming home soon* gustav

185ᵁ   Breslau, 22 October 1906ᴾ

My dearest Almschi,
How wicked of you to put Putzi & Gucki in my case, but not yourself! –
Two rehearsals are already over. I'm getting rather tired of running after
my Third Symphony,† but unfortunately nobody else knows how to do it.
The Neissers are very put out that you aren't with me. We're having marvellous weather, and I'm doing a lot of walking, but I'm still <u>pretty</u>
exhausted after the 'Franzosenwoche' in Vienna, and I look forward to a
few nice quiet days when I get home. Warmest greetings my Almschi from
Your Gustav

186ᵁ   Breslau, 23 October 1906ᴾ

My dearest,
Somehow you've contrived to send no letters at all. I hope only your laziness
is to blame, and that all is well. – Now (5.30 p.m.) I'm off to the final
rehearsal, and tomorrow my train leaves straight after the concert. I should
reach Vienna early the following morning (Thursday). And then I wouldn't
'object' to a nice hot bath. The train is due to arrive at about 6.30 a.m.
Rehearsals have run pretty smoothly, but they're tiring all the same. Warmest
greetings, my heart from Your G.

Love to Mama

---

* Orig.: 'glueckliche ankunft   herrliche unterkunft   baldige wiederkunft'.
† Since the world première in 1902, Mahler had conducted ten further performances of the work.

Before the year was over, Mahler was to undertake two further short trips. Two days after the opening night of Hermann Goetz's comic opera The Taming of the Shrew, *on 3 November, he left for Munich to participate in a charity concert with the reinforced Kaim Orchestra. The programme was unusually long, even for those times. It opened with the Munich première of Mahler's Sixth Symphony, followed by the prelude to* Die Meistersinger, *orchestral songs by Richard Strauss, Felix Weingartner and Hugo Wolf (sung by the Dutch alto Tilly Koenen) and Liszt's First Piano Concerto (with Ernst von Dohnanyi as soloist). The Sixth Symphony had been prepared by Bernard Stavenhagen, a conductor whom Mahler never held in particularly high esteem. On this occasion, however, he found him both agreeable and competent. As at the world première in Essen, the Andante was played before the Scherzo.*

187[U] Postcard   Vienna, 5 November 1906[P]

My Almschili,

You were so sweet today, and so were our dear little devils – entrancing. I've taken another powder, and now that I've reached the Westbahnhof my headache has gone. I hope the change of air will do me good as usual. Kisses to you and the children. Write to me straight away at Hotel Vier Jahreszeiten. Your G.

188 Telegram   Munich, 6 November 1906

in very best of health today* to the hotel did make my way then took a bath so nice and hot and drunk of coffee one whole pot poetic is today my cable as only munich makes one able for here the arts are more than fable one feels transposed to arcady and thats a thing that pleases me   gustav

189   Munich [7 November 1906]
                                          Hotel Vier Jahreszeiten

My Almschli,

Yesterday I didn't have a moment to write: rehearsal from ten to half past one, then lunch with Gutmann & Stavenhagen, who really is a very dear fellow. – Then I left visiting cards at the Intendant's office, at Mottl's and at the Austrian Embassy, where I was invited to dine this evening. I refused, of course. At four o'clock was the second rehearsal. Pringsheim was present at

---

* Orig.: 'eingetroffen', followed by forced rhymes with 'geloffen' (for 'gelaufen') and 'gesoffen' (vulg.). The complete original text is reproduced in the Appendix (p. 395).

both rehearsals, and once again made a brilliant show of conducting the cowbells. As a special embellishment, the Hoftheater has lent us a particularly large, single cowbell, which Pringsheim is playing himself. Evidently it represents the last word in the art of yodelling. It gives the symphony, as well as Pringsheim, an unusual aspect, and if you were here you would probably be moved to that same wistful nod of the head as last time. – But I must remain true to myself and reject every programmatic connotation. – After the rehearsal, Pringsheim (who was very pleased, in a yodelly kind of way) felt just as I did, so he took me to his parents, who live in a magnificent palace,* where I drank tea and felt very well in the company of such kind-hearted, well-educated people.

Then I went (alone) to the Residenztheater, where I watched a hugely amusing play by Oscar Wilde† and was really annoyed that you weren't with me. You would have enjoyed it immensely. Today at ten was the third rehearsal. The musicians are beginning to get a grip on things. As this is a charity concert, the haute volée will be turning out in force (even Gisela‡ has announced herself). – The impresario is urging me not to have the cowbells played offstage, but to let them be simulated on-stage. They want to tether the big bell around Pringsheim's neck and let him run up and down with it, which is the only way of producing the sound by natural means. This should tip the scales and cause a resounding success – perhaps even a knock-out success – with the ladies in the audience.§ I believe Stavenhagen will be repeating the cowbell passages in one of his popular concerts.**

And now farewell, my darling, and warmest greetings. I hope you'll be as sweet on my return as you were on parting.   Your Gustl

Since Mahler had to catch the night train back to Vienna, Stavenhagen took his place for the Liszt concerto. Mahler arrived home the following morning and conducted a performance of The Taming of the Shrew *the same evening. From his office he sent Alma the following message:*

190[U] Visiting card   [Vienna, 9 November 1906][E]

My dear Almschi,
I've just read the enclosed article from the Münchener Zeitung. So you see,

---

* Alfred and Hedwig Pringsheim, Thomas Mann's parents-in-law; they lived at Arcisstrasse 12.
† *The Importance of Being Earnest.*
‡ Gisela, Archduchess of Austria, a daughter of Kaiser Franz Joseph I.
§ Untranslatable puns on 'ausschlaggebend' and 'durchschlagend'.
** Stavenhagen conducted a further performance of the *Sixth Symphony* (complete!) on 14 November.

yesterday evening in Munich was my death by firing squad. Here too are the keys – and a big juicy kiss.

Your G.

Mahler's 'death by firing squad' was a review of the Sixth Symphony *by Rudolf Louis, who had also attended the world première in May. 'As in Essen,' wrote Louis, 'the Andante moderato in E-flat major made the strongest impression on the public. It sounds delightfully delicate, though admittedly its cloying sentiment is not to everyone's taste. It may be the most popular movement, but personally I prefer the opening Allegro and the grotesque Scherzo. The latter is by far the most original movement, disturbed only by the affectation of the 'altväterlich' [venerable] trio section. The finale sets out to scale lofty heights, but never quite reaches them.'*[10]

The next day Mahler travelled to Brno, where he was due to conduct a concert on 11 November which included his First Symphony. *On this occasion Alma travelled with him, though in AMM4 she mistakenly ascribed to the event as the early spring of 1907.*[11]

In early December Mahler travelled to Graz. The previous year his Lieder had created such a sensation there that audiences were now curious to hear one of his larger works. Originally he had been asked to conduct his Second Symphony, *but since the theatre in Graz was not equipped with an organ he opted instead for the* Third. *Preliminary rehearsals were taken by Friedrich Weigmann. The concert (soloist: Bella Paalen, a Hugarian-born contralto whom Mahler was about to engage for the Hofoper) was a charity event in aid of the theatre's pension fund. Shortly beforehand Ernst Decsey published a long article about the* Third Symphony *in the* Grazer Tagespost.[12] *Wilhelm Kienzl (best known as composer of the opera* Der Evangelimann) *reviewed the concert in the* Grazer Tageblatt. *Though deeply hurt by Mahler's refusal to perform his new opera,* Don Quixote, *he was ungrudging in his praise of Mahler's music, particularly the finale, in which, he wrote, 'the composer reveals the innermost secrets of his heart'.*[13]

191[U]   Graz, 1 December 1906[P]
                                              Grand-Hotel Steirerhof

My dear Almschili,

I didn't get much sleep last night. When I arrived here at 5.30 a.m., poor Weigmann had ceremoniously arrived to meet me at the station. So it appears he didn't get much sleep either. We walked to the hotel, then I sent W. home, took my time over washing and dressing, drank an excellent cup of coffee and ate a roll and butter. I'm including an article I found in a Graz newspaper (mainly for Mama, to whom you should take it <u>at once</u>).[*] – Now I'm waiting for Weigmann to take me to the rehearsal. – The hotel is really comfortable. Let's hope I can find a telephone somewhere so I can call you. Fondest greetings to you, my Almschi, and best wishes also to Mama. Your old Gustl.

Mahler was invited to repeat the concert three weeks later, on the afternoon of 23 December. Having left for Graz early in the morning, he wrote to Alma from the station.

192[U] Postcard   Vienna, 23 December 1906[P]

Dearest Almschi,
Let me take this opportunity to say 'good morning' and 'auf Wiedersehen' first thing tomorrow morning. It was pretty cold this morning. In return, I deserve a hot bath when I get home. I'm already looking forward to breakfast with you and the children. Fondly   Your G

Mahler did not often enjoy his guest engagements, but found them necessary in order to create a performing tradition for his symphonies. During the second half of 1906 his concert tours had become more frequent than ever before, so much so that at the end of the year Montenuovo accused him of neglecting his duties as Hofoperndirektor. Mahler replied that he was fulfilling his duties as administrator, conductor and stage director as faithfully as ever, and that his successes abroad could only enhance the prestige of Vienna and the Hofoper.

---

[*] Presumably the above-mentioned article by Ernst Decsey in the *Grazer Tagespost*.

1907

Following so soon after Montenuovo's reprimand, it was nevertheless unwise of Mahler to embark in January 1907 on a fifteen-day concert tour. He had just conducted the Vienna première of his Sixth Symphony, *this time with the orchestra of the Konzertverein rather than with the Philharmonic (hence his sad remark in letter 201: 'It makes me yearn for my Philharmonic, but alas, they won't have anything to do with me'). And now he embarked on a fresh round of guest appearances, beginning on 14 January with the first complete Berlin performance of his* Third Symphony.* *The concert was given at the Philharmonie, with the Berlin Philharmonic Orchestra and Chorus (chorusmaster: Siegfried Ochs) and the Dutch contralto Maria Seret as soloist. Immediately afterwards Mahler travelled to Frankfurt to conduct his* Fourth Symphony *at a Museumskonzert, then on to Linz for a performance of his* First Symphony.

193   Berlin [9 January 1907]
                                                    Conrad Uhl's Hotel Bristol

My Almschili,
Well, the first rehearsals are over.
The orchestra is not altogether <u>first rate</u>, but very experienced, very attentive (although I'm told this is exceptional and entirely for my benefit), but one notices the sloppiness of the local celebrities (tout comme chez nous). – So I hope for a respectable performance. The Wolff people have been giving me the cold shoulder, but that's fine by me: at least they'll leave me in peace. Fried sat there open-mouthed from beginning to end, swallowing it up root and branch, until at the end he just sat there with a glazed expression, like a sated boa constrictor. In the evening he joined me and Berliner at the restaurant† and grew quite profound. Finally he confessed that the sheer expediency of everything I did had come as a revelation to him, and that he himself was <u>totally</u> inept (but he promptly qualified his statement by adding self-assuredly that the others were even worse!).

* In November 1896 Arthur Nikisch had performed the second movement on its own; in March 1897 followed a performance of the second, third and sixth movements, conducted by Felix Weingartner.
† Orig.: 'Restaurang' (Berlin-style pronunciation).

Today I have time to catch my breath, so I'll see if I can get hold of Strauss about a ticket for Salome tonight. I've rid myself of Fried for today and tomorrow – I must have some time to myself. The way Berliner was enthusing about you yesterday, one would have thought he was in love. And Fried was really sad that you weren't here. – It's been raining ever since I arrived, worst luck. All this travelling is really too much, but I'm afraid it simply <u>has</u> to be.

Fondest embraces, my dear, and don't forget to write! Your   Gustav

194   Berlin [10 January 1907]
                                                   Conrad Uhl's Hotel Bristol

My dear, good Almschili,

<Your two dear letters arrived yesterday, and this morning your third. This time I have nothing but praise for you! Excellent idea to take Mama to Dr Kovacs.* We'll have to take the matter into our own hands. It's fortunate indeed that there's nothing organically wrong. If only Mama would accept the gravity of the situation and take good care of herself, everything would turn out fine.

Having heard Walter's trio, I have to say that I share your opinion.† Your 'review' is quite merciless, but it's the truth of the matter, I'm afraid. Such a fervent waste of effort is really regrettable. Now you understand why I was struggling to suppress my yawns. But now let me tell you about the life I'm leading here. I miss you dreadfully! We could have spent the last two days exploring Berlin together. I got rid of Fried, and have been taking my meals with Berliner, who's still the same loyal comrade he always was. Our main topic of conversation, naturally, is you. I also put him in the picture about Justi and all that. He was utterly astonished.>

I spent yesterday afternoon chez Strauss. She greeted me at the door – 'Pst, pst! Richard's asleep' – and dragged me into her (very untidy) boudoir, where her old mother was drinking coffee,‡ and inundated me with the floodwaters of every financial and sexual scandal of the past two years. Without even giving me time to reply, she hastily quizzed me about '1,001' other things, and under no circumstances would she let me leave. Richard had had a tiring rehearsal in Leipzig yesterday, she told me, then travelled back to Berlin to conduct Götterdämmerung in the evening. He was so exhausted, he'd decided

---

* Friedrich Kovacs, a Viennese heart specialist. Mahler himself was later also to consult him.
† Shortly before leaving Vienna, Mahler had attended a rehearsal of Bruno Walter's Piano Trio, played by the composer with members of the Rosé Quartet.
‡ Orig.: '<u>Káffee</u> (nicht Kaffee)'.

to go off for a nap, and she was taking the greatest care that nobody woke him. I found that very touching. Suddenly she blurted out: 'But now it's time to wake that scallywag.' And before I could stop her, she had grabbed me with both hands and dragged me up to his room, where she assailed him in stentorian tones: 'Get up! Gustav is here!' (For an hour I was 'Gustav', later she suddenly reverted to 'Herr Direktor'.) Strauss sat up with a resigned smile, and we resumed our lively discussion of scandals past and present, but now à trois. Tea was served, then he drove me back to my hotel in his car, but not before she had arranged that I join them for lunch on Saturday. At the hotel I found two front-row stalls tickets for <u>Salome</u> waiting for me, so I took Berliner along. – I was completely bowled over by the performance (orches-trally and vocally first class, but the stage production utter kitsch[*]). My dear Almschili, you have seriously underestimated the qualities of this score. It's absolutely brilliant, a <u>very powerful</u> work and without doubt one of the most significant of our time! Beneath a pile of rubble smoulders a living volcano, a subterranean fire – not just a display of fireworks. It's the same with Strauss's personality, which is why it's so hard to separate the wheat from the chaff in his music. But I've acquired a profound respect for the man as a whole, and this has confirmed my opinion. I'm absolutely delighted, and I go with him <u>all the way</u>. Yesterday the conductor was Blech[†] (superb). On Saturday Strauss himself will be conducting, and I'll hear it for a second time. [Emmy] Destinn was wonderful, and the Jochanaan ([Rudolf] Berger) pretty good too. All the others were mediocre, but the orchestra played magnificently. This afternoon I'll be at Frau Wolff's with Berliner. I promise you, my dear, not to fall in love. She isn't exactly the young girl you dreamt of – <you Traumgörgl![‡]> By the way, I dreamt of you last night: you had your hair the way you used to wear it as a girl, and I liked it like that! Almschili, why don't you have it done like that again? I far prefer it to your current Jewish look.[§] At twelve o'clock I have a rehearsal with my alto solo. I fear I'm in for a nasty surprise. – The last three nights I've been sleeping <u>ten</u> hours, and every afternoon an hour more. It's done me a power of good, and this lazy living is probably very good for me too. I kiss you, my dear heart! Why haven't you sent news of the <u>children</u>? Warmest greetings to Mammerl, and tell her to be <u>good</u>. Greetings also to Carl. Your old Gustl

[*] Orig.: 'Kitsch und Stoll' (probably an allusion to August Stoll, cf. footnote on p. 235).
[†] The composer–conductor Leo Blech. Mahler had conducted his opera *Das war ich* at the Hofoper in 1905.
[‡] Allusion to Alexander Zemlinsky's opera *Der Traumgörge*, which Mahler was due to perform later in the year at the Hofoper.
[§] Orig.: 'Verjüdlung'.

Yesterday at the Opera I bumped into Messchaert.* He was charming and is <u>delighted</u> with the songs! <The letter you found is not the reply to my application but a <u>second supplement</u> to his letter.>

195   Berlin [11 January 1907]
                                                    Conrad Uhl's Hotel Bristol

My Almschili,
I hope you've already received my two long letters. Yesterday was a »dinner« at Frau Wolff's, as I told you. The only other guests were Oscar Bie,† Fried and Berliner. It was generally pretty tedious, and afterwards I walked home with Bie & Fried. I spent a quiet evening in the restaurant with Berliner and <u>Ochs</u>, who's done a wonderful job with the chorus – a very fine fellow, by the way. To bed at eleven.
This afternoon I have my third rehearsal with chorus & soloist. I wonder how it will be. And today I shall also be calling on Hauptmann. I'd be perfectly happy to be back home with you all again. <It was crafty of you to plead ill-health. I envy you your hours of leisure, with time for reading and playing with the children.>
Ochs would like to be entrusted with the world première of my <u>Eighth</u>. Vederemo! At any rate, his chorus is the biggest and the best.
Judging by the stupidity of the critics, there's no point in giving a 'world première' in Vienna.
This evening I'm going to see a play by <u>Wedekind</u> (at Reinhardt's‡). I have to take the bull by the horns. Fried goes into ecstasies, Berliner finds it too disgusting for words.
Tomorrow I'll be seeing Strauss again, and in the evening I'm going to Salome. How deeply I regret your not being here. – You know, Almschi, the young girl with whom I fell in love was probably you. Maybe I was dreaming of you while you were dreaming of me.
All my love to you! This time you've been a <u>very good</u> girl. Your Gustl

---

* The Dutch baritone Johannes Messchaert, one of the most celebrated Lieder singers of his day. He was due to give a Mahler recital in Berlin on 14 February 1907, with the composer at the piano.
† Oscar Bie, music critic of the *Berliner Börsencourier* and Berlin correspondent for the arts page of the *Neue Freie Presse* in Vienna.
‡ Max Reinhardt's new theatre, the Kammerspiele.

196   Berlin [12 January 1907]
                                                    Grand Hôtel de Rome u. du Nord

My Luxl,
So the final rehearsal is over, and I'm well satisfied. Often enough the Wolff agency operates carelessly, but this time they've pulled all the stops out. Afterwards I joined <u>Strauss</u> for lunch, which was also feeding time[*] for Blech and his wife. Nobody was there when I arrived. But then along came Frau Strauss and struck up a lively conversation, which plummeted rapidly to the following depths: 'Lordy lordy, only a million? Not 'alf. Five million! Then Richard'll give up music.'
Dear Almschili: I have just been interrupted by <u>Hauptmann</u>, whose friendly face helped dispel the appalling emptiness caused by my visit to Strauss. – He wants me to go with him to Leistikow[†] tomorrow evening. But as I don't care for such invitations, we settled for an informal dinner in the hotel. We also found much else to talk about. I'll tell you everything when I get home, for my detailed account of the dinner chez Strauss has been nipped in the bud. Suffice it to say that I've come to loathe this 'de Ahna' person, and that he (Richard, I mean) scattered his pearls of wisdom like indiscriminate small talk between myself and Blech, with the result that the respectful and friendly attentiveness I always show towards him on such occasions went for a burton, indeed probably passed him completely by. – Every time I experience something of the sort, I feel utterly at loggerheads with myself and the rest of the world. Am I then so different from everyone else? Heavens above, it's enough to make you retreat into an impenetrable forest and cut yourself off from the outside world. <I've just received the enclosed telegram from Vienna. How should one react? Please show it to a few people! I don't trust the general peace and have a suspicion that the hall would be <u>empty</u>.
Unfortunately I have to reply to Baron Tucher straight away. I'll try to play for time. As soon as you receive this letter, cable me your reaction.>
Yesterday I went to <u>Reinhardt's Kammerspiel</u> (a delightful little theatre, decorated with immense taste, the like of which one had never seen before), where I saw Wedekind's Spring Awakening. The play is his opus 1, but it's already fifteen years old! You know, I was <u>bowled over</u>! Immensely powerful, talented and full of poetry. What a shame! To think what <u>that</u> man might have made of his career. Just think of the company he keeps: whatever came over him?

---

[*] Orig.: 'Abfütterung'.
[†] The painter Walter Leistikow, a founder member of the Berlin Secession.

Every second I was regretting that you weren't with me. <I sat with Berliner & Fried.>

This evening I'm going to Salome, and shall try once again to grapple with the problem of Strauss. My Almschili, I'll write again after tomorrow's public dress rehearsal. Warmest greetings for today, my heart, and thank you for all your dear, long letters. Your old   Gustl

<Greetings to Mammerl and Carl. Thank heaven you're not the daughter of an army general.*>

The telegram came from Baron Tucher in Munich: 'in view of the immense success of your symphony permit me to repeat my request for a performance of same on 16 february at a concert of the deutscher hilfsverein request immediate reply due to agreement with the konzertverein to reserve 16 february'. Considering that the success of the Sixth Symphony had been anything but 'immense', Tucher's offer appears surprising.

The long roster of Mahler's Berlin encounters in the midst of a strenuous rehearsal schedule testifies to his enormous reserves of intellectual energy and the constant widening of his horizons, even at this relatively late stage in his life. His remarks about Wedekind's Spring Awakening indicate that he was not necessarily the puritan Alma liked to make of him. Banned from most German theatres, this play about puberty and the awakening of adolescent sexuality was then considered shocking and immoral.

197   Berlin, 13 January 1907[P]
                                                      Grand Hôtel de Rome u. du Nord

My Almschl,

Well, yesterday I went to see Salome! My impression was even more favourable, and I'm convinced that this is one of the greatest masterworks of our time. I don't understand the situation at all, and can only guess that the voice of the 'Earth-Spirit' has spoken from the core of genius, and that this voice seeks an abode that appeals not to human tastes but [to understand more clearly] its own 'carapace'.[†]

Before the performance, by the way, I bumped into Strauss at the Opera. On his own he was his charming self again and insisted we should get together

---

* Pauline Strauss's father, Adolf de Ahna, was a general in the Bavarian army.

† In the original German, the last part of this sentence makes no sense. Alma, in her edition of this letter, expands the idea as follows: ' . . . that appeals not to human tastes but builds according to its own, inexplicable needs. Maybe in time I shall come to understand this "carapace" more clearly.'

afterwards. We all met up in a restaurant – he, his wife and his mother-in-law, Berliner and I – and discussed everything with good humour and at some length. It was thoroughly enjoyable, except when his Eternal Feminine* started firing off her temperamental 'intermezzos'.† But being in a good mood, she reverted to her 'Gustav' approach. – This morning Hauptmann joined me again (he's staying at the same hotel). At six o'clock we'll call on Leistikow, and afterwards, at eight, we go to see 'Das Friedensfest'.‡

The public dress rehearsal begins at twelve (an hour from now). My Third seems to me like a symphony of Haydn. If people hear me say that, they'll probably think I'm off my head. But that whole question leaves me fairly cold.

I received the enclosed letter from [Tilly] Koenen. I was so shaken that I cancelled Messchaert's Vienna recital. How would it look if every singer wanted me to accompany them in concert?§

Warmest greetings. How are the children doing?   Your Gust

198   Berlin, 14 January 1907ᴾ
                                                    Grand Hôtel de Rome u. du Nord

Well, my Almschi,

Today is my last day in Berlin, thank God! I'm no longer quite sure if I'm coming or going.

Yesterday's dress rehearsal went extremely well. I entered to a storm of applause and was warmly applauded after every movement, also at the close. After the concert there was a dinner in my honour at Luise Wolff's. From there I went off for an hour with Hauptmann and Leistikow. I still don't understand why he was so adamant about it. Then to the Deutsches Theater to see 'Das Friedensfest' (Hauptmann was very keen for me to see it, otherwise I would have stayed home). – A frightful, realistic affair. Those who warm to this kind of art certainly get their money's worth. In the effort to reach a fair judgement, I had to put myself entirely under the author's sway. (The following morning Hauptmann asked me up to his room to talk about it.) After the performance I was collected by Reinhardt and we went to a

---

* Orig.: 'ewig Weibliche'.
† A prophetic choice of word on Mahler's part, for it uncannily anticipates Strauss's depiction of intimate family affairs in his opera *Intermezzo*, first performed in 1924.
‡ Gerhard Hauptmann's play, premièred in Berlin in 1890, bears the subtitle 'a family catastrophe in three acts'.
§ Messchaert sang Mahler's *Kindertotenlieder* in Vienna on 28 January 1907, accompanied by Richard Pahlen. Shortly afterwards, on 21 February, Tilly Koenen sang the same Lieder in Berlin, accompanied by Coenraad Val. Bos.

wine bar, where we talked everything over, both performance and play. He's an extremely astute man of theatre, and it's wonderful to talk shop with him. Later – at Reinhardt's behest – we were joined by Wedekind. I was raring to go, and gave him a piece of my mind. But they all listened very carefully and sympathetically. Maybe I was even of some use to them. I was not displeased by Wedekind. Early this morning, immediately after breakfast, Hauptmann came into the room: 'I've come to collect my school-report.' So I told him what I thought of his play, and we chatted away most agreeably. After he had left, I was visited in my room by his delightful, (very) young son with his English governess.* She told me he couldn't bear it any longer and simply had to say 'Good morning'. Isn't that sweet? This little boy has shown me how I stand with the older generation.

<At midday Berliner will pick me up and take me to the National Gallery. I shall stay at home in the afternoon, and look forward to being alone for a while. Oh, I almost forgot: Osthaus† and his wife were at the concert and visited me in the green room. They were very enthusiastic. In the evening I met them again at the wine bar. They send their greetings to Carl. Leistikow made no impression on me at all. My train to Frankfurt leaves at eight o'clock tomorrow morning. I'll be staying at Hotel Imperial. It's been so sweet of you to write every day, and such nice long letters.>
Warmest greetings from   Your Gustav

<(I feel a little hungover today.)>

The Third Symphony *was well received by the public but panned by the critics, particularly by Leopold Schmidt in the* Tageblatt *and Otto Taubmann in the* Börsencourier. *Mahler was flattered to hear that the concert had been attended by Crown-Prince Ernst August (himself a keen amateur composer), who had found glowing words of appreciation. Richard Strauss heard part of the dress rehearsal and wrote to Mahler to express his admiration; at the same time he explained that he would not attend the concert, due to pressure of work.[1]*

Four days later, in Frankfurt, Mahler conducted a concert consisting of Beethoven's Coriolan *Overture, his own* Fourth Symphony *(soloist: Elsa Gentner-Fischer), and Schumann's* First Symphony *(the latter, no doubt, in his own version with substantially modified orchestration).*

---

* Hauptmann's seven-year-old son Benvenuto ('Buzzi').
† Karl Osthaus, art historian and founder of the Folkwang-Museum in Essen (the first museum of modern art in Germany).

199   Frankfurt, 15 January 1907[P]
                                                            Hotel Imperial

My dearest,

<u>Magnificent performance</u> yesterday! The public reacted with more under-
standing and warmth than I ever could have hoped for. – As for the reviews,
once again I mention them only in third place. At the station this morning I
read the Börsencourier, which states point-blank that I have no talent and
can't even orchestrate. – I was most upset that <u>Strauss</u> didn't attend. On
returning to the hotel, I found the enclosed card. Frau Pauline – judging by
my recent insights – probably wouldn't let him go. 'You're stayin' 'ome
tonight! One game o' skat, then off to bed with yer.' After the concert I dined
at the hotel with Frau Wolff, Fernow, Ochs and his wife, and Berliner. They
took a lot of trouble to keep me out of the public eye. <I didn't stay long.
Berliner brought me home and helped me pack. Up at six.> The train left at
eight, and at four o'clock I arrived here.

I was met at the station by Rottenberg and a man named Siloti[*] from St
Petersburg, who wants me to conduct there next year.

As usual, Rottenberg has prepared the programme in advance. He's the same
good colleague as ever.

<My room, which is snug and most attractive, costs only <u>6 marks</u> (special
artists price).>

Unfortunately I can look forward to a full bill of fare, with invitations from
committee members of the Museumskonzerte every evening. I'll do my best
to shirk them.

So the Viennese press is full of reports of my resignation? Some people probably hope I'll stay away for longer, is that right?

Warmest greetings for now. I'm going to bed soon. Farewell, my dearest.

Gustav

200   Frankfurt, 16 January 1907[P]
                                                            Hotel Imperial

My Almschl,

Well, I got through my first rehearsal all right. The players' attitude is positive and willing. – Just imagine, Siloti from St Petersburg is here at the
request of his orchestra, who want me at all costs to conduct two concerts

---

[*] The celebrated Ukrainian pianist Alexander Siloti. In 1903 he had inaugurated an orchestral
concert series in St Petersburg. Mahler did not accept his invitation, preferring instead to
entrust arrangements to his Russian impresario, C. M. Schröder.

with them. He said roughly the same as Gabrilovich: my rehearsals were unforgettable; they had learnt so much from me and would like me to conduct another <u>Haydn</u>, also the Choral Symphony, some Wagner and one of my own symphonies. They're offering 1,000 roubles per concert, so it's worth considering. The proposed dates are <u>21</u> and <u>28</u> December. Maybe you'd like to come along with me again –? <I couldn't make my excuses, so this evening, unfortunately, I have to eat my way through a dinner with the president of the Frankfurt Konzertgesellschaft.> It feels like a year since I last saw you (that's because you've been writing such dear letters, which make me feel homesick for you).

I myself no longer know what to make of Strauss. How can one explain such imbalance, so curious a mixture? But my opinion of Salome remains unshaken (just think of such people as Titian or <u>Bacon</u>, the philosopher).

The people in Vienna seem to be off their heads. Here the papers are full of telegrams from Vienna saying that I've resigned, that the Opera has an unbelievable deficit, that it would be impossible to keep me on etc. etc.

Gucki is so sweet – <of course!>

Love and kisses, my dear, from your   Gustav

Just one day before Mahler returned to Vienna, a caricature appeared in Die Zeit *(a weekly periodical) on the topic of Mahler's long periods of absence (reproduced on facing page).*

201   [Frankfurt, 17 January 1907]^E

My dear heart,

Your last letter gives me cause for great concern. Look, Almschili, it won't kill you – just look at Mama and her heart trouble – life goes on, and suddenly all this fuss.

I beg you, take proper care of yourself! I'll be back in three days, thank God, and then I'll take you away for treatment. – Today's rehearsal went pretty well. My symphony sounds excellent, and tomorrow we'll finish off the Schumann (in that wonderful finale I have to admit that the fiddles sound more abrasive than persuasive*). It makes me yearn for my Philharmonic, but alas, they won't have anything to do with me.

As a public figure, I'm not exactly being handled with kid gloves right now – more like a wild animal pursued by a pack of dogs. But I'm not the person to give up half way, and to me these body blows from all sides that

---

* Orig.: 'mehr kratziös als graziös'.

A month in the life of the Vienna Hofoperndirektor
Director Mahler is unavailable:

In the first week he rehearses his new symphony with an unknown orchestra.
In the second week he looks for an instrument with a completely novel sonority.
In the third week he is busy revising his symphonies.
In the fourth week he needs a break to recover from his holiday.
The sign on the office door reads:
Office hours from 6.00 p.m. to 2.00 a.m.

I'm having to dodge are no more than a massage (the Berlin press was almost unanimous in its 'contempt'). When my suit gets splashed with excrement, I brush it out. 'Boldly confront every hostile aggressor!'* Just as well that we have fifty thousand goads and an annual pension of five thousand to fall back on! – So now it's time to tighten our belts a notch or two. I received the enclosed letter from Mengelberg. Such loyalty does one a power of good! – By the way, I've a good mind to cancel Messchaert's concert in Berlin. What's the point of letting them piddle on me all over again? These little beasts evidently think of me as some kind of a cornerstone. – So tomorrow is the concert, then I take the night train to Linz, where I can breathe Austrian air again. I arrive at the Westbahnhof on Monday at 12.55. You'll meet me there, then home. I'd like the children to sit with us at table. There at least are two opuses the critics can't dismiss as miscarriages.
A thousand kisses, dear heart, from   Your Gustl

As these letters from Frankfurt show, Mahler considered his concert to have been a success. However, catcalls could be clearly heard in the midst of the applause, and, as usual, the critics found the Fourth Symphony *more 'interesting' than 'beautiful'. This did not upset Mahler unduly, for he had grown accustomed to rough handling by the press. In any case, he had far more serious cause for concern. The newspapers were presenting an ominous picture of the situation that would confront him when he returned to Vienna. Hell had indeed broken loose since his departure, and rumours were circulating about his imminent resignation, due to an unprecedented deficit of 200,000 crowns at the Hofoper.*

His last stop on the way home was at Linz, where his First Symphony *had been rehearsed in advance by a local conductor, Leopold Materna, who also conducted Beethoven's overture* Leonore no. 3 *and accompanied a tenor from Graz, Gustav Kaitan, in three of Mahler's songs. On his way to Linz, Mahler reported to Alma on the Frankfurt concert in a postcard mailed from Passau.*

202[U] Postcard   Passau, 19 January 1907[P]

My dear Almschi,
Today was a public dress rehearsal followed in the evening by the concert. Went very well – and the audience showed its appreciation. – In an hour or so I'm off to Linz (Hotel Erzherzog Karl). From there it's only four more

---

* Orig.: 'Allen Gewalten mit Trutz erhalten!' (Goethe's poem 'Feiger Gedanken bängliches Schwanken' from *Denksprüche und Merkreime*, slightly misquoted).

hours to you. Thank God. I always get on best with the orchestras. The players here behaved charmingly to me, as in Berlin. Warmest greetings   G.

On his return to Vienna, Mahler had to face the storm that was raging in the press, as well as prepare the new Roller production of Die Walküre, *which was due to open on 4 February.*

The press campaign had been launched during Mahler's absence, on 13 January 1907, with a virulent article in Die Zeit. *The author, Richard Wallaschek, claimed that the new* Walküre *was nothing but an attempt to disguise the fact that the repertory was much reduced and that the quality of performances had declined. He also alleged that Mahler's frequent absences undermined his authority, particularly with the singers, who found it unfair that they were constantly refused permission for guest appearances, while he himself was often absent for that very reason. According to Wallaschek, Mahler the symphonist had become the enemy of the Hofoper, which he had 'destroyed'.*

Mahler suggested to Prince Montenuovo that he should publicly counter at least the most blatant of these accusations. But the Prince's advice was that Mahler should reply with deeds, not words.

His first 'deed' was therefore the new Walküre, *but it was badly received by most of the critics, who found fault with its 'orgy of darkness', its 'modern' costumes, unaccustomed tempi and such insignificant details as Siegmund's brown wig, as opposed to the customary Teutonic blond. Otto Klemperer, in contrast, considered both Mahler and Roller to have achieved 'absolute perfection'[2] with this production, and Roller himself considered it his finest achievement to date.*

Mahler's enemies soon found new cause to cavil. Roller had recruited a gifted young dancer, Grete Wiesenthal, for the silent title role in his forthcoming production of Auber's La Muette de Portici. *The decision had been taken with Mahler's agreement but without the knowledge of the ballet director, Josef Hassreiter; indeed, rumour now had it that Roller intended to direct all future dance activities at the Hofoper himself. Hassreiter complained bitterly to Prince Montenuovo and threatened to resign. Montenuovo in turn summoned Mahler to his office and reprimanded him: 'Director Mahler, this is the first time you have stood up for an injustice. Being a court official at heart, I cannot and will not condone that.'[3]*

Other factors also contributed to Mahler's depression. For one thing, the censor was still refusing to pass the libretto of Salome; for another, funds were not granted for new productions of the remaining Ring *dramas,* Siegfried *and* Götterdämmerung. *Then there was the case of Fritz Schrödter, now nearing the end of his career who was frequently booed off the stage.*

Mahler had agreed to renew his contract only at a reduced salary, but with the support of people in high places Schrödter had intrigued against Mahler and got his way. By the end of April his contract had been renewed, and on the same terms as before.

By the middle of March, Mahler's resignation had become a topic of serious discussion at his meetings with Montenuovo.

On 5 March Bruno Walter conducted a new production of Meyerbeer's Le Prophète *with a promising young mezzo-soprano as guest soloist: Sarah Walker (also known as Madame Cahier). The same day, Mahler sent a courier to Alma, who was evidently unwell, with a news cutting and the following message:*

203^U Postcard [Vienna, 5 March 1907]

Dearest,
To while away the monotony of lying in bed, I'm sending you the enclosed clipping from the Abendblatt. I think you'll find it amusing. Typical of our friend Zuckerkandl. See you tonight. Greetings, your Gustav

The anonymous report which Mahler sent to Alma, headed 'Das Jubiläum des Hofrates Professors Zuckerkandl' (Hofrat Professor Zuckerkandl's jubilee), appeared in the evening edition of the Neue Freie Presse *on 5.3.1907. It gives a jovial account of the celebrations to mark Emil Zuckerkandl's twenty-fifth anniversary as director of the Institute of Anatomy at the University of Vienna.*

Mahler's attention was probably drawn to the article by a brief announcement, on the same page, of his forthcoming new production of Iphigénie en Aulide, *which was due to open on 18 March. With Gluck's classical tragedy Mahler brought down the curtain on one of the great eras of music theatre. Roller's sets and costumes were inspired by antique vases; with imaginative use of light and colour he contrived to bring these simple elements to life in an unforgettable way. Both Otto Klemperer and Lilli Lehmann later testified to the utter simplicity of this production, which they considered a triumph of harmony and classical beauty. This time the critical response was almost entirely positive. However, even an achievement of this stature failed to silence Mahler's adversaries, and performances were sometimes disrupted by demonstrations and counter-demonstrations. Shortly after the opening night Montenuovo publicly dismissed all talk of Mahler's resignation as an empty rumour. Nevertheless, savage attacks in the press, the hostility of the Philharmonic, the apathetic attitude of the public (houses for* Iphigénie *were*

266

by no means sold out): Mahler may have learnt to bear such setbacks with equanimity, but they were beginning to undermine his self-confidence.

Meanwhile, he had unwittingly violated one of the Hofoper regulations. Alma recalls: 'Mahler habitually entered his own schedule into the Opera's main repertoire ledger. Under the heading "After Easter" he added, perfectly innocuously, "Rome, three concerts."'[4] But the Opera was closed only until Easter Monday, and Mahler should have applied for special extra leave to conduct his third concert. One of his enemies took the ledger to Montenuovo, who immediately called for Mahler and asked him to explain himself. The discussion grew acrimonious and ended with Mahler agreeing to hand in his resignation.[5]

The day after the première of Iphigénie, Mahler set off for Rome, accompanied by Alma. He conducted two concerts there on 25 March and 1 April, and interrupted his return journey for a further concert in Trieste on 4 April.

Although the substance of his last meeting with Montenuovo had been kept secret, on returning to Vienna he found that the onslaught in the press was gathering impetus. News of Schrödter's re-engagement and of Montenuovo's interview with a prospective successor, Felix Mottl, added considerably to the pressure on him to resign, but still he could not bring himself to take this final step. Meanwhile, the Viennese première of Salome, given at the Deutsches Theater on 25 May by an opera company from Breslau, reinforced his sense of anger and frustration at the intrigue in higher circles, where his true adversaries remained invisible and unidentifiable.

In early May Mahler's younger daughter, Gucki, went down with scarlet fever, an infection that was circulating in a highly virulent form and with a high fatality rate, particularly amongst younger children. To avoid contagion, Mahler himself moved into the Hotel Imperial, where he stayed for four weeks, and Putzi was sent to stay with her grandparents on the Hohe Warte.

At the end of the month Mahler handed in an official letter requesting the termination of his appointment. Montenuovo would have accepted it at once, but Mahler had no actual contract with the Hofoper: his appointment as Operndirektor had been implemented by imperial decree and could hence be dissolved only by a new decree, and this could not be formulated until a successor had been appointed. However, the question of Mottl's appointment was by no means settled; indeed, Luitpold, Prince-Regent of Bavaria had refused point-blank to release him from his contract. Thus, for the time being, Mahler's future remained uncertain.

Meanwhile, he had been approached by Heinrich Conried, director of the

Metropolitan Opera in New York, who was searching for a new conductor for the German repertoire. New York society was flocking to hear Nelly Melba, Luisa Tetrazzini and Mary Garden – not at the 'Met', but at Oscar Hammerstein's Manhattan Opera House. If the 'Met' was to remain at the forefront, a star conductor would have to be engaged. This was the background to Conried's trip to Europe and his meeting with Mahler, at which he offered him a four-year contract and 'the highest salary ever paid to a musician'.[6] By European standards the offer was indeed munificent: 125,000 crowns for a six-month season in New York, compared with 36,000 crowns for a ten-month season in Vienna. Since Conried did not wish his coup de maître to be announced prematurely, it was agreed to keep the meeting a secret. And since Mahler was not officially permitted to engage in contractual negotiations at this juncture, he too was anxious to handle the affair with the greatest discretion.

In early June Mahler gave a long interview with Ludwig Karpath for the Neues Wiener Tagblatt, in which he stressed that he had not been 'overthrown', as some papers claimed, but was leaving of his own accord because he was tired of operatic life in Vienna and of the innumerable lies told about him in the press. One of these lies, he stressed, was the alleged deficit. He was glad to hear that Mottl had been chosen to 'take up the thread where he had left off', and congratulated himself and the Hofoper on a successor of such stature.[7] On 4 June he took the train to Berlin, where Conried had arranged to meet him the following morning. Mahler's tenure of office at the 'Met' was as yet undecided. This was a matter of great importance to him, since he wished to retain his Austrian domicile and devote more time to composition. After the meeting he sent Alma a telegram and a letter.

204[U] Telegram   Berlin, 5 June 1907

unable to reach you by phone   splendid contract with conried   letter follows soon   me too   fondly gustav

205   Berlin, 5 June 1907[P]
                                                           Hotel 'Der Kaiserhof'

My dearest Almschili,
For two hours I've been trying to reach you on the phone. I only hope I can get a connection soon. Meanwhile, I'm writing these few lines. – I left home with quite a migraine (didn't want to tell you), so Walter hastily fetched me an aspirin from his apartment. I slept very well and arrived here feeling rested. Took a bath (in my room), had breakfast, then went straight to Conried, who's staying at the same hotel. He's got endless plans, and wants to make something

of a Caruso out of me. Then [his terms]: eight months (180,000 crowns) – I
talked him down to six, and finally we settled on the following: three months
(15 January to 15 April) for 75,000 crowns all in, plus travel allowance and
subsistence (in a first-class hotel)! We still haven't agreed how long the contract
should run: he wants four years, I want just one. When I've spoken to you, I'll
go upstairs and see him again. He wants me to conduct Wagner and Mozart at
the opera plus six concerts (including my C-minor choral symphony).
Damnation take it: fifteen minutes of cursing, swearing and tearing my hair,
but to no avail. I'd better send a cable and forego the telephone call.
I'm leaving tomorrow, and the next day I'll give you all the details.
Warmest greetings from   your Gustav

Kiss   Kiss
   6 months a year for 4 years @ 125,000 crowns
   $^1/_2$ million crowns
   or annual guest contracts of 6–8 weeks @ 50,000 crowns fee
   total of 200,000 crowns in four years
Kiss   Kiss
   Auf Wiedersehen
   <at the Hennebergs?>

*Towards the end of June Mahler felt the need to escape the turmoil of the city
and the excitement caused by the on-going crisis at the Hofoper. In any case, he
had nothing more to tell the press; his decision was final, and until a successor
had been appointed he himself could make no commitments for the future.*

   *Alma was unwilling to leave for Maiernigg until Gucki had completely
recovered. Therefore Mahler travelled alone to Hochschneeberg on the
Semmering, where he planned to rest for a few days before joining his family
on the journey to Klagenfurt.*

206^U Postcard: Puchberg am Schneeberg,   [Puchberg, 23 June 1907^P]
rack railway

Reached Puchberg at two. Now straight to the top.* Stormy, squally
weather. More from the summit. Fondly, your G.

207^U [Hochschneeberg, 29 June 1907]

My dearest Almschl,
Since yesterday we've been engulfed in thick fog, and it hasn't cleared for a

---

* Orig.: 'aufi' (dialect).

moment. But it's lovely here all the same, and I really most regret that you're not with me. Now for my report. Yesterday, a quarter of an hour before the train left, I was sitting at the station when along came <u>Bahr and Mildenburg</u>,[*] both on their way to – Loretto, where they intend to spend the next four weeks. We travelled together as far as Wiener Neustadt. – Not very good news, in other words. Every afternoon for some weeks now I've been suffering from migraine, and yesterday was no exception. In the evening it got so bad that I spent an hour walking around in the fog, bareheaded. That made me feel better, and I slept pretty well. – I hope the symptoms don't recur while I'm here.

But Almschi, if the weather doesn't improve I have considerable qualms about you getting off the train tomorrow morning at half past four at Klagenfurt. I'm writing this letter here in the hope it will reach you at Maiernigg the morning before my arrival. I'll be leaving here at 8.30 to catch my train at 12.00 in Wiener Neustadt, so I hope I'll be with you around half past seven.

The book by Mereshkovsky[†] is wonderful, highly original and a welcome companion in my solitude. I'm almost completely on my own here (that's the good thing about bad weather: if it were fine, it would be swarming with people). But you must come back up here with me in the autumn, on our return journey. It's really most comfortable. And read the Mereshkovsky <u>immediately</u>. It's one of the finest things I know, indeed one of the few books I'd like to read for a second time.

I only wish it weren't so <u>cold</u> here.

Very well, my dear, by the time you read this I'll be in the train, steaming towards you.

Warmest greetings from   your Gustav

208[U] Postcard: Hotel Hochschneeberg   Hochschneeberg, 29 [June 1907][P]

I really must show you where I'm staying, and in what style. –

I've already chosen a wonderful room with a southerly view for you in September. – It's extremely comfortable here. Whenever you feel like it, you can go down to reception and call me at home or in the theatre, and a week or a fortnight here will do you a power of good. – I can come up here when-

---

[*] Much to Alma's distaste, Mildenburg liked to spend the summer months on the Wörthersee. She had recently celebrated her engagement to the writer Hermann Bahr.

[†] Presumably *Leonardo da Vinci*, the third novel of the trilogy *Christ and Antichrist* by Dimitri Mereshkovsky. Published in German translation in 1903, the book caused a furore in intellectual circles. Ferruccio Busoni, for instance, who read it in 1908, acknowledged its influence on the libretto of his opera *Doktor Faust*.

ever I like (on foot), because in September I'm still free in the afternoons.
Today, unfortunately, the weather has taken a turn for the worse   Gustav

*Since the danger of contagion from Gucki seemed to have passed, Putzi was
now sent home. It was a fatal decision: shortly after Mahler joined the family in Maiernigg, she fell ill with a high fever. The rest of the tragic story is
best told in Alma's own words:*

Fourteen days of anxiety, relapse, danger of suffocation. What terrible days!
Nature underlined the drama: storms, red skies. Mahler loved that child so
dearly, he would creep away to his study for hours at a time, as if trying to
come to terms with the impending loss. During that last night, when the doctor performed the tracheotomy, Mahler's serving man stood at his bedroom
door, so that if he were woken by the noise he could calm him down and lead
him back inside. And so he slept the night through. That terrible night, in
which the English nurse and I improvised an operating table and helped
anaesthetize the poor, suffering child. During the operation I ran along the
shore, shouting out loud, heard by nobody. It was five in the morning (the
doctor had not allowed me into the room) when the nurse came and said,
'It's over.' And I saw that beautiful child with her big eyes, lying there gasp-
ing for breath. We suffered for a whole day – until it was over. Mahler paced
up and down outside her bedroom door – or rather, outside mine, for as a
gesture of wilful self-destruction I had put her in my own bed. He fled. He
could not bear to hear the death-rattle any longer.'[8]

*Mahler never completely recovered from this tragedy. For Alma, who subse-
quently lost two further children (her baby son Martin and her teenage
daughter Manon, both fathered by Franz Werfel), the experience was no less
traumatic.*

*A few days after Putzi's death, Dr Blumenthal, the doctor who had
attended her, was called in to examine Alma, who was suffering from palpi-
tations. While he was there, Mahler asked him to examine him as well. For
the first time he was made aware that he was suffering, probably as a result
of his frequent throat infections, from valvular insufficiency (not a heart disease, but a minor malformation that reduces cardiac efficiency). As
Blumenthal predicted, the natural process of regeneration had already com-
pensated for this insufficiency: Mahler needed to avoid over-strenuous exercise, nothing more. Nevertheless, it was decided that he should leave
immediately to consult a specialist in Vienna. He was accompanied by the
neurologist Richard Nepallek, a cousin of Alma's, who had stood by the
couple during the harrowing weeks of Putzi's illness and death.*

209 Postcard   [in the train to Vienna] 17 July 1907[P]

Dearest,

We're sitting here in the dining car, and our eyes are in our stomachs (what a shame neither of you is here, you'd revel in it). I beg you, now your two guardians have left, don't <u>overdo</u> things and keep a hold on everything. Miss Turner,* Kathi and Anton should minister to your every need. When I reach Vienna, I'll take a quick bath and, just to be sure, I shan't go anywhere <u>near</u> Carl!† Shall stay at Hotel <u>Imperial</u>.

Warmest greetings   Your Gustav

<Kindest regards to you both [signed] Richard [Nepallek]>

210 Postcard   Vienna, 17 July 1907[P]

Just to let you know that we've arrived safely. I'll make my way straight to the hotel and take a bath. – Tomorrow I'll see Kovacs, and the following morning (Friday) you can expect a cable from me. Be prepared to leave for whatever destination Kovacs may determine. –

Almschili, don't forget to bring my <u>Oberon</u> papers.‡ They're on the book rack in my room, on one of the lower shelves. Don't leave any of them behind. <If you're to come to Vienna, I strongly <u>advise</u> you to take the train from <u>Krumpendorf</u>, the one that Richard and I took.> Please, you two, when it comes to the packing cases, don't handle anything <u>yourselves</u>.

Fondly   your Gustav

211   Vienna [18 July 1907]
                                                    Frohner's Hotel Imperial

My dearest Almscherl,

Now for a brief report. We arrived here at six o'clock. I went straight to the hotel, took a bath and ate a ham in the café. There I bumped into Karpath, who had it on the highest authority that Prince Lichtenstein had said, 'We won't let Mahler go, we won't accept his resignation.' – Well, vederemo. –

<At eight o'clock I met up with Nepalleck at Hartmann. I ate nothing but a compote, then we went for a short walk. At nine o'clock I went up to my room

---

* Gucki's English nanny, Lizzie Turner.
† i.e. to avoid the risk of infection.
‡ Mahler was working on a performing version of Weber's *Oberon*. His idea was to abridge the spoken dialogue, which had always been a stumbling block to staging the work, and fit it to music drawn entirely from themes used elsewhere in the score. His version was published in 1919 by Universal Edition; Gustav Brecher gave the first performance at the Cologne Stadttheater in 1913.

and straight to bed. Slept through until this morning at 7.30. I've just had breakfast, and am waiting for Carl, who should be here any minute.> I feel very well. If Blumenthal hadn't said anything, I would have wandered around much longer, and yesterday I certainly wouldn't have gone to bed before midnight. So you see, my love, everything has its good side. From now on I shall avoid all exertion, and if I don't have to stay here I shall run my whole life as Kovacs suggested (frequent trips with you to the Semmering etc.). My thoughts are constantly with you, my dearest ones, and I hope we'll be reunited tomorrow or the day after. I'll cable you this evening as soon as I've seen Kovacs. I think you'll both probably travel via Vienna, in which case you, Almscherl, should consult Kovacs too. I'll make all the necessary arrangements.

The weather here is simply dreadful: one storm after another. As far as that goes, it's certainly more agreeable in Maiernigg than anywhere else.

And now fondest kisses to you both. Live sensibly, and don't handle anything yourselves when you pack the bags. Don't forget my Oberon papers. And bring my cycling outfit with you – also Mommsen,* <Beethoven's letters and Hölderlin.> Of the books, bring everything except the Goethe and the Shakespeare. Bring the Rückert with you.

Warmest greetings, my dearest   Your Gustav

Mahler's love of strenuous exercise, mountaineering, cycling, rowing and swimming had always made Alma apprehensive. Dr Kovacs, whom Mahler consulted in mid-July, had already treated Alma's mother (cf. letter 194). Alma probably encouraged him to exaggerate the gravity of her husband's condition, so as to persuade him to adopt a less strenuous lifestyle. But Kovacs succeeded so well that for a few months Mahler became obsessed with his heart condition.

Since the death of Putzi, living in Maiernigg had become unbearable. Mahler therefore decided to spend the rest of the summer with Alma and Gucki at Schluderbach in South Tyrol (not to be confused with Alt-Schluderbach near Toblach, where the Mahlers were to spend the summers of 1908–10).

212ᵁ Note on the back of a railway timetable   [Toblach, July 1907]

Dearest Almschl,
There's a good hotel on the Toblachersee, between Toblach and Schluderbach. Would that be suitable? Cable at once per expr. to Toblach station.

* Mommsen's *Römische Geschichte* was one of Mahler's favourite books. On one occasion it was the topic of a lively discussion between him and Richard Strauss, who disliked it (AMM1 (p. 76–7).

How long the family remained in or near Schluderbach is not certain. A pho-
tograph, signed 'Alfred Liebig' and dated '10 August 1907', shows Mahler at
Fischleinboden near Sexten in South Tyrol. Soon afterwards, in mid-August,
the family returned to Maiernigg. From there Alma wrote to Alfred Roller:
'We got back from Fischleinboden yesterday, and don't feel as ill at ease in
the villa as expected. Our main concern is for our future, and since Gustav
finds Vienna more nauseating than ever (particularly the Opera), and is more
anxious than ever to leave – the question of our future abode remains unde-
cided.'9

'For a time,' Alma recalled, 'Mahler and I were alienated, our suffering had
driven us apart. Without realizing it, he felt I was to blame for the death of
our child.'10 Anna Mahler later recalled that tension also arose at this time
between the Mahlers and the Molls, for Mahler surmised that Putzi had been
sent home before her sister had fully recovered, and hence considered his in-
laws indirectly to blame for the tragedy. Whatever the case, he kept his grief
to himself.

The new season at the Hofoper opened on 18 August. Six days later
Mahler returned to Vienna in the company of Emil Freund, who had been
staying with the family at Maiernigg. From the railway station at Marburg
(Maribor, Slovenia), Mahler sent Alma two correspondence cards. As usual,
he also sent a brief note from Vienna to confirm his arrival. On this occasion
he also wrote the following day from Döbling. He was staying there with the
Molls until his servant returned from Maiernigg, where he was helping Alma
to pack.

213[U] Postcard   Marburg, 24 August 1907[P]
                                                                        11.30

Dearest,
In the train – a heartfelt greeting from the station. I feel really fine – far better than all the time at Maiernigg. – Clearly I just need to take my mind off
things a little. The <u>ticket</u> I sent you via Anton: you could use it for <u>Marie</u> (all
the more reason for her not to travel first class with you). – <u>At present</u> all
trains are chock-full! Don't forget to write to Banhans. Warmest greetings
from   your G.

I'm so happy!
[written by the signatory:] Greetings   Freund

214[U] Postcard   Marburg, 24 August 1907[P]

D.A. It's just occurred to me that I left my grey hat behind. It's probably
hanging downstairs on the coat-stand. Please send it at once, otherwise I'll
have to buy a new one.
Warmest greetings again   G.

215[U] Postcard   Vienna, 24 August 1907[P]

Just arrived. Carl met me at the station (Hassinger came too, poor fellow)
and now we're about to drive out to Döbling.* I'm feeling quite well.
Warmest greetings   Your G.

216[U]   Vienna, 25 August 1907[P]

My Almschili,
Had a good sleep and a good breakfast. Then into town with Carl. That little letter on manuscript paper was so sweet! My first hour at the office is
over too. I've already been stung for an interview by someone sent by
Korngold from the Neue Freie Presse. For Korngold's sake I sat it out. You'll
see it in tomorrow's edition. Now I'll collect Carl and drive home with him.
I'll stay there for the rest of the day, too.
I left my knitted waistcoat in Maiernigg! Please bring it with you. – There's
a smallpox alarm here too. Everyone's getting inoculated! Almscherl, why
don't you go to Blumenthal and get it done quickly, maybe Gucki too – also
Miss Turner. While you're there, ask him if I should be inoculated too. I hope
you won't stay away too long. I do feel at home out there in the
Osterleitengasse, but I'd prefer you to be with me, my Almscherl. Warmest
greetings, my dearest, from   Your Gustav

*As musical director of the Munich Hofoper, Felix Mottl was unable to obtain
a release from his contract and withdrew his candidacy. Montenuovo's attention now turned to Felix Weingartner, who since 1891 had been director of
the Berlin Hofkapelle. The court of Wilhelm II was a hotbed of intrigue and
artistic reactionism, and Weingartner had fallen foul of his superiors in circumstances similar to those which had led to Mahler's decision to leave
Vienna. Only too glad for an excuse to leave Germany, he responded to
Montenuovo's proposal with alacrity. At first he met with resistance from the*

---

* The Molls had rented an apartment at Osterleitengasse 2A, pending completion of their new
villa, designed by Josef Hoffmann, in the Wollergasse.

Prussian authorities, but on 9 August he informed Montenuovo that he was free to negotiate. The following day the Obersthofmeister duly informed Mahler of the situation, adding that his pension had been increased to 3,000 crowns with an additional bona fide payment of 20,000 crowns, and that in the eventuality of his death Alma would be entitled to the pension normally allotted to the widow of a Hofrat.[11]

In an interview with the Neue Freie Presse, *which appeared the same day it was given (26 August), Mahler discussed his plans for the future and emphasized that in New York he would be conducting more concerts than operas (a promise that Conried ultimately failed to keep).*

217[U]   [Vienna, 26 August 1907]

Dearest Almschili,
I've so enjoyed reading the enclosed article by Kalbeck that I'm forwarding it to you for your amusement. – The other cutting just arrived from Darmstadt.[*] Your Gustl

The article (in the Wiener Mittagszeitung *of 26 August) was not in fact by Kalbeck. Quoting the* Berliner Tageblatt *as his source, the anonymous author produced a work of purest fiction: Mahler had sold his house in Maiernigg, he wrote, and bought a small villa in Mödling; he had completed a symphony based on 'the death of Faust', which was to be premièred in the United States, as well as 'a number of chamber works'.*

218   [Vienna, 27 August 1907]

My Almschili,
Once again I had an excellent night's sleep. I'm sending you a few items from my 'in-tray', of which the love-letter from W[eingartner] will interest you most. Having read the Neue Freie Presse, he seems to be convinced that I could be either a help or hindrance to him. <Yesterday Nepallek came out to visit us. The more I see of him, the better I like him. I gave him our <u>box</u> for Lohengrin and Otello.[†]> We're having the most marvellous weather. I hope you're getting it too, so you can really enjoy your stay. – When are you coming back? I haven't seen anyone here yet, not even Roller or Arnold. <u>Przistaupinski</u> & <u>Wondra</u> are the only ones who know how to behave. Everyone at the Opera is greeting me <u>cordially</u> and <u>respectfully</u>. In other

---

[*] The cutting from Darmstadt has not been preserved.
[†] Performances on 28 and 31 August, conducted by Schalk and Zemlinsky, respectively.

33 Mahler in Rome (1907)

34 The Metropolitan Opera, New York

35 The baritone Anton Van Rooy

36 The soprano Marcella Sembrich

37 The soprano Olive Fremstad

38 The tenor Leo Slezak
   with Arturo Toscanini
   (1909)
39 Mahler with Bruno
   Walter in Prague (1908)

40 Akseli Gallen-Kallela: Gustav Mahler
    (October 1907)
41 Fjodor Ivanovich Chalyapin

42 Mahler at Fischleinboden (1909), photograph by Alfred Liebig

43 Gustav and Alma Mahler at Toblach (1910)
44 Mahler with his daughter Anna at Toblach (1909)

45 Carnegie Hall, New York (c. 1905)

46 The Concertgebouw, Amsterdam

47 Mahler (seated) with Dutch musicians in Amsterdam (1909)
(l. to r.): Cornelis Dopper, Hendrik Freyer, Willem Mengelberg, Alphons Diepenbrock

48 Mahler with Theodore
Spiering and daughter Anna

49 The Savoy Hotel, New York

50 Ossip Gabrilovich

51 Walter Gropius as a student (1909)

52 The Trenkerhof,
Alt-Schluderbach

53 Facsimile of a poem by
Mahler (letter 323)

54 Mahler's 'Komponierhäuschen'
(composing shack) in Toblach

55 Mahler rehearsing in Munich for the world première of his *Eighth Symphony*
(September 1910)

56 Caricature: Mahler is informed that no audience remains in the hall, because everyone
is needed to participate in the performance of his 'Symphony of a Thousand' (1910)

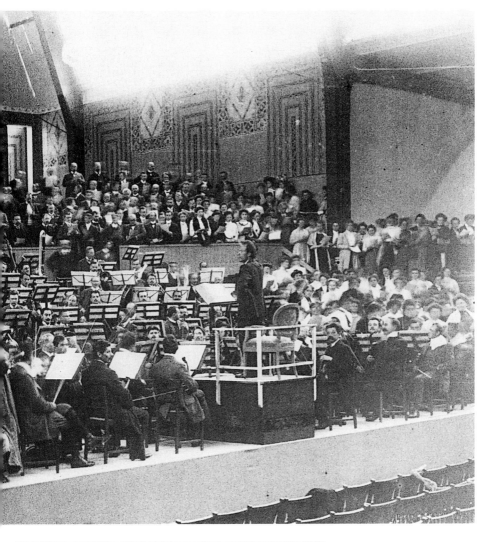

57 (l. to r.) Gustav Mahler, Alma Mahler, Maria Moll, Anna Mahler, Oskar Fried and Anna Moll at the Pragser Wildsee (1910)
58 Gustav and Alma Mahler with seamen and a fellow passenger on board the *Amerika* (April 1911)

EINLASS IN KIRCHE
UND FRIEDHOF
ZUR BEERDIGUNG
GUSTAV MAHLERS

59 Mahler's funeral carriage arriving at the cemetery in Grinzig (12 May 1911)
60 Admission ticket for Mahler's funeral

61 Bronze bust of Mahler by Auguste Rodin

words, it's got off to a better start than we imagined.

No letter from you today. I hope one will still arrive. Fondly Your Gustav

Weingartner wrote to Mahler as follows: 'Not long ago the prospect seemed almost beyond belief, but now it has come true: I am to be your successor in Vienna. There is much I could say, but permit me instead to express just one brief wish. I gather from the newspapers that you will be retaining your home in Vienna. In the past we cultivated friendly relations, and although these appear to have lain dormant for some years, I hope and wish that they can now be restored and maintained. I look forward with pleasure to seeing you again soon in Vienna.'[12]

Having conducted two movements from Mahler's Third Symphony in 1897, Weingartner considered himself to be Mahler's friend and colleague. After all, it was also at his behest that Mahler had conducted the world première of the Fourth Symphony in November 1901 with the Kaim Orchestra, of which Weingartner was then principal conductor. Weingartner himself had planned to conduct the work on tour with his orchestra. However, at the first concert, in Karlsruhe, he performed only the finale, replacing the other movements with two works of Beethoven, and at subsequent concerts in Nuremberg, Darmstadt, Frankfurt and Stuttgart he cancelled the Fourth altogether. Largely because of this, relations between the two musicians had broken down completely. Mahler did reply to Weingartner's 'love-letter', but only after a long delay, and with a curt acknowledgement.

219[U] Postcard   Vienna, 27 August 1907[P]

Just a few lines today, d.A., so that you hear at least something from me. Yesterday evening we visited Emil & Bertha [Zuckerkandl] at Purkersdorf.* They were thrilled, and Emil really rose to the occasion. His health has improved in the last few days. Just imagine, they're living entirely according to the <u>Lahmann</u> system[†] and are full of praise for it; they exhorted me to do the same. I found the food extremely tasty. I feel far better here. At least the nervous attacks have all but ceased. I'll probably get myself inoculated. It would be a <u>very</u> good idea if Blumenthal were to <u>do the same</u> for all of you. Kathi here should do so too. Evidently the epidemic is spreading. Warmest greetings from your   G.

---

* Sanatorium Purkersdorf, where Emil Zuckerkandl was undergoing a course of treatment.
† The German dietician Heinrich Lahmann. He revolutionized many aspects of nutrition, personal hygiene etc., and advocated a largely vegetarian diet.

220ᵁ Postcard

[Vienna, 28 August 1907]
Café Hohe Warte

Dearest Alma,
We're all feeling very cheery, and having partaken of a delicious high tea
we're now off to ramble in the country. The very warmest of greetings, to
Gucki too, from Emil Freund.

(I just wanted to make this into a <u>picture</u> postcard.) I've been in the ornamental gardens here
every afternoon. Today Freund came to fetch me.
Greetings   Gustav

221ᵁ

[Vienna, 29 August 1907]

Dearest,
But now you truly deserve a special commendation for your daily letters!
Reading them makes me feel like going off to Maiernigg and buying a villa.
– Yesterday I looked at Grete's house* from the outside. It made me really
envious, it's so lovely. Mama's house will be wonderful too. But we can manage it too, don't you think? – Just forget the gossip about the Theuers. These
people can't be taken seriously, neither their slanders nor their compliments.
As they have nothing to talk about, they poke fun at others, because it's the
easiest and most gratifying way of making conversation. Rest assured that
Theuer is fond of you – when you're there! Today I'm getting myself inoculated. Oh, I almost forgot: subjectively speaking, I'm feeling really well. If I
hadn't received that 'verdict', I wouldn't have anything to complain about.
However, I'm living very <u>cautiously</u> and taking care not to over-exert myself.
My bowels are back to normal too. All the same, I'm looking forward to the
arrival of my healing angel. Kathi just phoned to ask when you're arriving.
Warmest greetings from   Your Gustav

<u>What are your feelings about Ischl?</u>

---

* Grete and Wilhelm Legler were returning to Vienna after seven years in Stuttgart. They had
bought a plot of land on the Hohe Warte (Armbrustergasse 22) on which to build a villa. Like
the Molls' new villa, it was built to commission by the architect Josef Hoffmann.

222   [Vienna, 30 August 1907]

Dearest,
The heat here is getting rather tiresome. Yesterday I had my inoculation. Dr
Hamperl did it, and while he was about it he examined me too. He found a
<u>small</u> valvular deficiency which has been entirely compensated for, and
thinks nothing of the whole business. He said I could most certainly follow
my profession and I should live an absolutely <u>normal</u> life, except that I
should avoid <u>over-exerting</u> myself. The strange thing is that he actually said
the same as Blumenthal, but his whole manner had something comforting
about it. I have indeed lost my fear of conducting. Tomorrow I'll be seeing
<u>Montenuovo</u> for the first time. – Zemlinsky has already been to see me.
You'd be amazed to see how his face has filled out. Marriage seems to be
suiting him well.* – Actually I'd like to take a hike up the <u>Schneeberg</u>! And
would you perhaps also care for a little mountain air? Maybe Roller would
come along too, <he's really so kind to me. I can't wait to hear> when you're
due back. <But don't think of bringing Marie with you. That wretched
woman gets on my nerves.†> Your letters are so sweet, I'm glad to see you're
so full of beans, and wouldn't mind the benefit of it myself. Warmest greetings   Your Gustav

[Top of first page:] <Stay as long as you like, Almscherl, and come home
soon!>

223^U   [Vienna, 30 August 1907]

My Almschili,
It's just occurred to me that tomorrow's your birthday. Unfortunately it's too
late for a present, and for the life of me I wouldn't know what to get. You
know how hopeless I am about such things, my Almschi, don't you.
If I had my way, I'd spend the day with you on the Schneeberg. It must be
wonderful up there. – Tomorrow I'm moving back to the Rennweg; here in
the apartment it's a little overcrowded. I'll have to borrow towels and bed-
ding from Arnold, because you've got the key to the linen cupboard.
Warmest greetings from   Your Gustl

* Zemlinsky had joined the conducting staff of the Hofoper in May 1907, chiefly to assist
Mahler in rehearsing his new opera, *Der Traumgörge*, which was due to be premièred by
Mahler in October. He had married Ida Gutmann a few weeks earlier, on 21 June.
† Presumably the serving-maid mentioned in letter 213.

224[U]   [Vienna, 31 August 1907]

Dearest Almschi,

I'm just about to send you a money order for 1,200 crowns. I gave Freund his 1,000. You're absolutely right to be spending these wonderful days in the country. Here in Vienna it's terribly hot.

Apart from that, as an after-effect of the inoculation you're very likely to run a slight temperature. I've had one since yesterday, and have a nasty pain in the arm (swollen gland). Carl experienced the same. As from today, I'll get Kathi to cook for me at home. Yesterday at Freund's we ate Lahmann-style. Albi* phoned two days ago. We went for a walk and had a meal together. Otherwise I'm rather out on a limb. It's dreadful about Maria![†] Mama has had several sleepless nights again. Carl, who went there on Sunday, is expected back today.

Warmest greetings   Your Gustav

225[U]   [Vienna, 31 August 1907]

My dearest Almschili,

So I shan't send the money after all, and since you intend to return on <u>Monday,</u> I shan't go to the Schneeberg but wait for you here instead. Today I'm moving in at the Rennweg, though I'll still be going out to Carl's for lunch. It must be wonderful in Maiernigg right now. I can breathe that mild, clean air in your letters. – Yesterday and today I've been sitting for portrait photographs by <u>Nähr</u>[‡] under the supervision of <u>Roller</u>. According to Roller, the pictures have come out <u>extremely</u> well. – Physically, I'm feeling <u>really</u> well. I no longer feel <u>any</u> after-effects of that certain condition, but I'm living very quietly and carefully all the same. – Today, my Almschi, it's your birthday. When you get back, we'll take a stroll into town and find something nice for you. I hope this is the last time we're prevented from spending your birthday together. Yesterday Pollak came out to visit us. He had very interesting things to say about his trip to England. – Cable me at the <u>theatre</u> and let me know when you're arriving. I can scarcely wait. Your old Gustl

---

* i.e. Albine Adler (see footnote on p. 159).

† Maria Moll, Anna Moll's daughter by her marriage with Carl. The cause of dismay is not documented.

‡ Moritz Nähr, a photographer closely involved with the Secession. His portraits of Mahler are perhaps the finest ever made (cf. Plate 35).

226^U   [Vienna, 1 September 1907]

Dearest,
Enclosed is the letter from Emma [Rosé]. Maybe you'd care to answer it. –
I'm feeling pretty poorly. My swollen glands are causing me considerable
pain, particularly at night, and my digestion is also completely topsy-turvy.
Yesterday Hammerschlag came to see me, and we spent the evening with
Carl. He asked how you were keeping.
Freund waddles along here every morning too, and wants to know your
exact time of arrival. He's so touching. I scarcely see anything of Arnold.
Today Walter played me his symphony, the one he wrote last year.*
Unfortunately I could find absolutely nothing to say about it. He felt rather
put down, but I gave him my honest opinion. [Three lines obliterated.]   Your
Gustav

Now that Weingartner's appointment was certain, Mahler was free to final-
ize the details of his contract for New York. On 20 September he therefore
travelled to Munich for a further meeting with Conried. Before boarding the
train he sent Alma his customary greeting.

227^U Postcard   Vienna, 20 September 1907^P

M.A. I've a few minutes to spare, just enough to send a greeting. Somewhere
on my desk I've left a telegram from [Angelo] Neumann. Read it and tell me
what you think. I'm feeling pretty well. See that you get over your flu and
<u>stay in bed</u>! It's the best cure. Warmest   Your G.

The outcome of Mahler's meeting with Conried was set down in a supple-
ment to the original contract of 21 June, which Mahler then signed on 27
September. It was agreed that he should arrive in New York four weeks ear-
lier than originally stipulated, and that during this extra period he would
conduct two performances a week for an extra fee of 25,000 crowns.[13]

Mahler bade farewell to the Hofoper with single performances of his
favourite operas, given during the months of September and October: Don
Giovanni, Figaro *and* Die Zauberflöte, Die Walküre, Iphigénie en Aulide *and*
finally, on 15 October – the tenth anniversary of his appointment as
Hofoperndirektor – Fidelio.

---

* Bruno Walter, *Symphony no. 1* in D minor. It was first performed at the Grosser
Musikvereinsaal in Vienna on 6 February 1909, with the Orchestra of the Konzertverein
conducted by the composer.

*Before leaving for America, he made two further guest appearances, a con-
cert with the Kaim orchestra in Wiesbaden on 9 October, and a series of three
concerts in Russia and Finland. While changing trains at Frankfurt on his
way to Wiesbaden, he met his old friend Ludwig Rottenberg. The Wiesbaden
programme, given in the impressive new Kurhaus Hall, consisted of
Beethoven's* Coriolan overture and *Fifth Symphony, followed by the* Prelude
and Liebestod *from* Tristan *and the Prelude to* Die Meistersinger. *As usual,
he wrote to Alma before setting out on his journey.*

228[U] Postcard   Vienna, 6 October 1907[P]

Still enough time, my dearest, to send you a fond greeting! I hope you're
already asleep, and tomorrow, when the postman brings you this card, I shall
still be sleeping soundly. Your   G.

229[U] Telegram   Frankfurt, 7 October 1907

taken a stroll with rottenberg   travelling on refreshed to wiesbaden   gustav

230   Wiesbaden, 7 October 1907[P]
                                                       Hotel Nassau (Nassauer Hof)

Dearest Almschi,
Soon after my arrival I had quite a shock. At the hopelessly antiquated
Victoria Hotel I took one look at the room: with so much knocking of doors
and ringing of bells, I knew I wouldn't sleep a wink. So without even both-
ering to unpack, I drove straight to the Kurhotel in search of a better room.
Finally they found me one at the Nassauer Hof. It isn't particularly quiet, but
at least it's comfortable. So here, for the love of mercy, I'll give it a try.
'Who hath brought me into this land?', I call out every quarter-hour! All the
idiotic hurly-burly of a »fashionable« spa – I really could have done without
it. If it weren't for the indigestible dumplings and roast veal smothered in
garlic at the Theuer's, I would never have dreamt of accepting that telegraphic offer.*
Well, at least my programme is straightforward and ovation-provoking.[†]
Let's hope it will pay for my fur coat. Right now I'm sitting in my room
stark naked, waiting for my baggage, which I left at Hotel Victoria. It's a
way of combining pleasure with expedience: writing to you whilst giving

---

*Evidently Mahler had received a cable offering him this engagement whilst he and Alma were
dining in Maiernigg with their neighbour Alfred Theuer.
[†] cf. footnote on p. 117.

my body an airing, waiting undressed for my clothes to be brought, so as not to waste a minute later on. After the fodder in Frankfurt, namely, I'm looking forward to a good dinner. I just love this pen and the greasy writing paper.

Enough then – Greetings etc.   Your Gustav

231^U Telegram   Wiesbaden, 9 October 1907
                                                                          5.55

tried to contact you by phone but without success   my concert completely sold out whereas all previous ones empty   feeling fine in other respects too gustav

Ten days later Mahler was already making his way to Russia. Since Alma was still unwell, she decided not to travel with him but to take a course of treatment on the Semmering. Mahler's concerts in St Petersburg and Helsinki had originally been scheduled for December, but were subsequently brought forward to October to fit in with his schedule in New York.

232^U Postcard: Warsaw railway station   Warsaw, 20 October 1907^P

Shall shortly be travelling on to St Petersburg – here it's as dirty as ever! Had a very good night's rest. Warmest greetings. – I'm very sad that you're not with me.   G

233^U Telegram   St Petersburg, 21 October 1907

arrived safely greetings gustav

Mahler's first concert in St Petersburg, promoted by the Imperial Russian Musical Society, took place on 26 October in the main hall of the Conservatory. The programme consisted of Berlioz's overture Roman Carnival, *Beethoven's* Seventh Symphony *and concert aria* Ah perfido, *followed by orchestral songs by Richard Strauss, Max Fiedler and Hugo Wolf (soloist: Tilly Koenen) and Wagner's Prelude to* Die Meistersinger.

234^U St Petersburg [21 October 1907]
                                                              Hôtel d'Angleterre
                                                                          I

Dearest Almschi,
Just a short letter for now, so that you hear from me as soon as possible. – I

had a splendid journey, and was met, as before, by <u>Frank</u>,* who's as agreeable as ever. I've completed all arrangements with Schröder, corrected orchestral materials and met Gabrilovich's brother.† <u>Ossip</u> G. ceremoniously presented me with a crate of apples, and I've already eaten some of them. Now Frank is here (four in the afternoon) to take me for a walk. I'll write a longer letter tomorrow. For today, I just wanted to say how much I miss you, my Luxerl, and that I'm constantly being reminded of the days we spent here six years ago. I embrace you, my dearest. Write soon.
Your Gustav

Greetings to Mama and to Carl too, if he's already returned.
Frank sends best wishes as well. He received only one of our letters – and he answered it too!

235   St Petersburg [22 October 1907]^E
                                                              Hôtel d'Angleterre
                                                                            <2>

My Almschi,
Let me carry on (i.e. continue yesterday's letter), as it's not yet time to be carried off home!‡
With regard to my journey, I should add that I spent two enchanting hours at Warsaw station (that's how long I had to wait), where I was quite horrified to be served tea by a crotchety old waiter with a greasy tailcoat and grimy shirt. I couldn't bring myself to order anything else from the buffet, as it was swarming with bluebottles (even at this time of year the Poles manage to attract hordes of them). Instead, I unpacked my own treasures and amused myself for an hour. Then I wandered around in search of our old Jew. I couldn't find him, but I did find a number of younger ones (I thought it better not to bring one back as a souvenir for you). All the same, I had a most amusing time. It's a strange experience to observe such exotic people at close hand. One would like to question each of them in turn: their identity, their occupation, their hopes and wishes. There are older ones and younger ones, all mixed up. I was fascinated by a group of females – three generations:

---

* The graphic artist Gustav Frank, a cousin of Mahler's who had come to St Petersburg in 1890. In his capacity as a Member of the Royal Academy of Arts, he had prepared portraits of two tsars, etchings of Tolstoy and the celebrated actress Eleonore Duse etc. Since Mahler's last visit, he had also married.
† Arthur Gabrilovich, a solicitor.
‡ Orig.: pun on the word 'fortfahren'.

two old crones, one middle-aged woman (very personable) and three teenage girls lined up like organ pipes, the eldest with a handsome, gangling youth – all Slavic types. They seemed to be holding court – in one corner of the station, then in another – but they didn't board the train. What were they doing there, I wonder? –

Then followed a twenty-four-hour train journey. As long as there was still light, I marked up the parts of my Fifth Symphony; in the night I slept long and well. Frank, who is still the same kind-hearted, rather philistine gentleman he always was, comes to fetch me every day at five. Yesterday I dined at his home. <I didn't care for his children at all.> He longs for a change of scene, and can't stand it any longer. He'll probably relinquish his post and forfeit the pension attached to it (by the way, his title is indeed 'Excellency'). This morning was our first rehearsal. The orchestra gave me a warm welcome, rehearsed wonderfully and applauded enthusiastically when it was over.

Then I went home and was about to sit down to lunch when old Mrs Abaza[*] arrived. She was very keen to invite me to dinner. I refused, but promised to call on her. She's looking very well, and seemed intent on talking to me. Although I was hungry and not in the mood for conversation, she simply wouldn't budge. There was something curious about her exchange. She came to me as if I were a ministrant; evidently she's afraid of death and wanted to know what happens in the afterlife. I must have said something on the subject five years ago, and now, it seems, she has been waiting anxiously these five years to resume our conversation where it left off. Of my Second Symphony[†] she told me she found it most characteristic, and that it had made a considerable impression on her. I asked if she could still remember the text.

She: 'Is there a text? Oh yes, but the way the chorus sang, it was incomprehensible.'

I: 'Why don't you read it? Then you'll find the answer to your questions.'

She: 'I must get hold of a copy.'

And off she went right away. I'm convinced she went straight to the music shop to buy the score.

Unfortunately the hotel has deteriorated and the price has risen in inverse proportion. Everything looks so run down, and even the food is no longer

---

[*] Julia F. Abaza, a German singer who had married a Russian nobleman and was well-known in St Petersburg as a patron of the arts. She had been a good friend of Tchaikovsky.

[†] Oskar Fried had given the Russian première of Mahler's *Second Symphony* just a year previously, on 10 November 1906.

what it was. It's not quiet at night either – my room overlooks the courtyard. Next door is room 28, where we stayed last time. I took a peek inside as I went past. The old chambermaid is still there, and she promptly asked after you. – In fact, everyone is asking after you.

Walter (the concertmaster) is no longer in the orchestra (he's retired now). But he came to greet me and stayed for the whole rehearsal.

Do you remember the strange smell that pervades everything in Russia – even in the train on the way here? Something like a mixture of smoked wood and Russian leather. It reminds me of the time we spent together here.

<Now I'm waiting for Frank to join me for a stroll. I'll be going early to bed, because tomorrow's rehearsal starts at nine o'clock, as they do every day. I hope to receive post from you before long.

When I get back from Helsinki, I'll move into Hotel Europa. It's been renovated and is said to have improved considerably. Warmest greetings to you all.> Your Gustav

236   St Petersburg [23 October 1907]
                                                 Hôtel d'Angleterre
                                                       <3>

My Almschl,

All this time I've been racking my brains about something I was supposed to bring back for you from St Petersburg (we talked about it in Vienna), but I simply can't remember what it was. So please, write and tell me <u>at once</u>! <If you send me your measurements, they make wonderful <u>boots</u> here and use the softest <u>Chevreau</u> leather. At any rate, I'd like to buy myself a pair. If you like I can bring a pair for you too.>

Today was the second rehearsal. The orchestra is doing marvellously and they're as enthusiastic as ever. A little deputation came and asked me courteously if I would like to conduct two concerts with them next February, or at least agree on principle. Naturally, I told them that the journey from America was too long, but I'd be very happy to come another year. They even thanked me for promising that much.

What a pity you're not here. It really is a pleasure to rehearse under such conditions. <I received the enclosed note from Frau Abaza.* So I've promised to call on her for an hour this evening at nine o'clock.>

At the hotel I've moved to the top floor in the hope of escaping the noise. But it's dreadfully dirty here. I'm paying <u>eight roubles</u> a day. In Germany I can

---

* The enclosure has not been preserved.

get the finest suite for the same money.* And they say Hotel Europa is even dearer.

Almschili, I'm very disappointed that you haven't yet sent a single letter. Even if you're fully occupied, you could at least have sent me a postcard. Now I'm on the top floor and can look out on the beautiful square with the lofty St Isaac's Cathedral. I love to sit at my desk by the window all afternoon, reading, sleeping, dreaming and admiring the view.

<On Monday I'm off to Helsinki.>

Warmest greetings from   Your Gustav

<Such luck: one of my shirts was already missing a button when I got here, and the others are so loose that they fall off at the slightest touch.>

237^U   St Petersburg [24 October 1907]

Hôtel d'Angleterre

No. 4

Dearest Almschl,

What sad news your letter brings me today. Another of those nervous attacks. Go straight to <u>Kovacs</u>, I beg you, and do exactly what he tells you. You're still young – somehow you've simply <u>got</u> to get over this. Heavens, what I would give to rid myself of all my maladies, and you can't even keep it up for a fortnight. – Keep calm while I'm away, and use the time to attend to your disorders. – As for the plan to buy a plot of land in Heiligenstadt, I can venture no opinion. I believe we should place our trust entirely in Carl and simply do as he advises. After all, it's not so urgent that we'd have to exchange contracts right away. I'll be home in a fortnight. I'm sure they'll keep their word until then, and meanwhile we can argue out the pros and cons. – My first concert here will soon be past and gone. Frank and Gabrilovich are taking turns to keep me company. – The latter reminds me of his brother: so unbelievably sensitive and so kind and considerate, down to the last detail.

I've been wandering about in the hotel. It makes me almost indignant when I see someone come out of room <u>28</u> on the second floor. Today, as I was going up to my room on the third floor, out came a woman with her hair in curlers.† I almost felt like making a rude remark. On Sunday evening I'm leaving for Helsinki, where everything is said to be more civilized (cleaner).

---

* In 1907 the silver rouble was valued at approx. 2.25 marks. According to the 1907 edition of *Baedeker*, a room at Hotel Bristol in Berlin cost 5 marks.

† Orig.: 'mit Wuckerln'.

Write and tell me how you're getting on. Until <u>Friday</u> morning use my Petersburg address; as from Saturday write to <u>Helsinki</u>, Finland, c/o <u>Konzertbüro Fazer</u>.

<u>Now be a good girl</u> and avoid the <u>high life</u>, even if you're feeling better. You've got to get well for America. By the way, I sincerely hope the sea voyage and the stay sine cura will do you good.

With all my love   Your Gustav

238^U   St Petersburg [25 October 1907]
                                              Hôtel d'Angleterre

5

Dearest,

Still no letter! After what I wrote yesterday, I'm really worried now, for there can only be one explanation for your silence. Why don't you ask Mama or Justi to tell me what's up. – Time is dragging during this visit. Tomorrow it will be only a week since I left home, but to me it already feels like three.

Today was the public dress rehearsal – very full. Afterwards I was again approached by the committee, headed by Walter, who asked if I would at least agree to conduct two Benefit Concerts next year (a kind of philharmonic concert promoted by the orchestra itself). I must say, you'd be amazed at the kind-heartedness of these people.

Perhaps it would be agreeable for us to spend a fortnight here next October (naturally you'd come with me).

I can't leave for Helsinki until <u>Monday</u> evening, as I have to rehearse here on Sunday for my second concert. – How I detest rehearsals that begin at <u>nine</u> in the morning! You remember what it was like all those years ago?

I still haven't had time to visit the Eremitage because I have rehearsals every day from nine to twelve, after which I have a meal (lunch with Gabrilovich at 12.30), then sleep until five, when Frank comes to fetch me.

Tomorrow I hope to receive at least a card from you, otherwise I'll be really very anxious. Fondly   Your Gustav

239^U   St Petersburg [28 October 1907]
                                              Hôtel d'Angleterre

Dearest,

Another two days without a letter: you're being very lazy this time, and I'm very worried about it.

The concert was the day before yesterday (huge success). Next year the orchestra wants me to come for two concerts, and betweenwhiles the Intendant would like me to conduct two or three performances at the Opera. It might be possible in October.

This evening I'm off to Helsinki (the address is Hotel Societetshuset). Also don't forget to write 'H., Finland'. Mrs Saburov* has now arrived. When I get home, I'll just have to feed myself up; this time I haven't been dining out at all.

Let's talk your plans over when I get home. What does Carl think of it? Above all, what about Aussee? After all, in the coming years we'll need somewhere at least for the spring and the summer; but you're right: during the winter months we probably won't be at home. – Yesterday it turned cold at last, and I walked about proudly (and comfortably) in my fur coat. The sleeves have turned out a little too short and tight, so they'll have to be altered when I get back. Apart from that it's very fine and causes quite a stir. I'm finding the climate in St Petersburg very agreeable. What a shame you're not here with me. I beg you, make sure your heart is back to normal before I arrive, and above all let Hammerschlag come to see you. I mean it! Don't delay, you'll only regret it. Why haven't you sent any news of Gucki? And I'd also like to know how Mama and Carl are getting on. Fondly Your Gustav

(The orchestra here is really delightful and warm-hearted in its attitude towards me.)

Mahler's railway journey to Helsinki lasted approximately eight hours. Finland had been part of Sweden from the twelfth century until 1809; from then on (until 1917) it was a Russian grand duchy. For many years the Finnish language had been forbidden, and only in 1902 was it placed on an equal footing with Swedish. A national strike in 1906 had led to a reform of the parliamentary system, with equal representation for the Finns. Thus, when Mahler arrived in Helsinki, the nationalist movement dominated every walk of life, and notably music, literature and the visual arts.

On his first evening in Helsinki Mahler attended a concert of the Philharmonic Society conducted by Robert Kajanus. The programme included two works by Sibelius, the symphonic poem Vårsång (Spring Song) op. 16 and, as an encore, the celebrated Valse triste from Kuolema op. 44.

---

* Wife of the Russian statesman Andrei Aleksandrovich Saburov, whom the Mahlers had met on their first visit to Russia, in 1902.

240   Helsinki [30 October 1907]
                                                    Hôtel Societetshuset

My Almschili,

Well, yesterday was my first day in Helsinki. Unfortunately it's been raining here, so I've had to take off my lovely fur coat. In the evening I went to a popular concert, at which I made the acquaintance of my orchestra. It's astonishingly good and disciplined, which says much for the musical director, Kajanus, who enjoys an excellent reputation in the musical world, by the way. He called on me in the afternoon and stayed for quite a while. An extremely sympathetic man, serious and modest.

At the concert in the evening – with the audience seated round beer tables – I was surprised by Axel Gallen[*] and his wife, who came and sat with me. We stayed on after the concert, and were joined by Kajanus and his wife, as well as a pianist from Brussels.[†] Gallen was in immensely high spirits, and I liked him a lot. At eleven o'clock I bade them farewell and went to bed, which caused quite a stir, because here everyone drinks until dawn. On Saturday, the day after the concert, Gallen wants to show me his yawl and take us out on the water. Then in the evening I'll return to St Petersburg.

The programme included some pieces by Sibelius, the Finnish national composer, who has made a big name for himself, not only here but also in the outside world. The first composition was a standard piece of kitsch spiced with a national sauce prepared from those 'Nordic' harmonies we know only too well. 'Pui Kaiki'.[‡]

By the way, all these nationalist geniuses use the same formula. In Russia and Sweden it's no different – not to mention the whores and pimps of present-day Italy. Axel, who knocks back twelve glasses of schnapps before dinner and sails a yawl, cuts a very different figure. His health and high-spirits have something authentic about them. So far no news from you.

Warmest greetings, my dear Almschili!   Gustav

<My first rehearsal is at twelve o'clock.>

Mahler may have formed an unfavourable opinion of the works of Sibelius heard at the concert, but Sibelius himself remembered their subsequent

---

[*] Orig.: 'Galen'. The Finnish painter Akselli Gallen-Kallela. Mahler knew him from Vienna, where he had exhibited at the Twelfth and Nineteenth Secessionist Exhibitions, which opened in December 1901 and January 1904, respectively.

[†] The pianist and composer Arthur de Greef.

[‡] According to Alma (AMMI, 397), this was what came out when little Gucki attempted to say 'Pfui Teufel' ('Yuck').

meetings as friendly and illuminating. He and Mahler took several walks together, during which their discussion touched on questions of philosophy and musical form. Sibelius expressed the opinion that the essence of symphonic composition lay in deep, hidden relationships between musical ideas; Mahler disagreed: 'No, a symphony must be like the world. It must be all-embracing.'[14]

A certain tension must have been palpable during these meetings, for Sibelius was hoping that Mahler would offer to perform his music in New York.[*]

241[U]   Helsinki [31 October 1907]
                                             Hôtel Societetshuset

Dearest,
Just received your telegram from the Semmering with news of your 'well-being'. I'm really happy to hear it. Helsinki is wonderful, thanks to the sea. It surrounds the city on all sides, and wherever you are, you can always see it. I'm bored here all the same, because I have so little time to explore. After rehearsal I always take a rest (after lunch too). My address in St Petersburg remains unchanged: Hôtel d'Angleterre. I don't feel like changing, and anyway I've got used to it now.
It seems like an age since I left home. – I'm off to rehearsal again now, and want to get these few lines off to you quickly, so you know where to write to me in St Petersburg. So long   Gustav

242   Helsinki, 2 November 1907[P]
                                             Hôtel Societetshuset

Dearest,
Well, yesterday was the concert. People had gathered together from all over Finland. <u>Sibelius</u> had already called on me before lunch. Like all Finns, he too is extremely sympathetic. After the concert, Gallen joined us too. Now I'm sitting here, waiting for him to take me for a ride through the Finnish skerries in his motor boat. Unfortunately it's raining, and I fear this will rather dampen our pleasure. But wait! Would you believe it: this very moment, while I'm writing, the sun has started to emerge. So maybe it will be enjoyable after all.
I wasn't so pleased about the <u>dash</u> in the text at the point where you wrote that you have to leave the Semmering. But Almschi! What kind of reason is that? If it was doing you good, you should have stayed on. Somehow we'll

---

[*] Mahler did indeed programme the Sibelius *Violin Concerto* for one of his New York concerts in 1911 (with Maud Powell as soloist), but was unable to conduct it himself because he was already sick.

scrape the 100 crowns together! Now at last you know how much your health is worth to you.

This evening I'm off to St Petersburg. Thank heaven this episode is coming to a close. I'm already feeling very fed up, although I've been in good company both here and in St Petersburg.

<Here comes Gallen to fetch me. So I'd better close now with warmest greetings.   Your Gustav>

<Don't forget to buy the yoghurt machine so I can resume my milk diet when I get back. I'd also like to start my <u>massage</u> sessions straight away. Please make all arrangements, so that everything is ready.

[in Gallen-Kallela's hand:] Best wishes from Gallen.>

On Mahler's last morning in Finland, Gallen took him by boat to visit the architects Eliel Saarinen and Hermann Gesellius. The two had set up in partnership in 1896, together with a third architect, Armas Lindgren. They had won international acclaim with their Finnish pavilion at the 1900 Paris Exhibition, and at the time of Mahler's visit they were working on their best-known project, Helsinki Central Station. But arguably their masterpiece was the Hvitträsk residential complex, built in 1902. Saarinen and Gesellius lived there in villas built and decorated to their own specifications; Finland's finest craftsmen had worked with them on the project.

243   St Petersburg [4 November 1907]
Hôtel d'Angleterre

My dear Almschili,

For the past hour I've been ringing for the waiter to bring me some writing paper, but the scoundrel hasn't come. So I'll have to write on this telegram form – naturally in telegraphic style.

Since yesterday morning (when I got back from Finland), I've been correcting orchestral parts, and – with much wailing and gnashing of teeth – I've just finished. And now I have a large hollow in the middle finger of my right hand. – My day with Gallen turned out rather well. He and a celebrated architect, whose name escapes me, took me under their wing. They swathed me in rugs and fed me with smorgasbord until I felt quite sick. – I was frozen stiff (but so were they). After a three-hour voyage through the skerries, with constantly changing sea views, we reached our destination. There we were met with horse and carriage, and off we rode in the highest of spirits to a beautiful house (actually more like a villa) in purest Hoffmann style, where we were welcomed with the greatest hospitality.

This architect lives there all the year round with his partner (whose name I do remember: he's called Gesellius).

It's on a lake, and from the upper floor you can see the sea. The rooms are beautiful – rather like the Hohe Warte translated into <u>Finnish</u>. For just a year these two architects, sympathetic young fellows both, were married to two equally sympathetic young ladies, and they all lived happily together (they had known each other since childhood). One day, a year ago, it occurred to one of them that life without variety is no 'life' at all. So what did they do? They swapped wives,[*] and for the past year they've been living together as happily as ever, building houses for other people and living in their own. Isn't that a wonderful story? – In the evening, as it was growing dark, we sat in the twilight round the hearth, with massive logs glowing and flickering as if in a smithy. – Gallen, who had been staring at me fixedly all the way there (like a huntsman with his prey), suddenly brought out an easel and started painting my portrait – much in the style of Rembrandt, lit only by the flames from the fireplace.

He'd been working away for half an hour or so when I grew restless, so we all stood up and went off for a stroll in the woods. I was rather glad to have made my escape, and didn't once mention the portrait again. An hour later it was time to leave, and I was just saying my farewells, when up came our host with the easel, and to everybody's amazement there was the picture – complete in every detail. A magnificent painting and a remarkable likeness too.[†] You'd be amazed! What a splendid fellow! The mere sight of him steering his boat was quite wonderful. There he stood erect and alert, his eyes two fiery coals straining into the distance – tall and sturdy like a Viking. I can well imagine that the women just fall at his feet. – All these people made such a heart-warming impression, by the way, and for all their hospitality they never imposed on me. At one point, without saying a word, I took a nap on the sofa in the next room, and not a sound disturbed my slumbers.

As from yesterday I'm back here in the custody of Frank & Gabrilovich. The latter in particular kisses the ground I tread.

Today I received a cable from you: '<u>Everything all right</u>'. I hope this was merely your belated reply to my last letters. You know, these letters take <u>four days</u> to reach their destination. Why don't you write a nice long one? But you'll have to be quick, otherwise I'll already have arrived home. Warmest greetings from   Your Gustav

[*] In fact it was Saarinen's first wife, Mathilde, who left him for Gesellius; Saarinen later married Gesellius's sister Loja.
[†] See Plate 40. Gallen's portrait of Mahler is now housed at a private collection in Finland.

<Greetings to Carl & Mama and to Justi, who sent a very dear letter. Maybe I'll still find time to reply to it.>

Mahler's second concert in St Petersburg, on 9 November, was something of a marathon. It opened with his Fifth Symphony, *then followed Rachmaninov's* Second Piano Concerto *and two movements from an unspecified concerto in E-flat major by Mozart (both works played by Raoul Pugno and conducted by Mikhail Vladimirov). To conclude, Mahler returned to the podium for Beethoven's* Coriolan *overture and the* Prelude and Liebestod *from* Tristan und Isolde.

244[U]   St Petersburg [5 November 1907]
                                            Hôtel d'Angleterre

Today I received a second 'all well' telegram from you. But Almschi, this is an entirely new departure, and I really don't know what to make of it. My sense of logic tells me either all is <u>not</u> well, and your telegram is intended to reassure me a little, without telling me what's going on, or all is indeed well, in which case I don't understand why you can't manage to scribble a few lines on a postcard. – And then you want me to cable you my time of arrival? Today, a whole week in advance? But so much could happen before then. –
I have nothing new to report from here. I read a review by Burckhard in the Neue Freie Presse,[*] so let's hope he's feeling better.
I also read the unfortunate story of schoolmaster Kraus.[†] Mama and Carl will probably be very upset.
Yesterday I went to the Opera. <u>Onegin</u>. Very strong ensemble, but a coarse, amateurish performance – the same as everywhere – and the same as Vienna soon will be! You'll see.
I wonder whether I'll get to see anything from you this week other than telegrams. Warmest   Gustav

245[U]   St Petersburg [8 November 1907]
                                            Hôtel d'Angleterre

My Almschi,
Three days have passed with no news at all, and before that I received a

[*] Max Burckhard, 'Das Erlöschen der Notverordnung', *Neue Freie Presse*, 1.11.1907.
[†] At the Jewish Home for the Blind on the Hohe Warte a schoolmaster by the name of Siegmund Kraus had fallen into a well; some days later he died from his injuries (*Neue Freie Presse*, 2.11.1907).

telegram every day for three days, but nothing else. I just don't know what to make of it.

All your letters addressed to Helsinki seem to have reached me. The last one was a report on a performance of Madame Butterfly.* – Life here goes on as usual. The rehearsals for this concert were pretty taxing, but I hope I've survived it all.

Our final rehearsal today was completely sold out. Huge success. They seem to be acclaiming me as a second Nikisch. But nowhere, I must admit, have I met more serious-minded factions or more agreeable, enthusiastic young people than here. And so there are plenty of people who know very well to discern between Mahler and Nikisch (until now he was always the public's darling here). I've also spent several evenings in the theatre: quite interesting. All going well, I'll be leaving here on Sunday evening and should reach Vienna on Tuesday afternoon around 3.30.

This Kraus affair must have given Carl and Mama quite a jolt.

Today I received a 'friendly' letter from Freund.†

If all is well, as you cabled, I don't understand why you haven't written. I hope there's no serious trouble.

Warmest greetings from   Your Gustav

246ᵁ Telegram   St Petersburg, 10 November 1907

arriving tuesday three thirty   gustav

On this occasion the Fifth Symphony *received a frosty welcome. Commenting on the ovations accorded to the other works on the programme,* Novoye Vremya *thought that Mahler's pride must have been 'wounded to the quick'. Even if most critics disparaged the symphony, its orchestral mastery did elicit some praise, but Isaiah Moisievitch Knorozovsky, writing for* Teatr i Iskusstvo, *was alone in acknowledging Mahler to be 'one of the most original and brilliant representatives of modern symphonic music'.*[15]

Igor Stravinsky and his teacher, Nicolai Rimsky-Korsakov, were both present at Mahler's second concert. The former, recalling the occasion in his Conversations *of 1959, spoke of Mahler's conducting and personality as having made a greater impression on him than the music itself.*[16] *The latter, according to his biographer V. V. Yastrebtsev, found the music 'devoid of taste and talent', disapproved of Mahler's 'coarse and clumsy' orchestration and*

---

* Alma had evidently attended the opening night of Puccini's Madame Butterfly at the Hofoper on 31 October; the work was receiving its first performance in Vienna.
† Orig.: intentional pun on the word 'Freund'.

condemned the work as an 'arrogant improvisation' by a composer 'who never knows what will happen in the next bar'. [17]

In the afternoon of 12 November 1907, after a railway journey that had lasted more than two days, Mahler arrived back in Vienna. Twelve days later, with a performance of his Second Symphony, he bade the city a formal farewell. Contrary to Alma's recollections (in AMM4),[18] the hall was packed, both for the final rehearsal and the concert. All Mahler's friends, disciples and admirers were present, for most of them realized that they would probably never hear him conduct again. 'The audience simply would not leave,' reported the Neue Freie Presse. 'Mahler was called back to the rostrum time and again, to ovations, cheers and waving handkerchiefs, to which the members of both the orchestra and the chorus added their voices. [. . .] It was their way of bidding farewell to Mahler the composer, the Hofoperndirektor, the conductor – the whole fascinating personality of a man whom Vienna has now lost.'[19]

Such enthusiasm was by no means universal, indeed, some reactions to Mahler's farewell were singularly unkind. 'How sad that a man of such imagination, ambition and ability [. . .] should lack the spirit of true creativity, of naive originality,' wrote Richard von Perger, director of the Vienna Conservatory, 'for then he would rank amongst the foremost.'[20] And the critic Max Graf ventured the opinion that 'for all the brilliance of his artistic conception, Mahler's achievements as Hofoperndirektor have been largely negative. Despite the ten years he spent in Vienna, he has remained a stranger to the city. [. . .] He never saw eye to eye with Viennese society, never fell under the city's spell, nor do any of his compositions even hint at the fact that the man who wrote them lived and worked here'.[21] Hermann Bahr was one of the few who acknowledged the extent of Mahler's achievement as Hofoperndirektor. These ten years, he wrote, had been 'the greatest era in the history of opera in Vienna, a unique attempt to direct a theatre from the standpoint of purest artistry.'[22] In an epoch of radical changes, Mahler had been obliged to recognize the limitations of nineteenth-century music-theatre. As the train drew out of the station, carrying him and his family to Paris and thence to the United States, he turned to Alma and said: 'Repertoire opera has no future. I'm glad I didn't have to experience its demise during my term of office. To the very end, I managed to hoodwink the public into believing that they were witnessing something exceptional.'[23]

At eight o'clock on the morning of 9 December some two hundred friends and admirers convened at the Westbahnhof to bid Mahler a final farewell. 'When we arrived,' wrote Alma, 'everyone was already standing there with *hands full of flowers and eyes full of tears. They came into our compartment and decked it with garlands – the seats, the floor, everything. As the train drew out of the station we felt no remorse, no longing. The pain had been too great. All we wanted was to leave, to get as far away as possible.'*[24]

The following day the Mahlers arrived in Paris, where they took rooms at Hôtel Bellevue. On 11 December Mahler attended a performance of Tristan *with Ernest van Dyck in the title role, but left before it was over. On 12 December the family travelled on to Cherbourg, where they went aboard the* Kaiserin Auguste Viktoria. *On 20 December they disembarked in New York and settled into a suite at Hotel Majestic. Three days later Mahler took his place for the first time on the rostrum of the Metropolitan Opera.*

1908

On 1 January 1908 Mahler made his New York début with Tristan und Isolde after just nine days of rehearsal (in Vienna he would have prepared such a production for weeks and months). As compensation for the shoddy staging, the cast was splendid, with Olive Fremstad as Isolde, Heinrich Knote as Tristan and Louise Homer as Brangäne. Mahler's first appearance filled many columns in the New York press. His interpretation was compared to that of the greatest German conductors New York had known, such as Felix Mottl and Anton Seidl. Some critics expressed surprise at the subtlety and subdued level of his orchestral dynamics, which allowed the singers to be heard with unaccustomed ease. Lawrence Gilman, in Harper's Weekly, considered the interpretation on that account to lack 'fiery ecstasy', and found it 'emasculated, shorn of almost all its glory and its strength'.[1]

On 23 January followed Don Giovanni. Again, the production and stage direction were inept, and again the cast, which included Emma Eames, Johanna Gadski, Marcella Sembrich, Antonio Scotti and Fjodor Chalyapin, was scintillating. Some critics never missed a chance to vaunt their supposedly superior knowledge of music and its interpretation. Henry Krehbiel, for instance, writing for the Herald Tribune, censured Mahler for 'refusing to follow the traditional tempi'.[2] From then on most of Krehbiel's reviews were unfavourable.

Later in the month, Mahler received confirmation of a rumour he had heard before leaving Europe, namely that persistent ill-health had obliged Conried to stand down. Mahler was offered the post in his stead, but refused it, explaining that he was no longer willing to accept administrative duties. In due course Giulio Gatti-Casazza, director of La Scala Milan, was nominated as Conried's successor. He in turn announced the engagement of a star conductor, Arturo Toscanini, as co-principal conductor. Mahler could not foresee any problems arising from this appointment; after all, in Vienna he himself had entrusted much of the Italian repertory to Italian maestri.

Mahler's repertoire during his first season at the 'Met' included Die Walküre and Siegfried, both of which were again performed with strong casts and weak stage presentation. Yet his greatest success, indeed one of the greatest triumphs in his whole career, occurred shortly before the end of his stay, with a new production of Fidelio, premièred on 20 March. Mahler had *persuaded Conried to import Roller's 1904 sets from Vienna; this time he himself took charge of the stage production and was allowed a greater number of rehearsals. His interpretation of a work he loved above all others, but which had never been popular in New York, aroused tremendous enthusiasm both in the press and the public. At every performance, his incandescent interpretation of the overture Leonore no. 3 (inserted before the second scene of Act II) drew an ecstatic response. The 'driving eloquence'[3] of the performance, the 'dramatizing intensity that beat in every phrase and accent', the 'might, poignancy, irresistible emotion'[4] were praised to the skies. To Anna Moll, Mahler wrote: 'Fidelio has had a tremendous success. At one stroke it has completely changed my fortunes.'[5]*

The consequences of this triumph were far-reaching. In March 1908 Mrs George R. Sheldon, the wife of a prominent New York banker, formed a committee with the aim of creating a new 'Mahler orchestra', or rather of restructuring the New York Philharmonic, which hitherto had played only a subsidiary role in New York's musical life, on a permanent basis. Meanwhile, Walter Damrosch had engaged Mahler for three concerts with the New York Symphony, to be given in the autumn of 1908. When he heard of Mrs Sheldon's plans and of the trial concerts Mahler was to conduct with the Philharmonic the following spring, Damrosch flew into a rage. He himself was a mediocre conductor, but he had powerful connections. From the presence of such a formidable rival he had everything to lose.

Before returning to Europe, Mahler conducted a series of performances with the Metropolitan Opera company in Boston and New York. At a farewell benefit concert for Conried,* he gave another of his much-admired performances of the Leonore overture no. 3.

As the season closed, Mahler's feelings about America could be summed up as a combination of enthusiasm for a country in which he had discovered a refreshing lack of prejudice, a tolerant pragmatism which enabled him to make necessary concessions, and a desire to educate the New York public and improve standards of performance. In this respect he had already made some headway; indeed, he had been promised more rehearsal time for the coming season. Shortly before leaving America, he wrote to Zemlinsky: 'I'll be returning next winter. Both of us have found much to appreciate in this country; people go about everything with an alertness, sanity and candour that we find most attractive. Everything has a future.'[6] But this generally favourable disposition did not prevent him from regretting that he had left

* Conried died the following year.

Vienna: 'All this while, I have been plagued by homesickness,' he wrote to Countess Wydenbruck at the end of the season. 'Unlike my wife, who would gladly remain here altogether, I regret to say that my heart belongs to Vienna.'⁷ However, homesickness was not the root of the problem. Mahler was still worried about his health, and Putzi's death had left deep scars. Alma comments in AMM4: 'He was also aware of his own illness, and all else was of little consequence for him. He was nervous, quick-tempered and irritable. It was a very sad winter for me – and certainly for both of us.'⁸

On 23 April the Mahlers set sail for Europe aboard the Kaiserin Augusta Viktoria. *Having disembarked at Cuxhaven on 2 May, Mahler travelled on to Hamburg, then to Wiesbaden, where he was to conduct the Städtische Kur-Orchester on 8 May in a programme that included his* First Symphony, *Mendelssohn's 'Fingal's Cave' overture and Beethoven's* Leonore *overture no. 3. Alma stayed on in Hamburg for two days, presumably to visit her relatives, before joining Mahler in Wiesbaden. As usual, he sent her a brief message from the railway station before setting out on his journey.*

247ᵁ Postcard: The Outer Alster, Hamburg   Hamburg, 5 May 1908ᴾ

Warmest greetings, dear heart. I've got masses of time on my hands. G.

In Wiesbaden, Arnold Berliner and Ossip Gabrilovich attended Mahler's rehearsals. The concert itself was a disappointment, largely because it was poorly attended. Mahler and Alma returned to Vienna on 10 May, and stayed with the Molls on the Hohe Warte while their apartment in the Auenbruggergasse was made ready for them.

Ten days later, on 21 May, Mahler left for Prague, where he was to conduct a concert with the Czech Philharmonic Orchestra. Vienna was bustling with excitement as it prepared for the Emperor's jubilee celebrations on 12 June, while Prague had organized its own programme of festivities for Franz-Joseph's jubilee as King of Bohemia. Mahler's concert was the first of a series of ten to be given in an exhibition hall built specially for the occasion in Stromovka Park. His programme included Beethoven's Seventh Symphony *and* Coriolan *overture, Smetana's* Bartered Bride *overture, the* Prelude and Liebestod *from* Tristan *and the Prelude to* Die Meistersinger.

248ᵁ Telegram   Prague, 21 May 1908

arrived safely   feeling on top of the world   greetings gustav

249   Prague [22 Mai 1908]
                                                   Hotel Blauer Stern

My Almscherl,
I was very glad to receive your dear letter today. Yesterday was very pleasant, with an excellent and cooperative orchestra. – Here I'm continually surrounded by a crowd of young (very agreeable) people, including Bodanzky
and <u>Klemperer</u>, who has made a splendid solo piano arrangement of my
<u>Second Symphony</u>. – <I have a delightful room in an annexe of the <u>Blauer</u>
<u>Stern</u> – with furnishings by Fix und Portois.[*]
I <u>greatly</u> enjoyed the 'Northern' bread that Justi gave for me the journey, and
it seems to serve its purpose. <u>Please order me another loaf for Sunday</u>
<u>evening</u> (I'll probably arrive at half past seven, unless I travel back the night
before, but that doesn't make much sense).>
I wonder what we'll manage to find for the summer? I leave everything to
you. – Today we have our second rehearsal.
I was very taken with the conductor of the Czech orchestra here, a Dr
Zemanek,[†] who recently gave a performance of my Fourth Symphony to
great acclaim. Bodanzky and the others tell me it was first rate.
Many kisses, my Almschi. I look forward to seeing you soon!
Your Gustav

*Arthur Bodanzky was a former pupil of Zemlinsky and had worked for one
season (1900/1) under Mahler as a repetiteur at the Hofoper. In 1905 Angelo
Neumann engaged him as 1st Kapellmeister at the Neues Deutsches Theater
in Prague. In the autumn of 1908 he was due to take up a new, considerably
more influential appointment as 1st Kapellmeister at the Nationaltheater in
Mannheim.*

*Otto Klemperer first met Mahler in 1905 when he conducted the off-stage
orchestra in Oskar Fried's performance of the* Second Symphony *in Berlin. In
1907 Mahler gave him a written recommendation, on the strength of which
Neumann engaged him as chorus-master (and later Kapellmeister) at the
Neues Deutsches Theater in Prague.*

*Klemperer's impression of these rehearsals was so overwhelming, as he
wrote in his* Erinnerungen an Gustav Mahler, *that he began to doubt his own
conducting ability and even thought of abandoning the profession.*[9] *By all*

---

[*] A Viennese firm of cabinet makers that worked in close collaboration with the Wiener
Werkstätte.
[†] Vilém Zemanek, one of the first principal conductors of the Czech Philharmonic. Under his
direction the orchestra performed several of Mahler's works.

accounts, the concert was a phenomenal success. On the podium, Mahler was presented with a palm branch, decorated with red and white ribbons to symbolize the colours of Bohemia. Before leaving for home, he accepted an offer to return to the Czech Philharmonic in September to conduct the world première of his Seventh Symphony.

In Mahler's absence, Alma and her mother had travelled to Toblach in search of a summer house. On arrival, they found the Pustertal still buried in deep snow. In due course, however, they succeeded in finding what they were look-ing for: the Trenkerhof, 'a large, isolated farm-house with eleven rooms, two verandas and two bathrooms; a little primitive, to be sure, but wonderfully sit-uated. We immediately decided to rent it for the summer, then we returned to Vienna, packed our belongings and made our way back to Toblach.'[10]

They set out on 10 June. This hasty departure was probably a flight from the metropolis, for as the date of the Imperial jubilee drew nearer, the hustle and bustle grew in proportion. The Trenkerhof in Alt-Schluderbach is situ-ated within sight of the small market town of Toblach, on the southern side of the Pustertal. Mahler soon found a carpenter to build him a shack in the woods, where he would be able to work undisturbed. Once his new Komponierhäuschen *was ready – and apparently it was completed in a mat-ter of days – Mahler moved in with his upright piano and a few favourite books. Two letters to Bruno Walter, written around this time, show that he needed solitude to regain his peace of mind and stop worrying about his health. Soon afterwards he started work on* Das Lied von der Erde, *his first new composition since 1906.*

Many visitors came to Toblach during the summer, including Anna and Carl Moll, Paul Hammerschlag, Julius Korngold, Ernst Decsey, Alfred Roller, Oskar Fried and Gustav Brecher. On one occasion, Mahler complained to Moll of this constant coming and going, but to Alma it must have provided a welcome diversion from the daily round. Only one message to her has sur-vived from this period, a note presumably left by Mahler on the way to his shack, early in the morning while she was still asleep.

250[U]   [Toblach, August 1908]

Dearest,

I've just got up, and at present the weather is dull. If it cheers up later, and if you feel like going through with our plan, come and fetch me from the shack at eleven. I've all but finished, and have only one small item still to remove. We can time our departure so as to reach Schluderbach by midday. If you don't come, I'll see you at lunchtime, as usual. G

The last movement of Das Lied von der Erde, *'Der Abschied', was completed in short score on 1 September. Four days later Mahler left for Prague, where he had two weeks to prepare the world première of the* Seventh Symphony. *This time was to be spent not only rehearsing the work but also checking and refining the orchestration. From Vienna, where he briefly interrupted his journey, he sent Alma the following letter:*

251[U]   [Vienna, 5 September 1908]

My dearest Almschili,
Just a few lines, which I hope will still reach you in Toblach. – The night, or rather the sleeping car, was wonderful. I slept for most of the journey. Carl met me at the station in Vienna with the keys to the apartment, so I was able to drive straight to the Auenbruggergasse. I gave Fraenkel's[*] prescription to Carl right away. I hope it reaches you with this letter. Then off to the coffee-house. Roller[†] arrived soon afterwards; he was exceptionally kind and warm-hearted.
The situation at the Hofoper has become intolerable for him. He'd like to leave post-haste. Walter arrived at 10.30. Then we took a walk and had a chat, and Arnold joined us. Now we're on our way to Meissl und Schadn, where Pollak will be meeting us too. I phoned him in advance and tapped him for a <u>first-class</u> ticket on the Franz-Josefs-Bahn.
Everyone thought I was looking very well. Appetite and digestion are first-rate, as I expected.
Warmest embraces, my dearest. It was sweet of you all to follow me down to the station. Best wishes also to Mammerl,
Your Gustav

252 Telegram   Prague, 7 [September 1908]

corrected parts all day yesterday   rehearsed today   tomorrow free day   feeling very well   still no letter from you   fondest greetings gustav

---

[*] Joseph Fraenkel, who had emigrated to the United States in 1889 and was now director of the Montefiore Hospital in New York.
[†] Before leaving Toblach, Mahler had written to both Bruno Walter and Alfred Roller, arranging to meet them at Meissl und Schadn before he took the three-o'clock train to Prague.

253   Prague [8 September 1908]
                                            Hotel Blauer Stern

My dearest Almscherl,
So far I simply haven't had time to write. Yesterday I spent literally the whole
day correcting parts, and so far I've taken just one string rehearsal. I had
lunch and dinner with the youngsters. Hammerschlag turned up here too:
he's participating in a congress, and yesterday evening at six o'clock we took
a cab ride together. – This time I'm very dissatisfied with the hotel. The man
next door wakes me up every night at eleven o'clock, and snores so loudly
that it shocks me out of my sleep, as if there had been an accident.
He's leaving today, thank God, and Prague itself, which has been intolerably
noisy, is expected to quieten down a little now that the congresses etc. are coming to a close. Returning alone to the Blauer Stern last night, I bumped into the
inevitable Orlik (wherever I am, we seem to coincide). Naturally I sat with him
and let him talk away. I gobbled up* everything he had to say about Japan and
China. But he's a muddle-headed fellow, and his insights seem to be drawn not
from his own experiences but from hearsay. Later Bodanzky joined us. Orlik
told us all about his recent travels in Provence and what he'd learnt about art
there. He paints quite differently now, he said, adding that he learnt mostly
from the sunlight and the landscape, and that it had been uplifting to tread
'artistically virgin land'. My suspicion is that he took photographs and traced
copies of Cézanne and van Gogh. Apart from that, he seems to be a kind-
hearted person and an upright citizen (in the petit-bourgeois sense).
What would I give to have you here. But I'm really looking forward to the
six weeks of peace and quiet that will follow. <It must be wonderful in
Toblach. How absurd to have arranged things like this!
Fondest greetings, my Almschi. Write soon and, above all, come here soon.
Your Gustav>

*The German painter Emil Orlik was known above all for his graphics and
caricatures. Having travelled fairly extensively in the Far East, he was also
something of a specialist in Chinoiserie, a subject that will have interested
Mahler at this time with regard to his work on* Das Lied von der Erde.
*Mahler had met Orlik several times previously, in Prague and at Secessionist
exhibitions in Vienna. Alma notes in AMM1 that Orlik worked extensively
from photographs.[11] His well-known portrait of Mahler, which he claimed to
have done from memory, is based on one of the photo portraits of Moritz
Nähr, dating from 1907.*

* Orig.: 'räumte ich ihm abi' (dialect).

254   Prague, 10 September 1908[E]
                                                        Hotel Blauer Stern

My dearest Almscherl,
Motto:
   How blissful, how blissful –
   a hairdresser / a waiter / a tenor / a pensioner to be!
   President of the Allgemeiner Deutscher Musikverein[*]
   Deputy President of ditto[†]
'Who hath brought me into this land?'
Naturally enough, I have absolutely no mental energy left for letter-writing, no
matter what I have to write, where I write it or when I post it. – I have orchestral materials to correct, and meanwhile I'm wondering how I can transform
sausage cauldrons into timpani, rusty watering-cans into trumpets and a public
bar into a concert hall. From all this chaos I've managed to fish out just one
small ray of solace: a despondent trumpeter said to Bodanovich[‡]: 'I'd just don't
see what's beautiful about blasting out muted high notes all the way up to C-
sharp for bars on end.' The remark instantly called to mind the human soul,
which is likewise incapable of comprehending its own misery, its tormented but
muted struggle with the sublime, its failure to grasp the ultimate purpose or visu-
alize how such shrieks unite to form a great chord in the universal symphony.
Bodanovich's reply to this unhappy man was perfectly logical: 'Just wait! At
present you can't understand it because you don't have a view of the work as
a whole. When it comes together, you'll understand why it's written that
way.' (I had just taken a sectional rehearsal with the wind. Typical of this
Vale of Tears that we still lack the comfort and bliss of the violins, nor do we
yet have the lower strings, fundament and anchor of all else.)
Therefore let us bear this confusion with endurance.
Keussler[§] is also already here. A splendid fellow. After the Saturday evening
rehearsal I'll be joining him for a vegetarian meal.
So long, old Almschl. Get used to living with a damper. Sooner or later the
mutes must come off!
Your   Gustav

<Please, I urgently need the addresses of Pfitzner and Berliner.>

[*] i.e. Max von Schillings.
[†] Friedrich Rösch (cf. footnote on p. 139).
[‡] A playful reference to Arthur Bodanzky.
[§] The Latvian-born composer, conductor and musicologist Gerhard von Keussler, who came to
Prague in 1906 as conductor of the German-speaking Männergesangverein. Apart from con-
ducting choral concerts, he lectured on music history and aesthetics.

255   Prague [11 September 1908]
                                                       Hotel Blauer Stern
                                                       Friday morning, 8 a.m.

Just a few quick lines today, my dear Almschel. I was really thrilled by your
dear letter and the postcards from the train. <At times like this you seem to
understand me. I'm really very pleased to see that you're capable of such
insights.*> Unfortunately one tends to lose this marvellous gift of self-pos-
session as soon as one returns to the hurly-burly of everyday life. At such
moments one needs to concentrate one's memories of those moments of
bliss, and to get into the habit of searching whenever possible for a glimpse
and a breath of that world. – The sectional rehearsals are over, and tomorrow at last, at ten in the morning, is the first full rehearsal. The hotel and the
city itself are hideously noisy. To avoid the risk of another snoring neighbour
waking me up four or five times a night, I had to reserve the next-door room
(the man is leaving today, at last). Warmest greetings, my Almscherl. I wish
you were already here!
Your   Gustav

*Because the Sixth Symphony had met with little public and critical acclaim,
Mahler had difficulty in finding a publisher for the Seventh. Finally the rights
were acquired by Lauterbach und Kühn,[12] a small firm that was at that time
in the process of being taken over by Bote und Bock. This led to long delays
in preparing the performing materials; indeed, the full score did not appear
in print until the autumn of 1909.*

256[U] Telegram   Prague, 14 September 1908

spent all day correcting parts   no time to write   greatly looking forward to
your arrival tuesday afternoon in the hotel   room ready for you next to mine
very cold here   dress warmly & bring my winter coat   fond greetings gustav
berliner has just arrived

*The Swiss writer William Ritter has left a vivid eye-witness account of one of
the final rehearsals of the Seventh Symphony, held in the Concert Hall of the
Prague Exhibition, where waiters kept walking from table to table with
cutlery and napkins. Alma had now arrived, and for her benefit Mahler
decided to play the finale through for the first time.[13]*

---

* In ELM Alma explains: 'I had written to Mahler to say that I was reading Novalis, whom I
had just discovered.' In 1924 she published two settings of Novalis, *Hymne* and *Hymne an die
Nacht,* for voice and piano.

'*Mahler, anxious and sombre – and not because of his symphony – had only one thought in his mind: his wife. He had asked for a table to be placed in the main aisle, not more than thirty feet from the rostrum, where his idol could sit on her own. On this occasion she made a very strange impression on us ... As this formidable, boiling cauldron of a symphony came to an end, there was a stunned silence. On stage, Mahler gave the players a few instructions. Then, without looking at anyone, he closed his big score, came to the side of the stage, and like a sleepwalker hypnotized by the presence of this woman, slowly, with an expression of infinite sadness, almost of despondency, he went to sit with her. He sat at right angles to her, his face turned in our direction, but his eyes fixed upon her, as if in bewilderment ... and he whispered ... who will ever know what he said ...? And as he returned her gaze with those pensive, troubled eyes, he did so with such intensity that we were all frightened ... What was going on between them? ... The symphony was over. What was the delay, what were we waiting for, why did we simply not leave ...? Nobody dared to move ... I shall never forget Madame Mahler ... For all the respect I have always felt towards her, I cannot lie about my personal impression of this tête-à-tête. It was clear that she understood neither what was being said to her nor the music she had just heard, which he knew was written entirely out of reverence for her ... She forced a smile, ... cast embarrassed looks to the left and the right. She was aware that we were all watching! And it made her so nervous, poor thing ...! She felt not a jot of pity for the man of genius who, prostrated and entirely absorbed in his work, was virtually dying of love at her very feet. This obliviousness, this drama; we could all sense it. And it lasted a long time.*'[14]

Ritter's depiction of the dress rehearsal is less positive in tone. He was practically the only commentator who at this early stage observed the growing rift between Mahler and his wife, which eventually was to lead to the marital crisis of 1910.

At the première, on 19 September, the Seventh Symphony *received a fifteen-minute ovation. Most of the reviews were courteous, some even laudatory. Nevertheless, it was a* succès d'estime, *and during Mahler's lifetime the* Seventh *was performed only a handful of times. Its second performance, in Munich on 27 October 1908, was organized by the Munich impresario Emil Gutmann as the first of a series entitled 'Meisterdirigenten'. The symphony was followed by Beethoven's overture* Leonore no. 3 *and Wagner's* Meistersinger Prelude, *a fascinating choice, since the finale of the* Seventh *opens with a clear allusion to one of the themes in* Die Meistersinger.

257[U] Postcard   Vienna, 19 October 1908[P]

Warmest greetings before my departure. Fondly your G.

258[U]   Munich, 21 October 1908[P]
                                               Hotel Vier Jahreszeiten

My dearest Almscherl,

After today's rehearsal (with an unbelievably cooperative orchestra) it really does appear that it can be a 'pleasure' to be the 'composer' of a successful new symphony. – As you know, the players walked out on Kaim and organized themselves into an independent organization. It's really a delight to witness the energy and determination of these people. As yet they may be doing pretty badly, but even in their frayed jackets they scrape and blow indefatigably and with true enthusiasm. If it goes on like this, Munich will do me a power of good. NB something I have often noticed: Munich (which is 600 metres above sea level) has a splendid climate. I always feel in top form here, provided unrelated circumstances don't spoil it. I can still clearly recall, for instance, how I wandered around here some twenty years ago with no money in my pocket and no chance of finding work.[*] Later too, fifteen years ago, during the cholera epidemic in Hamburg, when I received my marching orders from Pollini.[†]

The idea of moving to <u>Munich</u> is growing on me. How would you feel about it? For about 3,000 marks one could find a villa in its own grounds, and in Vienna the cost of living is in fact twice as high. Here, with our income, we could live like princes. Right in the heart of Europe, with excellent railway connections in all directions.

Once again, I have a delightful suite in the hotel – and it isn't even expensive. I only wish you could see for yourself how cosy it is. I even have a private bathroom. I only hope you can decipher this scrawl. It's because of the room, which is so very inviting.

Warmest greetings from   Your Gustav

---

[*] This was in the summer of 1888, when Mahler had annulled his contract at the Leipzig Stadttheater and found himself temporarily out of work.

[†] This was in 1892. For fear of infection, Mahler had refused to return from his vacation in Munich. Notwithstanding the epidemic, Pollini decided to open the Hamburg Stadttheater season in mid-September, as planned, but Mahler ran the risk of dismissal by delaying his return by two weeks.

259^U Telegram   Munich, 23 October 1908^E

unable to write yesterday had to play skat all day[*] in the very best of health
rehearsals running satisfactorily   fondest greetings gustav

260^U   Munich, 25 October 1908^P
                                                Hotel Vier Jahreszeiten

Don't be angry, Almscherli. I've had <u>two full</u> rehearsals every day (except on
the day I wrote to you), and betweenwhiles I've been fully occupied with
exhausting games of <u>Skat</u>. All this time I've been feeling absolutely <u>top fit</u>. It
must surely have something to do with the Munich climate. Tomorrow is the
first day I can catch my breath a bit. If you decide to come, be sure to arrive
in time for the final rehearsal on Tuesday at twelve. Fried is coming too!
Warmest greetings. Cable me if you're coming.   Your Gustav

261^U Telegram   Munich, 26 October [1908]

skat skat nothing but skat[†] almscherl do your best to come here   dress
rehearsal tomorrow at twelve   fondest greetings gustav

*Once again, William Ritter was present for most of the rehearsals. Mahler,
who had just been rehearsing the Prelude to* Tristan, *made a remark which
struck him as revelatory: 'He came towards me, looking at me, but with an
expression that disclosed the lingering remnants of a inner vision: "This
Tristan is something beyond words!" And a moment later, as though speaking to himself, "Ah! A cherished head on one's shoulders – the woman we
love in one's arms – no matter! If I knew that I was neither in that head nor
in that heart, and that someone else was the ruler of that heart . . ." Much
embarrassed, I pretended not to hear this intimate thought, for it was clearly
not intended for my ears and actually sounded like a soliloquy. But how distressing to think of what we had seen in Prague . . .! Ossip Gabrilovich told
me he had heard something similar.'*¹⁵
    By all accounts, the Seventh Symphony *and the repertoire works that
followed it were enthusiastically applauded, but the press found it hard to*

---

[*] Skat: a card game popular in Germany, and of which Richard Strauss was particularly fond.
According to Alma (ELM), the reference is jocular, for Mahler never played cards. This was
his way of telling her that he was kept busy correcting proofs or orchestral parts.
[†] Whimsical allusion to Sachs's monologue in *Die Meistersinger*, Act III: 'Wahn, Wahn, überall
Wahn.'

forgive Mahler for his 'noisy cacophonies', 'strident dissonances' and 'audacious effects'. The virtuoso orchestration, the 'astounding technique' of this 'master of forms and colours'[16] was praised at the expense of the work itself. Rudolf Louis, as hostile as ever, considered the work 'a monster of impotence and superficiality'.[17]

During the summer and autumn of 1908, Mahler also attended to the sale of his house in Maiernigg. With the aid of Emil Freund, contracts were exchanged with the new owners during the first week of November.

Before setting out once again for America, Mahler accepted an invitation from the Hamburg Philharmonic to conduct a concert of repertory works similar to that of his Prague concert in May: Beethoven's Seventh Symphony and Coriolan overture, Tchaikovsky's fantasy overture Romeo and Juliet and the Prelude to Die Meistersinger.

262[U] Telegram   Hamburg, 6 November 1908

excellent journey   warmest greetings gustav

263   Hamburg [7 November 1908]
                                                      Hotel Esplanade

My dearest Almscherl,
Terrific trip in a superbly comfortable railway carriage. Mama will already have told you: you'll love it.
We arrived in Berlin, and Berliner was waiting for us. Then a two-hour drive by car to Grunewald, which is delightful but very cold. So don't forget to wear your furs and bring blankets. I've made all other necessary arrangements with Berliner.
On arrival, we were met here by Brecher with a magnificent automobile. Unpacked and got changed. Brecher had to conduct a performance, so I drove to Behn's (in Brecher's car, of course) and had dinner there (i.e. a late lunch at seven p.m.). I left for home at nine, this time in a hackney cab, which I considered as good as walking. Went to bed and slept until seven. The hotel is a delightful little place. What a shame you can't stay here longer with me. Everywhere here it's more homely and attractive than in Vienna. Everybody's asking after you and lamenting your absence.
Now I'm expecting Brecher to collect me by car, and off we go to the rehearsal. More this afternoon, I hope.

Warmest greetings from your Gustl

<I almost forgot the <u>letter</u>, which I didn't manage to read until I was on the train from Berlin to Hamburg (in fact I'd completely forgotten about it). I had better pass it on at once, before you die of curiosity. Please bring it when you come, so I can write a reply.[*]>

264[U] Postcard   Hamburg, 7 November 1908[P]
                                              Hotel Esplanade

M.d.A.,

Two rehearsals today! I'm sending just a brief greeting, so you have at least some news of me. Feeling very well. Greatly looking forward to your arrival. I trust you got my letter with the enclosure. I've heard nothing from Justi. Warmest greetings   Your G.

265[U]   Hamburg, 8 November 1908[P]
                                              Hotel Esplanade

Dearest Almscherl,

I hope you receive this greeting before you leave. – Don't forget the tickets for our passage. Also the address for the <u>digestive wine</u>. My rehearsals have been most enjoyable, and the stay altogether very pleasant.
I shall wait for you at <u>Dammtor station</u>. <u>In Vienna don't</u> forget to have the baggage marked for that destination, it has to be <u>specially requested</u>. I only hope this wonderful weather will last another week, also the sunshine, which we've been enjoying here the whole time.
Greetings to Mammerl and Carl. Justi's package has already arrived and is being processed at the customs. I can't wait to open it –
A courier has just delivered the package. I browsed through it for half an hour, as if spellbound. Now I have to leave for rehearsal. It makes me blush like a small child to think that <u>this</u> is what that . . . stole from me and gave a stranger to read. Ah well, never mind. Warmest greetings
Your Gustav

Roller was planning to stage a ballet at the Hofoper based on the folk-tale of Rübezahl. *He mentioned his plans to the Rosés, and Justine recalled that Mahler in his youth had written an opera libretto on that very subject, indeed that the unfinished manuscript was still amongst his papers. Accordingly, she sought it out and lent it to Roller. Mahler was horrified to hear that his sister*

[*] The letter in question has not been preserved.

had shown one of his youthful efforts to a less than intimate friend. According to Alma, Justine swore at first that she had burnt the manuscript as soon as Roller had returned it, but Mahler did not believe her. Indeed she later sent it to him in Hamburg.

When the package arrived, Mahler wrote to thank his sister, adding, 'I have to tell you that when I opened the package it wasn't Rübezahl *at all, but something* <u>completely</u> *different, namely* The Argonauts, *which is an opera libretto. Is that what you gave Roller? But he was talking about* Rübezahl! *I remember the book very well – it's in a smaller format. So what's going on? Nothing but riddles.'*[18]

Alma claims to have helped Mahler throw the manuscript of Rübezahl *into the sea during their voyage to America.*[19] *But in fact it was still among her papers when she died. She too seems to have confused* Rübezahl *with* The Argonauts *(the latter is indeed lost without trace).*

Meanwhile, news of The Argonauts *manuscript had somehow filtered through to the press, and at the end of November a Paris news agency announced that Mahler was working on an opera entitled* Theseus.[20] *Three weeks later the same agency issued the following* démenti: *'Much as the idea appeals to him, [Director Mahler] has at present neither the time nor the inclination to compose a large-scale dramatic work, and he will be quite satisfied, considering the wide range of his conducting activities, if his "symphonic goals" can be attained in the manner he visualizes.'*[21]

Mahler's Hamburg concert was enthusiastically received, although some critics found his interpretations 'too spiritualized', too 'detached' and intellectual, though 'intensely personal'.[22]

On 12 November, Mahler, Alma, Gucki and her English nurse, Maud Turner,* sailed from Cherbourg on the SS Amerika *(Hamburg–America Line). On arrival in New York, on 21 November, they settled at the Savoy Hotel, on the corner of Central Park, Fifth Avenue and 59th Street, an establishment favoured by many guest artists at the Metropolitan Opera.*

Since Mahler's first appearance at the Metropolitan, in November 1908, much had changed. It soon transpired that Gatti-Casazza's policies were far more enlightened than those of his predecessor. In this respect Toscanini brought his influence to bear, with demands no less stringent than Mahler's own. Unfortunately a bitter conflict had broken out the previous summer between Mahler and Andreas Dippel, the assistant manager, because Gatti-

---

* Maud Turner, aged twenty-two, had evidently taken up her appointment quite recently as successors to Lizzie Turner, who was eighteen years her senior (information drawn from Ellis Island ship manifests).

Casazza had promised Toscanini that he could make his New York début with Tristan. Mahler had conducted this carefully rehearsed production several times, and considered it his rightful property. He therefore refused to entrust it to Toscanini; indeed, he even threatened to resign. Thus the maestro made his eagerly awaited début, on 16 November, not with a work of Wagner's, but with Verdi's Aida. On 10 December, with a performance of Götterdämmerung, he demonstrated his skill as an interpreter of Wagner.

Upon arrival, Mahler set to work with the New York Symphony Orchestra at Carnegie Hall. For the first of three concerts, on 29 November, he had chosen to conduct Schumann's First Symphony, Beethoven's Coriolan overture, Smetana's Bartered Bride overture and Wagner's Prelude to Die Meistersinger. For his second concert, on 8 December, he enlisted the contribution of the Oratorio Society and its chorus-master Frank Damrosch (one of Walter Damrosch's brothers) in the US première of his Second Symphony. His third programme, on 13 December, included three classical masterworks: Wagner's Faust overture, Weber's Oberon overture and Beethoven's Fifth Symphony.

Sensing that Mahler had become something of a threat to him, Walter Damrosch did his best to diminish the success of these concerts by failing to have them adequately publicized. The rehearsals were plagued by absenteeism, the orchestra itself was mediocre, and since Damrosch had also made little attempt to distribute complimentary tickets, Mahler found himself conducting to half-empty houses. Nevertheless, the Second Symphony made a considerable impression on both press and public. Indeed, after the concert the performers themselves joined in the applause.

The poor quality of playing provoked more comment in the third concert than Mahler's actual conducting, which Krehbiel once again deemed 'too austere and intellectual'.[23] Through no fault of his own, Mahler also found himself at the centre of a controversy between Mrs Sheldon and Damrosch, with the latter going out of his way to make it known that Mahler's concerts had not only failed at the box office but had also been artistically disappointing.

At the 'Met', Toscanini was deeply offended by Mahler's uncompromising attitude about Tristan. From the outset he reigned supreme, swiftly winning the confidence of the public and the approval of the press. Mahler made his first appearance of the season on 23 December with Tristan, in which he opened some of the traditional cuts. On this occasion the press was unanimously enthusiastic, even if some critics still considered his interpretation more 'sophisticated' than 'warm-blooded'.[24]

1909

During Mahler's second season at the Metropolitan Opera, his chief task was to prepare two new productions with sets and costumes by the Viennese stage-designer Heinrich Lefler: Le Nozze di Figaro *on 13 January, for which Mahler was granted an unprecedented two weeks of rehearsal, and* The Bartered Bride *on 19 February. The* Figaro *cast was again made up exclusively of star singers, including Marcella Sembrich, Emma Eames, Geraldine Farrar, Antonio Scotti and Adamo Didur. Again Mahler reduced the number of strings and conducted from a piano with paper-covered strings to imitate the sound of a harpsichord.** *Again the critics enthused about the vivacity of the music-making, which 'foamed and sparkled like champagne', about the singers' acting and the close 'union between the orchestra and the doings of the stage'.[1] Mahler's calm gestures on the podium were universally admired, and the third act duet almost always had to be encored. For once Mozart triumphed at the Metropolitan. Despite critical acclaim, the production was performed only six times in New York, followed by one performance in Philadelphia and a further one in Brooklyn. The cast for* The Bartered Bride *included Emmy Destinn, Karl Jörn and Adamo Didur; a troupe of dancers with their ballet master, imported directly from Prague, contributed greatly to the production's appeal. Nevertheless, it proved no more of a box-office success than* Figaro.*

Now that the new management had emerged triumphant, with the Italian element strongly to the fore, Mahler bade farewell to the Metropolitan Opera with a last performance of Figaro *on 26 March. He left without regrets: clearly there was no room in one opera company for two conductors of the calibre of Toscanini and himself.*

The task now awaiting him was more stimulating and required all his time and energy. When he first conducted the New York Philharmonic, the number of permanent members had been only thirty-seven, and extra players had to be recruited for each concert in turn. Mahler's new plans were ambitious to say the least: the number of permanent members was to be increased to one hundred; in the course of the season, the orchestra was to give forty-six concerts in New York and embark on a mid-season tour of New England.

---

* In Vienna, Mahler had organized the purchase of a spinet for the *secco* recitatives in his Mozart cycle.

Mahler's first concerts, on 31 March and 6 April, demonstrated his command but laid bare the weaknesses of the orchestra. Essential as it was to replace some of the older players, the immediate realization of such plans was hampered by the Musicians' Union. Only a small quota of European musicians was permitted to join American orchestras, and then only after six months' residence in the US; the remaining musicians would have to be recruited from the ranks of other American orchestras. At the last Guarantors' Committee meeting, held three days before Mahler sailed back to Europe, he was authorized to engage a new concert-master and a new principal flautist from Europe. The concert-master incumbent, Richard Arnold, was persuaded to resign, but stayed on as orchestral manager.

Alma's description of Mahler's state of mind during this second American season shows that his depression of the preceding year had largely been dispelled. He looked to the future with greater optimism and was delighted to have a new orchestra completely at his disposal.

During their stay in New York, he and Alma accepted numerous invitations to the homes of artists, musicians, scientists and patrons of the arts. In a letter to Bruno Walter, Mahler wrote of the 'habit of living' (Gewohnheit des Daseins), which he found 'sweeter than ever', of moments when he felt 'entirely clear and secure' and could find 'definitive answers to every question'.[2] During the past year his health had improved considerably; Alma, on the other hand, was going through a period of nervous instability which her Viennese doctors attempted to remedy by sending her to take the waters at Levico, near Trent in Northern Italy.

In the spring of 1909 Anna Moll came to join her daughter and son-in-law in New York, and on 10 April all three left for Cherbourg, together with Gucki and her English nurse, on the Kronprinzessin Cäcilie. From there they travelled on to Paris, where Carl Moll (with the help of Paul Clemenceau) had secretly commissioned Auguste Rodin to sculpt a bust of Mahler. The sittings, which lasted ten days, were a severe trial of his patience.

The month of May was spent in Vienna, meeting old friends and auditioning musicians for the New York Philharmonic. Josef Weinberger, who had been instrumental in founding Universal Edition at the turn of the century, had recently appointed Emil Hertzka as his managing director. It was Hertzka who now negotiated the contract for the Eighth Symphony; he also

---

* Levico had been popular as a spa since the 1850s. The waters, which contain traces of iron and arsenic, were considered effective for the treatment of skin diseases; neurologists and gynaecologists also recommended Levico to their patients.

took steps to acquire the rights to the first four symphonies. Both contracts were signed in June.

On 9 June Mahler took Alma, Gucki and her nurse to Levico. He then returned to the Trenkerhof, near Toblach, where he stayed until 5 September. During this period he wrote twenty-five letters and postcards to Alma.

266[U]   [Toblach, 13 (?) June 1909]

Dearest,

Well, here I am. Everyone turned out to greet me (that's how it is, quite simply), and I satisfied the burning curiosity of these dear souls with repeated exclamations of 'How are you keeping? How did it go? I'm feeling very well,' whereupon each in turn repeated that the weather was none too good, and that it would be quite nice, or even very nice, if the sun were to start shining. Once I had reached my cosy little room, Anna* helped me unpack. – Unfortunately I found <u>no</u> apples, but <u>Freund</u> had sent two jars of honey, so for the time being I won't need to look for a further supply. – In the post I found amongst many other things a royalty payment of 475 crowns for the <u>Drei Pintos</u>! Isn't that splendid? On the assumption that the news will considerably hasten your recovery, I thought I'd let you know right away. – Would you like me to send you the cheque, which is made out to the <u>Länderbank</u>? Should I cash it and send you the money, or should I keep it here until you arrive? As you see, something always comes along to help you with your housekeeping money.

Now write soon. I must see how I can set things up. I shan't bother to reply to the telegram.

Fondest greetings, my darling.   Your Gustav

See to the apples, Almschi. There's a bill for 60 Crowns from <u>Gerold</u>,† which I'll pay by money order. I'm freezing to death here.

267   [Toblach], 13 June 1909‡

Dear Almschi,

My first morning here. It's freezing cold in the living room. The little stove seems to be no match for a proper oven, so there's no chance of a cosy room temperature, warm enough for me to sit here without wearing my

---

* Possibly Anna Trenker, the lady of the house.
† A bookshop in Vienna.
‡ Dated 13 June by Mahler, but probably written on 14 June.

boots and overcoat. The piano is already in the shack, but until the weather improves I shan't go down. <How glad I am that you and Gucki are in the South.>

Yesterday I wanted to give Trenker his money, but he wouldn't take it, saying he thought it would be safer in the strongbox (which I've had carried straight up to my room, by the way). <So far Kathi and Agnes* have served me well. Yesterday, for the first time, I ate a piece of that eagerly awaited speciality: Graham bread. It was delicious. The crate with the doll's house has arrived and stands unopened in my room. – Today, because of the frightfully cold weather, I've taken the precaution of putting on two layers of underwear.> If I had a grand piano here, I'd warm myself up with music. – <From the enclosed bill I see that when I go to collect the goods tomorrow I'll have to part with 66 crowns.

Yesterday I wrote to Bertha Zuckerkandl, turning down the Paris project in its present guise. I don't understand why these people didn't contact me directly, so I sent my reply through the same channels.>†

I'm enclosing the letter <from Fritz [Löhr]> to show you why I'm making my peace with old friends and acquaintances. <Be so kind as to support me in this.> Let's hope that all the joy and happiness it causes will reflect on us – I know it will. For me it's a great consolation to have straightened everything out with Lipiner – and 'to love as long as love can last'.‡ <I'll be interested to see what you have to report in your first letter – how you're feeling and how you and Gucki are getting on. You got there in the nick of time!>

Many greetings, my dearest, from   Your Gustav

This letter shows how much Mahler had suffered in the past seven years from the rift with his old friends, which resulted from his marriage to Alma and the strong dislike she had taken to them. Mahler had never entirely severed relations with Fritz Löhr; indeed, in 1906, while working on the Eighth Symphony, *he had written to him to obtain the complete text of 'Veni creator spiritus'.*

---

* Agnes Huizdova, Mahler's idiosyncratic cook, who later served as inspiration for one of the characters in Franz Werfel's novel *Der veruntreute Himmel*. Apart from her culinary talents, she also played the zither.
† Bertha Zuckerkandl's letter was presumably connected with the 1910 performance of Mahler's *Second Symphony*, which her sister Sophie Clemenceau was helping to organize.
‡ Orig.: 'zu lieben, so lange ich noch lieben kann' – quotation (slightly altered) from the poem 'Der Liebe Dauer' by Ferdinand Freiligrath.

268[U] Postcard: Drei Zinnen in the Pustertal   Toblach, 14 (?) June 1909[P*]

Just a few words of greeting for now. It's raining cats and dogs – how lucky you are. I'm in town at present – had my hair cut, bought an umbrella. Now homeward bound. Write soon, your G.

269   [Toblach, 14 June 1909]
                                                                            Monday

My dearest Almschi,
<I hope you received my last postcard and letter, as I'm not quite sure if they were adequately addressed. I'll pay the enclosed bills from here, seeing as I'm now the Croesus of the family; anyway, it will save you unnecessary trouble. So far, despite the wind and the rain, I've been walking into town every day for my 'afternoon tea'.[†] Apart from that, I'm perfectly satisfied with our two housemaids. – I fear the paraffin stove won't suffice – as I expected. I've been living in the Trenkers' quarters, because I haven't yet summoned up the courage to move into the cellar.[‡] – As soon as it turns a little warmer, I'll give it a try and also have my iron stove installed, as I did last year. Meanwhile, you, my dearest, can benefit from the paraffin stove to heat up your room before bedtime (and so shall I). That will put an end to all chattering of teeth. – I'll get them to heat the living room too. It's extremely comfortable – but unfortunately the writing desk is locked, so I can't use it for my work.>
All the same, the house and its location are a real joy – except for the noise, which is a continual annoyance. When these yokels whisper, the windows rattle, when they tiptoe, it shakes the rafters. All day their two sweet offspring chirp away: 'Bibi! Bibi!' (which happens to be their Volapük[§] and signifies: everything under the sun). The dog, too, likes to remind me that I am 'one among many' and barks from sundown until long after the yokels have entered the Land of Nod. Every quarter of an hour I'm woken by the dulcet tones of their snoring. – Damn it all: how wonderful the world would be if one could fence off a couple of acres and live within them completely undisturbed. –

---

[*] Postmark partly illegible.
[†] Orig.: 'jause' (*sic*). From Alt-Schluderbach to Toblach Post Office is over two kilometres. The fact that Mahler walked this distance every day shows that he was no longer unduly worried about his heart condition.
[‡] The 'cellar', according to Alma, was one of Mahler's words for his *Komponierhäuschen* (ELM).
[§] Volapük, the first synthetic international language (a predecessor of Esperanto). It was devised by Johann Martin Schleyer in 1879.

Every time I get back from my daily walk, I half expect to see you and Gucki running to meet me. Being alone during the day is agreeable – most agreeable – but by tea-time it begins to get on my nerves.
Warmest greetings my Almschili   Your Gustav

<I've just received your letter with the enclosed card from Hirth.* I'll leave it to you to reply. Let me know if my letters are reaching you.>

270   [Toblach, 16 (?) June 1909]E

Dearest,
The still-life down there is getting me down. The Massacre of the Innocents is nothing, the Battle of the Centaurs is a mere trifle compared with what goes through my mind when I hear the war cries of our happy Alpine warriors. – When all is said and done, I really must think about moving out. Oh, oh, oh! Would that I could live for once without disturbance. People make so much noise! –
<Berliner has just sent a delightful birthday present for Gucki: a big natural history book with magnificent animal drawings.† He obviously chose it with immense care. – Also your letter, with all your delightful news of Gucki. How wonderful it is when a child begins to take notice of the outside world and becomes aware of so many things that we adults have come to take for granted. Yesterday I received a card from New York announcing the death of Mr Wolfsohn.‡ –
I've thought up something lovely for you: why don't we set up the middle upstairs room as a studio? We could take out all the unnecessary furnishings, leaving just the sofa, the armchair and the table. You could model away there to your heart's content.§ It would also be most suitable, as the light falls from a northerly direction. If you agree, I'll arrange everything

---

* Friedrich Hirth, a German Sinologist. He emigrated to the United States, where he published several books and became head of the Department of Chinese Studies at Columbia University. Mahler and Alma met him during their first season in America. He recounted many tales of China to them, which Mahler must have recalled when composing *Das Lied von der Erde*.
† Anna Mahler had celebrated her fifth birthday on 15 June.
‡ The American impresario Henry Wolfsohn, who died on 31 May in New York. As chief conductor of the New York Philharmonic, Mahler often had dealings with his concert agency.
§ Alma had taken a few sculpture classes with Edmund Hellmer in Vienna, but her attempts proved short-lived. Her daughter Anna inherited the interest, and later became known as a sculptress of distinction.
** Josef Fraenkel, the Mahlers' doctor friend from New York, visited Toblach after Alma returned from Levico.

before you get here. Should Fraenkel** join us, I'll give him my second room, as I did last year with Nepallek. Mama can sleep downstairs in the room next to yours. All in all, with the extra upstairs room we have three guest rooms. I think that should suffice; anyway, I think it will be best to accommodate all our guests in hotels and invite them up here for the afternoons and evenings.

This summer I really want to see you back in form.>
Fondly   Your Gustav

<Rome is asking if I could give the concerts in <u>May</u>, as the second half of April is no longer free. What do you think?*>

271^U   [Toblach] 17 June [1909]

My Almscherl,
Your letter is really bad news, not because you say you're feeling weak and debilitated, but because it surprises you and you're thinking of leaving. Don't forget: they warned you that for the first two weeks you would feel only the negative aspects of the treatment, and that you would have to wait patiently. – The actual benefits only become apparent after returning home. So be sensible and don't throw in the towel.
Meanwhile, we have taken delivery of three packages from Vienna, also a crate of vegetables, a ham, oil, two trussed chickens and a whole pannier of live ones: all from the Grünwalds. – You'll have to thank them with a flourish of trumpets.
I enclose a telegram from New York and an article from the Arbeiterzeitung, which you should find interesting. – I'm working hard on concert programmes,† which is none too easy because of the rehearsals. But by the time Arnold arrives from NY it should be ready. – I'm keeping to an extremely regular daily routine, and hope to be in stable health by the time you return. The weather has been almost nothing but dull, cold and rainy. All the same, there have been many pleasant hours. Even when it rains I take my daily walk into Toblach, post my letters and drink an afternoon coffee (but only milky coffee) at the baker's.
My Almschi, can I expect another humorous letter tomorrow?
Fondest greetings, your Gustav

---

* The concerts were finally scheduled for 28 April and 1 May 1910.
† As Mahler wrote to Bruno Walter, 'I received an urgent request to submit twenty-four programmes for the coming season within two weeks' (GMB, no. 417).

272[U]   Toblach [18 (?) June 1909]

Dearest,

I'm enclosing Burckhard's letter. I'm happy to tell you, by the way, that the Tauernbahn is opening on 12 July, so if you'd like to visit your friend in the Salzkammergut, nothing will stand in your way.* The journey will take five to six hours. –

The flour, paraffin, modelling clay, soap and sculpting tools have also arrived, and Trenker has been to collect them. – As for my accommodation, I'm beginning to realize that the rooms I took last year would suit me far better, but only if the windows can be fitted with insect screens and if the lady of the house removes her cheeses from the basement (I know they're there: I only needed to follow my nose to find them). Then I'll need my paraffin stove in the largest room, and my old iron oven (my old, 'beloved' oven, as you would say) for the shack in the woods. What do you think? Is that the best arrangement? The advantage would be that the paraffin stove could be taken into your room for the evenings, to make your bed nice and cosy (perhaps for me too). – The skies cleared today, and I imagine you're also finding it pretty warm and snug now. But be patient, Almscherl. The hot waters with their iron content will do you both a power of good. – I wonder when they'll deliver the Bösendorfer. If it hasn't arrived by 1 July, I'll order one from Kohn so there's a piano in the house when you arrive. Today I'm going to close the windows in the downstairs (cheesy) room and try to heat it up with the paraffin stove. Maybe it will work.

Many greetings from your   Gustav

Your second letter has just arrived. It's very sweet of you to write every day, Almschi. Since you're taking no interest in 'the men-folk', I'll presumably have to assume the role of 'the flesh pots in the land of Egypt'.† Ouch! What a metaphor for a husband with vegetarian inclinations!

Alma wrote that her old friend Max Burckhard 'usually slept in a hut hidden away in the woods, because when he wasn't feeling well he didn't like to see people. [. . .] His villa on the Wolfgangsee was equipped with a drawbridge.

---

* The 'friend' mentioned here was Burckhard himself. The Tauernbahn railway between Mallnitz and Böckstein (a distance of over 83 km) passed over forty-seven viaducts and through ten tunnels, curtailing the journey from Toblach to Salzburg by several hours. The Mahlers travelled this route for the first time in August 1909.
† cf. *Exodus* 16:3: 'Would to God we had died by the hand of the Lord in the land of Egypt, when we sat by the flesh pots.'

When he didn't feel like receiving visitors, [. . .] he raised the bridge and was totally enclosed by the water. Sometimes he would disappear like that for days on end.'

273^U

[Toblach, 18 (?) June 1909]
Friday?
(I can't keep track of the days)

My Almschi,

Just for once there's a good reason for all the noise: our people are carrying the furniture back downstairs. I decided on this step primarily because the insect screens in the two rooms really do seem to keep the midges at bay, while letting the air in. When I asked whether the kitchen windows were in order, I was told that Agnes had refused point-blank to have the screens fitted, and anyway there wasn't enough <u>wire mesh</u> to go round. But that I don't understand, for so far we have only <u>two</u> insect screens (in my room upstairs), and I'm sure you brought more of the stuff with you. So it's up to you to read the riot act* to these beasts, make them do what they're told and ensure that in future I don't find flies in my spinach. I'm getting my meals <u>on the dot</u>, by the way, which is doing my digestive system a power of good.

All in all, this is a delightful place, if it weren't for the long evenings, which strain my stoicism and philosophic attitude to their limits. I haven't heard a word from Mama. Please send news of her from time to time. By the way, where are my garters and half-length socks, of which we bought such quantities last year? – The fields are entirely green now, but the flowers aren't yet in bloom. I'm so glad for you, because when you return they will all just be coming out. – If you were to live as I am here (as regular as clockwork, namely), you would soon feel as if you had been born again. Such an existence suits me extremely well: renunciation is bringing forth the finest of fruits.

If you're a good girl and stay the course, I might come and fetch you. But only if Bahr and Mildenburg† aren't there, for I could scarcely ignore them. Many greetings from your   Gustav

274

[Toblach, 20 (?) June 1909]

My Almscherl,

Your dear letter didn't arrive until yesterday afternoon (I always collect the second post myself); I was beginning to get really worried.

---

* Orig.: 'ordre du Mufti'.
† Hermann Bahr and Anna von Mildenburg were due to marry in Salzburg on 28 August.

How well I understand your changes of mood (provoked this time by a dream), for I myself am frequently subject to such things. This may come as a surprise to you, but let it also be a consolation and perhaps even an explanation of your own behaviour. Human beings – and probably all creatures on Earth – are incessantly productive.

At every level, this process is inseparable from the nature of life itself. When productive energy ceases to flow, its 'entelechy' dies with it, i.e. it needs a new body to be reborn. On that level at which higher forms of humanity exist, the creative act (which comes to most people in the natural guise of procreation) is coupled with a gesture of self-assurance. On the one hand this enhances the process, on the other it makes demands on our moral judgement. And this is what causes creative people such disquiet. Apart from the few brief moments in the life of a genius when these conditions are met, it's the long intervening periods of infertility that test the awareness and provoke unrequitable longings. Indeed, the distinguishing feature of the chosen few is an unceasing and truly agonized sense of striving. – Now you probably know or have some idea what I think of the 'works' of man. They are that part of him which is fleeting and perishable; whereas what a man creates of his own person, what his restless striving and vitality combine to make him, is that part of him which survives. In this sense, my dear Almschi, you have achieved all you need for your soul to expand and reach out towards higher things. And you have a long life ahead of you! Draw increasingly on your inner strength (indeed you do!), assimilate as much of the world's beauty and power as you can (more than this one cannot do – and even then it is given only to the few). 'Spread your wings', occupy your mind with all that is good and beautiful, never cease to grow (for that is true productivity), and be certain of what I have always preached to you: what we leave behind, no matter what it may be, is merely a husk, an outer shell. Die Meistersinger, the Choral Symphony, Faust – all these are nothing but discarded wrappings. In essence, our bodies are also no more than that. Now I am not saying that the act of creativity is pointless. Mankind needs it in order to grow, to rejoice, for that too is an expression of well-being and potency. – But why music, of all things? How often do I picture you in the joyous mood (I know it only too well) that pervades you when you 'open yourself out'. <The last time was in the Prater.

Above all, get well – for then 'creativity' of one sort or another comes of its own accord, as does the joy that comes with it. Yesterday we took delivery of the Bösendorfer grand, a magnificent instrument and brand new. You'll love it. I've now moved all my things downstairs, where I'm finding it

wonderfully snug. Yesterday I wrote to Fraenkel. Credit Lyonnais: is that the address?> I haven't yet ventured into my shack. Moving into the 'shack' is always <u>such a radical step</u>, and I haven't yet plucked up the courage. Warmest greetings my Almschi
Gustav

Send more news of Gucki soon.

275^U   [Toblach, 21 (?) June 1909]

But Almschi, my dearest!
Why such a sad letter today? You complain about being lonely, but Gucki is with you and at least you're in the company of human beings – even if it's only Miss Turner. Just think of my solitary existence here, day in, day out. When evening approaches, I feel tempted to pack my case and join you. But I grit my teeth and stay put; for one thing, I know you're in Levico for health reasons and you'll be joining me in a few weeks' time – for another, it happens to be my duty (ask Gucki: she knows exactly what that is) to stay here and collect my thoughts. Tomorrow I'll go down to the shack. So far I haven't had the courage, because it was too cold. But now it's high time to experiment with the stove. Old Georg told me today that they probably won't have time to install my old oven next week. So tomorrow I must see whether I can make do with the paraffin stove. – Almschi, I can't tell you how sorely I miss you, already now! [Ten lines obliterated]. I just can't wait to board the train and fetch you home. – Yesterday we received a consignment of clothes for you; I shan't open it. And Fraenkel's pills have arrived from Paris. Do you need them? If not, I'll keep them here. – The insect screens are proving very effective, and I feel really comfortable in my two rooms. As I said, I lack nothing except – something <u>very important</u>! Do you understand – you gloomy child of nature?[*]
Should I send a cheque to Vienna for the paraffin stove? Or shall I defer all such matters until you get here?
Once you've completed your treatment, I confidently expect you to find your form again. I'll grant you your daily dose of melancholy, for it's a luxury I also enjoy. And when you're feeling sad, remember that I share your feelings. Soon we shall be reunited, and then we can really relish the fact and make <u>good use</u> of being together. Don't you agree, Almschi? Fondly your   Gustav

---

[*] Orig.: 'melancholische Wildanten'. The expression originates in Act I/ix of Ferdinand Raimund's romantic pantomime *Das Mädchen aus der Feenwelt oder der Bauer als Millionär* (Vienna, 1826). Mahler knew the play from his years in Kassel.

276   [Toblach, 22 (?) June 1909]

My Almscherl,

That was a dear letter (the second today, what's more) [two lines obliterated]. You see, one really does need to establish a spiritual focus; after that, everything looks quite different. And the fact that you have chosen Goethe, of all writers, reveals much of your inner self and shows that you are developing by leaps and bounds – outwardly as well as inwardly.

Your interpretation of the final stanza* is splendid, and I'm convinced it's better than that of even the most learned commentators, who don't come close to understanding it (admittedly I haven't read them, but I do know that they've been tussling with this problem for the best part of a hundred years). You see, the interpretation of an art-work is something out of the ordinary [one and a half lines obliterated]: its _rational_ aspects (i.e. those that can be logically explained) are rarely important; in fact, they are a veil that obscures the object itself. – But when a soul is in need of a body – and to that there can be no objection – the artist has to find his means of expression from within the rational world. And if his concept is not entirely clear, if he has not yet grasped it in its _entirety_, the rational element involuntarily obscures the underlying artistic idea, and the work becomes inordinately hard to understand. –

In this respect, Faust is quite a jumble, and since it was written over the course of a _long_ lifespan, its ingredients do not always blend, and many of them _remain_ raw _material_. This means that one has to approach the work from a wide range of aspects and angles. But the essence of it actually lies in its _artistic entity_, which cannot be expressed in dry words. Truth is a subjective concept, and it varies for each of us and in every new epoch. Consider the symphonies of Beethoven, which make a new and different impression on every listener. – Would you like me to outline the progress I have made towards 'rationalizing' these closing verses? I'll try, but I don't know if I'll succeed. Well then: I understand these four lines as being closely linked to all that has gone before – not only as a direct continuation of the preceding stanza, but also as the peak of that vast pyramid which constitutes the work as a whole and which expounds a world of characters, situations and developments. Each scene (particularly in Part II, by which time the author has matured to his task) points ever more clearly, if at first indistinctly, towards

---

* Mahler is discussing the closing stanza of Goethes's _Faust, Part II_: 'Alles Vergängliche / Ist nur ein Gleichnis; / Das Unzulängliche, / Hier wird's Ereignis; / Das Unbeschreibliche, / Hier ist's getan; / Das Ewig-Weibliche / Zieht uns hinan.' (Everything transitory is but an allegory; the inadequate is here achieved; the inexpressible is here accomplished; Eternal Femininity leads us onward.)

this <u>one</u> final, inexpressible, scarcely imaginable and most intimate of ideas. So here everything is an <u>allegory</u>, a means of expressing an idea, which is by definition <u>inadequate</u> to fulfil the requirements. While it may be possible to describe <u>transitory</u> things, we can feel or imagine but never <u>approach</u> what underlies them (i.e. all that which 'here is <u>achieved</u>'), for it is transcendental and unchanging, hence <u>inexpressible</u>. That which leads us forwards with mystical strength – which every creature, perhaps even every stone, knows with absolute certainty to be the centre of its existence, and which Goethe here calls <u>Eternal Femininity</u> – here too, <u>an allegory</u> – namely a <u>fixed point</u>, the <u>goal</u> – is the antithesis of eternal longing, striving, motion towards that goal – in a word, Eternal Masculinity. You are quite right to characterize the latter as the <u>love force</u>. There are myriads of metaphors and designations for it (just consider how children, animals, people on a lower or higher plane of existence delve and spin). With ever increasing clarity, Goethe himself presents an endless hierarchy of such allegories, and towards the close he intensifies them still further: Faust's impassioned search for Helena, the Walpurgis-Night, the inchoate Homunculus, the numerous entelechies of lower and higher degree, all presented with conviction and transparency. Mater Gloriosa, the personification of Eternal Femininity, is the culmination. Thus, with direct reference to the closing scene, Goethe turns to his audience, and this is what he says:

'<u>All transitory things</u> (i.e. everything I have shown you in these two plays) – are <u>allegories</u>. These, by the very nature of their worldliness, are <u>inadequate</u> – <u>but when</u> freed from their outer shell of human frailty, they are <u>accomplished</u>, and there is no further need for circumlocution, comparison – or <u>allegory</u>. For all I here have attempted to express, which is in fact <u>inexpressible</u>, is <u>accomplished</u>. What then have I been attempting to express? I can outline it only in the form of a further allegory:

<u>Eternal Femininity</u> has <u>carried</u> us <u>forward</u>. We have arrived, we are at rest, we are in possession of that which on earth we could only desire or strive for. Christians speak of "eternal bliss", and for the sake of my allegory I have made use of this beautiful, sufficiently mythological concept [two lines obliterated] – and the one most accessible to this era of world history.' I hope I have expressed myself clearly. In any discussion of such incredibly subtle, <u>irrational</u> concepts, as I said, there is always the risk of talking rubbish, which is why the commentaries all have something repugnant about them.

<Your telegram has just arrived: but you'll have to explain it in greater detail. Therefore I shan't reply until I've heard from you.> That will be all for today. Many greetings from   Your Gustav

<Wednesday? I think I lost track of the date several days ago. And now your letter has arrived. Look, this needs careful thought. Such strenuous exercise five evenings a week seems too much to me! I'll think it over, and when I reply I'll send you a copy.

I'm enclosing a bill from Cormaldi, which you can pay from your account. A postcard from Grünwald: does it by any chance include the address?>

This, one of the longest and most substantial letters Mahler ever wrote, is clearly the one that Alma was referring to when she wrote in AMM4, 'We exchanged letters about abstract concepts.'³ The final scene of Faust, *which Mahler had set to music in the* Eighth Symphony, *was still very much on his mind, and the meanings he read into it are of primary importance. Siegfried Lipiner's thesis, written in 1894 while he was studying in Vienna, was entitled* Homunculus, a Study of Faust and the Philosophy of Goethe. *Mahler had certainly had many discussions with him on the subject of Goethe's masterpiece and the many possible interpretations of the closing scene. He did not mention Lipiner in his letter to Alma, for she had taken a strong dislike to him, yet his analysis undoubtedly propagates some of Lipiner's ideas.*

277ᵁ   [Toblach, 23 (?) June 1909]

Dearest,

The weather is simply dreadful, and I'm not sure whether to go for my daily »walk« today. – Down in the shack it's impossible. Up in the house it's too hot (I've been fighting off a migraine), while my feet are frozen. I'll have the oven brought down again. Last year it was always comfortable there, even when the weather was really bad. – The paraffin stove will be a boon. Wherever one goes, one is in constant need of added warmth. –

Yesterday I paid those two bills. – <u>Grünwald sent another basket of eggs!</u> What should I do?

I wrote to Deckner* yesterday, asking for details of his proposed contract. – At least we have something to amuse ourselves with for a while. – Zacherl sent a bill for the insurance. Shall I pay the 22 crowns and 13 pfennigs he's asking?

Now I'm going to ask them to light the big oven. There's nothing more comforting than a roaring fire. – My fountain pen has run dry, and there's no ink in the house, hence the pencil. Good Lord, what weather. I can't even set foot outside the house, so I can neither post this letter nor collect yours. I can't wait to hear what your barometer is reading.

Fondest greetings for today   Your Gustav

* The Berlin concert agent Hermann Deckner.

I wish you were already here!

Hermann Deckner was trying to interest Mahler in a Wagner cycle (sung in Italian) at the Teatro Colon, Buenos Aires. It may seem surprising that Mahler even considered the offer, for he already had firm commitments in New York. Admittedly, the funds assembled by the Guarantors' Committee of the New York Philharmonic were sufficient only for three seasons, but the aim was to endow New York with a permanent symphony orchestra, and Mahler almost certainly intended to stay for two years, especially after working hard to weld the new ensemble together.

278   [Toblach, 23 (?) June 1909]

<But Almschi, that's terrible!
I ask myself what kind of treatment this is, if it results in disturbed nights and long hours of restlessness, and why it's having such an effect on you. Please send me a description of your activities (i.e. the kind of baths they've prescribed), so I can figure it out for myself.
Gucki is making such wonderful progress, but it saddens me to think that she's never quite so sweet and natural in my presence. Since yesterday I've been working in the shack. Maybe it will be satisfactory. But I must say, a real oven makes it cosier by far. Maybe I'll get used to it. I'm annoyed that Anton hasn't yet sent the blanket. The floor is decidedly chilly – but then, it started raining again yesterday and it's turned pretty cold.
I've decided to negotiate with Buenos Aires, but I'll delay my decision at least until your return, so we can talk it over together. – [Richard] Arnold will be arriving soon from New York. I wonder what news he'll have. Apparently they engaged a timpanist from Pittsburgh, and he's quite good.
Why don't you tell me exactly <u>what</u> the doctor <u>told</u> you, whether he's satisfied with your progress etc. Are you having good weather? And is Gucki drinking the spa water too? Did you receive my reply to your questions about Faust? And has Hammerschlag sent the money? Mama asked for a 'wish list', so I'll make one today. I believe I have found the keys.> Keep your spirits up, Almschi! It will be <u>well worth while</u>, believe me – and I have plenty of experience in such matters. – I'm writing this at the bedroom window, where there's a wonderful view over the meadows (the room next door is far too cold). The sun is just coming out; already the butterflies have returned, and the flowers are raising their heads. They've had a bad time of it in the last two days, and I'm sure they all feared for their lives. One ray of sunshine, and the horrors of rain and a chill wind are soon forgotten.

<It's really wonderful outside. So now I'll fetch my walking stick and be off for my daily afternoon walk.
Fondest greetings   Your Gustav

When you write tomorrow, I expect something happy and gay, and that's how I want you to pass the time too, so you won't have to spend the next day in bed.>

279[U]   [Toblach, 24 (?) June 1909]

My dear Almschili,
Judging by your latest, crazy-contented* letter, I note with satisfaction above all that your energy and good humour are steadily improving, but that the treatment isn't doing much to help you relax. Despite all my complaints and entreaties, you still haven't told me what the treatment actually is.
Meanwhile, I've been trying the patience of our dim-witted landlord and his family, and in the process they've probably come to take a dim view of my wits too. First I ask them to bring the oven down, then I tell them not to bother, but to use the paraffin stove instead. I've been in two minds about it for a fortnight, and today I decided yet again: I'll keep to the stove. The weather has again taken a turn for the better, which means that conditions in the shack have become more bearable. Admittedly it would be better still if one could do without the risky business of the oven altogether. If you need it in your room, they can fetch it for you every evening.
I'm expecting my visitors now – after which I look forward eagerly to the day when we're united again. I very much hope that your treatment, followed by the days you spend here, will do you a power of good.
Fondest greetings my Almscherl   Your Gustav

280[U]   [Toblach, 25 June 1909]

Dearest Almschi,
I was just off to the post to collect your letters, when Arnold arrived – straight from New York – and in a jovial mood. There's no chance of writing any more today, but for your amusement I'm sending you a pile of correspondence. The Pintos royalties are a godsend: a few scraps on an empty plate.
I'll cash the cheque and keep the money for you. So far I've put 1,300 crowns to one side for Trenker, as you requested. – I'm very upset about Gucki. You say she caught a cold the other morning? Despite Miss Turner's severity and the short skirts, she's so sickly that she catches a cold at the slightest provo-

* Orig.: 'pudel-närrisch', from 'pudelwohl' (coll., 'on top of the world') and 'närrisch' ('crazy').

cation. We've made her go bare-legged, we've forbidden her warm clothing, and all that's come of it is – anaemia. Sad!

I must close now: Mrs Arnold is teetering towards me with her husband at her side.

Warmest greetings   Gustav

281[U]   [Toblach, 26 June 1909]

Dear Almschi,

The profound tedium of our American friends is casting a shadow over the entire countryside. The moment I clapped eyes on the spouse of my »management«, I realized just how inhospitable I really am, and decided that [Hotel] Germania should be honoured with the custom of our »distinguished foreigners«. This evening I'm expecting Freund, whom I shall invite to enjoy all that our home and castle has to offer. He may be 'taken aback', but once he's left he won't return.

For the moment my life is nothing but orchestral affairs. From the Arnolds one expects nothing else. We also have a good deal to attend to. – The Arnolds have deigned to extend their stay at the Germania until <u>Thursday</u>. – For tomorrow (Sunday) I've invited them to »lunch«.

The Grünwalds have sent me yet another basket of <u>eggs</u>. It's a great shame, as I've renounced my daily egg at breakfast, and I have no idea what Agnes is doing with them. – A parcel arrived for you from your shoemaker in Vienna, which I have sent on to Levico.

Spiering's letter was in reply to an enquiry from me.[*] – I have replied to Deckner, stipulating the following conditions: 18,000 dollars, first-class cabin, performances to be shared with an »assistant conductor«, engagement of van Rooy.[†]

I sent Berliner a <u>very warm-hearted</u> letter. I can't imagine anyone writing more cordially to a friend; indeed, he should be very proud of it.

Gutmann has announced his arrival in August to discuss the Music Festival. So we'll have plenty of diversion.

Send Pollak my warmest greetings. It was very kind of him to keep his promise.

Now I shall leave for my rendezvous with our illustrious representatives of American music.

[*] The American violinist Theodore Spiering, who had been recommended to Mahler by Fritz Kreisler. After a successful audition, Mahler engaged him as concert-master of the New York Philharmonic.
[†] The Dutch baritone Anton van Rooy, leading Wagner baritone of his generation.

When Pollak sets out on his homeward journey, he could take a day off and visit me here. Neue Freie [Presse, Vienna], [Neues] Wiener Journal, Arbeiter Zeitung, Frankfurter [Zeitung]. At [Hotel] Germania: Die Zeit, Münchener Neueste [Nachrichten], Berliner Tageblatt. Or perhaps he could let us know when he'll be passing through; then at least I could meet him at the station. Many greetings dearest Almscherl   Gustav

[top of first page:] How is Gucki?

282   [Toblach, 27 June 1909]

My dear Almscherl,

<How silly that Pollak should be proving so tiresome – but I don't expect he'll want to stay much longer.> At present I'm very much tied up with social life. An endless run of celebrations – except that there's nothing to celebrate.* – Every evening our carefree Alpinists have a get-together (whenever I'm out, they're out harvesting; whenever I'm at home, so are they). They pass the time with jolly jokes and cheerful songs. Occasionally they also play an exhilarating game, something between bowls and shot-putting (the players keep themselves fit by waving their arms about and kicking their legs excitedly, fortifying their lungs all the while with raucous cries). When the excitement rises to fever pitch, they all contrive to shout at once. – This evening I was expecting Freund, but late in the evening he wired to say he'd taken the wrong train and had to spend the night in Villach. So I didn't see him until today, when we had »lunch« together in the highly stimulating company of the Arnolds. She, in particular, is very quick on the uptake, which I hadn't expected. Like all such people, she babbles away cheerfully and always has plenty to bring up (i.e. feelings, not food). As a fitting gesture, Agnes concocted a »lunch« from what she considered to be American or even Canadian recipes, and the fairer sex entertained our small but select gathering with a dazzling succession of ideas and impressions. At the end she ran out of steam, and I had a brilliant idea: I asked for the <u>horse</u> to be bridled, and hustled our guests into the open two-seater. For two people of such ample girth it was rather a squeeze, but all the more fitting as a 'cosy corner for a happy pair'.† – Then I went for a nap, but was so agitated that I couldn't sleep. I'll spend the rest of the afternoon in pondering poses and sentimental aperçus (my wretched fountain pen has run dry again). The weather took a turn for the better today, by the way, and soon it promises to be as pleasant as ever. –

---

* Orig.: 'Ein Fest erschlägt das andere. Ich erschlage sie alle' (untranslatable pun on 'erschlagen').
† Orig. (unidentified quotation): 'kleiner Raum für ein glücklich liebend Gespons'.

Almschi, take it easy, won't you, and do <u>everything</u> the doctor tells you. You'll love it here, I know. I can't wait for you to arrive. <Trenker asked for 1,000 crowns, which I've already paid.> Warmest and fondest greetings   Gustav

283^U   [Toblach, 28 June 1909]

Dearest Almschel,
And now I have to fetch new writing paper – which goes to show how diligently I've been corresponding. Life goes on here as ever. – Meanwhile, I have acquired deeper insights into the mind of Mrs Arnold – yesterday, while writing postcards to our friend Leifels.* At first I thought she was a dullard,† but I was wrong: she's a tease, the quintessence of playfulness. Yesterday she was enthusing over the beauties of nature, which she knows chiefly from pictorials. Curiously enough, I suddenly thought of the barouche. So tomorrow (on Tuesday instead of Thursday) they'll drive up the new road into the Dolomites and can look at all the places of interest on the way. – A great idea, don't you think?
Freund is here chiefly for health reasons, though he makes no show of it.‡ I second him in this, and we've been doing deep-breathing exercises together – through the nose, with the mouth closed. [Eighteen lines obliterated.]
No letter from you today. I only hope there's one at the post office, as I'm going to fetch it now. – It will be better not say anything to Pollak about his visiting us here.
In view of Agnes's rustic tastes, I'm not quite sure about all those menus. – It will be splendid when we are all reunited. But I shan't come to fetch you, Almscherl, because it's more expensive than one might think. And we should take advantage of our rare luck with that unexpected royalties payment. – You know, I'm gradually warming to the Plankenberg idea. Maybe it would be just the thing. Must close now – the flies don't give you a moment's peace. Fondest greetings, Gustav

284^U   Toblach [30 (?) June 1909]

My Almscherl,
Strange: we were both fantasizing about Plankenberg simultaneously, our thoughts crossed. Of late, I've often dreamt about it. I can see us in the park,

---

* Felix Leifels, assistant manager of the New York Philharmonic.
† Orig.: 'Strunk' (literally: stump). In ELM II, Alma explains: 'We had a family friend whose word for infantile or unresponsive people was "Strunk", and we adopted the word for our own family vocabulary.'
‡ Emil Freund was helping Mahler to negotiate a contract with Universal Edition.

in spring and autumn, seasons which for the past twenty years I've spent in the stifling heat of big cities. Oh for peace, peace! It would be wonderful if it worked out. At any rate, the first thing we'll do when we get home in the autumn is visit Plankenberg. But you must be the first to see it, for to revisit people or places that one loved in one's early years is often a very special experience.

Heppner's* letter is charming: an essay in the naively romantic style of an unspoiled, kind-hearted rural who's been living fifty years behind the times. He's never progressed beyond Romanticism, which is what I like. He's a believer – and that's the society I'm fond of. We should let him bring his influence to bear on Gucki.

Burckhard's letter is indeed very good news, but now you must keep your word. I think, once all our guests have departed, I want a little peace for you; then in late August or early September we can pay a visit to Salzburg, which I'd also be glad to see again. While you're visiting Burckhard, I'll stay there and wait for you, then we can return to Vienna via Plankenberg (which is on our route). Meanwhile, Gucki would stay with Mama in Toblach, then travel back with her. What do you think? – The Arnolds left yesterday. High time too, they were getting on my nerves, and I couldn't put up with them any longer. – Freund is staying until Saturday. – There are some visiting cards for you here from a certain Werner, for which I paid cash on delivery (4 crowns at the post office). I'm really thrilled to hear that Uchatius is coming to stay,[†] but don't hurry back on her account. If need be, I'll receive her on my own. It's essential that you don't curtail your treatment. I have to write to New York, so I'll close now. Greetings to Pollak. – Please write and tell me if Gucki has recovered completely.

So long[‡] Gustav (bad examples spoil good habits)

285[U]   [Toblach, 1 (?) July 1909]

Dearest Almschi,

I'm so happy about your news. At first I didn't understand the reason for your state of mind, which I found quite unbearable, but now I do. All the same, your new request (to keep a record of the bills I pay) fills me with

---

* Identity unknown.
† Marie von Uchatius studied Art and Art History with Alfred Roller at the Kunstgewerbeschule in Vienna. She was with the Mahlers at Hotel Majestic on 16 February 1908, and witnessed with them the fireman's funeral recalled in the finale of the *Tenth Symphony*.
‡ cf. footnote on p. 231.

horror. In this respect I've been living from hand to mouth, and I think I've already sent you everything. Apart from that, I only pay the bills that reach me. As far as I know, Kathi or Trenker have also paid some of them, and I'm sure they'll show you everything when you arrive.

Should I pay the enclosed bill? And please return that press cutting about fly repellents. Don't forget, above all, that by the time you arrive these blessed creatures will be in their prime. I expect the enclosed advertisement for Australian apples will be of interest to you. Business people in Vienna are so dreadfully impractical, as you can see.

Buenos Aires is giving me no rest – but I'm resolved to cancel. Fifty Wagner performances in three months, with no chance to rehearse betweenwhiles except for warming-up sessions.

Will you pay the enclosed bill from Brandweiner? Or should I?

Please send Carl the key to the apartment, for otherwise, as he writes, he can't get in. Apart from checking the cash box, he'll need to send my garters and half-length socks, which we left behind.

Please write with full details of the treatment you're receiving. Baths – drinking water etc. – and let me know if you're letting Gucki participate too. – Look after yourself properly and stay in bed for four days.

Fondest greetings   Your Gustav

The wild flowers have started to blossom. They've just reached the yellow phase.

286^U [Toblach, 2 July 1909]
Friday

Dearest Almscherl,

Just a short letter today. As I emerged from my shack, Fried and Brecher were there, with broad grins on their faces (or narrow ones, as the case may be)! Freund was there with them, though he didn't really belong. Freund negotiated with Agnes to improvise a hasty meal, which both guests greeted with repeated roars of delight. I kept telling myself how sad it was that you weren't with us. It would have been such fun. Brecher has to leave this afternoon – for Bad Gastein. I couldn't persuade him to stay any longer. Shamefacedly he stammered something about Walker* waiting for him.

How about Fried? Shall I send him on to you? He'd be delighted to go and

* The American contralto Edyth Walker. She was engaged at the Vienna Hofoper when Mahler arrived there in 1897, but in 1903, after a series of bitter conflicts, he persuaded her to resign.

would certainly cheer you up. He has a terrific contract for next season in St Petersburg, so he can pay his way. Please wire me <u>as soon as this letter arrives</u> to say whether he should come, and if not, whether I should <u>keep him here until you get back</u>. – Judging by your last letter, it sounds as if it might not be out of the question for you to spend a further week in Levico. Please do everything you can that does you good.

Many greetings from your Gustav

Freund is leaving tomorrow.

From the following letter, and particularly the paragraph beginning 'since leaving Levico', it could be surmised that Mahler interrupted his Toblach vacation at this juncture to visit Alma in Levico. Indeed, she describes this very scenario in AMM4:

Mahler was very worried about me, and finally he came in person. I travelled up to Trient to meet him. When he got off the train, I didn't recognize him. Before setting out, he had intended to beautify himself, but the hairdresser in Toblach had shaved his pate almost bald (Mahler had been reading the paper, and hadn't noticed a thing). Without those bushy side-tufts which gave his long, gaunt face its proper form, he looked as hideous as a convict. I found it too strange for words, and couldn't overcome the incongruity. Two days later he left in dismay.[4]

The absence of any reference in telegrams or letters to a trip to Levico at this juncture suggests that Alma's memory ran away with her. She may have been thinking of the summer of 1910, when Mahler did indeed visit her, but at Tobelbad (cf. letter 315). Mahler's 'since leaving Levico' can be explained by the fact that he had accompanied Alma, Gucki and Miss Taylor on their journey there four weeks earlier. And the scene of dismay over his new hairstyle was probably enacted at the station in Niederdorf, when Alma arrived from Levico on 13 July.

287[U]   [Toblach, 4 July 1909]

My dear Almschili,
So Fried has moved in, and Brecher has been saying (for the last two days) that he's going to visit Walker in Gastein. By the time you arrive, he should have taken the train (at any rate they make very pleasant company – discreet and easy-going as they both are). Brecher is staying at the Südbahn Hotel. It has a splendid »hall«, in which I've been taking afternoon coffee every day. – Freund has gone off, protesting eternal devotion. So now it's up to you to

decide whether I should let Fried stay on (he's very quiet and pleasant). Tell me exactly what you want. I don't think he'd disturb us. I'll let it be known that you're in need of rest, and it's also agreed that we see nothing of each other until lunchtime.

Today I'm sending you 200 crowns. Don't be sparing with it! Next winter we'll make it up; after all, it's only a trifle. I very much approve of your plan for us to go away – if the house gets too full – without saying where we're going. We could find ourselves a cosy hideout.

Since leaving Levico I've been taking one Saiodine* tablet a day, and there have been no ill effects. As from tomorrow I'll increase the dosage to two a day, as prescribed by Dr Liermberger.†

Maybe that will do me good too.

Yesterday I gave Agnes a bonus of five crowns. But if I don't keep my eyes skinned, she'll keep putting Trenker's butter on the breakfast table. Today, having got wise to her tricks, I stole up to the kitchen window and started up a conversation which I surreptitiously brought round to that very topic, and said I'd be most grateful if she were to serve Niederdorf butter, because Trenker's butter sometimes makes me throw up. I closed with a few seasonal jibes – though this time I didn't pinch her cheek – then I sauntered off, chuckling familiarly. – Thank heaven you'll soon be running the house again. Grünwald has sent another basket of vegetables. Just imagine it, the Leifels have already reserved a state cabin: it's costing them $1,800! I've sent Mrs Sheldon a friendly letter together with all my concert programmes. I know she'll think all the more highly of me for it. Please let me know your exact time of arrival. But I beg you: there's no need to hurry just for the sake of a few days or a few crowns. We'll soon make them up. Many greetings my Almscherl   Your Gustav

I've asked Hammerschlag to send 2,000 crowns. More details when you arrive.

[Top corner of first page:] Ask Dr Liermberger if I should still be on Saiodine, and whether I should also be taking his prescription, in combination or on its own.

---

* Saiodine (calcium iodobehenate): a drug for treating syphilis, arteriosclerosis and bronchial asthma, developed by Emil Fischer and J. von Mering in 1907, and marketed by Bayer and Hoechst.
† Dr Otto Liermberger, head of the medical institute at Levico and author of two books on the ferruginous properties of the spa waters, *Die Kuren und das Klima von Levico und Vetriolo in Südtirol, Vienna*, 1903 (English trans.: Vienna, 1908) and *Levico-Quellen und ihre Anwendung in den Tropen*, Vienna (undated).

The following letter is unique in that it documents a full-scale domestic quarrel. Kathi, the cook, evidently wrote to Alma complaining of her master's 'surly' behaviour. Mahler's reply to her accusations may appear flippant, for an argument about locked doors and rancid butter must have struck him as trifling. Nevertheless, he was clearly annoyed with Alma – and perhaps understandably so, for she always tended to treat her servants as confidantes and willing slaves.

288[U]   [Toblach, 8 July 1909]

Dear Almscherl,

Words <u>fail</u> me! Reading Fräulein Kathi's letter (and I'm writing 'Fräulein' to keep myself out of further trouble), and yours, I don't know whether to laugh or to cry, dearest Almscherl. – Very well: I give you <u>my word of honour</u> that I never spoke a surly word to Fräulein Kathi; I've been feeling far too indolent for that. On the contrary, I've been holding my tongue for the best part of four weeks (even though her complete lack of care and attention has been most upsetting) in the hope – which Frl. Kathi shares with me – that it will soon be over. I have <u>only</u> ever ventured remarks on two or three occasions when she served things I couldn't eat (such as semolina pudding), or if the awful taste betrayed the fact that Trenker's butter was on the table. She actually attempted to <u>smuggle</u> it in for breakfast, but it smelt so awful that I couldn't eat it, and anyway I could see that it lacked the factory wrapping. As it is, the house smells far too strongly of Trenker. Kathi (or rather, Fräulein K.) has been leaving the door to the balcony in Gucki's room open (overnight), so I locked it and took the key away (I believe that's the main reason for her annoyance).

But as I say, all this time I have <u>never</u> spoken harshly or unkindly to her. This is the most insolent allegation I have ever heard from one of our servants. Heaven knows, there must be some ulterior motive. And that I should have to answer to you for it is all the more aggravating. At home you always reproach me for taking a back seat: 'Why don't you say something – why don't you tell her – why don't you kick up a fuss' etc. But I don't, because I prefer to avoid all contact with the personnel. I keep my <u>distance</u>, in fact, I don't speak to them at all. They may find that annoying, but I have my reasons. I hope this will suffice, and that in future the good lady will never darken our door. In the light of these two letters, I also don't know whether I can make my peace with her, for never in my life has a »servant« so annoyed me. At any rate, <u>until</u> you return I shall say nothing. Maybe it's already been discussed in the household – my allegedly arrogant behaviour –

338

for contact with the Trenker family has always been my greatest 'delight' – and my 'arrogance' probably never made itself felt before, since you, with your 'way with people', probably helped to soften the impact.

I hope you don't hold any of this against me, and don't feel that I should be 'spreading the word of humanity' amongst my fellow human beings.[*]

I also hope I have the right to choose the company I cultivate and to talk to people only when it suits me. Can I not expect my cook to prepare the dishes I wish for (not to mention the fact that you drew up a diet sheet which she has completely ignored)? And when I expect good butter from Niederdorf and find Trenker's pigswill on the table instead (perhaps this is the reason why I make such an unpleasant impression), I certainly have the right to an opinion! I give you my word of honour: all this time I have not once raised my voice, and I've taken every precaution not to jeopardize your position. That she should come running to you and wilfully distort the facts is the height of impertinence. For my part, I could well complain about her resentful attitude and the unpleasant atmosphere she's been creating. You know how such things take all the pleasure out of a vacation. During the four weeks I've been here, she has been a constant source of annoyance and discontent.

Maybe I'll finish this letter in the afternoon. I had to get at least some of the spleen off my chest before lunch. The only consolation is your letter, which has just arrived. –

I take it that Gucki is now completely restored to health. As for you, I'm still waiting for you to reply on that score.

Back again, after wolfing down a hasty meal. Prost, Mahlzeit! By the way (to add a little more fuel to the fire), what a curious idea to split on me to the lady of the house! What does the dear woman actually want? Give notice? Get rid of me? It's she or I: one of us has got to go!

I've just sent a telegram to Fried: very agreeable. I gave him your address and asked him to look you up and bring you some convivial company. Has he already called? I've heard nothing more.

Now I must explain about yesterday's telegram. No letter arrived on Sunday. Worried by your news of Gucki, I cabled you. No answer. On Monday morning I received your letter with the many enclosures, but no word of Gucki. Since your letter was dated Sunday, i.e. before my cable had arrived, I worried all the more. Tuesday morning: no letter. The same afternoon: still no letter. That's why I sent the express cable.

Ninety-six kilos of comestibles have been delivered from Klagenfurt. And yesterday (7 July) we received a crate of apples from Justi.

[*] Orig.: '"menschliche Menschen" menschlich bemenschen'.

So you plan to arrive already on Tuesday? Once again, I beg you, don't miss out on your treatment. The water is appalling here, and I thank the Lord for every day you can spend in beautiful Levico. Please think it over carefully and be sure to leave the final decision to Dr Liermberger.

Putting on weight really doesn't matter right now. Going for walks is a good idea. But eating too little is idiotic! In heaven's name, why do you do such foolish things?

You haven't mentioned Pollak in your letter. I seem to think I've offended him (I also know why; when you arrive, I'll tell you).

Must close now. Many Greetings   Gustav

Let's not argue about this business any longer – we have time for that later (not to argue but to discuss, when we're together). I would gladly have spared you the trouble, but one tends to forget, and meanwhile you've fallen for Fräulein Kathi in a big way and can't stop talking about her.

I've sent off the money for Toch* and Redlich.

To be fair, Agnes cooks very well (except when she ignores my diet).

[Top corner of first page:] I have nothing against Agnes. She seems to be inoffensive and good-humoured.

289[U]   Toblach, 10 July 1909[P]

My dear Almscherl,

Only one more day until we meet again! Then I won't need to write any more, thank heaven.

And now for something very important: please bring as much honey as possible. My supply has already run out. It's the best honey I ever tasted, and I do believe it's put me right. It seems to agree with me very well. So bring as much as you can! On Tuesday evening I'll meet you at Niederdorf all on my own. And be sure to bring an evening meal with you. – Brecher has left, and just as he was going, Decsey arrived. He's staying with us, due to a curious chain of circumstances, in the upstairs room next to Fried's. But he won't stay long, of course. Incidentally, Brecher is due to return in a few days. When you get here, you'll have to explain Zuckerkandl's letter to me. – I can hardly wait for you to arrive! Let's make a jolly time of it. Subjectively speaking, I'm in excellent form. Fraenkel seems to be right: if my bowels are in order (and for the past week they have been), everything is fine. Now I must

---

* The twenty-year-old composer Ernst Toch, whose Sixth String Quartet had been performed to great acclaim at the Vienna Musikverein in 1905 by the Rosé Quartet. In 1909, on the recommendation of Mahler and other adjudicators, Toch was awarded the Mozart Prize of the City of Vienna

do what I can to keep it that way.

Thank heaven you're capable of walking longer distances. We can take a stroll every afternoon.

Farewell for now. Fondest greetings   Your Gustel

It's pouring with rain. <u>Bring honey</u>! And Regalia!*

Alma arrived in Toblach on 13 July. During the preceding four weeks, Mahler had been as busy as ever, studying scores for his New York Philharmonic concerts and working on the short score of the Ninth Symphony *(which he completed towards the end of September).*

In mid-August he and Alma left for Salzburg. On their return to Toblach, at the end of the month, they were joined on 3 September by Richard Strauss and his wife, who stayed for two days. To mark the occasion, Strauss invited Mahler and all his house guests (including Alfred Roller and Anna Moll) to dine with him at the Südbahn Hotel. On this occasion, according to Alma, Pauline Strauss behaved as outrageously as ever. Strauss motioned to Mahler to sit next to her, whereupon 'Pauline called out: "Only if you don't fidget, 'cos I can't put up with that!" Mahler was, in fact, just about to sit down, but he stood up and found a seat at the other end of the table.'[5]

Mahler left Toblach on 6 September. From the station, he sent the following card to Alma:

290[U] Postcard   Toblach, 6 September 1909[P]

D.A. A hundred more greetings.

My <u>ticket</u> cost about <u>60</u> crowns, and I paid 10 crowns in baggage charges. Cable me if you want me to send money. What a magnificent walk! I hope your throat doesn't play up. Please write at once, at least a postcard. A thousand greetings   Your G.

I also forgot [Wilhelm Meister's] Years of Travel. Let them fetch you one volume after another (the white ones) until you find it. Goethe, Works – small edition, Goethe Conversations – large format.

Back in Vienna, Mahler spent two days at the Hohe Warte with Carl and Anna Moll.

---

* A brand of cigarette.

291^U   [Vienna, 7 September 1909]

So, my dearest Almscherl,
At one o'clock I had an excellent and abundant meal with Mama here, then
I took a nap. Now we're both off to Grinzing for an extra-special high-tea in
the gardens we once visited together.
I take it you received this morning's telegram and the letter from Nord-
deutscher Lloyd, telling us that we've been allotted <u>not only</u> 5 but also 3.*
For today simply warmest greetings. Mama has also written to you.
Tomorrow I'm seeing Walter and Arnold. They're dining at 'Sandor'; I shall
eat at home, and afterwards they'll collect me. Justi is coming on Monday.
Your G.

Write!

292^U   [Vienna, 8 September 1909]

My dearest Almscherl,
Your dear letter reached me here this morning. I slept, bathed and breakfasted very well. Frightful hammering noises downstairs: the apartment is
being redecorated! Then I took a stroll with Walter – he left for rehearsal,
while I went on alone, meeting Arnold on the way. We took a fiacre together;
I drove in it to Mama's and he to 'Sandor'. Had an excellent meal and slept
there too. Now I'm waiting for Walter & Arnold to take a walk with me.
Spent the evening at the Erzherzog Karl, where Freund joined us. Yesterday
I called on Pollak: not at home; telephoned the Ministry, then booked a table
at Café Imperial. There I ate a supper of eggs and Graham bread, followed
by mocha with cream. At 8.30 Pollak arrived, in high spirits. We had a long
chat, and at 10.30 he walked me home. If the noise in the house doesn't stop,
I've a good mind to spend next week at Göding. Warmest greetings my
dearest,
Your Gustav

*Alma returned to Vienna earlier than usual, because she had arranged for
herself and Gucki to have their tonsils cauterized. Mahler had intended to
remain in the city and work. However, since the noise in the downstairs
apartment did not abate, he travelled on to the Redlichs at Göding. Alma,
meanwhile, was recuperating at the sanatorium.*

---

* Presumably cabin bookings on the *Kaiser Wilhelm II* for the forthcoming voyage to America.

293[U]   [Göding, 18 September 1909]

By now, my dearest, your torments should be over. I'll phone you later.
I'm having a splendid time here! What a shame I didn't come here straight
from <u>Toblach</u>. I'm spending all my time in the fresh air, even in the mornings,
as I've been working at an open window. A further decided advantage as far
as I'm concerned is that meals are served absolutely on time. I'll be leaving
on Wednesday at 10.40 and arriving in Vienna at 12.15. Then I'll join you
straight away on the Hohe Warte. I hope to find you in fine form by then;
perhaps you'll even feel up to joining me for a brief excursion. – I've already
received a reply from Colonne, which shows that his intentions are entirely
serious. Still no news from <u>Mengelberg</u>, however.* What a dreadful correspondent! Today Redlich said that if we were to rent a country residence à la
Plankenberg, he would make you a present of a dainty carriage, and help us
find a couple of splendid, low-priced horses.
If only we had it all arranged. We really must see to it! This fretting and
freezing in summer is simply too much. Apart from that, you two, with your
tender throats, could then weather every storm (with a bit of luck).
So long, Almscherl, see you soon.   Your Gustav

Greetings to Mammerl.

294   [Göding, 18 September 1909]

My dearest Almscherl,
You put a very brave face on it. I've heard all the news: twenty-four incisions
– and no anaesthetic. I'm delighted with you both. I'm sure it will be of <u>great</u>
<u>benefit</u> to you for the rest of your days. I was very worried, particularly
because I had to wait from four o'clock to five-thirty for the telephone call.
I had already resolved to pack my case (with the lightning speed for which
I'm so renowned) and drive to the sanatorium. – Take care of yourself until
Monday, my dearest. I'll probably return to Vienna on Wednesday, and come
to lunch with you. Meanwhile, I've settled in here very well. But when you're
not with me, outings in the coach give me little pleasure. The rooms are very
comfortable, as is the whole lifestyle. But the factory and the trains are a continual disturbance, day and night.
All the same, I'd like to have something of the kind myself – without a

---

* The conductor Eduard Colonne had written about the Paris performance of the *Second
Symphony*, scheduled for April 1910. At this time, Mahler was also in touch with Mengelberg
about his forthcoming series of concerts in Amsterdam.

factory or a railway line. A comfortable house and a big garden with fruit, flowers and vegetables.

Carl says he'll keep looking until he finds something of the kind near Vienna for us. – –

And now fondest greetings, my brave little Almscherl. Is Gucki enjoying her barrel-organ? I hope so!   Your Gustav

<Greetings to our dear Mama.>

295   [Göding, 19 September 1909]

My Almschi,

I wrote to you yesterday, but when I spoke <with Mama> on the telephone, I was told you hadn't yet received the letter. By now I hope you have. Yesterday, for all my good intentions, I had an anxious day. – I feel wonderful here! To be able to sit and work at an open window and breathe in the scent of trees and flowers: this joy is entirely new to me. Only now do I realize the error of my ways in the summer.

My pleasure hasn't even been diminished by the infernal din that goes on night and day. – I simply <u>must</u> find something of the sort. Carl says he won't rest until he's found us something. – Altogether, my stay here has done me a power of good. I can feel that it has put me at my ease. There's nothing for it: everyone needs warmth and sunshine. The thought of my various composing shacks fills me with horror. I may have spent the finest hours of my life in them, but my health has probably suffered in the process.

We've been taking coach rides twice a day. Most of all, I regret that you aren't here. I just love these plains! One day we must have something like this – but without the noise. I hope to surprise you on Wednesday on the Hohe Warte. Warmest greetings, my love! You have been wonderfully courageous (but I expected nothing less).   Your Gustav

Mahler returned from Göding on 22 September. According to Alma, he had spent most of his time there on final retouchings to the full score of Das Lied von der Erde, *which he planned to send to Emil Hertzka before leaving for America. Bruno Walter met him at the station in Vienna, and now that the* Ninth Symphony *was finished, Mahler spoke to him for the first time of the new work. Apparently he was afraid of being overcome by emotion, and therefore lent Walter the score to play it for himself. As the latter recalled: 'I shall never forget the expression on his face when he told me of his visit to Moravia, and that the world had never seemed more beautiful than during those few days in the country, where the smell of the earth rising from the fields had filled him with a strange, heartfelt joy. His words concealed an inner turbulence, not unlike that of his Hamburg years, which was causing him to ponder the great questions of existence, but with even greater urgency and agitation.'*[6]

Several members of Mahler's circle have spoken of his illness and forebodings of early death, yet to Bruno Walter he spoke of his plans for the future and of the house he intended to purchase for his retirement. To Alfred Roller he confessed that since the diagnosis of his cardiac condition he had taken care to avoid unnecessary physical exertion, primarily because he was looking forward to his old age, when he would have time to catch up on the many books he had always wanted to read, such as the letters of Goethe.

In the autumn of 1909 Mahler was preparing for an American season no less strenuous than his Hofoper schedules: between 1 November and 2 April he was to conduct forty-six concerts.

Before joining Alma in Paris, en route for Cherbourg and America, Mahler had agreed to conduct a performance of his Seventh Symphony *in The Hague on 2 October, followed by further performances in Amsterdam on 3 and 10 October. It was also planned to take the Concertgebouw Orchestra to Frankfurt, but the concert was cancelled, evidently due to lack of time. In the first two programmes, Mahler's* Seventh Symphony *was followed by Beethoven's* First Symphony, *conducted by Mengelberg; Mahler himself concluded the third concert with the Prelude to* Die Meistersinger, *as if again drawing attention to the quotation from that work in the finale of his* Seventh.

En route to Amsterdam, he wrote to Alma in Vienna.

296[U]   In the train [28 September 1909]

My Almscherl,

I slept wonderfully and had a particularly good breakfast. The Westbahn is using brand new sleeping cars now. They offer approximately the same facilities as the old ones, but there are improvements all round. Above all they're cleaner, better designed and a little more spacious. You should book two half-compartments in the middle of the carriage and be sure to do so in good time. The one (for Gucki and Miss Turner) will cost the price of two sleepers, the other (for you) costs the equivalent of $1\frac{1}{2}$ sleepers. So if, for instance, you book nos. 9/10 and 11/12, there'll be an adjoining washroom (if you make your reservation five days in advance, you're sure to get them), so you'll sleep soundly and feel more at home. But don't forget. After all, it's a matter of spending twenty-four hours in decent surroundings rather than in a pigsty.

345

Take a big flask of tea with you, a butter-cooler and some Graham bread, then you'll have a splendid breakfast. When I left, I was sad to leave you looking so poorly, and sad indeed at having to leave at all. This time it was your 'only three days' that was to blame, for otherwise I wouldn't have left under any circumstances. Warmest greetings to Mama and Carl. I shall miss them sorely. Your Gustav

297   Amsterdam [29 September 1909]
Het Concertgebouw

My Almscherl,
Brief report: Mengelberg waiting for me at the station. Good-natured and hospitable as ever. Long chat, then to bed, tired. Didn't sleep too well. Following morning, rehearsal at 9.30. Everything excellently prepared. Sounds magnificent. Hailed a cab in the afternoon and went for a ride, also walked a while. Six o'clock: »dinner«; nine o'clock to bed and slept very well until six o'clock. Today at 9.00 second rehearsal. – Once again, I'm thoroughly enjoying Holland. Their most endearing characteristic is their love of cleanliness. Kitchens are spick and span, which is typical of everything in this country. When one eats a meal here, one thinks with horror of the squalor elsewhere. Diepenbrock was already at the first rehearsal. Such a splendid fellow. How very sorry I am that you're not here. I'm sleeping in a big twin-bedded room, and there's a small adjoining room with a child's bed (the connecting door has been removed). They've taken so much trouble to get everything ready for us. – Mengelberg is absolutely determined to perform the Eighth, and Bodanzky and Hagemann from Mannheim have also announced themselves.*
The orchestra is <u>wonderful</u> and has taken me very much to heart. This time it's not work but pleasure. – Yesterday a deputation came and asked me to conduct the other items on the programme at least once (at the first concert Mengelberg will conduct them). They so much wanted to rehearse Beethoven or Wagner with me. Isn't that marvellous? Especially when one considers that they'd have to sacrifice two free mornings. 'Tout comme chez nous!'
I embrace you, my dear. <Do the same for me for Mama and Carl.> Write! Your Gustav

<Did you get my scribbled note about railway tickets?>

* Bodanzky had meanwhile completed his first season at the Mannheim Nationaltheater. He and his Intendant, Carl Hagemann, were planning a Mahler Festival for the spring of 1910. Mahler agreed to conduct several concert and opera performances for them, but later cancelled.

298   Amsterdam [1 October 1909]
                                              Het Concertgebouw

Dearest Almscherl,
I'm very worried. Your silence surely implies that your liver is playing you up. Take care not to make things worse when you start packing.* Please, Almschi, if a few cups get broken in the process, it really doesn't matter. And if the worst comes to the worst, you don't need to join me until the 11th. The few days' rest might do you good. – Here everything is going superbly. Mengelberg definitely wants to organize a performance of the Eighth. The conditions would be ideal: a very well-trained chorus, orchestral forces better prepared than anywhere else, and all of them available for unlimited rehearsal. Vederemo! Bodanzky and Hagemann, Bock† & Fried have announced themselves per telegram.
The Clemenceaus are arriving on Sunday already, so we can expect a few hectic days. The orchestra is wonderful – so refreshing after my experiences in New York. Kreisler is giving concerts here and has been attending my rehearsals. I'm exceptionally fond of him, both as man and artist. <I can't say the same for his wife – but then, I have no need for her.‡>
The Mengelbergs are as warm-hearted and hospitable as ever, in a way that only the Dutch understand. Diepenbrock is a joy: profound and loyal. – If only I had news of you, to put my mind at rest.
Today is the last rehearsal. In the third concert I'll probably conduct the whole programme (Wagner Faust overture, Siegfried Idyll, Meistersinger overture, followed by my Seventh).
Warmest greetings to you all, my dearest   Your Gustav

299   Amsterdam [1 October 1909]
                                              Het Concertgebouw

Dearest,
At last a letter from you! I'm so happy to hear that twenty cases have already been packed. That means your liver isn't giving you trouble. Take care not to overdo it. Tomorrow we're off to The Hague, and for the sake of a little relaxation after these last few very taxing days I've hired an automobile (it

---

* Mahler had decided to vacate the apartment in the Auenbruggergasse, because he and his family had spent so little time there during the past two years.
† Hugo Bock, director of the Berlin music publishers Bote und Bock, who had acquired the rights to the *Seventh Symphony*.
‡ After a tour of the USA in 1901 Kreisler had returned to Europe aboard the *Prince Bismarck*, where he made the acquaintance of the American-born Harriet Lies. They married in New York the following year.

costs 40 fl.). – I'm anxious, rather anxious about the next days, when I'll be surrounded by so many people. It will be nothing but confusion, and I can see myself taking my meals in bed again. Fond as I am of the people themselves, I can't stand the crowds. It's no small thing when people sit in a train for eight hours just to hear one of my works. Nowadays such enthusiasts are still pretty rare (although matters do seem to be improving a little). Please Almscherl, give the enclosed note to <u>Carl</u> and ask him to attend to it soon. I'd like to do at least something to return Mengelberg's hospitality, for he has really put himself out. A few days ago he remarked on my filter-tipped cigarettes, and asked for the address of the manufacturer. <It will cost about 6 fl.> Warmest greetings my Almschi,
Your Gustav

Yesterday I played Mengelberg and Diepenbrock a few passages from my Eighth. – It's funny: the work always makes the same, typically powerful impression. It would be absurd if my most important work happened to be the easiest to understand.

300   Amsterdam [6 October 1909]
                                                    Het Concertgebouw

My Almscherl,
When this letter arrives, please cable me at once at
    Mahler / Amsterdam / van Eeghenstraat 107 / bei Mengelberg
and tell me when you're arriving.
Wait! That won't be any good. The day after tomorrow, Friday the 8th, I'll be travelling on to Paris, Hotel Bellevue, where I'll wait to hear from you. Some days ago I caught a frightful cold, and all this staying in strange places has taken its toll.
Since yesterday I've had the apartment to myself <and am relishing the peace and quiet.>
The enclosed letter from Reiter* shows that there's more to him than your typically philistine orchestral musician.
I almost forgot: my symphony was a huge success. Altogether, the ground has been exceedingly well prepared for me here. Nevertheless, I've decided not to give the Seventh in New York, but to start with the Fourth.† For an audience unfamiliar with my music, the other work is too complex.

* Orig.: 'Reitler', i.e. Xaver Reiter, whom Mahler had recently engaged as principal horn of the New York Philharmonic.
† In the event, Mahler introduced himself in New York as a composer not with the *Fourth* but with the *First Symphony* (on 16 and 17 December).

If those women continue to plague me, they shall have their Tchaikovsky (at least it will keep them quiet). I can well understand your fatigue. You see, my dearest, having a lot to do takes it out of you – it's as simple as that! Warmest greetings   Your Gustav

<Best wishes to Mama and Carl.>

Have just received your letter. All right, I'll check in at Hotel Majestic (I'll be arriving on Friday). Please tell everyone in Vienna.

Mahler and the ladies of the Guarantors' Committee had failed to agree on some of the programmes for his concerts. Tchaikovsky had visited New York in April 1891 (two years before his death) and conducted four concerts for the inauguration of Carnegie Hall. Since then New York audiences had taken a strong liking to his music. Although Mahler preferred Tchaikovsky's operas to the symphonies, he yielded to the wishes of the committee by adding the Romeo and Juliet *overture,* First Piano Concerto *and the* Sixth Symphony *('Pathétique') to his programmes. The following season included even more Tchaikovsky.*

During his three days in Paris with Alma, Mahler sat for Rodin for a few more hours and discussed the performance of his Second Symphony *due to be given at the Théâtre du Châtelet in April 1910. On 12 October he and his family boarded the* Kaiser Wilhelm II *in Cherbourg for their fifth Atlantic crossing. This time the sea was particularly rough, and the ship docked in New York with several hours' delay. According to Alma, Mahler hardly left his cabin during the whole voyage.*

Plans for the Philharmonic's first season as a permanent orchestra were ambitious. The concerts were divided into four series: eight Thursday sub-scription concerts, repeated on Friday afternoons; a Beethoven cycle of six concerts, also on Friday afternoons; five 'popular' concerts at reduced prices on Sunday afternoons; and a series of six 'historical' concerts on Wednesday evenings, modelled on those which Hans von Bülow had conducted in Hamburg many years before, and perhaps also on the celebrated 'historical' piano recitals of Anton Rubinstein and Ferruccio Busoni. Two extra concerts were planned for New York, a further concert for Brooklyn, two for Philadelphia and, in the last week of February 1910, a tour of New England.

Theodore Spiering, the orchestra's new concertmaster, has testified to the tremendous zeal and enthusiasm with which Mahler embarked on this new enterprise, so unlike any he had undertaken before:

'*Rehearsals in New York began at once, and Mahler set to work with enor-mous enthusiasm. Every day he rehearsed with great care. [. . .] His rehearsals were unfailingly interesting, but he was also very demanding. He* never kept to a specified schedule, but we rarely exceeded the 3 ¹/₂ hours stip-ulated by the Musicians' Union. Sometimes ninety minutes sufficed, or even seventy-five. When Mahler worked, it was always at full stretch. Every minute counted. There were no breaks. Almost never did we simply play through. It was a continual struggle against all odds, to be fought until it was won. The orchestra was not accustomed to such intensity, and at first the players reacted unwillingly. Soon, however, they fell into line and learnt to admire the man who spoke so harshly to them but got them to play better than they had never imagined would be possible. As an interpreter Mahler remains unequalled.'7

   The programme of the first subscription concert, on 4 November, included Beethoven's overture The Consecration of the House and Eroica Symphony, followed by Liszt's Mazeppa and Richard Strauss's Till Eulenspiegel. Five months later, on 1 and 2 April, the season closed with Beethoven's Choral Symphony, preceded by the Choral Fantasy. Several concerts, particularly those of the 'historical' cycle, attracted only small audiences, but on the whole the season was a great artistic success. While most of the critics were lavish in their praise, Henry Krehbiel and William Henderson systematically took Mahler to task for his alleged wilfulness, iconoclasm and over-dramati-zation, complaining that he tampered with the scores of the great masters. Soon it transpired that these regular slatings were motivated less by aesthet-ics than by intrigue: most of Mahler's admirers were opponents of Walter Damrosch and his New York Symphony concerts; Krehbiel and Henderson, on the other hand, were on the teaching staff of the Institute of Music Art, a school owned and directed by the Damrosch family. Mahler's refusal to let Krehbiel publish the programme of his First Symphony, which he had long since discarded, only served to aggravate the situation. Krehbiel's animosity became obsessive and made itself felt in every review, indeed even in his obit-uary of Mahler.

1910

On 6 and 7 January Mahler conducted a programme consisting of Berlioz's Symphonie Fantastique, *Beethoven's 'Emperor' Concerto (with Busoni as soloist) and Wagner's Prelude to* Die Meistersinger. *Krehbiel was alone in disparaging the Berlioz, and considered Mahler to have overtaxed the orchestra's resources. Clearly he was exasperated by the public's enthusiasm, echoes of which filled many columns of the New York newspapers and musical journals.*

A letter to Bruno Walter gives a clear indication of Mahler's state of mind at this time:

I hope my silence has given you no cause for concern. It was for no other reason than that I have been immensely busy (it reminded me of my time in Vienna) and have had time only for four activities: conducting, writing music, eating and sleeping. I realize that I am incorrigible. People like me have no alternative to being thorough, and that, as I have come to realize, means being overworked. [. . .] My orchestra is typically American: apathetic and untalented. One has to move heaven and earth to get them to play. It's not so agreeable for me as a conductor to have to return to first principles. My only pleasure is rehearsing works that are new to me. And I still derive immense pleasure from making music. If only the musicians themselves were a little better![1]

The tour of New England in February 1910 included concerts in New Haven, Springfield, Providence and Boston. The centrepiece of all four programmes was the Symphonie fantastique. *Mahler also gave three performances of his Bach Suite, conducting (as in* Figaro *at the 'Met') from a modified piano that sounded like a harpsichord. From Springfield he wrote to Alma.*

301[U]   Springfield, 24 February 1910[P]

Dearest,
It gets more »old-fashioned« every day. O Savoy! What a »nice«, peaceful Arcady* you are. – I'm staying in a hole of a place (there's no alternative here), with a never-ending din of machines, »cars« etc. And my stomach is

---

* Orig.: 'Tusculum'.

no longer behaving itself. Maybe it's the butter, so from now on I'll do without it. It's very cold too, lots of ice and snow. Fortunately I have my fur coat. – This »tour« wouldn't have suited you at all. All the servants are blacks. Here, by the way, they're most agreeable, unassuming and eager to please. Spiering as travelling companion is like a character from an operetta. It's hard to talk to him. He mulls over every word, one's mind begins to wander and eventually one completely loses the thread of his conversation. – At any rate, New Haven is a pleasant little place with a dreadful hotel. Springfield is a hideous dump, and the hotel quite impossible.

So long for now! Please don't forget to prepare my package for Gucki. Gustav

Did you give notice that I had moved out?

In AMM4 Alma describes her social life as fairly active during this third period in New York. She records a trip to the Roosevelts' country estate at Oyster Bay, and a visit, in the company of Otto Kahn and his wife, to Eusapia Palladious, a celebrated Italian medium. She accompanied her husband to several parties thrown by American millionaires, and one night they toured the less reputable areas of downtown Manhattan with Rudolf Schirmer, the publisher of Mahler's Bach Suite.[2]

At this time, relations between Mahler and Alma were evidently good, though tension arose when she became strongly attracted to the Russian pianist Ossip Gabrilovich. From her unpublished diaries it transpires that the 'affair' never went beyond an exchange of kisses, but on one occasion Mahler overheard their conversation, and must have been deeply hurt. [3]

It would appear that Alma was also harshly criticized by Mahler's friends. A letter of Mahler's to Guido Adler shows that he sometimes felt obliged to speak up for her:

This brings me to the subject of my wife. Your opinions and remarks do her great injustice. Take my word for it, her sole concern is for my well-being. During eight years at my side in Vienna she never let the apparent glamour of my position go to her head, never succumbed to the temptation of extravagance nor indeed even lived up to our social status – despite her temperament, despite the lures of the Viennese way of life and the 'good friends' in that place (who all live beyond their means). Even now, her sole concern is to support me in my striving for financial independence, which would afford me the necessary peace of mind to compose (and I repeat, by the way, that this is no unattainable goal, as it was in Vienna). You've known her long enough. When did you ever observe her behaving extravagantly or egoistically? Do you really think she would suddenly have changed since you last saw her? [. . .] Or is it perhaps our duty to live a life of penury on my pension from the Hofoper? Why, since it was offered to me, should I not earn a good living with honest, artistic work? I assure you once again that my wife is not only a valiant help-mate who shares my intellectual interests (a rare alliance), but she also runs the household with care and common sense. For all our prosperity, she helps me economize; indeed, our stability and material comfort are entirely of her doing. I could prove this to you in actual figures. But surely this is not necessary. With a little goodwill (and recollections of your own impressions), you should be able to figure things out for yourself.[4]

At the end of the season Mahler wrote to his mother-in-law:

I've come through the year with flying colours, and haven't actually spared myself. Of the three of us, I alone have uninterruptedly enjoyed good health. It's certain that Almschi hasn't had a better winter in years – a few chills, but nothing serious, and she soon picked herself up. Gucki doesn't seem to have settled in here quite as well. She went down with a chronic catarrh (combined with a touch of fever), but she's over it, thank heaven. Now she's feeling as fit as a fiddle, the very picture of health. [. . .] Is there any chance of renting a country house, something like Göding etc., as I mentioned to Carl?[5]

Despite all his exertions – and during this season Mahler conducted an aver-age of ten concerts a month – on 1 April he was able to notify Bruno Walter that 'the fair copy of the full score of my Ninth [Symphony] is now finished'.[6]

He was also much occupied with the plan conceived by Emil Gutmann for the first performance of the Eighth Symphony, *which was to take place in September 1910 in Munich. At first he tried hard to discourage the impresa-rio, reminding him that printed vocal scores were not yet available, although they should have been delivered to the various choruses by 1 January. However, such were Gutmann's enthusiasm and efficiency that his plans did finally come to fruition.*

Towards the end of the season, Mahler found time to rehearse and conduct four performances of Tchaikovsky's Pique Dame *at the Metropolitan Opera, for a fee of $5,000. The cast, headed by Leo Slezak and Emmy Destinn, was uniformly brilliant and, as with* Figaro, *Lefler's sets were imported from Vienna. According to the press, Tchaikovsky's opera was successful with the public, and only Mahler's departure curtailed the series of performances. However, the New Yorkers do not appear to have taken to this darkest and gloomiest of Tchaikovsky's operas, and it was not revived.*

Nor did the first Philharmonic season end in a climate of optimism. The intelligentsia had supported and admired Mahler, but the halls had rarely been filled to capacity. Rumours of Mahler's discouragement found their way into the press, even though he himself firmly denied them. It was obvious that policy changes were necessary, and he himself insisted on the engagement of a professional manager for the next season. Despite the deficit, which had entirely wiped out the Guarantors' fund, he obtained permission from the committee to improve the quality of the orchestra by dismissing twenty-six musicians (seventeen of whom had been under contract only since the opening of the 1909–10 season) and engaging sixteen new ones – more than a quarter of the total membership of the orchestra – in their place.

The Mahlers left New York on 5 March on the Kaiser Wilhelm II, reaching Paris a week later in time for rehearsals of the Second Symphony. The performance followed on 17 April at the Théâtre du Châtelet, with the Colonne Orchestra under Mahler's direction (soloists: Povla Frisch and Hélène Demellier). Although the success was far greater than has often been alleged, most of the critics expressed more respect for Mahler as artist and conductor than enthusiasm or understanding for his music. He was introduced to Fauré, Debussy and Dukas at a luncheon party given by the Clemenceaus, and Alma asserts that he was greatly offended when he heard that Debussy, Pierné and Dukas had left the hall before the performance was over. Her story is not entirely credible: Dukas was noted for his unfailing politeness and generosity, while Pierné, who had himself opened the programme with Lalo's overture to Le Roi d'Ys and a Handel organ concerto, is unlikely to have taken his leave immediately afterwards. As for Debussy, documentary evidence does support Alma's claim, indeed Mahler came to regard Debussy as his principal adversary within the French musical scene. In his eyes this was a particularly uncourteous gesture, for he had included several of Debussy's works in his New York programmes.

From Paris, Alma accompanied Mahler to Rome, where he was to give three concerts with the Accademia di Santa Cecilia at the recently inaugurated Augusteo. The season was nearing its end, and many of the orchestra's regular members had already left for a South American tour. Not surprisingly, the standard of playing at the first two concerts, on 28 April and 1 May, was abysmal, in fact the biggest disaster of Mahler's entire career. After a bitter conflict with the musicians, Mahler cancelled the third concert and returned to Vienna. Alma pleaded with him to stay in Rome and fulfil his contract, but he would have none of it. Later (in letter 310), he rebuked her for having opposed him.

They arrived back in Vienna on 3 May. Shortly afterwards, Emil Gutmann came from Munich to discuss the schedule for the world première of the

Eighth Symphony, *which Mahler was to rehearse in the second half of June. Gutmann had arranged for two large choral societies to participate, the Vienna Singverein and the Riedel-Verein in Leipzig.*

On 21 May Mahler signed contracts with Universal Edition for the Ninth Symphony *and* Das Lied von der Erde. *Choral rehearsals for the* Eighth Symphony *were delayed, because the vocal score had been in print for only a month. In Vienna, Mahler attended several rehearsals of the Singverein, conducted by Schalk, and was far from satisfied with the results.*

Alma's nervous condition had not improved, and it was decided that she should take the waters at Tobelbad, a popular spa in the neighbourhood of Graz. Her stay was to be longer than the one of the preceding year at Levico – six weeks in all – and again she was accompanied by Gucki, who was now six years old, and her governess Miss Turner. Once again, Alma gives an inaccurate account of her journey: 'Having taken Mahler to Toblach, I went under doctors orders to Tobelbad, in search of a cure for my nervous disorders.' Letter 302 shows that it was exactly the other way round: Mahler took the family to Tobelbad on 1 June, then returned to Vienna the following day. On the way back he visited a disused vicarage ('provost's lodge') that he may have been considering as a new country home.

302^U   [Vienna, 6 June 1910]

My dear Almschili,
It's taken all this time to write to you. Since my return (which was entirely presto rabiato, as my return journeys usually are), I didn't get a moment to myself. The provost's lodge is a delightful little place – particularly to look at. Truly romantic. But I'm not sure whether it would be comfortable to live in. Carl, whose opinion in such matters can be trusted, says it could be. Whatever the case, you'd have to take a look at it yourself. And we'd certainly have to invest something in it. The four big rooms are just wonderful, as is the kitchen, which has a separate dining area and adjoining quarters for the servants. But everything else would have to be built on, including sanitary facilities. I don't quite see how it can be done, as there's only <u>one</u> staircase, which separates the kitchen from the other four rooms. As all the other rooms are on the other side, the only access to them would be through the kitchen. – But as I said, I'd prefer to let Carl [two lines obliterated].
I'm certain Tobelbad will do you good. I left you with a heavy heart this time. How I'd love to be there and roam around with you in a little place like that – without any work – just peace and contentment. That's something we've never done together! But first you must be restored to health. Maybe

in September, all going well. At present I'm using your little room, where my thoughts are often of you. Yesterday I sat at the window (after lunch) for the best part of an hour, bathing in the wonderful sunlight that shines up here. The bells were ringing, and in the distance was a confused din of Sunday trouble-makers – harmonicas, hurdy-gurdies etc. It was as if my whole childhood was welling up within me! I can't tell you how much I adore it. And everywhere before my eyes your cherished picture. [Six lines obliterated.] Today I'm sitting at the window again – but on the building site next door the urchins are making a ghastly racket. I'd dearly love to give them a good hiding. Please write and tell me all about your life in Tobelbad. I have come to regret my domineering behaviour at table. I was in such high spirits – and you were so downcast (next time you'll probably be kicking over the traces, while I'm suffering from stomach cramps).

Warmest greetings, my Almschi, from your Gustav

Freund was here today. A surprise visit at lunch. Even better than a piece of Sacher Torte!

[top of first page:] Mama and Carl are so unbelievably good to me.

303   [Vienna, 8 June 1910]

My dearest Almschili,

<Yesterday, on returning from a twelve-hour motoring trip (Winter[*]) in search of a country house, I found your letter. This morning, early as it still is, I shall reply. Above all: you're a scamp.[†] Why trouble your head with such nonsense? Don't you know yourself well enough by now, and me too? I've never been more fond of you than I am now – really never! And> when I mentioned your good looks that last morning in Tobelbad, it was an involuntary expression of delight at the sight of you. As you came towards me, you looked so unbelievably sweet and charming. Surely you know me by now? «If something is expected of me, I never shirk it.» In art, as in life, I rely entirely on spontaneity. If I were obliged or compelled to compose, I know for sure that I couldn't put a single note to paper. Four years ago, on

---

[*] Josef von Winter, a Viennese surgeon whom Mahler had met in his youth in the German Nationalist circles of Richard von Kralik. His wife Josefine was artistically inclined, both as painter and composer.
[†] Orig.: 'Afferl'. In her last letter, Alma had evidently asked Mahler whether he still loved her. A few days earlier, on 2 June, she had made the acquaintance of Walter Gropius and fallen in love with him (cf. J. Rothkamm, 'Wann entstand Mahlers Zehnte Symphonie?' in *Gustav Mahler Durchgesetzt?*, Musik-Konzepte 106, X/1999, 110).

the first morning of our summer at Maiernigg, I went up to my shack, resolved to take it easy (for I was in dire need of rest at the time) and to gather new strength. – As I entered that all-too-familiar room, the creator spiritus took possession of me, held me in its clutches and chastised me for eight weeks, until the work was all but finished. – The previous summer I'd been intending to complete the 7th (of which the two Andantes were already finished). For two weeks I plagued myself to desperation, as you surely recall – and finally I made off for the Dolomites. But there it was the same story. Finally I gave up and drove home, convinced that the summer had been wasted.

You weren't waiting for me at Krumpendorf because I hadn't announced my arrival. I got into the boat to be ferried across. At the sound of oars plying through water I was suddenly inspired to the theme (or rather the rhythm and atmosphere) of the introduction to the first movement – and within four weeks the first, third and fifth movements were completely finished. Do you remember? Look, my dear, you know enough of me and my ways to understand that I could never hurt you in any way. Particularly since you know very well that I live only for you and Gucki, and that no other living thing could ever come between you and my love for you. Everything else pales beside it – like a poor woodcut compared with a Titian! Get well soon, my Luxerl, so you can soon keep pace with me, and we can enjoy life together like two good comrades. [Three lines obliterated.] <Let yourself never fall victim to doubt.> Life and love will seem to you like the blossom of a tree that grows ever taller – and sometimes ever broader; and even if the blossom may fall, and later the fruit – one can confidently expect the next spring, when everything germinates once again. <No more foolish ideas! Get well soon – that's the main thing. And now, I beg you, minister systematically to all your needs, and stay put until you feel completely restored.> On Friday night I have to travel to Leipzig (there's a rehearsal on Saturday), so unfortunately I can't visit you. Just <u>one day and one night</u> would be too <u>risky</u> for me too. However – I finish in Munich on <u>2</u> June [sic]. One word from you, and I'll travel straight to you via Vienna for a few days 'con amore' at your side. Or I could travel directly to Innsbruck and Toblach, catch my breath and recover from the exertions of rehearsal, then come down and collect you. It all depends which course of treatment you find most suitable. But once again <u>I beseech you</u>: get well – do all that's needed!

Just a cursory account of the last few days. At rehearsal on Monday evening the Vienna Männergesangsverein demonstrated its worthlessness (nobody turned up, at the start only fourteen people were there) and Schalk his incompetence (I let him conduct to begin with – I was so annoyed that I had refused – and he got all the tempi wrong).

Later the ranks began to swell. I left my corner like a sulky schoolboy and took up the baton. Things went better immediately, but soon it became apparent that the gentlemen hadn't yet studied their parts. And now I'm still not sure whether the concert can take place, because I'm absolutely determined <u>not</u> to tolerate artistic slovenliness. Admittedly, the women are terrific and make up for many of the men's misdemeanours. <(You see, exactly comme chez nous!)> The following day the Winters collected us with their car <(Carl had arranged everything)> and we set off on a three-hour drive to Pöchlarn to view a country house. Beautifully located, but totally dilapidated and swarming with gnats.

We then drove back along park-like alleys through the Wachau, following the course of the Danube past Dürrenstein and Weissendorf as far as Mautern. Delightful little places all of them, and completely unspoiled. Then we took a right turn, passed Göttweig and drove through a hilly area of meadows and woods. Quite by chance we ended up near Neulengbach, and suddenly we found ourselves driving past <u>Planken</u>berg. It looked utterly delightful, and I was thinking so intensely of you that your ears must have been burning. – All the way, Carl and I almost wept at the thought that you and Mama weren't with us (though at one stage I actually fell asleep – that was the fault of Frau Winter, who was sitting next to me). All going well, I have resolved to take exactly the same trip with you by car in September. And now farewell, my dear. Write me a happy letter, otherwise I shall set out on my journey with a heavy heart.

A thousand kisses from your Gustl

Josefine Winter wrote a detailed account of this outing in her diary:

'8.30 a.m. In brilliant sunshine with Mahler (and at his request) to Krummnussbaum, where he wanted to look at a country mansion; over the Rieder Berg; Mahler delighted by the sight of it all, particularly by the poplars; horrified that they're being felled because they're considered worthless. "Don't people do worthless things too? Such as playing tarock or performing 'The Merry Widow'?"

'Already the drive down the Sommerheidenweg and through the Schottenwald met with great enthusiasm; Moll had never been there before! St Pölten, a larger town and quite appealing; then Pöchlarn, a smaller place; then along a winding alley ("a crazy approach road, how appropriate", observed Mahler laughingly) to Krummnussbaum, where the property itself met with his disapproval (directly opposite a sawmill!).

'*In Melk many fine old houses. Lunch there at the Goldenes Schiff. The landlord asked Mahler for his autograph, but he passed the guestbook on to Josef, saying that he was the car-owner.*

'*With Moll to the monastery. Down a narrow path and through a side door into the magnificent church. The open main entrance afforded a superb view over the Danube valley, framed as if in a triptych by balustrades and columns. Wonderful.*

'*Unfortunately it started to rain; later it cleared up. Magnificent drive through the much-vaunted Wachau. It was like a park, a regular alternation of hills and quaint riverside villages. Mahler took great pleasure in it all; later too, as the rocks receded and we left the Danube valley to cross undulating hills towards Tulln. Mahler much appreciated the beauty of Schloss Walpersdorf, standing in splendid medieval isolation. Rain again. Mahler ate a supper of ham and eggs and apples, then devoured a quantity of nuts. I intimated that I would love to hear the close of* Faust II *in his new symphony, but he didn't take the hint.*

'*Home at 8 o'clock.*'[7]

304[U]   [Vienna, 10 June 1910]

Dearest,

It's five o'clock in the morning, and I must make full use of the early hour to write you a few lines, otherwise I won't have time for the rest of the day. I've been so terribly busy of late, and today it's particularly bad, because I also have rehearsals and must attend to preparations for the autumn. If only I knew how you're getting on in Tobelbad. You haven't written a single word on the subject. – This evening I go to Leipzig, <u>Hotel Sedan</u>, where I hope to receive at least one letter from you. I stay there until the night of the <u>13th</u>, then on to Munich, where I arrive on the morning of the 14th and shall be staying at Hotel Regina. Dearest, I took the <u>portefeuille</u> out of the strongbox and gave it to you to keep in your room. Just now I wanted to put a contract into it (for the 9th Symphony), but couldn't find it. I thought you might have given it back to Carl. Have you taken it with you? Or where could it be? All our American currency is in it too!

We still don't have a tenor for the 8th Symphony. Neither Senius nor Maikl seems to be up to it. [Bruno] Walter has come up with a tenor (an Italian stagione singer, but an American who speaks German) with a really magnificent voice, and he's learning the part.

I shan't take the big suitcase with me. Instead Mama will buy a new grip,* so we have one in reserve. Why should I carry so much ballast for just ten days?

* Orig.: 'Sprüngerl'.

I hope to hear from you soon – – – Your letters were sweeter than ever (you've sent three so far). Such warmth radiates from them.

Addio, my dearest, and don't forget to tell me about Gucki. Fondest greetings, your Gustav

After some deliberation, Mahler chose one of the most celebrated concert singers of his generation to sing the solo tenor part in the Eighth Symphony: *Felix Senius. Georg Maikl, whom he also considered for the part, had been a member of his ensemble at the Hofoper since 1904; as a lyric tenor, he would have had difficulty with the more dramatic passages in the score. The American singer mentioned here was probably William Miller, whom Bruno Walter later engaged for the world première of* Das Lied von der Erde.

305[U] Telegram   Leipzig, 12 June 1910

worked hard with chorus[*] pretty good and solo tenor very good also corrected orchestral parts as usual kisses your gustav

306[U] Telegram   Leipzig, 13 June 1910

rehearsing and erasing solo tenor first rate travelling on tonight to munich hotel regina shall write from there in excellent health fondest greetings gustav

307[U] Telegram   Munich, 16 June 1910

hallo almschili no time to write parts copied by kornfeld[†] full of mistakes spending every minute correcting sounds overwhelming all the same so far only sectional rehearsals please write gustav

308   Munich [17 June 1910]
                                       Regina-Palast-Hotel

My Almschl,

I'm writing this for you just as a sign of life. What this copyist has done to me (the one who made such an affected, unpleasant impression on us at the time) is simply too dreadful. In every part, wherever an instrument has a longer passage of rests, instead of writing them out in full, the lazy pig has merely written <u>tacet</u> (which is normally done only when an instrument is

---

[*] Mahler was rehearsing with the Riedel-Verein, whose conductor, Georg Göhler, was one of his most ardent admirers (cf. p. 370).

[†] Karl Kornfeld, a staff copyist at Universal Edition in Vienna.

silent for a whole movement). – So now, not only are the players unable to find their bearings, but when I, poor devil, want to change the orchestration, instead of simply writing in the necessary bars at the appropriate place, I also have to write out the entire tacet passage, and sometimes have to delete several lines to make room for it. This is wasting hours and hours of my time. I know what you'll be saying: 'Vienna!' (or perhaps: 'Jews!') – but remember, in Vienna I also have the finest, most reliable of copyists (Forstik). And in future I shall insist that only he should copy my music. I had a very pleasant time in Leipzig. The whole choir (250 of them) was waiting for me punctually at eight o'clock, and stood up respectfully when I came in, as if we were at school. They were extremely well prepared and, without a trace of unruliness,* very enthusiastic. Afterwards they waited on the street to cheer me. Their conductor, Dr Göhler, is known as a vehement opponent of Strauss and one of my staunchest supporters – a very capable, conscientious fellow. Senius (Dr Marianus) was there too, and sings magnificently – you'll love it. The Munich orchestra is attentive and very fine, not a chair is empty. Gutmann is doing a terrific job, and in future I'll take care to treat him with the greatest respect. But my strength is beginning to fail me <(my stomach too). Of course Grethl Remy should come; she's a splendid person – and you're fond of her, that's the main thing.† Because of that I'm already fond of her too.> Greetings to you, my Almscherl!
Your Gustav

<What's Gucki up to?>

[upper corner of first page:] <Did you find the portefeuille?>

309   Munich [18 June 1910]
                                                          Regina-Palast-Hotel
                                                          In the morning

My Almscherl,
<Today was the first full rehearsal. It was sheer purgatory! – When I've finished here, I don't know what I should do. My return ticket is booked for Toblach via Innsbruck. If you want me to come to you straight away, I'd have to forfeit the ticket and travel via Vienna. But then the journey would take an extra eight hours. – In my opinion it would be best if I first went to Toblach for a breath of fresh air and a good rest, then spent a couple of days

---

* Orig.: 'Pahöl' (Viennese dialect, from the Hungarian 'páholni': brawl).
† Grethl von Remy: identity unknown.

in Tobelbad and brought you home. – Mama wants to spend a few days with you too, but then you'll be caught up in the hurly-burly, and that can't possibly be beneficial to your cure. Please think it over, my dear. If you're feeling utterly lonely and want me to be with you <u>right away</u>, I really don't mind forfeiting my ticket to Toblach. But as I said, personally I'd prefer to come and <u>fetch</u> you. –

Gutmann is doing a wonderful job. – Just imagine whom I chanced upon on the street a few days ago? Krzyzanowski!* Since then, every evening after rehearsal I have actually been dining with him in an inn over the road. Just like in old times. –

At this time I don't think I'd really enjoy your utter isolation. What would I give if you could attend my rehearsals and chat with me afterwards.

I only hope you're doing <u>all</u> you can to get out of this muddle.† On the 22nd and 23rd all the soloists will be here, so we have ensemble rehearsals and rehearsals with the orchestra. –

Sometime soon I'd like to send you a rather curious book, written ten years ago by someone I'd never heard of.> As for Plato, what you write is the crux of the matter. Plato uses Socrates as a mouthpiece for his own outlook on life, which has been passed down through the centuries to people of lower intellect as that much-misrepresented concept, 'Platonic love'. – Its essence is Goethe's belief that all love is founded on procreation and creation; that procreation is an activity not only of the body but also of the soul, and that the two together constitute an outlet for this 'eros'.*) – In the closing scene of Faust the concept is represented symbolically. [Three lines obliterated.] The surface attraction of The Symposium lies in the vitality of its narrative and the dramatic fire of its 'story'. – When I read it at school, I remember enjoying the moment when Alcibiades rushes in, all youthful impetuousness, garlanded with vine leaves. And later, in the closing scene, Socrates provides a delightful antithesis as the only person still on his feet, while his friends are lolling about in a drunken stupor; calmly he stands up and makes his way to the marketplace to philosophize. Only later does one appreciate the diversity of opinions proffered, and only at the very end does one realize what this carefully planned rise in intensity is actually leading to: that wonderful dialogue between Socrates and Diotima, in which Plato outlines and summarizes his entire world. In everything that Plato writes, Socrates is the wineskin into which he pours his own wine. What immense stature that man

---

* Rudolf Krzyzanowski, a fellow student of Mahler's at the Vienna Conservatory. For some years he and his brother Heinrich (a writer) belonged to the closer circle of Mahler's friends.
† Orig.: 'Schlemastik'.

must have possessed to draw so endless a stream of memories and protesta-tions of love from such a pupil. One is tempted to compare him to Jesus Christ; indeed, every era has involuntarily drawn such parallels. – All con-trast is determined by milieu and Zeitgeist. On the one side, the radiance of culture in its highest form, with pupils and commentators of greatest intel-lectual brilliance; on the other, the darkness of a naive, infantile world, in which the child serves as a vessel for the marvels of worldly wisdom, an out-come of pure instinct, of a direct and intense way of looking at things and understanding them.

For today, my love, many greetings and don't forget to write. Your Gustav

*) Eros in both cases as creator of the world!

[top corner of first page: <What about the portefeuille? And Gucki?>]

310[U]   Munich [20 June 1910]
                                                    Regina-Palast-Hotel

What a sad little letter this morning, my Almschi! It makes me feel »really down.« – Today, for my part, I rehearsed the children. Dear little imps, some of them. Most of them are girls, I'm sorry to say, but they're really sweet and chatter away like sparrows. Unfortunately they've learnt the music with sev-eral dreadful mistakes (instilled by their various teachers). This has become quite a problem, and somehow I'll have to find a way round it. – The full rehearsal of the first movement was magnificent. Tomorrow we do the sec-ond. – Before we departed from Rome (you won't have forgotten this), I remember being irritable and indeed annoyed, because you were doing your utmost to persuade me to stay and carry on. I simply didn't understand you. Perhaps meanwhile you've come to see things differently. Whatever the case, in future I shall never put up with anything like those rehearsals and con-certs.

I've already heard every passage in detail at least once, and 'do believe he's a genius!'* So far the world has experienced nothing of the kind, and billions of years ago those primeval cells were pretty well organized, if one considers that even then they contained the seed of future works such as this. You'll love it in September, as long as nothing gets in the way! So long my darling Gustav

* In ELM, Alma writes: 'It was concertmaster Walter of the St Petersburg orchestra who said to me in 1902, with reference to Mahler, "I do believe he's a genius!"'

311   Munich [21 June 1910]
                                                        Regina-Palast-Hotel

My Almschi,

After yesterday's sad letter, I'm worried not to have heard from you at all today. Are you concealing something from me? I keep sensing something between the lines.

Today was the full rehearsal of Part II. Here, too, 'the Lord (Mahler) looked on it, and saw that it was good'!*

Tomorrow the soloists arrive. On Sunday, all going well, I'll return to Toblach, unless you suddenly decide that I should come directly to Tobelbad, in which case I'd ask you to send a cable. – If you agree with my plan, please see to it that everything is ready for me when I arrive.

If necessary, send me the appropriate keys. I'll need access to my books and possibly my wardrobe. Please also arrange for plenty of good, fresh butter, as I eat more of that than anything else. I've already ordered everything else from Vienna. The coming week promises to make considerable demands on me. Hordes of people are milling around: Rosé with his quartet, R. Strauss with the [Vienna] Philharmonic, critics from all over the world etc. Lord knows how many visitors etc. I shall receive. Well, I'll try to make the best of it. But from now on I'm taking my meals in my room. With all this exertion, I simply must have peace and seclusion. Warmest greetings, my Almscherl. Write every day, even if it's just a card.

Your Gustav

The first paragraph of this letter reads like a premonition of coming events. Around this time, Mahler wrote to his mother-in-law: 'I'm so worried about Almschi's letters, which have such a curious ring to them. What's the trouble?'[8]

For the summer of 1910 Emil Gutmann had arranged a full-scale music festival, which opened in May with concerts to celebrate the 100th anniversary of the birth of Robert Schumann. From 23 to 28 June followed a Richard Strauss week, which included performances of Feuersnot, Salome *and* Elektra, *three concerts with the Vienna Philharmonic conducted by Felix Mottl, Ernst von Schuch and Strauss himself, and two chamber music matinées. On 24 June Arnold Rosé played the Strauss* Violin Sonata, *accompanied by the composer; the Rosé Quartet then joined with Ignacy Friedman in a performance of the* Piano Quartet op. 13. *Mahler attended Strauss's*

---

* Mahler had used the same biblical paraphrase on at least one previous occasion, namely in 1902 at a rehearsal of the *Third Symphony* in Cologne.

orchestral concert the following day, which ended with a performance of
Don Quixote. Writing for a newspaper in Breslau, Arthur Neisser later
recalled that Mahler had applauded wildly from his box.

312   Munich [23 (?) June 1910]
                                                    Regina-Palast-Hotel

Between two rehearsals, Almscherl (and today's a hectic day), I send you
these words of greeting. Today was the first orchestral rehearsal with
soloists. – Highly inadequate as the singers may be, the impression was over-
powering. After the rehearsal the orchestra went literally wild. –
Just imagine, as I entered the hall <u>Fried</u> and <u>Klemperer</u> came to pay their
respects. That was nice of them. On the other hand, when I got home I found
Arnold Rosé's visiting card (after all, he could have found out where I was
rehearsing). Now, at four o'clock, I'm going to have a meal (as usual), to
which I've invited Fried. We start again at six, and tomorrow morning the
children's chorus will be there too. All going well, I shall travel to Toblach on
Sunday, and expect to arrive there at about four o'clock. – While I'm there,
I solemnly swear not to pick up a single sheet of manuscript paper, but only
to eat, go for walks and, above all, <u>sleep</u>. In Munich I've been quite incapable
of the latter, due to the automobiles with their interminable hooting.
My publisher (Hertzka) is here too, and is as pleased as Punch.[*]
It sounds overwhelming, I assure you. Every note is in place, both high and
low. Greetings, my Almschi, your Gustav

<All I have ordered is <u>bread</u> and dried fruit. I left Mama to look after the
apples. I leave all the other commodities (caffeine-free Café Hag) to you. I
ordered the bread personally from Fritz the baker. – Everything else can wait
until you arrive – but if I'm not to die of boredom I'll need my <u>books</u> right
away.
If it looks as if I can't bear it on my own, I'll come straight from Toblach.
However, I believe it will do me a power of good to 'withdraw into myself'
for a while – (I've quite forgotten what it looks like in there). See to it that
the butter on Sunday is really of the <u>finest quality</u>.>

313[U] Telegram   Munich, 25 June [1910]

why no news   am very worried   please send express reply   all going very
well here   letter tomorrow gustav

[*] Orig.: 'freut sich wie ein Schneekönig'.

314^U Munich [26 June 1910]
Regina-Palast-Hotel

Dear Almscherl,
Fried is with me right now. He's been a great help. – I'm pretty exhausted (no heart problems). While conducting, I made such fiery gestures that I strained a muscle in my upper arm, and that has done little to improve my state of health. Tomorrow – thank God – I'll be leaving for the wonderful air of Toblach, where I intend to relax completely. No news from you for two days! Almschi, surely you could have managed a postcard, if nothing else. Just this brief greeting for today, my Almscherl   Your Gustav

Worried by Alma's long silence, Mahler suddenly changed his travel arrangements. On 27 June he took the train to Vienna, and from there he travelled on soon afterwards to Tobelbad.

315^U [Vienna, 28 June 1910]

Well, my Almscherl, just these few lines and then I'll be with you. – Everything's going fine, and tomorrow I'll be shot of it all. – I'm very pleased with the publishers. This time the work has been much easier and more agreeable than ever.
Here I found more encouraging news of you, thank heaven. In Munich I was beginning to feel very depressed. –
I'll be leaving in two days' time (Thursday) on the same train as we took last time (lunch in the dining car), and would ask you to send a car (just a small one) to collect me at the station. This time I'll take the precaution of not having my hair cut beforehand (I'll have to do it later, though, as I'm already looking rather shaggy). I can scarcely wait, my dearest, to hold you in my arms again. But I beg you, for heaven's sake, be reasonable! Don't expect any new symphonies from me. They have to come of their own, otherwise they won't come at all, or they'd be suites. I'll stay until Sunday, and after dinner I'll leave for Graz and head off for Toblach on the night train, which I've already booked. Then you'll be on your own again for a few days, but Mama will join you on Tuesday. That's the schedule, and it's well thought out. And now farewell, my Almschl, and 'be good to me' when I arrive. Your Gustl

Mahler's promise not to have his hair cut before meeting Alma is a reference to the summer of 1909, when the barber in Toblach had cut his hair so short that Alma almost failed to recognize him.
On 30 June Mahler left Vienna for Tobelbad, where he spent two days

with his family. To Anna Moll he sent a positive report on Alma's state of health: 'In just a few words, I found Almschi much fresher and sturdier, and I'm convinced that her treatment has done her a power of good.'⁹

Before returning to Toblach on 4 July, Mahler stopped off in Graz to meet two old friends and admirers, Ernst Decsey and Julius von Weis-Osborn (on 14 March the latter had conducted a performance of Das klagende Lied).

316 Postcard   Graz, 4 July 1910ᴾ

D.A., I arrived in pouring rain, and I'm leaving in pouring rain. D. and O. greeted me like a reception committee, and accompanied me triumphantly to the inn, where they thawed out appreciably. Their truly detailed knowledge of the Complete Works of Mahler was most endearing, and we took turns in singing themes from the symphonies and songs. We resolved to found a Mahler Society and put up several memorial plaques. So long! Write! G.

317ᵁ   [Toblach, 5 July 1910]

Dearest Almschili,
Our country cousins are all happily united.* As before, they like to cut their capers directly beneath my window (I'm sleeping in my old room, the one that's so incredibly cosy). As soon as I move into my shack in the woods, no doubt they'll follow me there. –
Downstairs on the ground floor is a fidgety little nipper who spends most of the day bawling his head off. –
Our happy Bibis† are inseparable villains who slink around and spend most of the day japing and making raucous noises. Ah, if only these yokels brought their children into the world as deaf-mutes! Country life would be such a joy! Apart from that, everything is wonderful here again, and suits me down to the ground. –
Dearest, I don't have:
   1) apples
   2) the big piano lamp
   3) the key to the small Wertheim safe
   4) my half-length socks
   – I don't know where they are.

---

* Orig.: 'Also die munteren Landbewohner sind wieder all vereint' (a favourite phrase of Mahler's, quoted from Auber's *La dame blanche*, to describe the implausible reunion in Act III of Weber's *Euryanthe*).
† cf. letter 269.

Carl passed through this morning and deposited his paintbox with me. He himself will be joining us in a week's time.

Not a word from you! Almschi, can't you find even five minutes for a postcard for me? – Today Rottenberg announced himself. – And yes, I almost forgot: we received a huge basket of eggs, vegetables, lettuces etc. from Krumpendorf (evidently from the Grünwalds), and a second one with <u>twenty</u> live chickens. – The two serving-maids have settled in very well. What a relief to be rid of Kathi. She was a real shocker. –

I had to cough up another 12 crowns for the Bachverein.* Enclosed are the receipts from Gerold and the Bachverein.

I trust that Mammerl has already joined you. That should make you feel better straight away! She'll pick you up, I know. Warmest greetings to you both from Gustav.

What's Gucki up to? You could at least send more news of her.

As in 1906, Mahler intended to spend several days resting, and had no plans to compose. Soon, however, circumstances beyond his control caused him to start work on a new symphony, his Tenth. *Some commentators have suggested that he had sketched out ideas for the work already in New York, but there is no evidence to support the idea.*

On 7 July Mahler celebrated his fiftieth birthday in virtual solitude at Toblach. Much to his annoyance the event brought forth a flood of 'meaningless telegrams and postcards', and he was occupied for several days with the writing of replies and acknowledgements.

318^U   [Toblach, 7 July 1910]

Dearest Almschi,

I was really delighted to receive your letter.

If I understand you correctly, Gucki has [an overproduction of] uric acid. But that's much too early in life for such a little mite, isn't it? What are you going to do about it? Can it be treated with a sensible diet? Whatever the case, I beg you: never make her eat anything against her will. Eating too much can also produce too much uric acid (and is perhaps the prime cause of it). Children know when they've had enough. – It's wonderful here, and I could be living in paradise were it not for the dreadful noise, which could easily make a misanthropist of me. When these people make conversation, it sounds like a flock of

---

* The Neue Bach-Gesellschaft. Mahler had been subscribing to the Bach Complete Edition since 1894.

overfed parrots. The mother with her rasping voice is particularly nauseating. – On the other hand, I know no other place that's so isolated yet so close to the outer world, so beautiful and so healthy. I've been taking quiet strolls on my own, reading, eating, walking, watching. My bodily functions are all in perfect order. The servants are marvellous. Agnes may be terribly stupid, but that doesn't bother me, because she's obedient and serves me only what I ask for. The heavens have been raining down volumes of Rosegger on us. Mammerl has again excelled herself. Actually I wanted to give her the books, but never mind, she can read them here instead – otherwise I would have had to read them in her home. – Please pass on my warmest thanks, also for her kind words. Her letter and yours were the only ones that gave me any pleasure. Despite all the bans and interdicts, I've been more or less inundated with meaningless telegrams and postcards. Be consoled with the knowledge that I feel far better today than I did ten years ago. This diet, which I shall continue to observe, has been my salvation. That's for certain, and you too should make no mistake about it. Dear Almschili, once again I beg you:

1. I URGENTLY need the key to the Wertheim strongbox!
2. the lamps
3. I can't find my half-length socks
4. I don't have any apples
5. The thermos-plate (with hot water, it would be of immense benefit to me). Where can I get one?

[One line obliterated; closing page missing].

319   [Toblach, 8 July 1910]

My Almscherl,
My fingers are sore from writing letters; so much had accumulated that couldn't be put off any longer. I'll tell you about it when you arrive.
Gucki's drawings are a sheer delight. They made me laugh until I cried. – The idea of the five parallels is no proof. If anything quite the opposite, namely that Hodler's imagination and artistic sense are still those of a child. Without wishing to criticize him, I would say: Hodler may be a towering artistic figure, but Gucki, with her delightfully childish imagination, cannot prove the point.
<Almscherl, I implore you, stay as long as you can. You're on the road to recovery, but if you suffer another relapse, make sure that you're still being cared for. – If you don't have the patience to hold out, I fear the summer will be disrupted, as it was last year. Now that Mammerl is with you, you're in good hands. Today the weather was fine for the first time. Every day I thank my lucky stars that you're not here.> I've been shivering like a greyhound,

like a snow hare or (if they don't shiver) like our friend Pollak.

Göhler's article about me is the best and finest I've ever read. – I'm returning it to you not for that reason, but because I noticed something else, which I've underlined in red. It's sublime! You simply must read it! One could explain it as genetic selection, survival of the fittest or whatever other term the academics may think up. But this is <u>my</u> territory! The creator spiritus, my dear! It's just as uplifting, indeed more so, than a Choral Symphony, a Missa [Solemnis] or an Eighth Symphony (arrogant fellow!).

Fondest greetings to you both. Thank Mammerl for the wonderful nuts, and tell her that the ones I brought from Munich are all rancid.   Your Gustav

<Of late, old Trenker's behaviour has been more smarmy* than you could ever imagine.>

In AMM1, Alma comments on the second paragraph of this letter by explaining, 'I had made a remark about Hodler's eurhythmics',[10] a reference to Hodler's painting Die Eurhythmie *(1895, now housed at the Museum Berne). Mahler met the celebrated Swiss painter in 1904, when his work was exhibited at the Vienna Secession.[11]*

George Göhler had published an appreciation of Mahler's music in the monthly periodical Die Musik. *A second essay of his followed shortly afterwards in* Der Kunstwart, *and he also contributed to a volume of collected essays edited by Paul Stefan.[12] The principal characteristic of Mahler's music, according to Göhler (in his first article), was that its starting point was 'the sound, the individual note, and not an idea or a programme. His music does not depict or paint superficial things, it aims neither for artistic or technical effect, but is content merely to sound and, purely through these sounds, to awaken the same feelings in a sympathetic listener as were present in the mind of its creator when he wrote them down.' Göhler claimed that musical taste had been perverted by 'sexual abnormalities' and 'theatrical bombast', with the result that it was becoming ever harder to hear the human message in Mahler's music. Listeners perverted in this way 'cannot understand that in Mahler's music all inner sensation and experience is directly connected to extraneous forces, and that each and every detail is a reflection of higher, universal things'. On 9 January 1913 Göhler was the first to conduct the definitive version of Mahler's* Fifth Symphony.

Unfortunately the copy of Die Musik *enclosed with Mahler's letter has not been preserved. Hence it is impossible to establish what it was that he 'underlined in red' as a mark of disdain and disagreement.*

---

* Orig.: 'So was von Schmierampel'.

320^U   [Toblach, 9 July 1910]

Dearest Almschi,
Another two days without word from you! I simply don't understand it.
The weather here is lousy. If it goes on like this, it will be quite unsuitable for
Gucki. Unfortunately you haven't answered my questions. Hence it would
make no difference if I were to add that Agnes tells me we're running out of
coffee (Café Hag). Both our doñas seem to think that caffeine-free living is
good for the system.
I'm very satisfied with them both, by the way. They are willing and attentive.
Rottenberg, poor devil, is evidently bored in Landro, so sometimes he comes
over to see me. I don't blame him, but it does disrupt.
The isolation here is really heavenly. – Currently I'm exchanging sharply
worded letters with New York. We're having quite a spat, and unfortunately
it's been taking up a good deal of my time. I'll show you all the papers when
you arrive. – There's a long letter from [Lilli] Lehmann and another one from
[Lilly] Lieser.* I'll keep everything until you get here. I'm sending you
Bodanzky's article merely to show that enthusiasm and good will can inspire
even a musician to literary flights, and move even illiterates to quoting in
Latin.† You could do better, Almscherl, write more, answer my questions
[four words obliterated], 'be nice to me'. Warmest greetings to Mama.
Your Gustav

[on a separate sheet of paper:] Pollack coming to Tobelbad.

*Mahler's 'sharply worded' exchange of letters with New York concerned his
fee for the twenty additional concerts he had agreed to conduct during the
coming season. His contract had stipulated a maximum of forty-five concerts; now he was insisting on an extra $25,000, while the committee was
offering only $20,000. The dispute was settled later in the year, when a com-
promise was reached at $23,000.*

321^U   [Toblach, 10 July 1910]

Dearest,
The last three days have been anxious ones for me. – I don't understand why
you can't summon up the energy to send me another card. If I felt like
expressing resentment and had the heart to do so, I'd stop writing to you

---

* Lilly Lieser-Landau, widow of a prosperous industrialist and a patron of the arts. Later she
also offered financial support to Schoenberg.
† The article by Bodanzky was published in the Prague German-language newspaper *Bohemia*.

altogether. But how should one react towards such a 'woman-child'? Write and put up with it. You still haven't told me where the keys to the Wertheim strongbox are. And it's so important to me. Now please, let me know the day and time of your arrival. Trenker needs to know too, because of the carriage. You're bound to reply to that.

Carl has still not arrived, and I've heard nothing from him. Two letters for him from Mama arrived today. Yesterday I received an unexpected message from [Julius] Korngold, requesting an interview for the Neue Freie Presse. I answered him very precisely.

The children are very noisy here. Judging by the intolerable din, the youngest appears to be being weaned on sauerkraut and pork meat. These beasts need a good hiding. Even new-born calves are treated better. But there's plenty of other noise and commotion. The two toddlers, sweet and adorable as they may be, drive me to distraction with their strange babbling and noisy games. At least if Gucki were here I could laugh with one eye and cry with the other.

Mend your ways! Kisses to all from   Gustav

322^U News cutting   Toblach, 14 July 1910^P

This article was written by Carl. He said I should send it to you.

The article, published in early July, was about the memorial to Kaiserin Elisabeth ('Sisi'), in the Vienna Stadtpark, which was unveiled on 4 June 1907.

Shortly after arriving in Tobelbad, Alma had made the acquaintance of Walter Gropius, a young architect who was also taking the waters there. In the few weeks they spent together, he and Alma fell in love. In the original English version of her memoirs, And the Bridge Is Love, *Alma gives the following account of the affair:*

In the sanatorium I lived completely withdrawn, as always when I was alone somewhere. Barefoot, clothed in a horrible nightgown, I meekly took the out-door exercise in rain and wind that was the hallmark of the therapeutic faith adhered to at this institution. I lived on its lettuce-and-buttermilk diet, which made my little girl sick to her stomach. I bathed conscientiously in the hot springs – although the very first time I promptly fainted and had to be carried back to bed.

The German doctor in charge of the place prescribed dancing! Well, it made more sense than the boiling baths. Feeling responsible for me and worried by my despondency and loneliness, he introduced young men to me; one was an extraordinarily handsome German who would have been well cast as Walther von Stolzing in Die Meistersinger.

We danced. Gliding slowly around the room with the youth, I heard that he was an architect and had studied with one of my father's well-known friends.*
We stopped dancing and talked.

Soon there remained no doubt that young Walter Gropius was in love with me and expected me to love him in return. I would have treasured his friendship; I felt that it could have been a more beautiful friendship than any I had known – but now I left Tobelbad.[13]

Alma returned to Toblach some time after 15 July. The narrative continues in a slightly modified version, as published in AML:

Mahler met me at the railway station [. . .]. He was fonder of me than ever. Maybe the love of that young artist had helped me regain my self-assurance, for I felt happier and more optimistic, but I had no intention of embarking on anything new. About a week later came a letter, in which he [Gropius] wrote that he could not live without me, and that if I felt the slightest affection for him I should drop everything and return to him. The letter, though intended for me, was clearly addressed to 'Herr Direktor Mahler'. It has never been ascertained whether this young man had erred in the heat of the moment, or whether it was indeed his subconscious wish that the letter should fall into Mahler's hands.[14]

Having parted in Tobelbad, the two lovers continued to exchange passionate letters, with Gropius sending his, at Alma's insistence, to Toblach poste restante. Since it could scarcely have been his intention to write the wrong address on the envelope – 'Villa Trenker' or 'Alt Schluderbach', rather than 'Postlagernd Toblach' – his alleged error must in fact have been deliberate. Whatever the case, the consequences, as Alma relates, were dramatic:

During an excursion, I spotted the young man hiding under a bridge. Later he told me he had been in the neighbourhood for quite some time, hoping to meet me and persuade me to answer his letter. My heart was in my mouth, not for joy but for fright. I told Mahler at once, and he said, 'I'll go and get him.' He walked down to Toblach, found him and said simply, 'Come!' Meanwhile night had fallen. They walked all the way without exchanging a word, Mahler leading the way with a lantern, the other following. The night

---

* Gropius studied in Munich with Peter Behrens, whom Alma had met when visiting the artists' colony at Darmstadt in May 1900. On that occasion she travelled with her stepfather, Carl Moll.

was pitch-dark. I had stayed in my room. Mahler came to me with a very grave expression on his face. After much hesitation, I went to him [Gropius] . . . I interrupted our brief conversation after a few minutes, because suddenly I feared for Mahler. He was pacing up and down his room. Two candles were burning on the table. He was reading the bible. He said, 'Whatever you decide, you will be doing the right thing.' But I had no option! I may have grown despondent over the years at the rapid passing of my youth, but there had never been any question for me of a life without Mahler, least of all of a life with another man. [. . .] Mahler had always been the centre of my universe.

Alma wrote to Gropius:

I have to make up my mind. In my marriage I am experiencing something utterly unimaginable, namely that love is so infinite that if I remain with him – despite all that has occurred – he will live, and if I leave him he will die.[15]

She may have resolved not to leave Mahler, but it soon became clear that she also had no intention of abandoning Gropius. Ultimately she decided that both men were essential to her. After eight years of 'enforced asceticism', a young and handsome lover had become a necessity.

When Gropius left the house that night, Mahler accompanied him to the boundary of the estate. Before leaving Toblach, the young architect sent him a further letter: 'Unfortunately we found so very little to say to each other. It pains me to think that my behaviour was so offensive. Permit me at least to thank you for the dignified manner in which you treated me, and to extend my hand to you for one last time.' Alma went on corresponding with Gropius, but urged him to be cautious and to send his replies either to Toblach poste restante, as before, or to her mother (though Anna Moll had always been very close to her son-in-law, she was perfectly willing to serve as go-between). Alma's letters to Gropius burn with passion: 'I know that I am living for the moment when I can be utterly and completely yours,' she wrote. She calls herself 'Your wife' and adds: 'My Walter, I want to be the mother of your child, I want to lavish all my attention on that child until we can fall into each other's arms, joyously and for evermore, in security and without scruples.' Gropius's letters (of which several first drafts have survived) are just as ardent, but perhaps more controlled.

It would appear that Mahler was in fact not deceived, but would never openly admit to his knowledge. However, there were times when it must have been hard for him to feign ignorance. In October 1910, for instance, when he and Alma were due to cross the Atlantic, he agreed to travel alone to

Cuxhaven, where he had no commitments of any kind, leaving Alma free to meet Gropius in Munich and travel with him to Paris. There she spent several days with him before joining her husband at Cherbourg. Mahler would scarcely have made such an arrangement had he not been party to Alma's affair.

And so he ruefully accepted his wife's infidelity, provided that it was never made public, and, above all, that she did not leave him. For days and nights after the meeting with Gropius in Toblach he was haunted by the fear of losing her. Already during their engagement their age difference had aroused feelings of guilt in him. These same feelings now grew so acute as to drive him to distraction. Evidence of this pathological condition is provided by a frantic protestation of love and despair that he scribbled onto the manuscript of the Tenth Symphony. *Terrified that Alma might leave him, Mahler required constant reassurance of her physical presence, as she recounts:*

Up in the night. He stood before me in the dark. I started as if I had seen a ghost. From now on, at mealtimes I had to fetch him from his shack. I did so with great caution, for he was afraid of losing me, afraid he had already lost me. And often, in his hyper-anxious state, he would lie on the ground in his shack, weeping. Like that, he explained, he felt closer to the earth.[16]

A note from the Komponierhäuschen, *where Mahler 'lay prostrate', repeats the epithet 'my lyre-play' (Mein Saitenspiel) that he had written into the short score of his new symphony:*

323   [Toblach, August 1910]^E

My darling, my lyre-play,
I am possessed by dark spirits; they have cast me to the ground. Come and dispel them. Abide by me, my rod and staff. Come soon today, that I may rise up. Here I lie prostrate and await you; and silently I ask whether I may still hope for salvation, or whether I am to be damned.

Mahler sought desperately to show his love and expiate the neglect of which Alma had accused him. He took the unpremeditated step of dedicating the score of the Eighth Symphony *to her. He also 'discovered' her Lieder and persuaded Hertzka to publish them. Sometimes she found little notes from him on her writing desk or her bedside table. And then there were his poems, reproduced here* (faute de mieux) *in the same order as they appear in AMM.*

375

Embedded in these effusive verses are small but incontrovertible clues to the progress of the new work. The first dated poem (letter 329) reads as a general declaration of intent: 'Let me condense the tremors of my yearning, / Th' eternity of bliss divine in your embrace, / Into one great song.' As yet, however, Mahler had not yet experienced the moment of intuition, akin to the 'sound of oars plying through water' which had inspired the opening of the Seventh Symphony: 'The time has come, the quill is in my hand – / Yet the idea continually eludes me.' His next poem (letter 330) stresses that the igniting spark will grow from pain, which only the creative act can assuage: 'Spring up, o life-force, from my wounds again!' By the time he pens the poem of letter 325, the long-awaited flame of inspiration has been kindled: the tone is now jubilant, 'the notes fly high'.

324   [Toblach, August 1910]^E

Beloved,
I slept wonderfully, but not for a moment did my senses slumber. Never again, I believe, shall I lack that blissful certainty: <u>she loves me!</u>
These words are my life's essence. If I may no longer speak them, I am dead.
– Today, when I come, you will not be there. How I long to see you and take you in my arms. You, my dearest, most dearly beloved. – Like stars, your*
dear songs, blissful heralds of your divine being, shall illuminate my heaven, until the sun of my life shines in my firmament once again.

325 [written on manuscript paper]   [Toblach, August 1910]^E

Fairest, dearest one,
My lyre-play,
My storm-song,
You wondrous being! What music could I write
Whose words conveyed to you my mortal plight?
My breath, my very being is not mine!
No longer one, my self and I are driven forth –
And find no rest in heaven nor on earth,
Until they've slaked their thirst with your sweet wine.

The springtime forced itself on our alliance,
I yielded instantly, without defiance.
I died – how gladly – and its kiss restored my life.

* Orig.: 'My dear songs': evidently a slip of the pen.

376

The notes fly high, my heart beats quicker –
The words, like wedding candles, burn and flicker –
My very being flows to you, my wife.

326   [Toblach, August 1910]^E

Breath of my life,
I smothered your slippers in kisses and stood longingly at your door. You
took mercy on me, glorious woman, but once again, my dearest, the demons
have punished me for putting my own interests before yours. I cannot stir
from your doorstep, and would stay here until I can hear the sweet sound of
your breathing. – But I must! My princess has sent me down and away.*
Bless you, my love [three words obliterated] – for what you have granted me
– my heart beats only for you.

327^U [Toblach, August 1910]

Don't come for me today, because it's raining too hard, and your dear feet
would get wet. But if you do come – wear galoshes!

328   [Toblach, August 1910]^E

My Almschilitzili,
If you feel like it, stay in bed today – it's the best place to take it easy. I'll sit
at your bedside and stay with you all day. Shall bring something to read.
My Almschilitzilitzilitzi! Remember what you told me yesterday and repeat
it to me today.

329 [written on manuscript paper]   [Toblach,] 17 August 1910

For my dearest one,
My absent, omnipresent friend:
The time has come, the quill is in my hand –
Yet the idea continually eludes me.
To me the staves are like some desert land,
Their five straight lines a mirage that deludes me.
For still I am as dazzled by that light
Which shone on me at Aphrodite's sight.

---

* Orig.: 'hinunter'. The path from the Trenkerhof to the *Komponierhäuschen* has a slight
downward incline (cf. Rothkamm, *op. cit.*).

No matter what my heart desires or sings,
My senses rove and wander without aim.
My longing to that creature ever wings
Whose mouth so sweet breathed life into my frame.

Let me condense the tremors of my yearning,
Th' eternity of bliss divine in your embrace,
Into one great song that, like the sun a-burning,
Illuminates the beauty of your face.

From deepest depths that fairest form disclosing,
It sinks aflame upon the nuptial bed.
In you I'd find, as once in my composing,
A place to quench desire and rest my head.

330   [Toblach, 17 August 1910]^E

O sweetest hand that ever held me,
O dearest bond with which you weld me,
Take me but captive in your sensual clasp,
That as your slave I ne'er may flee your grasp.

O come to me sweet death in this, my hour of pain!
Spring up, o life-force, from my wounds again!

By the middle of August it had become clear that Mahler was in need of psychiatric assistance. Richard Nepallek therefore arranged for him to consult Sigmund Freud, who happened to be on holiday in Holland. Mahler deferred the appointment several times, which Freud rightly interpreted as itself being a symptom of the patient's neurosis. Finally he let it be known that he would soon be leaving for Sicily, and that a meeting would have to take place at once or not at all. Reluctantly, Mahler set out from Toblach on 25 August on the long journey to Leiden. From each stopover he sent something to Alma: three telegrams in all, and a poem.

331^U Telegram   Franzensfeste, 25 August 1910
                                                    2.42 [p.m.]

fondest greetings my dear ones   feeling well and thinking only of seeing you
again   I long for it as if I had been gone for days   gustav

332 Telegram   Innsbruck, 25 August 1910
                                                              6.35 [p.m.]

all my good and evil spirits are with me   you the victor rule us all   good
night my lyre-play   I feel only happiness and longing

333 Telegram   Cologne, 26 August 1910
                                                              1.30 [p.m.]

feeling constantly well   perfectly normal   nostalgic journey down the rhine
in search of lost happiness   every second spent with you returns to life here
the last two words of your telegram open new horizons   your gustav

*The operative words of Mahler's next poem seem to be those which open the
third verse, 'God gave me the gift to speak of my sorrow'. As a creative artist
he was in a position to translate sorrow into sound. Hence he possessed a
safety valve which protected him against the destructive potential of his inner
self.*

334   Amsterdam, 26 August 1910[P]

And far away those visions still are shining,
A shroud of grey obscures the picture-hall.
I weep for long-lost years, my soul is pining,
My heart grows still as recollections pall.

'Turmoil infernal – anguish unending' –
Friends on life's voyage, memories revered,
Harden the soul into iron unbending,
Show how to healing a pathway is cleared.

God gave me the gift to speak of my sorrow –
What bliss that my parting is but for the morrow.
One heart is still mine, and it throbs homeward-bound.
'O Heavenly turmoil – love – and almost no wound!'

Dearest,
I wanted to wire this to you, but now realize it would make no sense, so I'll
send it by post instead. My one and only beloved, your Gustav

335^U Telegram   Leiden, 26 August 1910
                                                                    7.40 [p.m.]*

just arrived   feeling quite all right   have written from the train   expect no
cable because too late after the meeting   more tomorrow   your gustav

*In AMM4 Alma summarizes Mahler's interview with Freud,[17] held during a
long afternoon walk in the streets of Leiden. Freud, it seems, told Mahler not
to worry unduly about his age, because it had in fact attracted Alma, who
had been in need of a mature man to replace her father. Mahler, on the other
hand, identified Alma with his mother; when he married her, he wished that
she had already 'suffered' and seen more of life. To his disciples Freud later
confirmed that the interview had indeed revealed Mahler's mother-fixation
(Mutterbindung), also that he was amazed by the composer's intuitive grasp
of the mechanisms of psychoanalysis. Mahler's first telegram to Alma, on his
way back to Toblach, shows that Freud had at least partly helped him to
recover his mental and emotional equilibrium.*

336^U Telegram   Leiden, 27 August [1910]
                                                                    8.48 [a.m.]

feeling cheerful   interesting discussion   motes swollen to planks   ready to
depart for Toblach   exact arrival time tomorrow   please cable sunday morning sleeper train 633 from cologne   your gustav

337^U Telegram   Emmerich, 27 August 1910
                                                                    12.51 [p.m.]

small mistake in last telegram   should be train 118   fondest greetings

338 Telegram   Cologne, 27 August [1910]
                                                                    4.23 [p.m.]

decided to take the later train   strolled for 2 hours   visited old haunts   as if
it all happened only yesterday   can scarcely believe it   going through it all
over again   hope to find a dear message tomorrow morning   your gustav

---

* Time of transmission.

*The last poem of this group not only muses on the outcome of the meeting
with Freud, but also reveals something of the motivation behind that grind-
ingly dissonant nine-note chord (the so-called 'cry of pain') with which
Mahler built shattering climaxes in the opening adagio and the finale of the
Tenth Symphony: 'In one single chord my hesitant notions / Converge with
the power of searing emotions.' The words 'ich starb der Welt' in the last line
allude again, as so often in Mahler's later letters, to the Rückert song* Ich bin
der Welt abhanden gekommen.[18]

339   [in the train] 27 August 1910

In the train on my return journey

> The nightmare's dispelled by force of persuasion,
> Dispersed are the torments of self-contemplation,
> In one single chord my hesitant notions
> Converge with the power of searing emotions.
>
> 'I love you!': three words that support and maintain me,
> Life's melody rising from sorrow and pain.
> O love me! – three words that I know, that sustain me,
> The bass-note to each and to every refrain.
>
> 'I love you!': three words that remain what I live for.
> With joy will I forfeit the world all around.
> O love me! – you that tempests blew ashore!
> Bless me – dead to the world – my haven found.

*Freud may have identified the cause of Mahler's neurosis, but he could do
nothing to alter the cruel situation in which his patient found himself. Now
that Mahler's thoughts centred more strongly than ever on Alma, his fear of
losing her remained obsessive. 'He attempted to propitiate her,' writes the
psychoanalyst Stuart Feder, 'as if she were some capricious goddess whose
decree could be favourably influenced by giving up burnt offerings'[19] – all the
more so since her efforts to conceal her passionate infatuation with Gropius
cannot have been very successful.*

*When Mahler left Toblach for the final rehearsals and world première of the
Eighth Symphony in Munich, Alma accompanied him to the station. On alight-
ing from the buggy, she experienced a series of trivial mishaps which provoked
considerable mirth amongst the bystanders. Having sent her a brief, sarcastic
telegram while changing trains at Innsbruck, on the second leg of his journey*

Mahler retold the story in doggerel rhymes quite different from his effusive verses of the previous weeks and days.

340[U] Telegram   Innsbruck, 3 September 1910
                                                              6.35 [p.m.]

shaken by the catastrophe but accepting my fate with manly composure whiled away the time with philosophical contemplation in the dining car fondest greetings gustav

341   [in the train to Munich, 3 September 1910]

On a tedious train journey – as in past times!

> My love sits beside me – it fills me with pride
> To be riding to town with my wife at my side!

> The sunshine laughs down on us both, oh how pretty!
> My heart is aglow with a sweet little ditty.

> Our journey's just ending when something disturbs it:
> A face flushes coyly, a grimace perturbs it.

> Her hat's lost its moorings, it flies, it is grounded!
> The lackeys all laugh, and my sweetheart's confounded.

> O shame! To the loneliest closet away!
> For where one derides her, she never will stay.

> New calamities follow, the shock never ceases:
> Her stocking is laddered, her skirt full of creases.

> Her eyes are a-flow now, the waterfall gushes.
> The nobler her anguish, the deeper my blushes.

> What's to do? Let's remove to the furthest compartment,
> Where officials protect us from theft and bombardment.

> Comes a fellow and asks: 'Is it this, ma'am, you seek?'
> The bystanders snigger and sneer – what a cheek.

> Most wretched of hats, for this I must scold you:
> A Wanderer found and yet wished not to hold you.

> Though I'm brave, at such scenes I'd prefer not to linger,
> Were it not for the ring that I wear on my finger.

There's no doubt that I love her with joy and elation,
But in future I'll go on my own to the station.

My beloved,
I'll be arriving in half an hour, so I have to bid you good night. This train is a frightful boneshaker. But even if my thoughts are agitated from tip to toe, there's one that predominates at all times, for my every thought is one and the same: always of you, my beloved! Good night, my Almschili. Have you got some dear gift for me? And what are you up to? Your
Gustav

Greetings to my dearest Mama
Make your day your gift to me.

The concluding (prose) passage of letter 341 was not available to the editors of the German edition, and is published here for the first time.
   Having arrived in Munich, Mahler immediately wrote two short letters.

342[U]   Munich, 3 September 1910[P]

Good morning, my beloved!
I found the enclosed quite by chance and was so struck by it that I've cut it out for you to read over breakfast. –
In my present state, wherever I look I keep finding answers to that one central question.
But it's curious that Bahr, of all people, should be able to explain something to me. It reminds me of Pythia: a foolish woman sitting in clouds of vapour uttering nonsensical remarks which wise men interpret as pearls of wisdom. O my girl, my sweetest girl! How I long for you!

Hermann Bahr's essay in the Neue Freie Presse, *entitled 'Unser Goethe',*[20] *elaborates on the theme of the transience of an artist's works as opposed to the perpetuity of his existence. Mahler himself had expounded on this topic to Erica Conrat in July 1904 (cf. pp. 175–6) and again to Alma the previous summer (letter 274): 'The "works" of man [...] are that part of him which is fleeting and perishable; whereas what a man creates of his own person, what his restless striving and vitality combine to make him, is that part of him which survives'. Bahr's essay echoes and expands this very idea: 'How trifling everything would appear', he writes, 'if only that part of a creative artist's achievement were valid of which he himself was conscious.' He cites the case of a young friend who had been contemplating suicide but desisted upon hearing a gramophone record of a particular song. This leads him to muse on the untold possibilities opened up through the new medium of recorded sound: 'Today we can scarcely measure the extent to which technology will guarantee us this entirely worldly kind of immortality.' Returning to the topic of Goethe, he concludes that 'a hundred years later, it is not the achievement of a creative artist that makes him an influence on all spiritual and earthly life, but his very existence'.*

As soon as he had settled down in Munich, Mahler wrote to Alma at greater length. In his next letters he sometimes speaks of himself as a schoolboy (Gymnasiast). The word involuntarily recapitulates his first letter to Alma (letter 3), in which he had confessed that he would be 'counting the hours like a schoolboy' until he saw her again.* But these documents also reveal the state of submission and emotional regression into which he had been plunged by Alma's reproaches and his fear of losing her.

343   Munich, 4 September 1910
                                        Grand Hotel Continental

Well, my beloved Almscherl, I've finished with the humdrum part (sleep, breakfast etc.), and now follows something far more enjoyable: translating my thoughts – which flutter unceasingly around your dear, blonde locks – into words. But if this is to be more than a mere schoolboy's essay, I must give myself a jolt and tell you the whole story. – And that, my dear, is what I'd like you to do too. Never fail to recount to me every detail of your daily round; every little sneeze, every ham roll is of interest to me. – Well then: once I'd sent off the express letter and the telegram from Innsbruck, the journey grew tedious. Until then, like an enamoured cockerel,[†] I was blind and deaf to the outside world. But later I realized I had spent too much time sitting down, so I warmed myself up a bit. – I was met by Gutmann, who was as kind and obliging as ever. He tells me that the first concert is bound to be sold out. At the hotel I found the vocal scores with the dedication, and hope that Hertzka has had the good sense to send a copy to Toblach as well. – It really was strange and stimulating to see that <u>dear</u>, <u>sweet</u> name on the title page, for all the world to read – like a joyful confession. How gladly I would have it graven onto every one of my vocal scores.[‡] But that too would be a schoolboy's way of doing

---

[*] In letter 3 Mahler describes himself as a *Junge* (boy, youth); here and subsequently he uses the more specific *Gymnasiast*, for which the nearest equivalent would be grammar-school boy (UK) or high-school boy (USA).

[†] Orig.: 'wie der verliebte Auerhahn'.

[‡] Orig.: 'Ach, ich schnitt es gern in alle Clavierauszüge ein' (allusion to *Ungeduld*, the seventh song of Schubert's *Die schöne Müllerin*: 'Ich schnitt es gern in alle Rinden ein').

things. And I want the world to take this seriously, I want people to realize that this is more than just a lover's fancy. This all reads like a marriage announcement, doesn't it? – Unfortunately I didn't sleep too well – four hours at the most – and all the while I was thinking of that perfumed bed and of how sorely I missed the comforting sound of gentle breathing that enlivens my nights like the ticking of a favourite clock. I even think I heard you calling out, 'Gustav'. How gladly I would have leapt out of bed to respond. Today my throat is sore and a little inflamed, but I'll take good care of myself, for when I return to my Lady and Saviour I want to be feeling fresh and healthy. Almschili, all these words seem so superfluous: just three would suffice, and I could write them, speak them, sing them over and over! My love, would that you could spend just half an hour every Sunday afternoon sharing in that sense of delight and sorrow which fills my entire days and nights with sighs!

It was so sweet this morning: when I woke up (at 4.30 a.m.), the first thing to catch my eye was that sparkling little ring – I kissed it and revelled in the solace it has given me during these days of separation. You know, if you had made me a present of it, it would have given me no pleasure. But the chance to wear a ring from your own finger means so much to me. Almschili, have you lived down your mishap at the railway station?

Gutmann is collecting me at ten o'clock, because I'd like to hear the final rehearsal of the Choral Symphony.[*] Maybe I'll skip the concert and go to bed at nine o'clock. My rehearsals start tomorrow. If only I had some news from you! Fondest greetings, my dear ones. My beloved, I long for a dear word from you. Your Gustav

Look at the supplement. Isn't it nice of them to build a new road for us![†]

In AML Alma wrote: 'When we got engaged, Mahler said, "Most people have the tastelessness to exchange rings, but surely you have as little desire to do so as I?"'[21] In view of this, it seems odd that Mahler should write of the 'sparkling little ring' that Alma gave him before he set off for Munich.

344[U]   Munich [4 (?) September 1910]
                                                      Grand Hotel Continental
                                                             <u>second letter</u>

Dearest,

I'm enclosing a letter addressed to you, which I opened by mistake. – Altogether, there's a good deal of post – but not a word from my Almscherl.

---

[*] The conductor was Ferdinand Löwe, of whom Mahler held no particularly high opinion.
[†] The 'supplement' has not been preserved.

It makes me so sad.

Alma had evidently understood Mahler's telegram from Innsbruck (letter 340) not as a joke, but as something more alarming:

345[U] Telegram   Munich, 4 September [1910]
                                                                    12.55

was only a joke   hope my letter and telegram made this clear   fondest greetings gustav

346   Munich [5 September 1910]
                                                   Grand Hotel Continental

But Almschilitzilitzilitzili!
What on earth did you read into that wretched telegram? Surely you must have realized it was a joke? How could I of all people have ever meant such bombastic nonsense seriously? You've blown the whole thing up into a giant balloon, so please deflate it and let it fall. – But now let me tell you about yesterday. Just imagine: when I checked in at the hotel I was feeling a little feverish, but the following morning (while writing to you, in fact) it got worse. I took fright, went straight back to bed and sent for a doctor (all because of the coming week). His examination revealed that my whole throat was inflamed and that the right-hand side was coated with a whitish layer of pus. – It came as a terrible shock, and immediately I called for them to swathe me in blankets, so I could sweat it out. The doctor didn't want to swab my throat, but instead prescribed a wonderful disinfectant, which would work brilliantly for you too: half a tablet every half hour (it's only been in use in Germany for a year or so). – I had to mobilize the whole hotel staff to get my blankets etc.; at the same time I sent for Gutmann and told him that I needed nursing. For three hours I lay prone, sweating profusely. Several times Gutmann had to mop my face and brow with a towel.
Oh, how fervently was I hoping for a sign of life from my saviour! But nothing arrived, until finally I received your 'stunned' telegram, which drove me to despair for fear of having unintentionally upset my dear Almschili. – Finally, in the afternoon, came the second telegram, which left me with no idea of how my dearest was feeling. Gutmann had to leave and attend to business, so I spent the afternoon in the most abject state and horribly alone. – When the doctor returned in the evening he observed a slight improvement. I spent the night[U] peacefully, and when I awoke today the fever had subsided. I ate a healthy breakfast, the doctor arrived and found me in far better shape, so he

gave his permission for the rehearsal. Don't worry, my Almscherl, I'll take the greatest care of myself, and by the time you arrive I'll be fit and well. But still no dear letter from you, which makes me so anxious. Without the sight of your dear eyes and the sound of your sweet voice, life is not worth living. And evidently you have no need of me at all, for otherwise you would have written. It's one thing to read a message written by the young lady in the telegraph office, but quite another to see one written in your own dear hand.

By the way, I've discovered something very strange. You know, whenever I was far away I used to sit at my writing desk thinking of you, just as now and with the same sense of longing. Freud is quite right: this utter dependence on you has always been latent in me, you have always been my light and the centre of my universe. Admittedly, the inner light that shines over us all, and the consciousness of sanctity – no longer diminished by inhibitions – heightens these sensations infinitely. What torment, what pain that you can no longer reciprocate them. But just as love always engenders love, fidelity always wins through to fidelity, and as long as Eros remains the master of men and gods, I too shall succeed in winning back what was once mine, in regaining the heart that once beat for me and can indeed be united only with mine [one line obliterated] on its journey towards God and serenity. –

Dearest, I had to interrupt my writing for five minutes. Fried has just returned and is sitting here again. But don't worry, I'm being very nice to him. He means so well – and at rehearsal he'll be of great service to me. – I've also just received the express delivery from Carl. So, dear Almschili, you needn't worry about me. Like Endymion or other figures from the 'age of opulence', I shall make it my business to frequent the restaurants and night clubs, even at the railway station. And no 'tragic catastrophe' shall force me to assume poses of 'manly composure' or indeed of 'philosophical serenity'. – Gutmann has just arrived with the reception committee, and the room is full of people.

And now farewell, breath of my life. – If only people realized how little all this means to me!

Greetings to our dear Mama   Your Gustav

347 Telegram   Munich, 5 September 1910
                                                                4.30 [p.m.]

just received your two dear letters   they make me happy and fill my whole day with sunshine   warmest thanks to you my dearest   your gustav

348   Munich [5 September 1910]
                                                        Grand Hotel Continental

Beloved, madly beloved Almschili,

Believe me, I'm wasting away for love of you. I haven't lived since one
o'clock last Saturday. Thank heaven for your two dear letters, which have
just arrived. Now I can breathe again. For half an hour I was in seventh
heaven. But now I can bear it no longer! If you stay away for another
whole week, it will be my death. Your two letters were so sweet – so
delightful. They told me something you never ever said to me. Repeat those
words often, that I may renew my belief in them over and over. – Today
was the first rehearsal. It went well, and my 'corpus' held out valiantly.
Whenever I interrupted, I instinctively turned round and tried to imagine
how lovely it would have been if my goddess were sitting in the stalls,
where I could glance unobtrusively across and catch a glimpse of that
sweet face. – Then I would understand the purpose of my life and the cause
of all my strivings.

The enclosed letter has just arrived.* I'm forwarding it to you for curiosity's
sake. What nitwits they are! – As if I had time to respond to all their ques-
tionnaires. I wouldn't dream of it. I'm inundated with paperwork, and it's all
going straight into the waste bin. Why has this numbskull arrived in Munich
so far ahead of time?

Yesterday afternoon, before I lay down to sweat, in came old Hirth. The
poor devil looks terribly old and scrawny now. He appears to have abandoned his pose of youthfulness, and when he sat down he cut such a sorry
figure that I felt quite scared. I murmured something about a virulent
infection, whereupon he turned whiter still, and soon he was gone. Peace
and quiet was thus restored, and my thoughts turned to the light of my
life. – And that's what I'm in need of at the moment. – If you can't be here,
at least I need to think about you or write to you. Almschili, if you had
left me at the time, I would simply have been snuffed out, like a candle
starved of air. When will you be arriving, dear heart? And how are you all
getting on? Please write and tell me. – As you know, I am a schoolboy at
heart, but a trace of the paterfamilias, husband, or whatever you prefer to
call it, still remains, and that part of me wishes for news of my dearest and
of all my dear ones! But your letter should open with the salient point,
which must fill the first three pages: that you love me, my dearest love.
Then on page four I'll need to know what you have been up to and how

---

* The enclosure has not been preserved.

you are feeling. At four o'clock I have my second rehearsal. I'm longing for you! Longing! Longing!

<u>As ever</u>, your Gustav

349   Munich [5 September 1910]
                                                            Grand Hotel Continental

My beloved,

So here I am again! The afternoon rehearsal is over – closing scene – every note addressed to you. I found it terribly exciting, as if I were at your bedside again – during those wonderful days – and recounting everything to you. – Oh, how wonderful it is to love. And only now do I know what it means. Pain loses its power and death its sting. How right Tristan is when he says, 'I am immortal – for how could Tristan's love ever die?'* I shall spend the evening quietly again. I'm all but restored to health, and have eaten a hearty meal. When my darling arrives I want to be in fine fettle. I can think of nothing but that moment: 'Is it true? Are you mine again? Can it be true? At last! At last!'† If only I knew when to expect you. Tomorrow is Tuesday. I thought that was when you wanted to arrive.

I've just received a postcard from Gustav Frank telling me that he's in Munich and would like to see me. Please write and tell me if you'd like me to sleep in the spare room, and Gucki with you, or what <u>other</u> scheme you might have thought out. You see, I'd like to fix up our little love-nest before you arrive. <The package of clothes from Carl has already arrived. What an incredibly prompt and dependable man he is!>

Our rooms here are very pleasant and unbelievably quiet. It's the first time I've visited Munich and been able to sleep at night. The windows actually open onto an inner courtyard of sorts. However, just to be sure that Almschi, dear heart, doesn't get upset, I've also booked a small salon overlooking the street, where we can dine and receive our guests.

If only for that reason, I'd like to know exactly when you're arriving, so that the rooms can be vacated in good time. Your latest letter was so sweet. For the first time in eight weeks – actually for the first time in my life – I could sense the bliss that springs from love when one loves with total conviction and knows one's love to be reciprocated. – My dream was quite to the point: 'dead to the world – my haven found!' But Almschi, you must keep repeating this to me, for

---

* 'Doch stürbe nie seine Liebe, wie stürbe dann Tristan seiner Liebe?' (Wagner, *Tristan und Isolde*, II/ii, slightly misquoted by Mahler.)

† '*Tristan:* Hab' ich dich wieder? *Isolde:* Darf ich dich fassen? *Tristan:* Kann ich mir trauen? *Isolde:* Endlich! Endlich!' (*ibid.*, ditto.)

I know that by tomorrow I shall no longer believe it! For this is 'bliss without repose'.* And now good night, my fairest, my sweetest one. Do you find him laughable perhaps, your schoolboy husband? Cable me your arrival time!
My beloved, your Gustav

After eight weeks of torment and despair, Mahler's last long letter ends on a more optimistic note. Alma had evidently been able to convince him that her love was not altogether dead, and that she would stay with him, come what may. Yet her letters to Gropius spoke with increasing openness of erotic feelings and desires. She made an assignation with him in Munich, so that they could meet clandestinely while Mahler was rehearsing the Eighth Symphony. *A month later they met again in Munich, this time to board the Orient Express to Paris, where they spent a few days together. Throughout the winter and spring they continued to exchange ardent love letters.*

The triumph of the Eighth Symphony *filled column after column of the German and Austrian press. At last Mahler's dearest hope had been fulfilled: he had been heard and understood by a wider public. His detractors were unable to explain such unanimous enthusiasm.*

Mahler arrived in Paris two days after Alma, on 17 October. The following day she accompanied him on the train journey to Cherbourg, where they boarded the Kaiser Wilhelm II *for the Atlantic crossing. In New York Mahler rehearsed the orchestra for a whole week before the first concert. The second Philharmonic season was far more successful than the first. By lowering ticket prices, Laudon Charlton, the new manager who had been engaged on Mahler's advice, had been able to attract new subscribers. Since it was Charlton's ambition that the Philharmonic should play a role in the cultural life of New York equal to that of the Metropolitan Opera, the number of concerts was increased and twenty-three musicians were replaced. As a result, the level of playing improved beyond measure. Mahler earned particular triumphs with such works as Schubert's 'Great' C major Symphony, Beethoven's 'Pastoral' Symphony and a number of Wagner concerts. As with the* First Symphony *in 1909, the critics did not warm to his* Fourth Symphony, *although it was a great success with the public. On Charlton's advice, Mahler made a number of concessions, such as increasing the number of popular and out-of-town concerts, abandoning the historical cycle and the Beethoven cycle, which had attracted only small audiences, and replacing them with a series devoted to national schools of composition. Thus Mahler*

---

* Orig.: 'Ein Glück ohne Ruh', quoted from the last verse of Goethe's poem 'Rastlose Liebe'. The German edition of this book adopted these words as its title.

conducted a German programme, a French programme (including the American première of Debussy's latest Images, Ibéria and Rondes de Printemps), an Anglo-American and an Italian programme (including the world première of Busoni's Berceuse élégiaque as well as Mendelssohn's 'Italian' Symphony [!]). In less than four months, Mahler conducted forty-nine of the sixty-five concerts planned for the season.

During the autumn and winter, his letters to family and friends were fairly optimistic. Several times he announced that he was surrounded with 'such affection and goodwill' that he would probably continue in his post as musical director of the Philharmonic. However, as the season neared its end, a conflict broke out between him and the Guarantors' Committee concerning the choice of programmes and the dismissal of an orchestral musician whom Mahler had befriended. Indeed, the committee reduced his administrative powers for the coming season, and accordingly he hesitated before signing a new contract. On 8 March he wrote to the Committee, accepting their proposal of ninety concerts for a fee of $90,000.

On 20 February 1911 Mahler woke up with a sore throat and a temperature, and Fraenkel was called in. This was by no means the first time that Mahler had succumbed to tonsillitis, and he thought nothing of conducting his 'Italian' concert on 21 February. The following days brought signs of improvement: the angina seemed to have been cured, but the fever persisted, decreasing at night, but increasing again as the day wore on. He was unable to conduct his next concerts, in New York and Boston, and Spiering had to step in. Mahler still believed he would recover, but a week later his condition had still not improved. Fraenkel therefore called in a specialist, who identified the infection as streptococcus viridans. Mahler's hereditary disorder, which had been diagnosed only two years earlier as Osler's disease, was now exacerbated by endocarditis (inflammation of the lining of the heart).

Rumours of Mahler's conflict with the Guarantors' Committee had been leaked to the press, and at first it was tacitly assumed that his illness was simulated. The critics, most of whom judged the season successful, acknowledged that the Philharmonic concerts had been much better attended than during the previous season and that the technical level was far superior. Mahler's letters indicate that he had every intention of returning to New York the following season. Hence they corroborate those press reports which allege that only illness and death prevented him from doing so. It was an interview that Alma gave to a New York correspondent in Paris[22] which was largely responsible for circulating the myth that 'America had killed Mahler'.

On 31 March Anna Moll arrived from Europe on the Mauretania to help her daughter nurse the patient. To his doctors, Mahler expressed his dearest wish: to return to Europe, to die and be buried in Vienna. When he left the Savoy Plaza Hotel, on 8 April, he was still able to walk to the elevator, but during the crossing his condition deteriorated steadily. In Paris he was treated by a French bacteriologist, André Chantemesse, who could only confirm the New York diagnosis. A further specialist came from Vienna on 10 May, but he too held out little hope for a recovery. Nevertheless, Mahler's face lit up when he heard that he was to return home.

His return to Vienna resembled that of a dying monarch, with reporters boarding the train at each station in the hope of fresh bulletins. As soon as the train arrived at the Westbahnhof on 12 May, Mahler was taken to Sanatorium Loew on the Mariannengasse, where he had been operated on ten years earlier. Innumerable bouquets and baskets of flowers already filled every corner of his room as well as Alma's. Many more arrived the next day, and soon they filled even the corridors. Mahler survived for a further six days, but gradually the infection spread to his whole body. On 17 May he lapsed into a coma, and he died the following day, 18 May, at 11.05 p.m., during a thunderstorm. He was buried at Grinzing cemetery in the late afternoon of 22 May. In observance of his wishes, the funeral rites were performed with no oration and no music.

Six months previously, Mahler had been on tour with the New York Philharmonic in Pittsburgh, Cleveland, Buffalo, Rochester, Syracuse and Utica. Alma and he had arranged to meet in Buffalo and visit the Niagara Falls. During her return journey to New York, she whiled away the time with one of Mahler's favourite books, Dostoevsky's The Brothers Karamazov, and on arrival she sent him the following telegram: 'Splendid journey with Alyosha'. Mahler replied as follows:

350^U Telegram — rendered as: 350[U] Telegram   Syracuse NY, 9 December [1910]
1.08 p.m.

my journey with almiosha even more splendid   wonderful snowy weather
today woo Gustav

This was Mahler's last message to Alma, a message of fervent love like all the
preceding ones, particularly since the crisis of the previous summer.

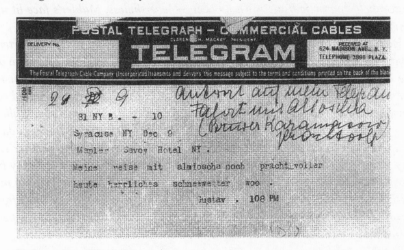

The last telegram to Alma Mapler (*sic*), with added comment in her hand: 'Reply to my
telegram, Journey with Alyosha (Brothers Karamazov) splendid.'

Whether his nine-year 'journey with Almiosha' had in fact been a 'splen-
did' one is debatable. Incompatibilities and animosities had been evident
from the start, were never fully reconciled and continued to smoulder
beneath the surface. Between two people so different in age, background and
character they were perhaps inevitable. Nevertheless, Alma transformed and
enriched Mahler's life. She gave him two handsome children and motivated
him to live, fight and compose. From the very beginning she had been his
'Heimatshafen' (home port), the object of his love and the centre of his life.
Until his last hour, Mahler cherished the image of a 'comrade', a 'faithful and
courageous helpmate on life's journey'. She had hoped at first that 'he would
raise her to his level'; later she could not be blamed for wishing to be a per-
son in her own right and not the mere reflection of her husband's glory.

The disaster of her affair with Gropius taught Alma to respect and admire
Mahler as an 'example to all'. Until his illness shattered the idyll, their last
winter in New York was a time of happiness and serenity. If love is devotion,
then Alma loved Mahler during the last months of his life because she was

indeed devoted to him. And yet she was never a truly 'happy' woman – whether with Mahler or the many who followed after him – if only because of the violent conflict between her instincts, impulses and aspirations.

Were the great men with whom she shared her life mere feathers in her cap, trophies, rather than human beings to be loved for what they were? Her letters to Mahler might have helped clarify the situation, but she destroyed them for fear of being judged harshly by posterity.

It was the same fear of posterity that moved her to expurgate or wilfully distort her memoirs. But then, by the time she sat down to write them, her recollections of people, places and events had themselves parted company with reality. There had never been anything academic, literal-minded or conventional about Alma, least of all when she put pen to paper. For in her world nothing was ever quite real.

Appendix: German texts of Mahler's poems

2

Das kam so über Nacht!
Hätt' ich's doch nicht gedacht
Dass Contrapunkt und Formenlehre
Mir noch einmal das Herz beschwere.

So über eine Nacht
Gewann es Übermacht!
Und alle Stimmen führen nur
Mehr homophon zu einer Spur!

Das kam so über Nacht
– ich habe sie durchgewacht –
Dass ich, wenn's klopft, im Augenblick
Die Augen nach der Türe schickt'!

Ich hör's: ein Mann – ein Wort!
Es tönt mir immerfort –
Ein Canon jeder Art:
Ich blick' zur Tür – und wart'!

64

Bei Piesporter u. Giesshüble
im gemüthlich Wirthsstüble
Bei Mandeln und Zibeben
lassen wir unser Almscherl leben.

188

im besten wolsein eingetroffen dann munter ins hotel geloffen gebadet und
kaffee gesoffen poetisch ist mein heutges kabel wie man in muenchen nur
capabel denn kunst erfuellt hier mann und wabel man fuehlt sich hier
beinahe griechisch darueber freue ich mich viechisch

325

Holdeste! Liebste!

Mein Saitenspiel!
Und mein Sturmlied!
Du Herrliche! O könnt ich Töne finden –
mein stammelnd Seufzen Dir in Worten künden!
Mein Athem ist – mein Wesen nicht mehr meins!
Nicht ich mehr – ich bin von mir selbst geschieden
– nicht eher kann mich Himmelsruh befrieden
als bis ich trunken deines süssen Weins!

Der Lenz hat mich und dich zu sich bezwungen.
Ich gab mich gleich, nicht hab ich erst gerungen.
Ich starb – wie gern – und süss küsst er mich wach!
Die Töne brausen – wüthen mir im Herzen
die heissen Worte flammen – Hochzeitskerzen –
Es strömt mein Wesen dir in's Brautgemach!

329

Meiner Holden!
Immer Gegenwärtigen!
Die Zeit ist da, die Feder ist zur Hand –
doch die Gedanken wollen nicht verweilen.
Auf die fünf Linien blick' ich unverwandt
– Es flimmern vor den Augen mir die Zeilen –
denn noch bin ich geblendet von dem Licht,
das mir gestrahlt von Aphroditens Angesicht!

Und was mein Herz auch singt und dringt –
es schweifen alle Sinne in die Runde!
O Sehnen, das mich ewig an die Stelle zwingt,
wo mir das Leben ward aus süssestem der Munde!

Zusammenfassen will ich alle Schauer meiner Lust,
der Gotteswonne Ewigkeit an ihrer Brust
zu einer Melodie, die wie der Sonnenbogen
den Himmel ihrer Holdheit kühn durchzogen –

in tiefste Tiefen tauchend ihrer Schöne,
dann flammend niedersinkt zum Hochzeitsbett!
O fände doch bei <u>Dir</u>, wie ehmals meine Töne,
mein Liebessehnen Heimathsruh und Stätt'!

330

Du süsse Hand, die mich gebunden!
O holdes Band, das ich gefunden!
Mit Wollust fühl' ich mich gefangen
und ewge Sklaverei ist mein Verlangen!

O wonniger Tod in schmerzenvollsten Stunden!
O Leben – spriesse auf aus meinen Wunden!

334

In lichten Fernen noch ein traumhaft Glänzen
ein grauer Schleier deckt der Bilder Saal
das Auge thränt noch nach entschwundnen Lenzen –
das Herz verstummt schon in Erinnrungsqual.

»Höllische Unruhe – fast nur Schmerz«
Gesegnet des Weges treue Gesellen
Umgürtet die Seele mit dreifachem Erz
Schliesst auf das Leiden Lindrungsquellen!

Auch mir gab Gott zu sagen, was ich leide –
O Wonne, dass ich nicht für ewig scheide.
Ein Herz blieb mein – und schlägt mir heimathwärts
»O Himmlische Unruh – Lieb – und fast kein Schmerz!«

339

Nachtschatten sind verweht an einem mächt'gen Wort,
Verstummt der Qualen nie ermattend Wühlen.
Zusammen floss zu einem einzigen Akkord
Mein zagend Denken und mein brausend Fühlen.

Ich liebe Dich! – ist meine Stärke, die ich preis
die Lebensmelodie, die ich im Schmerz errungen,
O liebe mich! – ist meine Weisheit, die ich weiss,
der Grundton, auf dem jene mir erklungen.

Ich liebe Dich! – ward meines Lebens Sinn
Wie selig will ich Welt und Traum verschlafen,
O liebe mich! – Du meines Sturms Gewinn!
Heil mir – ich starb der Welt – ich bin im Hafen!

397

341

Wie sass ich gar stolz – mein Liebchen zur Seite.
Ich konnt's gar nicht glauben, dass sie mich begleite!

Die Sonne sogar, sie lachte hernieder,
es sprossten im Herzen die luftigen Lieder.

Bald sind wir zu Stelle – O weh! Wie stutzig!
Mein Liebchen macht Äuglein, gar scheu und trutzig!

Erst kollert der tückische Hut zur Erde
drob lächeln die Öbstler, die Hausknecht', die Pferde!

O Schmach! Mein Liebchen sucht einsamste Orte,
zu fliehen der Menschheit böse Cohorte.

Doch oh! Welcher Schrecken, fast ungezügelt
– der Strumpfen verkehrt, das Gewand verbügelt!

Fast stürzen die Thränen in wilden Cascaden
– der Schmerz wird erhaben – Ich schuldbeladen!

Was thun? O fort zu den letzten Wagonen
wo die Schützer des Staates gewaltig thronen.

Da kommt ein Mann: »Hab'ns des da verlor'n?«
Gewaltig Gelächter der Helden mit Sporn!

Der tückische Hut – er war's, der Verruchte,
den ein Wanderer fand, der ihn gar nicht suchte.

Da kam selbst mein heldischer Muth in's Wanken,
Nur das Ringlein am Finger gab gute Gedanken!

Dass ich liebe mein Liebchen – wird Niemand bestreiten!
Dir nie lass ich mich mehr zum Bahnhof begleiten!

Bibliographical Notes

Foreword

1 AML, 83.
2 AML, 143.
3 Paul Stefan, *Gustav Mahler*, Vienna, 1920.
4 Natalie Bauer-Lechner, *Erinnerungen an Gustav Mahler*, Vienna, 1923.
5 Unpubl. letter from Alma Mahler to Arnold Schoenberg, 21.7.1921, Library of Congress, Washington DC.
6 Franz Werfel, *Verdi. Roman der Oper*, Vienna, 1924.
7 AML, 161–62.
8 AMM4, 9.
9 AML, 162.
10 AML, 277.
11 Jon Newsom, 'Introduction', *The Rosaleen Moldenhauer Memorial. Music History from Primary Sources. A Guide to the Moldenhauer Archives*, Washington DC, 2000, xxi.
12 Günther Weiss, 'Gustav Mahlers Briefe an Alma', *Musica*, Kassel, XLV, July–August 1991, 230.
13 S. v. Moisy (ed.), *Gustav Mahler. Briefe und Musikautographen aus den Molden-hauer-Archiven in der Bayerischen Staatsbibliothek*, Munich, 2003.
14 Unpubl., undated letter from Zemlinsky to Alma Schindler (*c.* 26.10.1900), van Pelt-Dietrich Library Center, University of Pennsylvania, Philadelphia, Mahler-Werfel Collection: Zemlinsky correspondence.
15 AML, 162.
16 GMB, no. 201.

Introduction

1 Stefan Zweig, *Die Welt von Gestern, Erinnerungen eines Europäers*, Frankfurt/Main-Hamburg, 1970, 41–2.
2 *ibid.*, 36.
3 Julius Epstein, 'Erinnerungen an meinen Schüler Gustav Mahler', *Illustriertes Wiener Extrablatt*, 19.5.1911.
4 Bruno Walter, *Gustav Mahler*, Leipzig–Zurich, 1936, 20.
5 Josef Bohuslav Foerster, *Der Pilger, Erinnerungen eines Musikers*, Prague, 1955, 444–5.
6 Ludwig Karpath, *Begegnungen mit dem Genius*, Vienna, 1934, 10.
7 H. Killian and K. Martner (ed.), *Gustav Mahler in den Erinnerungen von Natalie Bauer-Lechner*, Hamburg, 1984, 116.
8 AMM4, 29.
9 AMM4, 26.
10 AMD, 24.2.1901, 377.
11 AMM4, 26.
12 Stuart Feder, 'Mahler, Dying', *The International Review of Psycho-Analysis*, London, 1978, 125.
13 Killian *op.cit.*, 184–6.
14 *ibid.*, 187.
15 AML, 13.
16 *ibid.*, 14.
17 AMD, 27.7.1900, 307.
18 *Fremden-Blatt*, Vienna, 17.12.1877.
19 *ibid.*, 28.12.1878.
20 Heinrich Fuchs, *Emil Jakob Schindler*, Vienna, 1970, 19.
21 AML, 14.
22 AMD, 27.7.1900, 307.
23 AML, 15.
24 AML, 16.
25 Fuchs, *op. cit.*, 31
26 AML, 21.
27 Karen Monson, *Alma Mahler-Werfel*, Munich, 1986, 352.
28 AML, 15
29 AMD, 24.12.1898, 83.
30 AMD, 24.12.1899, 219.
31 AML, 21.
32 AML, 26.
33 *ibid.*
34 AML, 27.
35 AML, 28.
36 AML, 29.

37 *ibid.*
38 AMM4, 13.
39 Diary fragments (manuscript), van Pelt-
Dietrich Library Center, entry for
18.5.1920.
40 AML, 231–2.

Overtures (1898–1900)
1 AMD, 6.
2 AMD, 76.
3 AMD, 84.
4 AMD, 101.
5 AMD, 161.
6 AMD, 161–2.
7 AMD, 162–3.
8 AMD, 185.
9 AMD, 14.12.1899, 216.
10 AMD, 2.8.1900, 308.
11 AMD, 3.4.1900, 272.
12 AMD, 3.10.1900, 327.
13 AMD, 9.10.1900, 329.
14 AMD, 11.11.1900, 342.
15 AMD, 282.
16 AMD, 253–4.
17 AMD, 344–5.

1901
1 AMD, 441.
2 AMM4, 13.
3 AMM4, 14–15.
4 AMD, 442–3.
5 AMM4, 14.
6 AMD, 443.
7 AMD, 8.11.1901, 444.
8 AMM4, 27.
9 AMD, 444.
10 AMD, 10.11.1901, 445.
11 AMD, 445.
12 *ibid.*
13 AMM4, 28.
14 AMD, 445–6.
15 AMM4, 29–31.
16 AMD, 446.
17 Unpubl. letter from Alexander Zemlinsky
to Alma Mahler, undated (spring 1901),
van Pelt-Dietrich Library Center.
18 *ibid.*, 22.5.1901.
19 *ibid.*, 27.5.1901.
20 AMM4, 31.
21 Carl Moll, *Erinnerungen*, unpubl. typescript, MmM Paris.

22 AMD, 446–7.
23 AMM4, 32.
24 *ibid.*
25 *ibid.*
26 *ibid.*
27 *ibid.*
28 AMD, 447.
29 *ibid.*
30 AMD, 448.
31 AMD, 448–9.
32 AML, 31.
33 AMD, 450.
34 *ibid.*
35 AMD, 450–5.
36 AMM4, 34.
37 AMD, 455.
38 AMM1, 259
39 GMB, no. 301.
40 AMD, 455–6.
41 AMD, 456–7.
42 AMD, 457.
43 AMD, 457–8.
44 University of Western Ontario, London-
Ontario, Music Library, Rosé-Collection.
45 *ibid.*
46 AMD, 459.
47 *ibid.*
48 AMD, 459–60.
49 University of Western Ontario, London-
Ontario, Music Library, Rosé-Collection.
50 AMD, 460.
51 AMD, 460–1.
52 AMD, 461.
53 AMM4, 35–6.
54 AMD, 462.
55 AML, 31.
56 AML, 47–8.
57 Johann Peter Eckermann, *Gespräche mit
Goethe in den letzten Jahren seines
Lebens*, Munich, 1984; conversation of
16.12.1828, 259.
58 AMM4, 43.
59 AMD, 462
60 AMD, 462–4.
61 AMD, 464.
62 AMD, 464–5.
63 AMD, 465.
64 *Neue Freie Presse*, 28.12.1901.
65 AMD, 465.
66 Edward R. Reilly, *Gustav Mahler und
Guido Adler. Zur Geschichte einer*

Freundschaft, Vienna, 1978, 37.
67 Bruno Walter, *Briefe 1894–1962*, Frankfurt/Main, 1969, 52–3.
68 AMD, 466.
69 AMD, 466–7.

1902

1 AMM1, 280.
2 AMD, 467.
3 AMD, 467.
4 AMM4, 38.
5 AMM4, 39.
6 AMD, 468.
7 AML, 182.
8 AMD, 468.
9 AMM4, 41–2.
10 Strauss's copy was acquired by his biographer Willi Schuh; a photocopy is preserved at MmM.
11 AMM4, 47.
12 University of Western Ontario.
13 *ibid.*
14 AMM4, 57–8.
15 ELM. A comparison of these quotations demonstrates how Alma processed her own material for inclusion in AML. The spontaneity of the original is distilled, the content itself often distorted (here, for instance, by compounding three separate diary entries into a single paragraph).
16 AML, 33.
17 *ibid.*

1903

1 Alfred Roller, *Die Bildnisse von Gustav Mahler*, Vienna, 1922, 13.
2 University of Western Ontario.
3 *Münchener Neueste Nachrichten*, 24.6.1903.
4 AML, Summer 1903, 36–7.

1904

1 AMD, 54.
2 Oscar Bie, 'Mahlers Achte', *Neue Rundschau*, XXI, 1910.
3 AMM4, 58.
4 AMM4, 86.
5 Eduard Reeser (ed.), *Gustav Mahler und Holland. Briefe*, Vienna, 1980, 47. Letter

postmarked 'Amsterdam, 29.6.1904'.
6 AMM4, 90.
7 *ibid.*
8 AMM4, 91.
9 Unpublished letter to Emma Rosé, MmM.
10 AMM4, 92–3..
11 AMM4, 93
12 Letter from Schoenberg to Mahler, 12.12.1904, quoted in H. H. Stuckenschmidt, *Schönberg. Leben, Umwelt, Werk*, Zurich-Freiburg, 1974, 95–6.
13 Letter from Zemlinsky to Alma, dated '1905', actual date: 13.12.1904, van Pelt-Dietrich Library Center.
14 AML, 37–8.

1905

1 AMM4, 103.
2 AMM4, incorrectly dated by Alma as '22 March'. Mahler conducted the performance of *Fidelio* mentioned here on 25.3.1905; the letter was written the following day.
3 ELM I, 14.
4 Herta Blaukopf (ed.), *Gustav Mahler/Richard Strauss, Briefwechsel 1888–1911*, Munich, Zurich, 1980, 70.
5 Letter from Zemlinsky to Alma, van Pelt-Dietrich Library Center (erroneously dated '1906' by Alma).
6 ELM I.
7 AMM4, 115–17, quoted from Alma Mahler, *Gustav Mahler. Memories and Letters*, ed. Donald Mitchell and Knud Martner, trans. Basil Creighton, London, 1990, 92–3.
8 AMM4, 111.
9 AMM4, 109.
10 AMM4, 51.
11 AMM4, 91.
12 Quoted from the original manuscript version (van Pelt-Dietrich Library Center), which differs in several respects from the version in AML (p. 40).
13 AMM4, 112.
14 Reeser, *op. cit.*, 46.
15 AMM1, 340.
16 Reilly, *op. cit.*, 46.
17 Blaukopf, *op. cit.*, 102.

18 AMM4, 112.
19 ELM.
20 ELM.
21 AMM4, 105.
22 *Triester Zeitung*, 2.12.1905.

1906
1 Austrian National Library,
Theatersammlung-Oper, Z 268-1906.
2 AMM4, 122.
3 Klaus Pringsheim, 'Zur Uraufführung
von Mahlers Sechster Symphonie',
Musikblätter des Anbruch, II, 1920, no.
14, 497-8.
4 GMB, no. 360.
5 *Neue musikalische Presse*, 15 (1906),
353ff.
6 AMM4, 126.
7 Lilli Lehman, *Mein Weg*, Leipzig, 1913,
430.
8 Julius Korngold, *Die Korngolds in Wien:
Der Musikkritiker und das Wunderkind*,
Zurich, 1991, 107ff.
9 AMM4, 127.
10 *Münchner Neueste Nachrichten*,
10.11.1906.
11 AMM4, 130.
12 *Grazer Tagespost*, article reprinted in
Ernst Decsey, 'Stunden mit Mahler', *Die
Musik*, op. cit., 18, 352ff.
13 *Grazer Tagblatt*, article reprinted in
Wilhelm Kienzl, *Im Konzert*, Berlin,
1908, 51.

1907
1 H. Blaukopf, *op. cit.*, 121.
2 Otto Klemperer, *Meine Erinnerungen an
Gustav Mahler*, Freiburg-Zurich, 1960, 7,
23.
3 AMM4, 142.
4 *ibid.*
5 *ibid.*
6 Undated telegram from Joseph Conried
in ELM, 24.5.1907.
7 *Neues Wiener Tagblatt*, 5.7.1907.
8 AMM4, 147.
9 Otto Pausch, 'Mahlerisches in den
Rollerbeständen', *Studio Musicologica*,
Budapest, XXXI, 1989, 351.
10 AMM4, 156.
11 AMM1, 408.

12 AMM1, 409.
13 Zoltan Roman, *Gustav Mahler's
American Years, 1907-1911*, New York,
1988, 503.
14 Erik Tawastjerna, *Sibelius*, vol. II,
1904-14, London, 1986, 76.
15 *Teatr i Iskusstvo*, (Theatre and Art),
no. 44, *Novoye Fremia*, 4.11.1907
(Russian calendar).
16 Igor Stravinsky and Robert Craft,
Conversations with Igor Stravinsky, New
York, 1959, 38.
17 V. V. Yastrebtsev, *Nicolai Rimsky-
Korsakov*, Leningrad, 1960, 439.
18 AMM4, 151.
19 *Neue Freie Presse*, 25.11.1907.
20 *Die Zeit* (Vienna), 25.11.1907.
21 Max Graf, 'Wandlungen in der
musikalischen Gesellschaft Wiens',
Österreichische Rundschau, November
1907, 201.
22 Kurt Diemann, *Musik in Wien*, Vienna
etc., 1970, 18.
23 AMM4, 153.
24 *ibid.*

1908
1 *Harper's Weekly*, 25.1.1908, 30.
2 *New York Tribune*, 28.1.1908.
3 Richard Aldrich, *New York Times*,
21.3.1908.
4 Henry Parker, *Boston Evening
Transcript*, 3.4.1908.
5 GMB, no. 388.
6 GMB, no. 389.
7 GMB, no. 390.
8 AMM4, 156.
9 O. Klemperer, *op. cit.*, 9.
10 AMM4, 166.
11 AMM1, 413.
12 AMM1, 418.
13 William Ritter, 'Souvenirs sur Gustave
(*sic*) Mahler', *Schweizerische
Musikzeitung*, Zurich, CI, 1961, 34.
14 *ibid.*, 35-6.
15 *ibid.*, 37.
16 *Neues Münchener Tagblatt*, 2.11.1908.
17 Rudolf Louis, *Die deutsche Musik der
Gegenwart*, Munich, 1909, 183.
18 Letter to Justine Rosé, University of
Western Ontario.

19 AMM1, 181.
20 *Neue Badische Landes-Zeitung*, 30.11.1909.
21 *Neue Badische Landes-Zeitung*, 21.12.1909.
22 Review by Ferdinand Pfohl in *Hamburger Nachrichten*, 10.11.1908.
23 *New York Tribune*, 9.12.1908
24 *The Sun*, 24.12.1908 and *World*, 24.12.1908.

Gustav Mahler Durchgesetzt?, Musik-Konzepte 106, X/1999, 115.
19 Feder, *op. cit.*, 125.
20 Hermann Bahr, 'Unser Goethe', *Neue Freie Presse*, 26.08.1910, 1–3.
21 AML1, 226.
22 Charles Henry Meltzer, 'Gustav Mahler Is Desperately Ill in Paris', *New York American*, 6.5.1911.

1909

1 *New York Tribune*, 14.1.1909.
2 GMB, no. 404.
3 AMM4, 182.
4 *ibid.*
5 *ibid.*, 183.
6 Bruno Walter, *Gustav Mahler. Ein Porträt*, Wilhelmshaven, 1981, 55.
7 Theodore Spiering, 'Zwei Jahre mit Gustav Mahler', *Vossische Zeitung*, Berlin, 21.5.1911.

1910

1 GMB, no. 429.
2 AMM4, 192.
3 AML, 44–5.
4 GMB, no. 430.
5 GMB, no. 434.
6 GMB, no. 436.
7 Josephine von Winter, 'Tagebuch', *Nachrichten zur Mahler-Foschung*, 11, Vienna, March 1983
8 GMB, no. 441.
9 GMB, no. 437.
10 AMM1, 458.
11 AMM4, 80.
12 Georg Göhler, 'Der Künstler und seine Zeit' in Paul Stephan (ed.), *Gustav Mahler. Ein Bild seiner Persönlichkeit in Widmungen*, Munich 1910, 68–79.
13 Alma Mahler, *And the Bridge Is Love*, 50
14 AMM4, 203.
15 Reginald R. Isaacs, *Walter Gropius, der Mensch und sein Werk*, 3 vols, Frankfurt/Main etc., 1985–6, 100.
16 AMM4, 204.
17 AMM4, 206.
18 Jörg Rothkamm, 'Wann entstand Mahlers Zehnte Symphonie? Ein Beitrag zur Biographie und Werkdeutung',

Index of Letters

411

Index of Names

Captions to illustrations in the text are indicated in *italics*.

Index of Works

Die Argonauten (opera libretto, c. 1877) 313

Suite from the orchestral works of J.S. Bach 351, 352

Songs from *Des Knaben Wunderhorn* (1892–1901) 6, 12, 42n, 131n, 192n, 195

Kindertotenlieder (1901–1904) 12, 174, 177, 192n, 195, 229, 230

Das klagende Lied (1878–1880) 3, 4, 52, 53, 95, 131n, 229, 230, 231, 367

Piano Quartet in A minor (c.1877) 0

Das Lied von der Erde (1908–1909) 20, 99, 136n, 303, 304, 305, 344, 355, 360

Lieder eines fahrenden Gesellen (1884–1893) xviin, 4, 42n, 199n, 223

Lieder und Gesänge (3 volumes) 42n, 131, 223

Rübezahl (opera libretto c.1887–1880) 312–3

Rückert-Lieder (1901–1902) 12, 192n, 195, 196, 208n, 229, 380

Symphony No.1 ('Titan') (1888–1969) 5, 6, 11, 26, 28–9, 99–100, 113, 114, 116n, 118,
   131n, 132, 135, 137, 250, 253, 264, 301, 317, 350, 390

Symphony No.2 ('Resurrection') (1888–1959) 5, 7, 11, 48, 55, 56, 63, 64–5, 76, 77,
   99, 100, 120, 121–2, 131n, 137, 141, 149, 178, 186–9, 199n, 218, 221, 250, 260, 269,
   285, 296, 302, 314, 317, 343n, 349, 354

Symphony No.3 (1893–1896) 7, 56, 99, 100, 104–5, 107, 110, 112, 122, 131n,
   132, 133–4, 138, 139, 143, 144, 146, 149, 152, 153, 154, 186, 188, 189, 192–3, 242n,
   247, 250, 253, 277, 317, 364n

Symphony No.4 (1899–1901) 7, 11, 41, 57, 69, 77, 95–100, 107, 110–111, 119, 131n,
   137, 149, 151–2, 176, 178, 183–8, 223, 253, 260, 264, 277, 317, 348, 390

Symphony No.5 (1901–1904) 7, 12, 105, 124n, 132, 138, 139, 154, 156,
   157n, 177, 179, 181, 182, 183, 186, 190n, 191, 192, 196, 201, 223–4, 225, 227–30, 234,
   243, 285, 294, 295, 370

Symphony No.6 ('Tragic') (1903–1904) 20, 21, 100, 122–3, 158, 174, 177, 181,
   182, 185n, 186, 209, 212n, 214, 217n, 219n, 227, 231–4, 236n, 245, 248, 249n, 250,
   253, 258, 307

Symphony No.7 (1904–1905) 20, 21, 177, 209, 211–12, 213, 304, 307, 308, 310,
   345, 347n, 348, 376

Symphony No.8 ('Symphony of a Thousand') (1906–1907) 198, 234, 236n, 237–8, 242,
   256, 316, 318, 328, 346, 347, 353, 354–5, 359, 360, 375, 381, 385, 390

Symphony No.9 (1909–1910) 344, 353, 355, 359

Symphony No.10 (fragment; 1910) xiv, 334n, 368, 375, 380